Readings on
Behavior
in Organizations

Edited by

Edgar F. Huse
James L. Bowditch
Dalmar Fisher

Boston College

 ADDISON-WESLEY PUBLISHING COMPANY
Reading, Massachusetts
Menlo Park, California • London • Amsterdam • Don Mills, Ontario • Sydney

PREFACE

In writing textbooks or assembling books of readings, authors are concerned with a number of issues. Frequently, the approaches to these issues conflict. For example, the student and the professor each have different needs. Authors writing for professors may get their book adopted, but students may find it unreadable. On the other hand, books written to appeal to students and their needs may be regarded as simplistic by professors.

We have tried to deal with this problem in a new way. In order to keep the students' interest, as well as develop their knowledge in the field of organizational behavior and management, we have utilized material from the more popular, less scholarly press wherever possible. Students can be encouraged to read these "popular" selections first, so as to delineate the issues and to become alert to the level of sophistication of the informed general public. The students will then be in a better position to fully understand the issues as explored by more scholarly authors and researchers. This "dual-level" approach is an attempt to raise the students' level of sophistication by a "build-up" method.

A second important feature of this collection of readings is the emphasis on integrated contingency approaches to leadership, management, and organization development. As the field of organizational behavior and management matures, it is becoming increasingly clear that no one approach to leadership, management, and organization development is uniformly appropriate to all situations. Instead, the organization and its environment must be analyzed in detail prior to making any decisions about what types of organizational structure, leadership styles, and organization development might be most useful and effective.

The book is divided into four parts. Part I, "History and Perspectives," stresses the importance of examining an organization from multiple viewpoints, since social organizations are complex and are made up of many kinds of component parts. These parts can be considered as a total system comprising interrelated and interdependent subsystems; a change in one organizational subsystem has an effect throughout the entire system.

Part II carefully examines the two basic building blocks of a social organization—individual and group behavior. After a consideration of individual motivation, the emphasis turns to the way in which people perceive the world and communicate with one another. Next, the work group is examined—the nature of effective work groups and the basic elements of intergroup interaction. Part II concludes with four articles dealing directly with leadership and managerial roles.

The first thrust in Part III is on objectives and control systems, including such areas as long-range planning, management by objectives, human resource accounting, and specific illustrations of how work groups can subvert organizational policies and control systems. The second section of Part III is concerned with current issues and problems in selection, including the selection of hardcore unemployed, as well as complications resulting from recent laws and court rulings.

Part IV focuses on organization development, one of the most exciting new concepts emerging in the area of behavioral science. Here, the importance of organizational structure and its impact on behavior is examined, including organizational design and flows through the total system. The next several articles describe specific techniques in organization development. The section concludes with articles describing integrated approaches to organization development, including documented results.

Although this book of readings is designed to be used as a primary source book, it can also be used in conjunction with *Behavior in Organizations: A Systems Approach to Managing*, a more general text, by E. Huse and J. Bowditch and published by Addison-Wesley in 1973. We have used these readings at both the graduate and undergraduate levels and have found that they are a helpful addition to this basic text.

A number of people have been helpful in the preparation of this book. We give thanks to the Reverends J. Donald Monan, S.J., and Charles Donovan, S.J., for their encouragement, to Dean Albert J. Kelley and Associate Dean Christopher Flynn for arranging for secretarial support, to Rebecca Dorson, Anne Shenkman, Pamela R. Bomhard, M. Linda O'C. Jurgela, and Anne E. O'Reilly for providing that support, to Raymond Graber for his cataloguing effort, to Stephen Fix for suggesting an article which we incorporated, and to our wives—who initially groaned but later supported our newest venture.

Chesnut Hill, Massachusetts   E.F.H.
December 1974   J.L.B.
                                                                      D.F.

CONTENTS

PART I
History and Perspectives

PART I

What we see depends on how we do our looking. A circle, viewed from one angle, will look something like a football. Viewed from another angle, a circle will appear to be a straight line. The way to find out its "real" shape is to walk around it and view it from more than one perspective.

Organizations, things that happen in them, and the people in them are also seen more clearly when viewed from several perspectives. Unfortunately, we often look from just one angle, perhaps because it has yielded a vivid "first impression" which does not seem to require verification, or perhaps because we are so skillful and experienced at looking from that one angle that we decide to leave the other perspectives to someone else.

Government is nothing but a lot of red tape. The ball team is losing because the manager keeps his starting pitchers in too long. This office is inefficient because the workers are just plain lazy. Test yourself. How often in the past 24 hours have you made a one-angle, single-perspective statement of this sort?

Obviously, when anything as complicated as an organization is being viewed, a single perspective provides the viewer with an incomplete and often distorted impression. Even experienced managers and professionals are not immune to the single-perspective error. The plans for a new city parking garage recently won an architectural award. When the garage was completed, however, it was discovered that the garage had no exit ramp. The architects involved had become so concerned with the architectural beauty of the job that they had neglected to consult with the work force. The architects' single-perspective approach so dissatisfied the workers that they decided, "O.K., we'll just follow the plans to the letter." In another example, a telephone company executive could not understand why his outdoor repair crews had

History and Perspectives

high morale and were very productive while his office workers, who worked in heated, air-conditioned comfort and had just received a pay raise, were dissatisfied and inefficient. He failed to recognize that morale and productivity depend on many more factors than just physical working conditions and pay. Gradually, he came to realize that the repair men valued their membership on small, close-knit teams, the opportunity to solve challenging problems, and the freedom to plan and organize their own work. As he gained these additional perspectives, he became a better manager. He decided to reorganize the office and redefine the office workers' jobs in ways that provided them with more challenging work and opportunities for meaningful teamwork. He was pleased to find that performance in the office improved substantially.

The selections in Part I imply, each in its own way, that organizations and the work and people in them are best understood when viewed from several perspectives. Irving Bluestone, as might be expected of a union executive, argues that organizations are people, not simply command structures for enforcing strict work rules. His proworker, prounion sentiments notwithstanding, Bluestone makes a vivid and convincing case for the need to view organizations differently from the way they have been viewed in the past.

The selection by Warren Bennis, as well as those by Harold Leavitt and Jay Lorsch, provide their own summaries of the ways in which views of organizations have changed through history. Bennis begins by reviewing the work of the German sociologist Max Weber (1864–1920), who saw large organizations as "bureaucracies." He goes on to describe the newer ways in which organizations have been viewed since Weber's time and the still newer ways he believes they will need to be viewed in the future.

The selection by Harold J. Leavitt shows the historical development of

3

"structural approaches," "technological approaches," and finally "people approaches." His paper convinces us of the value of multiple perspectives by showing that different, alternative kinds of managerial action are implied by each of the three "approaches." Further, Leavitt notes that structure, technology, and people are interdependent parts of any organization, comprising a "system" in which a change in one part is likely to affect the other parts as well. Thus, our knowledge of an organization is dangerously incomplete until it includes all three perspectives.

The selection by Jay W. Lorsch makes still more explicit use of the concept of organization-as-system. He develops the notions of *differentiation* and *integration,* two fundamental attributes of any system, and shows how these concepts were used as the basis for research, explaining why certain organizations studied were more effective than others. Lorsch's research, conducted in collaboration with Paul Lawrence, James Garrison, and others, establishes the importance of looking at the degree of fit or lack of fit between an organization and its environment. This "contingency approach" has contributed to many current research efforts aimed at learning more about organizational effectiveness.

Part I begins on a historical note, with a selection from Frederick W. Taylor's classic, *Scientific Management.* Taken out of context, Taylor's instructions to worker Schmidt provide an excellent example of a one-perspective viewpoint. Taylor, much discussed by management writers, is often said to have been just that, a single-perspective viewer of organizations, but his writings are seldom read. Perceptive readers, recalling the cultural context within which Taylor's piece was written, can reach their own conclusion as to whether Taylor fits the stereotype others have made for him.

HISTORY

Taylor's Instructions to Schmidt
Frederick W. Taylor

One of the first pieces of work undertaken by us, when the writer started to introduce scientific management into the Bethlehem Steel Company, was to handle pig iron on task work. The opening of the Spanish War found some 80,000 tons of pig iron placed in small piles in an open field adjoining the works. Prices for pig iron had been so low that it could not be sold at a profit, and it therefore had been stored. With the opening of the Spanish War the price of pig iron rose, and this large accumulation of iron was sold. This gave us a good opportunity to show the workmen, as well as the owners and managers of the works, on a fairly large scale the advantages of task work over the old-fashioned day work and piece work, in doing a very elementary class of work.

The Bethlehem Steel Company had five blast furnaces, the product of which had been handled by a pig-iron gang for many years. This gang, at this time, consisted of about 75 men. They were good, average pig-iron handlers, were under an excellent foreman who himself had been a pig-iron handler, and the work was done, on the whole, about as fast and as cheaply as it was anywhere else at that time.

A railroad switch was run out into the field, right along the edge of the piles of pig iron. An inclined plank was placed against the side of a car, and each man picked up from his pile a pig of iron weighing about 92 pounds, walked up the inclined plank and dropped it on the end of the car.

From pp. 41–48, "The Principles of Scientific Management" in *Scientific Management,* copyright 1911 by Frederick W. Taylor; renewed 1939 by Louise M. S. Taylor. By permission of Harper & Row, Publishers, Inc.

We found that this gang were loading on the average about 12½ long tons per man per day. We were surprised to find, after studying the matter, that a first-class pig-iron handler ought to handle between 47 and 48 long tons per day, instead of 12½ tons. This task seemed to us so very large that we were obliged to go over our work several times before we were absolutely sure that we were right. Once we were sure, however, that 47 tons was a proper day's work for a first-class pig-iron handler, the task which faced us as managers under the modern scientific plan was clearly before us. It was our duty to see that the 80,000 tons of pig iron was loaded on to the cars at the rate of 47 tons per man per day, in place of 12½ tons, at which rate the work was then being done. And it was further our duty to see that this work was done without bringing on a strike among the men, without any quarrel with the men, and to see that the men were happier and better contented when loading at the new rate of 47 tons than they were when loading at the old rate of 12½ tons.

Our first step was the scientific selection of the workman. In dealing with workmen under this type of management, it is an inflexible rule to talk to and deal with only one man at a time, since each workman has his own special abilities and limitations, and since we are not dealing with men in masses, but are trying to develop each individual man to his highest state of efficiency and prosperity. Our first step was to find the proper workman to begin with. We therefore carefully watched and studied these 75 men for three or four days, at the end of which time we had picked out four men who appeared to be physically able to handle pig iron at the rate of 47 tons per day. A careful study was then made of each of these men. We looked up their history as far back as practicable and thorough inquiries were made as to the character, habits, and the ambition of each of them. Finally we selected one from among the four as the most likely man to start with. He was a little Pennsylvania Dutchman who had been observed to trot back home for a mile or so after his work in the evening, about as fresh as he was when he came trotting down to work in the morning. We found that upon wages of $1.15 a day he had succeeded in buying a small plot of ground, and that he was engaged in putting up the walls of a little house for himself in the morning before starting to work and at night after leaving. He also had the reputation of being exceedingly "close," that is, of placing a very high value on a dollar. As one man whom we talked to about him said, "A penny looks about the size of a cart-wheel to him." This man we will call Schmidt.

The task before us, then, narrowed itself down to getting Schmidt to handle 47 tons of pig iron per day and making him glad to do it. This was done as follows. Schmidt was called out from among the gang of pig-iron handlers and talked to somewhat in this way:

"Schmidt, are you a high-priced man?"

"Vell, I don't know vat you mean."

"Oh yes, you do. What I want to know is whether you are a high-priced man or not."

"Vell, I don't know vat you mean."

"Oh, come now, you answer my questions. What I want to find out is whether you are a high-priced man or one of these cheap fellows here. What I want to find out is whether you want to earn $1.85 a day or whether you are satisfied with $1.15, just the same as all those cheap fellows are getting."

"Did I vant $1.85 a day? Vas dot a high-priced man? Vell, yes, I vas a high-priced man."

"Oh, you're aggravating me. Of course you want $1.85 a day—every one wants it! You know perfectly well that that has very little to do with your being a high-priced man. For goodness' sake answer my questions, and don't waste any more of my time. Now come over here. You see that pile of pig iron?"

"Yes."

"You see that car?"

"Yes."

"Well, if you are a high-priced man, you will load that pig iron on that car to-morrow for $1.85. Now do wake up and answer my question. Tell me whether you are a high-priced man or not."

"Vell—did I got $1.85 for loading dot pig iron on dot car to-morrow?"

"Yes, of course you do, and you get $1.85 for loading a pile like that every day right through the year. That is what a high-priced man does, and you know it just as well as I do."

"Vell, dot's all right. I could load dot pig iron on the car to-morrow for $1.85, and I get it every day, don't I?"

"Certainly you do—certainly you do."

"Vell, den, I vas a high-priced man."

"Now, hold on, hold on. You know just as well as I do that a high-priced man has to do exactly as he's told from morning till night. You have seen this man here before, haven't you?"

"No, I never saw him."

"Well, if you are a high-priced man, you will do exactly as this man tells you to-morrow, from morning till night. When he tells you to pick up a pig and walk, you pick it up and you walk, and when he tells you to sit down and rest, you sit down. You do that right straight through the day. And what's more, no back talk. Now a high-priced man does just what he's told to do, and no back talk. Do you understand that? When this man tells you to walk, you walk; when he tells you to sit down, you sit down, and you don't talk back at him. Now you come on to work here to-morrow morning and I'll know before night whether you are really a high-priced man or not."

This seems to be rather rough talk. And indeed it would be if applied to an educated mechanic, or even an intelligent laborer. With a man of the mentally sluggish type of Schmidt it is appropriate and not unkind, since it is effective in fixing his attention on the high wages which he wants and away from what, if it were called to his attention, he probably would consider impossibly hard work.

What would Schmidt's answer be if he were talked to in a manner which is usual under the management of "initiative and incentive"? say, as follows:

"Now, Schmidt, you are a first-class pig-iron handler and know your business well. You have been handling at the rate of 12½ tons per day. I have given considerable study to handling pig iron, and feel sure that you could do a much larger day's work than you have been doing. Now don't you think that if you really tried you could handle 47 tons of pig iron per day, instead of 12½ tons?"

What do you think Schmidt's answer would be to this?

Schmidt started to work, and all day long, and at regular intervals, was told by the man who stood over him with a watch, "Now pick up a pig and walk. Now sit down and rest. Now walk—now rest," etc. He worked when he was told to work, and rested when he was told to rest, and at half-past five in the afternoon had his 47½ tons loaded on the car. And he practically never failed to work at this pace and do the task that was set him during the three years that the writer was at Bethlehem. And throughout this time he averaged a little more than $1.85 per day, whereas before he had never received over $1.15 per day, which was the ruling rate of wages at that time in Bethlehem. That is, he received 60 per cent higher wages than were paid to other men who were not working on task work. One man after another was picked out and trained to handle pig iron at the rate of 47½ tons per day until all of the pig iron was handled at this rate, and the men were receiving 60 per cent. more wages than other workmen around them.

The writer has given above a brief description of three of the four elements which constitute the essence of scientific management: first, the careful selection of the workman, and, second and third, the method of first inducing and then training and helping the workman to work according to the scientific method. Nothing has as yet been said about the science of handling pig iron. The writer trusts, however, that before leaving this illustration the reader will be thoroughly convinced that there is a science of handling pig iron, and further that this science amounts to so much that the man who is suited to handle pig iron cannot possibly understand it, nor even work in accordance with the laws of this science, without the help of those who are over him.

Worker Participation in Decision Making
Irving Bluestone

The history of mankind has been marked by struggle between those who govern and those who are governed. In each major conflict, regardless of time, place and circumstances, the voice of rebellion against authority has manifested itself in the cry for freedom, liberty, human rights, human dignity. Stripped of the emotional right ("Give me liberty or give me death") the underlying motivation is the right to participate in the decisions that affect one's welfare.

Monarchs claim to rule by "divine right of kings." And who would be so brave as to challenge the right of rulers whose reign is inspired by the divine embrace of God? Yet, challengers there were—and challengers there will continue to be. The yearning of people to have something to say about how they will be governed is unceasing, even as history records setbacks along the road from time to time.

The same drive that has moved people and nations toward political freedom exists as well at the workplace—between employer and employe. The owner of capital in the early years of the industrial revolution assumed the same mantle of the divine right of kings in his firm as had monarchs of an earlier day in nations. We are, of course, familiar with the oppression and oppressiveness of the factories of the early industrial revolution. Authoritative control over the employes was almost absolute—short of the right of the worker to quit and take his chances of being blackballed from other employment.

Zachary U. Geiger, proprietor of the Mt. Corry Carriage and Wagon Works, listed the rules and regulations for his employes to observe. The date was April 5, 1872. Today, they appear ludicrous. They were the norm in their day.

1. Employees will daily sweep the floors, dust the furniture, shelves and showcases.

2. Each day fill lamps, clean chimneys and trim wicks, wash the windows once a week.

Presented at the Conference on Strategy, Programs and Problems of an Alternative Political Economy at the Institute for Policy Studies, Washington, D.C., March 2–4, 1973. Reprinted by permission of Irving Bluestone.

3. Each clerk will bring in a bucket of water and skuttle of coal for the day's business.

4. Make your own pens carefully. You may whittle nibs to your individual taste.

5. This office will open at 7 a.m. and close at 8 p.m. daily except on the Sabbath on which day it will remain closed.

6. Men employees will be given an evening off each week for courting purposes, or two evenings if they go regularly to church.

7. Every employee should lay aside from each pay a goodly sum of his earnings for his benefits during his declining years so that he will not become a burden upon the charity of others.

8. Any employee who smokes Spanish cigars, uses liquors in any form, gets shaved at a barber shop, or frequents public halls will give good reason to suspect his worth, intentions, integrity and honesty.

9. The employee who has performed his labors faithfully and without fault for a period of five years in my service and who has been thrifty and attentive to his religious duties and is looked upon by his fellowmen as a substantial and law abiding citizen will be given an increase of 5 cents per day in his pay provided that just returns in profits from the business permit it.

Contrast this relationship with the following:

In 1967, the UAW was in negotiations with each of the big three automobile companies, General Motors, Ford and Chrysler. These negotiations take place separately since the auto industry and the UAW do not engage in industry-wide national contract bargaining. When the contracts were about to come to their terminal date (each of them had the same date of termination) the Union proposed to each of the automobile companies that the contracts be extended on a day-to-day basis while negotiations continued toward a conclusion. Each of the companies refused this proposal. As a result, the contracts expired and the workers were free at any time to strike. One of the union's tactics was to curtail the overtime worked in order to forestall the buildup of car inventories.

In one of the plants, the local management called a meeting with the committee after the workers had walked out rather than work overtime. The management said to the committee: "You fellows won't let us set our own schedules, so okay, you set the schedules."

The chairman of the union committee pondered this a moment and then asked: "You mean you want to give up management's prerogative to schedule overtime? You want workers to make that decision?" The company spokesman replied: "Look, we are asking you to do it." The chairman without blinking an eye retorted: "The hell with you. You set the schedules and we won't work them!"

AUTHORITARIAN RULE AT THE WORKPLACE

In a society which prides itself on its democratic system of freedom for the individual and rejection of dictatorial rule, the workplace still stands as an island of authoritarianism. The organizational mold of business, especially big business and the material objective of maximizing profits in and of themselves obstruct, or at the least, deter the fulfillment of democracy at the workplace to match the democratic goal of society at large. In fact, the workplace is probably the most authoritarian environment in which the adult finds himself in a free society. Its rigidity and restriction of freedom lead people to live a kind of double life: at home they enjoy a reasonable measure of autonomy and self-fulfillment as free citizens; at work they are subject to regimentation, supervision, and control by others.

A society anchored in democratic principles should insure to each individual the dignity, respect and liberty worthy of free people; it should afford opportunity for self-expression and participation in the shaping of one's own life. At work, however, personal freedom is severely curtailed, each worker having to adapt himself to tasks, work speeds, and behavior decided upon by others or by the demands of machines which dominate and direct his work life.

The American mode of life rests on the concept that in public life the "governors" are subject to the will of the "governed." In the private life of the business enterprise, however, leadership does not stem from the confidence of the "governed" but rather it is directed toward protection of the interests of the firm, most often against the "governed" (the workers), whose activities and patterns of life at work are organized, directed and dominated by the "governors."

In a democracy, the rules of society are fashioned with the consent of those who must live by them, and the individual is guaranteed a fair trial on the basis of the principle, "innocent until proven guilty." In the workplace, management decides the rules to be lived by and arbitrarily imposes its will by exercising its authority to impose disciplinary sanctions in case of individual transgression.

The argument in support of the authoritarianism of the workplace is that the organization of production and the goal of maximizing profit make it mandatory. Ownership means control. Ownership means rule by decree in the workplace. Thus, the pattern of relations between the "governors" and the "governed" in the business enterprise is contradictory to the democratic way of life.

Moreover, the power of ownership is then reinforced in society by custom, tradition and law. The rights of property often supercede the rights of people and these property rights are buttressed by protective legislation.

"PROFITS BEFORE PEOPLE" OR "PEOPLE BEFORE PROFITS"

This contradiction lies at the heart of the problems with which labor-management relations must grapple. Workers who organize into unions bring an increasing measure of democracy into the workplace. In the broadest possible sense, this is an essential task of unionism and collective bargaining. Moreover, once organized, the workers, as citizens, move to alter the law and to make the rights of people superior to the rights of property and profit. This, too, is an essential task of unionism.

In perhaps oversimplified terms, it becomes a question of "Profits Before People" vs "People Before Profits."

Present-day industrialized society holds certain economic precepts. Among them are:

1. Technological progress is inevitable and desirable.

2. A better living standard for all depends on increased productivity and an expanding gross national product.

3. The purpose of business is to make and maximize profit.

Thus, the underlying thrust of our economic system, anchored in the precepts noted above, led management to develop a production system which is maximally advanced technologically, with maximum production at lowest possible unit cost, and maximum profitability.

The pursuit of maximum profit received remarkable stimulus with the advent of industrial organization and its system of production. Very soon the individual and his needs became extensions of the tool. Skills were broken down to the least common denominator so that they became as interchangeable as machine parts. Specialization through fractioning the job into the simplest, most repetitive acts of performance reduced skill requirements to the minimum possible. The production process became "scientific management."

The granddaddy of the principles of "scientific management," Frederick Taylor, once held that the average working man is "so stupid and so phlegmatic that he more resembles the ox in his mental makeup than any other type." Obviously, this is more than mere exaggeration. It is a cynical expression concerning human beings who happen to be workers.

Over the years "scientific management" evolved into refinements which have robotized workers, removing from them to the greatest degree possible, requirements of education, knowledge, skill, creativity, brain power and muscle power. The assembly line, with its repetitive, monotonous sameness developed into the ultimate symbol of "scientific management." Taylor's principles have served industry well as guide toward ever increasing productivity, lower unit costs, and higher profits; and they dovetailed neatly into the concept of "Profits Before People."

"Scientific Management" is perhaps best epitomized by the system of internal competition within huge multi-plant corporations, where similar work spewing out vast quantities of similar products is performed in many factory units simultaneously. The General Motors Assembly Division (GMAD) will serve as a not untypical, even classical, example of the ultimate in corporate administrative structure thus far, utilizing the principles of "Scientific Managements" constantly to increase profit.

There are, as of now, eighteen auto assembly facilities managed by this Division of General Motors Corporation. The Division has developed an intricate auditing procedure which constantly manages the efficiency (unit cost) and quality of the production in each of the eighteen plants. The plant manager whose plant stands at the bottom of the efficiency or quality rating, in short order receives a visit from the general manager of the Division. Plant managers are expendable and, in addition, executives' incentive bonuses have been quite handsome in General Motors Corporation and no plant manager would like to forego his share in the bonus. One such visit sets the wheels in motion. The general manager meets with his production manager. The production manager feels the pressure. He in turn holds sessions with general foremen and foremen. At the end of the pressure chain is the worker. It does not take much imagination to appreciate the pressure points for more production in this kind of situation.

This type of competitive rating system has built-in economic advantages for the Corporation. At the point number eighteen on the totem pole moves to higher (more efficient, lower unit cost, better quality) position, some other plant manager finds his plant is number eighteen on the list and the process starts over again. One plant is always number eighteen and the plant manager strives to move his plant up from the "cellar."

Further competitive pressure faces the plant manager even if he should succeed in moving his plant up the audit ladder. For every department in the plant is also audited, so that even if a plant is rated, say, number twelve, it may be that a department in the plant—the cushion room, for instance—is number eighteen. The pressure then is to bring that department into a higher efficiency rating.

Where is the end of this pressure spiral? There is none. As an article on this subject in the New York *Times* of April 16, 1972 noted:

> The ranking system is endless, since improvement in one plant pushes another down the scale; so there are no final goals.

This appears to be the ultimate in a competitive system within the same corporation. Its success is measured not by the quality of life in the plant but by that additional dollar that is saved, the additional penny by which unit costs are pared, the extra bit of profit that is squeezed out of the system. The human element is reduced to the least common denominator; and the worker—from plant manager to sweeper—is made to feel the incessant pressure bearing down upon him, much as the assembler faces the inevitability of the next unit coming down the assembly line. They all become pawns in the profit game.

WINDS OF CHANGE IN THE PRODUCTION SYSTEM

Times and circumstances are beginning now to modify the 80-year old habits of "scientific management"—in part because workers' attitudes toward the meaning of work are changing and society as a whole is paying closer attention to the totality of its environment and the quality of life.

Around the time that Henry Ford announced the Five-Dollar Day he remarked: "The assembly line is a haven for those who haven't got the brains to do anything else." His "enlightened" wage scale was accompanied by rules which recalled the type of controls exercised by Zachary U. Geiger in his Mt. Cory works.

Mr. Ford's hiring practices were strict and stifling. No women were to work in his factories; they belonged at home in the kitchen and with the children. Men who failed to support their dependents would find no work at Ford. Similarly, divorced men or others who were "living unworthily"—that is, those who smoked or drank hard liquor.

Once hired, the workers were subject to a spy system. "Social workers" on the Ford payroll would enter the workers' homes and report on living habits: did the worker raise his own garden as instructed, did his family house male boarders (which was taboo); did the worker complain to his family about his job and factory conditions, etc.

Today, the employer no longer has control of the worker outside the workplace as in the past; and unionization has wrested from him a measure of the control he exercises at the workplace. The next step is to provide for the worker a measure of control over his job through his participation in the decisions affecting his job.

Contrast Henry Ford's stifling authoritarianism with the promise expressed in 1972 in the words of Mr. Richard Gerstenberg, Chairman of the Board of Directors of General Motors Corporation:

> "Productivity is not a matter of making employes work longer or harder . . .
>
> "We must improve working conditions and take out the boredom from routine jobs . . .
>
> "We must increase an employe's satisfaction with his job, heighten pride of workmanship and—as far as is feasible—involve the employee personally in decisions that relate directly to his job . . ."

In its own way and within its limited meaning, such an expression, yet unfulfilled, marks an unfashioned awareness of Robert Heilbroner's thesis that:

> " . . . the ultimate challenge to the institutions, motivations, political structures, lifeways and ideologies of capitalist nations is whether they

can accommodate themselves to the requirements of a society in which an attitude of 'social fatalism' is being replaced by one of social purpose."

In perhaps an over-optimistic sense, Mr. Gerstenberg's statement hopefully represents a conscious departure from the historic trickle down theory that profits come first, that profits exemplify good in themselves and can only rebound to the benefit of all of society. For more income and more material wealth, in and of themselves, do not guarantee a life of satisfaction or worth and certainly cannot compensate for lives converted into the deadened extensions of the tolls of production.

New directions are stirring as new problems arise. Cracks are occurring in the traditional discipline of the workplace. Absenteeism has been increasing. The "Monday" and "Friday" absentee is more commonplace. Tardiness shows an upward trend. Labor turnover increases. The boredom and repetitiveness of jobs are accompanied by "job alienation" and departure from the "work ethic," in turn resulting in a deterioration of attention to production and quality. Workers feel a loss of individuality, dignity, self-respect. Job dissatisfaction grows. And workers question the current ways of doing things as they seek to change the inflexible restrictions put upon them by the production process.

Malcolm Denise, Vice President of Ford Motor Company, posed the problem succinctly in a speech to Ford management in November, 1969.

> "Many employees, particularly the younger ones, are increasingly reluctant to put up with factory conditions, despite the significant improvements we've made in the physical environment of our plants. Because they are unfamiliar with the harsh economic facts of earlier years, they have little regard for the consequences if they take a day or two off.
>
> "For many, the traditional motivations of job security, money rewards, and opportunity for personal advancement are proving insufficient."

Research studies now abound, reporting in the language of the sociologist and the industrial psychologist the changes on worker attitudes described by Mr. Denise.

In 1969, the Survey Research Center of the University of Michigan reported the results of a study of 1533 workers at various occupational levels. It concluded that workers ranked interesting work, enough equipment to get the job done, enough information to get the job done and enough authority to get the job done ahead of good pay and job security.

An extensive study recently undertaken by Harold Sheppard and Neal Herrick, published under the title "Where Have All the Robots Gone?" concluded that job dissatisfaction is indeed widespread—and not alone among blue collar workers—and that workers entering the labor force are increasingly anti-authoritarian, better-educated, less income-oriented than past generations of workers and more resistant to meaningless repetitive and boring job assignments. They look to enhancing the quality of work life.

The Gallup organization, each year, has been taking a poll aimed at determining the "job satisfaction" expressed by workers. Between 1969 and 1971 those indicating satisfaction with their work dropped by 7 points, from 88 to 81.

The Bureau of Labor Statistics has found absenteeism rates have increased an average of 35% since 1961.

One significant aspect of American life which has been undergoing rapid change relates to the freedom (in a realistic sense) that people have to enjoy the autonomy of self-employment. In 1950, 16% of the labor force was self-employed. A decade later, the figure dropped to about 12%. Another decade, and it was around 8%. Thus, the percentage of the self-employed dropped by half in a brief 20-year period. Increasingly the people have been losing even this bastion of control over their working lives.

A recent study, undertaken by the HEW, entitled "Work in America" and released by Secretary of HEW, Eliot Richardson, leaves no doubt that worker dissatisfaction with jobs—both blue collar and white collar—is widespread and on the ascendancy and represents an urgent problem for management, union and government concern. The report notes:

"Significant numbers of American workers are dissatisfied with the quality of their working lives."

"Dull repetitive, seemingly meaningless tasks, offering little challenge or autonomy, are causing discontent among workers at all occupational levels."

The report makes a point that the failure to meet this problem will mean increased social costs. It points to the interrelationship between job dissatisfaction on the one hand and mental health, alcohol and drug abuse, heart disease, longevity, etc. on the other, and urges that unless correction is made society can expect these costs to increase as a tax burden on the total community.

Many leaders in industry have reached the conclusion that the problem is serious and something must be done about it. Spokesmen for ITT, General Foods, Jervis Corporation, Ford Motor Company, IBM to name a few, have made public statements on the subject.

Ed Cole, president of General Motors Corporation, addressing the College of Engineering at the University of Michigan stated:

"The work force has been changing. It is somewhat younger, . . . better educated . . . and more interested in being involved. These characteristics are advantages for any employer . . . if they are recognized and considered in making manufacturing changes. In many GM operations, we are involving the hourly rate employees more in decision making . . . asking for their suggestions when new processes are introduced, increasing their freedom of choice, and encouraging their initiative to do a better job."

At an International Conference on the Quality of Working Life in September, 1972, the issue was summed up as follows:

" . . . it became clear that there is already enough known both about what makes for a high quality of working life and about methods of obtaining organizational change to justify concerted effort to translate what is known into action."

Contrasted with the wealth of information based on sociologically scientific studies establishing the fact of growing job dissatisfaction and the reasons for it, the management consulting firm of Imberman and DeForest, Chicago, Illinois, reported contrary findings in its study of assembly line workers.

This study summarized:

"Our findings on the subject of worker alienation were that most employes (about 80%) are not alienated by assembly work, while about 20 per cent are."

In describing the study's result, Mr Imberman noted:

"In all cases, employes were asked what suggestions they might have to make their job situations happier, more productive, and more satisfying. In analyzing the thousands of interview responses, most employes were found to prefer jobs with less high-quality demands, with less direct responsibility, with less troublesome variety."

Even if the statistical results of the Imberman Study were valid, however, it is surprising that the analysis should downplay the significance of 20% of assembly line workers dissatisfied with their jobs. Such a figure is of epidemic proportions—and all indications are that job dissatisfaction is on the rise. Rebellion has been spawned by far less.

It is important to understand that reasonable satisfaction with meaningless, repetitive work may simply mean that man, being the highly adaptable creature that he is, has made his peace with an unhappy situation. There is strong evidence that workers write off deadening jobs as "inevitable" and seek their satisfaction in other pursuits. The HEW study makes a point of the interrelationship between the meaninglessness of the job and the adverse effect on the physical and mental well-being of the worker.

It is also important to note that workers who have been given the opportunity to enlarge their horizons at work, to participate in the decisions affecting their job, to lend their innovative in-put toward getting the job done have a focal point against which to compare their previous work experience.

These workers usually do not want to return to the simple, monotonous tasks of little or no responsibility. They have tried a better way and they like it.

(For an excellent analysis of the critics of the theme of growing job dissatisfaction, I would refer you to an address by Harold L. Sheppard of the W. E. Upjohn Institute for Employment Research at the 25th Meeting of the IRRA, Toronto, December 28, 1972. The address is titled: "A Simple Simon's Partial List of Issues About the Current Controversies Surrounding the Quality of Working Life.")

JOB DISSATISFACTION—SYMPTOM OF GROWING CYNICISM IN SOCIETY

The increase in job dissatisfaction is rooted not only in the production system of "scientific management." It feeds as well on the growing cynicism and frustration expressed toward public life.

Citizens feel more alienated toward their government and their public leaders as decision making in a complex world becomes more removed from them and they sense an inability meaningfully to affect the decisions of government. With the unique exception of a Nader, the average citizen feels an inadequacy in influencing the direction and thrust of society.

How widespread are complaints about the hypocrisy of elected leaders and the disillusionment over promises made and not kept? And how often are voices raised against corruption, dissembling and the lack of moral leadership on high? Even political spying, bugging, bribery on a large scale raise less a ripple than a deep freeze or a vicuna coat.

It is axiomatic that people respond more affirmatively to their role in society as they share in the opportunity to participate more significantly in the decisions that affect their welfare. History teaches moreover that at some point the people, denied this opportunity, will reach out and grasp it.

This is equally true at the workplace. The stirrings of job dissatisfaction, in my judgement, relate in large measure to the denial of participation in the decision-making process, the denial of the opportunity to be creative, innovative, to apply one's brain power to the job at hand, to control the machine instead of being controlled by it.

PROGRESS THROUGH UNIONISM

The ferment of union activity in the 1930's and 1940's consolidated the organizing strength of industrial workers. It was the first stage toward accomplishment of a larger goal: industrial democracy. It provided the base on which workers then were able to improve their standards of living, win better working conditions, and achieve a greater measure of dignity and security as important members of society. Every gain constituted an incursion into the traditional authority wielded by management. The vast array of benefits won in collective bargaining over the years relates essentially to protecting the worker and his family against the hazards of insecurity, and responding to company action or inaction at the workplace. Workers, young and old, continue to aspire toward a better life—to be won at the bargaining table and in legislation. Their unions will of course persist in innovative collective bargaining effort as well as improving upon already established benefit programs. They mobilize politically cognizant of the intimate relationship between "the bread box and the ballot box."

There is little need to spell out the enormously important progress which workers have made through their unions. In *quantitative* terms organized workers have won, and continue to win, a larger share of economic well-being. Unorganized workers have of course reaped the advantage of these gains made by unionized workers. Working conditions have been vastly improved under the pressure of collective bargaining. Yet in *qualitative* terms workers have not made as marked progress and are still struggling to play a more meaningful role in the decisions that affect their welfare in the business enterprise.

Emphasis on qualitative improvement of life on the job is, I believe, the next step on the road toward industrial democracy.

WHITHER WORKER PARTICIPATION?

Two distinct, somewhat overlapping, directions are indicated. The one relates to "managing the enterprise"; the other relates to "managing the job." The latter is of course part and parcel of the former but it is of more immediate concern to the worker in direct relation to his work

Experiments with regard to worker participation in "managing the enterprise" are underway in Yugoslavia (worker control of management), Germany (Mitbestimmung—codetermination established by law), Sweden (voluntary acceptance of worker representation on the Board of Directors), and Israel (union owned and operated cooperative enterprises).

In the United States, labor contracts, with their hundreds of provisions establishing and protecting the rights of workers, leave substantially to management the "sole responsibility" to determine the products to be manufactured, the locations of plants, the schedules of production, the methods, processes and means of manufacturing and the administrative decisions governing finances, marketing, purchasing, pricing and the like.

Unions in the United States traditionally have moved in the direction of improving wages, benefits and working conditions. Generally, they have left "managing the enterprise" to management, reacting to managerial acts objectionable to the workers. They have not embraced a political philosophy to motivate their overall policies and programs. This is not to say that U.S. unions have no socio-political-economic concepts. Quite the contrary; but they are not married to an "ism" governing and directing their behavior.

Rather, U.S. unions move to meet practical problems with practical solutions. It would be highly improbable that they will approach the problem of worker participation in decision making by way of fierce ideological struggle founded in socio-economic theory. They are not prone to beat their wings in ideological frustration.

Where workers feel victimized, they combine their forces to correct the situation—case by case, problem by problem. Gradual, persistent change—not revolutionary upheaval—has marked the progress of the American worker. When explosions occur—as they did in the 1930's—they are responses to specific problems in the search for specific solutions.

We can anticipate that worker participation will manifest itself in this way: a step-by-step effort to meet specific problems affecting the welfare of the worker.

Decisions regarding purchasing, advertising, selling, financing are far more remote from the immediate problems facing the worker than are decisions concerning his job. In the vast range of managerial decision that are made, the immediacy of impact on the worker varies enormously. Thus, the average worker in a gigantic enterprise usually displays less interest in the selection of the chairman of the board than in the amount of overtime he receives.

What direction, then, will the drive toward worker participation in decision making take? To begin with, it seems safe to say that any further encroachment on so-called management prerogatives will spell "revolution" to management, while to the worker it will simply represent a non-ideological effort to resolve a problem that bothers him.

Certain areas of possible confrontation come to mind.

Management, by way of example, controls the decision to shut down a plant or move all or part of it to another location, often hundreds of miles away. The union bargains for severance pay, early retirement, the right of the worker to transfer with the job and to receive moving allowance, etc. But the worker—often with long years of service—is the victim of such a decision. He is permanently thrown out of work, or, even if he is given the right to transfer with the job, he must pull up stakes, cut off the roots he has in his community, leave family ties and friends, and begin a new life in a strange place, with no assurance of permanence. Management wields the decision making authority; the worker (and the community) dangles at the end of that decision.

Similarly, management generally controls the final decision to subcontract work out or to move work about among its many facilities in a multi-plant corporation. It is the worker who faces the ultimate insecurity.

Management holds the authority to discipline. All places of work (like society at large) require rules and regulations for people to live by; but discipline can be a fearful weapon in the hands of a ruthless employer, even when subject to a collectively bargained grievance procedure.

Production scheduling can be a serious source of friction. In an auto assembly plant, for instance, changes in line speed to meet changes in production schedules, or changes in model mix, require re-balancing of jobs and operations. This in turn gives rise to disputes over production standards and manpower. Frequent changes in line speed or model mix disturb agreed upon production standard settlements and manpower agreements, often resulting in crisis bargaining and, on occasion, strike action.

The never-ending yet necessary introduction of technological innovation and the concomitant alteration of jobs, cutbacks in manpower need and effect on skill requirements are a constant source of new problems, emphasizing the concern workers naturally have for their job security.

The call for excessive overtime is a constant source of unhappiness and discontent.

These are but a handful of the kinds of confrontation issues directly affecting workers which increasingly are subject to "worker participation" bargaining.

There are other types of issues also, relating directly to life at the workplace, which will command attention, for democratizing the workplace carries considerations beyond the worker's immediate job.

The double standard that exists between the managers and the workers comes into question. Symbols of elitism, traditionally taken for granted in industrial society, are challenged: salary payment and its normally recognized advantages (vs. hourly payment); time clocks; paneled dining rooms (vs. plain Spartan type cafeterias); privileged parking facilities nearest the plant entrances; etc.

Democratizing the workplace may entail organizing the work schedule to enable the worker to manage his personal chores; visiting the dentist or doctor; getting his car repaired; visiting the school to discuss his children's problems with the teacher, etc.

It is easily discerned that worker participation in decision making will more readily spring up with regard to those aspects of working life most immediately and noticeably affected. "Managing the job" is more immediate and urgent. Worker concern for "managing the enterprise" is more variable and is best measured by the immediacy of impact on the worker's welfare.

Increasing attention is currently being devoted to this problem of "managing the job." Rising rates of absenteeism, worker disinterest in quality and quantity of production, job alienation, the insistence on unit cost reduction are motivating some employers to reevaluate current practices and customs governing management-worker relationships. Concurrently, the worker rebels against the authoritarian atmosphere of the workplace, the subordination of his personal dignity, desires and aspirations to the drive for more production at lower cost; he finds little challenge, satisfaction or interest in his work. While his rate of pay may dominate his relationship to his job, he can be as responsive to the opportunity for playing an innovative, creative and imaginative role in the production process.

One of the essential tasks of the union movement is to "humanize the workplace." A pleasant, decent management is desirable, but does not alter the basic managerial design. "Human engineering" concepts may make for more comfortable employer-employe relationships, but here, too, managerial administration of the workplace remains fundamentally unchanged. "Humanizing the workplace" must include not only the normally recognized amenities of life in the workplace; it must move to a higher plateau and relate to job satisfaction, a closing of the widening gap between the ever-increasing mechanization of production by "scientific management" and the participation which the worker can enjoy in the productive and decision making process. "Humanizing the workplace" in this sense represents one additional step toward the fulfillment of industrial democracy.

But humanizing the workplace must not become simply another gimmick, designed essentially to "fool" the worker and having as its primary goal an increase in worker productivity. Manipulation of the worker will be recognized for what it is: another form of exploitation; it will breed suspicion and distrust.

In this respect, Delmar Landen, an expert in personnel development for General Motors Corporation has said:

" . . . where we have to aim is participation—it is the only way to work in this increasingly complex society. The man at the top can't have all the answers. The man doing the job will have some of them."

Worker participation in decision making with regard to the job is one means of achieving democratization of the workplace. It should result in a departure from the miniaturization and oversimplification of the job to a system which embraces broader distribution of authority, increasing rather than diminishing responsibility and accountability, combined with the engineering of more interesting jobs, with the opportunity to exercise a meaningful measure of autonomy and to utilize more varied skills. It requires tapping the creative and innovative ingenuity of the worker to the maximum extent of his mental capabilities.

Hundreds of experiments have been and are being undertaken in American industry, following the European lead, directed toward opening up opportunities for meaningful worker participation. The HEW Report describes some of them. In the auto industry, the industry with which I am more closely associated, a myriad of demonstration projects is being attempted covering innumerable facets of the problem—including a sharp departure from use of the assembly line concept.

It is too early to describe precisely what form or forms new inroads toward the achievement of humanizing the workplace will take. Certain criteria, however, deserve serious consideration.

1. The worker should experience genuinely that he is not simply an adjunct to the tool, but that his bent toward being creative, innovative, inventive, plays a significant role in the production (or service) process.

2. The worker should be assured that his participation in decision making will not erode his job security or those of his fellow workers.

3. Job functions should be engineered to fit the worker; the current system is designed to make the worker fit the job, on the theory that this is a more efficient production system and that in any event economic gain is the worker's only reason for working. This theory may be proven wrong on both counts.

4. The worker should be assured the widest possible latitude of self-management, responsibility and the opportunity for use of his "brain power." Gimmickry and manipulation of the worker must not be employed.

5. The changes in job content, the added responsibility and involvement in decision making should be accompanied by concomitant upward movement in rates of pay.

6. The worker should be able to foresee opportunities for growth in his work and for promotion.

7. The worker's role in the business should enable him to relate to the product being produced, to the services being rendered, and to its meaning in society; in a broader sense, it should enable him as well to relate constructively to his role in society.

The unions, as representative of the worker, will naturally share with management in implementing these and other criteria. Finding the precise means to achieve the goal of "humanizing work" is not conducive to crisis negotiations. It is not the same as settling a wage dispute in the face of a twelve midnight strike deadline. Rather, it requires careful experiment and analysis. While issues of economic security (wages, fringe benefits) and continuing encroachment on what management terms its sole prerogatives will remain adversary in nature, there is every reason why humanizing the workplace and humanizing the job need not be matters of confrontation but of mutual concern for the worker, the enterprise and the welfare of society.

Admiral Rickover, concerned over the frightening prospect of man ruled by the machine, admonished:

> "A society is free when it centers on man; that is when it gives paramount consideration to human rights, interests and needs. Powerful forces are driving us towards a pattern of life in which technology, rather than man, would be central to the purpose of our society. The evidence is all around us. There is a marked propensity to regard technology as an end in itself,

when actually it is no more than a means to an end that man determines. There is a tacit assumption, whenever technology contravenes human desires, that man must adapt himself to technology instead of technology being made to serve man."

Today, more and more people are clamoring for the dignity and freedom which being "part of the action" insures.

Professor Jaroslav Vanek of Cornell University has put it succinctly:

"The quest of men to participate in the determination and decision making activities in which they are actually involved is one of the most important socio-political phenomena of our times. It is very likely to be the dominant force of social evolution in the last third of the 20th century . . ."

Today's worker stands on the threshold of this social force.

The Decline of Bureaucracy and Organizations of the Future
Warren G. Bennis

Most of us spend all of our working day and a great deal of our nonworking day in a unique and extremely durable social arrangement called "bureaucracy." I use the term "bureaucracy" descriptively, not as an epithet about "those guys in Washington" or as a metaphor *à la* Kafka's *Castle,* which conjures up an image of red tape, faceless masses standing in endless lines, and despair. Bureaucracy, as I shall use the term here, is a social invention, perfected during the Industrial Revolution to organize and direct the activities of the firm. To paraphrase Churchill's ironic remark about democracy, we can say of bureaucracy that it is the worst possible theory of organization—apart from all the others that have so far been tried.

The burden of this book rests upon the premise that this form of organization is becoming less and less effective, that it is hopelessly out of joint with contemporary realities, and that new shapes, patterns, and models—currently recessive—are emerging which promise drastic changes in the conduct of the corporation and in managerial practices in general. So within the next twenty-five to fifty years, we should all be witness to, and participate in, the end of bureaucracy and the rise of new social systems better able to cope with twentieth-century demands.*

The argument will be presented in the following sequence:

1. A quick look at bureaucracy: what it is and what its problems are;

2. A brief survey of how behavioral scientists and practitioners have attempted to modify and alter the bureaucratic mechanism so that it would respond more appropriately to changing times (in this section I shall

---

Adapted from an invited address presented to the Division of Industrial and Business Psychology at the American Psychological Association Meeting, Los Angeles, Calif., September 5, 1964. Published by permission of Transaction, Inc. from *Transaction,* Vol. 2, No. 5, July/August 1965.

*The number of years necessary for this transition is, of course estimated from forecasts for the prospects of industrialization. Sociological evolutionists are substantially agreed that within a twenty-five- to fifty-year period, most of the people in the world will be living in industrialized societies. And it is this type of society that concerns me here, not the so-called underadvanced, semiadvanced, or partially advanced societies.

show how these emergency remedies have been only stopgap measures and how more basic changes are required);

3. A general forecast of how most organizations of the future will operate.

BUREAUCRACY AND ITS DISCONTENTS

Corsica, according to Gibbon, is much easier to deplore than to describe. The same holds true for bureaucracy. Basically, though, it is simple: bureaucracy is a social invention which relies exclusively on the power to influence through reason and law. Max Weber, the German sociologist who conceptualized the idea of bureaucracy around the turn of the century, once likened the bureaucratic mechanism to a judge qua computer: "Bureaucracy is like a modern judge who is a vending machine into which the pleadings are inserted together with the fee and which then disgorges the judgment together with its reasons mechanically derived from the code."[1]

The bureaucratic "machine model" Weber outlined was developed as a reaction against the personal subjugation, nepotism, cruelty, emotional vicissitudes, and subjective judgment which passed for managerial practices in the early days of the Industrial Revolution. Man's true hope, it was thought, was his ability to rationalize and calculate—to use his head as well as his hands and heart. Thus, in this system roles are institutionalized and reinforced by legal tradition rather than by the "cult of personality"; rationality and predictability were sought for in order to eliminate chaos and unanticipated consequences; technical competence rather than arbitrary or "iron" whims were emphasized. These are oversimplifications, to be sure, but contemporary students of organizations would tend to agree with them. In fact, there is a general consensus that bureaucracy can be dimensionalized in the following way:

1. A division of labor based on functional specialization

2. A well-defined hierarchy of authority

3. A system of rules covering the rights and duties of employees

4. A system of procedures for dealing with work situations

5. Impersonality of interpersonal relations

6. Promotion and selection based on technical competence[2]

These six dimensions describe the basic underpinnings of bureaucracy, the pyramidal organization which dominates so much of our thinking and planning related to organizational behavior.

It does not take a great critical imagination to detect the flaws and problems in the bureaucratic model. We have all *experienced* them: bosses without technical competence and underlings with it; arbitrary and zany rules; an underworld (or informal) organization which subverts or even replaces the formal apparatus; confusion and conflict among roles; and cruel treatment of subordinates, based not upon rational or legal grounds, but upon inhumane grounds. Unanticipated consequences abound and provide a mine of material for those comics, like Chaplin or Tati, who can capture with a smile or a shrug the absurdity of authority systems based on pseudologic and inappropriate rules.

Almost everybody, including many students of organizational behavior, approaches bureaucracy with a chip on his shoulder. It has been criticized for its theoretical confusion and contradictions, for moral and ethical reasons, on practical grounds such as its inefficiency, for its methodological weaknesses, and for containing too many implicit values or for containing too few. I have recently cataloged the criticisms of bureaucracy, and they outnumber and outdo the Ninety-five Theses tacked on the church door at Wittenberg in attacking another bureaucracy.[3] For example:

1. Bureaucracy does not adequately allow for personal growth and the development of mature personalities.

2. It develops conformity and "group-think."

3. It does not take into account the "informal organization" and the emergent and unanticipated problems.

4. Its systems of control and authority are hopelessly outdated.

5. It has no adequate juridical process.

6. It does not possess adequate means for resolving differences and conflicts among ranks and, most particularly, among functional groups.

7. Communication (and innovative ideas) are thwarted or distorted because of hierarchical divisions.

8. The full human resources of bureaucracy are not being utilized because of mistrust, fear of reprisals, etc.

9. It cannot assimilate the influx of new technology or scientists entering the organization.

10. It will modify the personality structure such that man will become and reflect the dull, gray, conditioned "organization man."

Max Weber himself, the developer of the theory of bureaucracy, came around to condemning the apparatus he helped immortalize. While he felt that bureaucracy was inescapable, he also thought it might strangle the spirit of capitalism or the enterprenuerial attitude, a theme which Schumpeter later on developed. And in a debate on bureaucracy he once said, more in sorrow than in anger:

> It is horrible to think that the world could one day be filled with nothing but those little cogs, little men clinging to little jobs and striving towards bigger ones
> —a state of affairs which is to be seen once more, as in the Egyptian records,

playing an ever-increasing part in the spirit of our present administrative system, and especially of its offspring, the students. This passion for bureaucracy . . . is enough to drive one to despair. It is as if in politics . . . we were deliberately to become men who need "order" and nothing but order, who become nervous and cowardly if for one moment this order wavers, and helpless if they are torn away from their total incorporation in it. That the world should know no men but these: it is such an evolution that we are already caught up in, and the great question is therefore not how we can promote and hasten it, but what can we oppose to this machinery in order to keep a portion of mankind free from this parcelling-out of the soul from this supreme mastery of the bureaucratic way of life.[4]

I think it would be fair to say that a good deal of the work on organizational behavior over the past two decades has been a footnote to the bureaucratic "backlash" which aroused Weber's passion: saving mankind's soul "from the supreme mastery of the bureaucratic way of life." At least, very few of us have been indifferent to the fact that the bureaucratic mechanism is a social instrument in the service of repression; that it treats man's ego and social needs as a constant, or as nonexistent or inert; that these confined and constricted needs insinuate themselves into the social processes of organizations in strange, unintended ways; and that those very matters which Weber claimed escaped calculation—love, power, hate—not only are calculable and powerful in their effects but must be reckoned with.

MODIFICATIONS OF BUREAUCRACY
In what ways has the system of bureaucracy been modified in order that it may cope more successfully with the problems that beset it? Before answering that, we have to say something about the nature of organizations, *all* organizations, from mass-production leviathans all the way to service industries such as the university or hospital. Organizations are primarily complex goal-seeking units. In order to survive, they must also accomplish the secondary tasks of (1) maintaining the internal system and coordinating the "human side of enterprise"—a process of mutual compliance here called "reciprocity"—and (2) adapting to and shaping the external environment—here called "adaptability." These two organizational dilemmas can help us organize the pivotal ways the bureaucratic mechanism has been altered—and found wanting.

Resolutions of the Reciprocity Dilemma
Reciprocity has to do primarily with the processes which can mediate conflict between the goals of management and the individual goals of the workers. Over the past several decades, a number of interesting theoretical and practical resolutions have been made which truly allow for conflict and mediation of interest. They revise, if not transform, the very nature of the bureaucratic mechanism by explicit recognition of the inescapable tension between individ-

ual and organizational goals. These theories can be called, variously, "exchange," "group," "value," "structural," or "situational," depending on what variable of the situation one wishes to modify.

The exchange theories postulate that wages, incomes, and services are given to the individual for an equal payment to the organization in work. If the inducements are not adequate, the individual may withdraw and work elsewhere.[5] This concept may be elaborated by increasing the payments to include motivational units. That is to say, the organization provides a psychological anchor in times of rapid social change and a hedge against personal loss, as well as position, growth and mastery, success experience, and so forth, in exchange for energy, work, and commitment.[6]

I shall discuss this idea of payment in motivational units further, as it is a rather recent one to gain acceptance. Management tends to interpret motivation by economic theory. Man is logical; man acts in the manner which serves his self-interest; man is competitive. Elton Mayo and his associates were among the first to see human affiliation as a motivating force, to consider industrial organization a social system as well as an economic-technical system. They judge a manager in terms of his ability to sustain cooperation.[7] In fact, once a cohesive, primary work group is seen as a motivating force, a managerial elite may become obsolete, and the work group itself become the decision maker. This allows decisions to be made at the most relevant point of the organizational social space, where the data are most available.[8]

Before this is possible, some believe that the impersonal value system of bureaucracy must be modified.[9] In this case the manager plays an important role as the instrument of change, as an interpersonal specialist. He must instill values which permit and reinforce expression of feeling, experimentalism and norms of individuality, trust, and concern. Management, according to Blake,[10] is successful as it maximizes "concern for people"—along with "concern for production."

Others [11,12] believe that a new conception of the structure of bureaucracy will create more relevant attitudes toward the function of management than formal role specifications do. If the systems are seen as organic rather than mechanistic, as adapting spontaneously to the needs of the system, then decisions will be made at the critical point, and roles and jobs will devolve to the "natural" incumbent. The shift would probably be from the individual to cooperative group effort, from delegated to shared responsibility, from centralized to decentralized authority, from obedience to confidence, and from antagonistic arbitration to problem solving.[13] Management which is centered around problem solving, which assumes or relaxes authority according to task demands, has most concerned some theorists. They are as concerned with organizational success and productivity as with the social system. [14,15,16,17]

However, on all sides we find a growing belief that the effectiveness of bureaucracy should be evaluated on human as well as economic criteria. Social satisfaction and personal growth of employees must be considered, as well as the productivity and profit of the organization.

The criticisms and revisions of the *status quo* tend to concentrate on the internal system and its human components. But although it appears on the surface that the case against bureaucracy has to do with its ethical-moral posture and the social fabric, the real *coup de grâce* has come from the environment. While various proponents of "good human relations" have been fighting bureaucracy on humanistic grounds and for Christian values, bureaucracy seems most likely to founder on its inability to adapt to rapid change in the environment.

The Problem of Adaptability

Bureaucracy thrives in a highly competitive, undifferentiated, and stable environment, such as the climate of its youth, the Industrial Revolution. A pyramidal structure of authority, with power concentrated in the hands of few with the knowledge and resources to control an entire enterprise was, and is, an eminently suitable social arrangement for routinized tasks.

However, the environment has changed in just those ways which make the mechanism most problematical. Stability has vanished. As Ellis Johnson said: " . . . the once-reliable constants have now become 'galloping' variables. . . ."[18] One factor accelerating change is the growth of science, research and development activities, and intellectual technology. Another is the increase of transactions with social institutions and the importance of the latter in conducting the enterprise—including government, distributors and consumers, shareholders, competitors, raw-material and power suppliers, sources of employees (particularly managers), trade unions, and groups within the firms.[19] There is, as well, more interdependence between the economic and other facets of society, resulting in complications of legislation and public regulation. Thirdly, and significantly, competition between firms diminishes as their fates intertwine and become positively correlated.[20]

My argument so far, to summarize quickly, is that the first assault on bureaucracy arose from its incapacity to manage the tension between individual and management goals. However, this conflict is somewhat mediated by the growth of an ethic of productivity which includes personal growth and/or satisfaction. The second and more major shock to bureaucracy has been caused by the scientific and technological revolution. It is the requirement of adaptability to the environment which leads to the predicted demise of bureaucracy and to the collapse of management as we know it now.

A Forecast for the Future

A forecast falls somewhere between a prediction and a prophecy. It lacks the divine guidance of the latter and the empirical foundation of the former. On thin empirical ice, I want to set forth some of the conditions that will dictate organizational life in the next twenty-five to fifty years.

1. *The environment.* Those factors already mentioned will continue in force and will increase. That is, rapid technological change and diversification will lead to interpenetration of the government and legal and economic policies in business. Partnerships between industry and government (like Telstar) will be typical, and because of the immensity and expense of the projects, there will be fewer identical units competing for the same buyers and sellers. Or, in reverse, imperfect competition leads to an oligopolistic and government-business-controlled economy. The three main features of the environment will be interdependence rather than competition, turbulence rather than stability, and large rather than small enterprises.

2. *Aggregate population characteristics.* We are living in what Peter Drucker calls the "educated society," and I think this is the most distinctive characteristic of our times. Within fifteen years, two-thirds of our population (living in metropolitan areas) will attend college. Adult education programs, especially the management development courses of such universities as M.I.T., Harvard, and Stanford, are expanding and adding intellectual breadth. All this, of course, is not just "nice," but necessary. As Secretary of Labor Wirtz recently pointed out, computers can do the work of most high school graduates —more cheaply and effectively. Fifty years ago, education was called "non-work," and intellectuals on the payroll (and many staff) were considered "overhead." Today, the survival of the firm depends, more than ever before, on the proper exploitation of brainpower.

One other characteristic of the population which will aid our understanding of organizations of the future is increasing job mobility. The lowered expense and ease of transportation, coupled with the real needs of a dynamic environment, will change drastically the idea of "owning" a job—and of "having roots," for that matter. Participants will be shifted from job to job even from employer to employer with much less fuss than we are accustomed to.

3. *Work-relevant values.* The increased level of education and mobility will change the values we hold vis-à-vis work. People will be more intellectually committed to their jobs and will probably require more involvement, participation, and autonomy in their work. [This turn of events is due to a composite of the following factors: (1) There is a positive correlation between education and need for autonomy; (2) job mobility places workers in a position of greater influence in the system; and (3) job requirements call for more responsibility and discretion.]

Also, people will tend to be more "other-directed" in their dealings with others. McClelland's data suggest that as industrialization increases, other-directedness increases;[21] so we will tend to rely more heavily than we do even now on temporary social arrangements, on our immediate and constantly changing colleagues.

4. *Tasks and goals of the firm.* The tasks of the firm will be more technical, complicated, and unprogrammed. They will rely more on intellect than on muscles. And they will be too complicated for one person to handle or for individual supervision. Essentially, they will call for the collaboration of specialists in a project form of organization.

Similarly there will be a complication of goals. "Increased profits" and "raised productivity" will sound like oversimplifications and clichés. Business will concern itself with its adaptive or innovative-creative capacity. In addition, *meta*-goals will have to be articulated and developed; that is, supra-goals which shape and provide the foundation for the goal structure. For example, one *meta*-goal might be a system for detecting new and changing goals; another could be a system for deciding priorities among goals.

Finally, there will be more conflict, more contradiction among effectiveness criteria, just as in hospitals and universities today there is conflict between teaching and research. The reason for this is the number of professionals involved, who tend to identify as much with the supra-goals of their profession as with those of their immediate employer. University professors are a case in point. More and more of their income comes from outside sources, such as private or public foundations and consultant work. They tend not to make good "company men" because they are divided in their loyalty to professional values and organizational demands. Role conflict and ambiguity are both causes and consequences of goal conflict.

5. *Organizational structure.* The social structure in organizations of the future will have some unique characteristics. The key word will be "temporary"; there will be adaptive, rapidly changing *temporary systems.* [22] These will be organized around *problems-to-be-solved.* The problems will be solved by groups of relative *strangers* who represent a set of diverse professional skills. The groups will be conducted on *organic* rather than mechanical models; they will evolve in response to the problem rather than programmed role expectations. The function of the "executive" thus becomes *coordinator,* or "linking pin" between various project groups. He must be a man who can speak the diverse languages of research and who can relay information and mediate among the groups. *People will be differentiated not vertically according to rank and role but flexibly according to skill and professional training.*

Adaptive, temporary systems of diverse specialists, solving problems, linked together by coordinating and task-evaluative specialists, in organic flux, will gradually replace bureaucracy as we know it. As no catchy phrase comes to mind, let us call this an "organic-adaptive" structure.

As an aside, what will happen to the rest of society, to the manual laborers, to the less educated, to those who desire to work in conditions of high authority, and so forth? Many such jobs will disappear; automatic jobs will be automated. However, there will be a corresponding growth in the service-type of occupation, such as the "War on Poverty" and the Peace Corps programs. In times of change, where there is a discrepancy between cultures, industrialization, and especially urbanization, society becomes the client for skill in human interaction. Let us hypothesize that approximately 40 per cent of the population would be involved in jobs of this nature and 40 per cent in technological jobs, making an *organic-adaptive* majority, with, say, a 20 per cent bureaucratic minority.

6. *Motivation in organic-adaptive structures.* The section of this chapter on reciprocity stated the shortcomings of bureaucracy in maximizing employee effectiveness. The organic-adaptive structure should increase motivation and thereby effectiveness because of the satisfactions intrinsic to the task. There is a congruence between the educated individual's need for meaningful, satisfactory, and creative tasks and flexible structure or autonomy.

Of course, where the reciprocity issue is ameliorated, there are corresponding stresses between professional identification and high task involvement. Professionals are notoriously disloyal to organizational demands. For example, during the Oppenheimer hearing, Boris Pash of the FBI reported: "It is believed that the only undivided loyalty that he [Oppenheimer] can give is to science and it is strongly felt that if in his position the Soviet government could offer more for the advancement of scientific cause he would select that government as the one to which he would express his loyalty."[23]

There will be, as well, reduced commitment to work groups. These groups, as I have already mentioned, will be transient and changing. While skills in human interaction will become more important because of the necessity of collaboration in complex tasks, there will be a concomitant reduction in group cohesiveness. I would predict that in the organic-adaptive system, people will have to learn to develop quick and intense relationships on the job and to endure their loss.

In general I do not agree with the emphasis of Kerr *et al.*[24] on the "new bohemianism," whereby leisure—not work—becomes the emotional-creative sphere of life, or with Leavitt,[25] who holds similar views. They assume a technological slowdown and leveling off and a stablizing of social mobility. This may be a society of the future, but long before then we will have the challenge of creating that push-button society and a corresponding need for service-type organizations with the organic-adaptive structure.

Jobs in the next century should become *more,* rather than less, involving; man is a problem-solving animal, and the tasks of the future guarantee a full agenda of problems. In addition, the adaptive process itself may become captivating to many. At the same time, I think the future I describe is far from a utopian or a necessarily "happy" one. Coping with rapid change, living in temporary systems, and setting up (in quickstep time) meaningful relations—and then breaking them—all augur strains and tensions. Learning how to live with ambiguity and to be self-directing will be the task of education and the goal of maturity.

NEW STRUCTURES OF FREEDOM

In these new organizations, participants will be called on to use their minds more than at any other time in history. Fantasy and imagination will be legitimized in ways that today seem strange. Social structures will no longer be instruments of repression (see Marcuse,[26] who says that the necessity of repression and the suffering derived from it decreases with the maturity of the civilization) but will exist to promote play and freedom on behalf of curiosity and thought.

Not only will the problem of adaptability be overcome through the organic-adaptive structure, but the problem we started with, reciprocity, will be resolved. Bureaucracy, with its "surplus repression," was a monumental discovery for harnessing muscle power via guilt and instinctual renunciation. In today's world, it is a prosthetic device, no longer useful. For we now require organic-adaptive systems as structures of freedom to permit the expression of play and imagination and to exploit the new pleasure of work.

Notes

1. Bendix, R., *Max Weber: An Intellectual Portrait,* Doubleday & Company, Inc., Garden City, N.Y., 1960, p. 421.

2. Hall, R. H., "The Concept of Bureaucracy: An Empirical Assessment," *The American Journal of Sociology,* vol. 69, p. 33, 1963.

3. Bennis, W. G., "Theory and Method in Applying Behavioral Science to Planned Organizational Change," MIT Paper presented at the International Operational Research Conference, Cambridge University, Cambridge, Sept. 14, 1964.

4. Bendix, *op. cit.,* pp. 455–456.

5. March, J. G., and H. A. Simon, *Organizations,* John Wiley & Sons, Inc., New York, 1958.

6. Levinson, H., "Reciprocation: The Relationship between Man and Organization," Invited Address presented to the Division of Industrial and Business Psychology, Washington, D.C., Sept. 3, 1963.

7. Mayo, E., *The Social Problems of an Industrial Civilization,* Harvard University Press, Cambridge, Mass., 1945, p. 122.

8. Likert, R., *New Patterns of Management,* McGraw-Hill Book Company, New York, 1961.

9. Argyris, C., *Interpersonal Competence and Organizational Effectiveness,* Dorsey Press, Homewood, Ill., 1962.

10. Blake, R. R., and J. S. Mouton, *The Managerial Grid,* Gulf Publishing Company, Houston, 1964.

11. Shepard, H. A., "Changing Interpersonal and Intergroup Relationships in Organizations," in J. March (ed.), *Handbook of Organization,* Rand McNally & Company, Chicago, 1965.

12. Burns, T., and G. M. Stalker, *The Management of Innovation,* Quadrangle, Chicago, 1961.

13. Shepard, *op. cit.*

14. McGregor, D., *The Human Side of Enterprise,* McGraw-Hill Book Company, New York, 1960.

15. Leavitt, H. J., "Unhuman Organizations," in H. J. Leavitt and L. Pondy (eds.), *Readings in Managerial Psychology,* The University of Chicago Press, Chicago, 1964, pp. 542–556.

16. Leavitt, H. J., and T. L. Whisler, "Management in the 1980's," in Leavitt and Pondy, *ibid.*

17. Thompson, J. D., and A. Tuden, "Strategies, and Processes of Organizational Decision," in J. D. Thompson, P. B. Hammond, R. W. Hawkes, B. H. Junker, and A. Tuden (eds.), *Comparative Studies in Administration,* The University of Pittsburgh Press, Pittsburgh, Pa., 1959, pp. 195–216.

18. Johnson, E. A., "Introduction," in McClosky and Tretethen (eds.), *Operations Research for Management,* The Johns Hopkins Press, Baltimore, 1954, p. xii.

19. Wilson, A. T. M., "The Manager and His World," *Industrial Management Review,* Fall, 1961.

20. Emery, F. E., and E. L. Trist, "The Causal Texture of Organizational Environments," Paper read at the International Congress of Psychology, Washington, September, 1963.

21. McClelland, D., *The Achieving Society,* D. Van Nostrand Company, Inc., Princeton, N.J., 1961.

22. Miles, M. B., "On Temporary Systems," in M. B. Miles (ed.), *Innovation in Education,* Bureau of Publications, Teachers College, Columbia University, New York, 1964, pp. 437–490.

23. Jungk, R., *Brighter than a Thousand Suns,* Grove Press, Inc., New York, 1958, p. 147.

24. Kerr, C., J. T. Dunlop, F. Harbison, and C. Myers, *Industrialism and Industrial Man,* Harvard University Press, Cambridge, Mass., 1960.

25. Leavitt, *op. cit.*

26. Marcuse, H., *Eros and Civilization,* Beacon Press, Boston, 1955.

PERSPECTIVES IN MANAGEMENT

Applied Organizational Change in Industry: Structural, Technical and Human Approaches
Harold J. Leavitt

This is a mapping chapter. It is part of a search for perspective on complex organizations; in this instance, through consideration of several classes of efforts to change ongoing organizations. Approaches to change provide a kind of sharp caricature of underlying beliefs and prejudices about the important dimensions of organizations. Thereby, perhaps, they provide some insights into areas of real or apparent difference among perspectives on organization theory.

To classify several major approaches to change, I have found it useful, first, to view organizations as multivariate systems, in which at least four interacting variables loom especially large: the variables of task, structure, technology, and actors (usually people). (See Figure 1.)

Figure 1

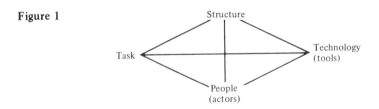

Roughly speaking, "task" refers to organizational *raisons d'etre*—manufacturing, servicing, etc., including the large numbers of different, but operationally meaningful, subtasks which may exist in complex organizations.

By "actors" I mean mostly people, but with the qualification that acts usually executed by people need not remain exclusively in the human domain.

By "technology" I mean technical tools—problem-solving inventions like work measurement, computers, or drill presses. Note that I include both machines and programs in this category, but with some uncertainty about the line between structure and technology.

Finally, by "structure" I mean systems of communication, systems of authority (or other roles), and systems of work flow.

These four are highly interdependent, so that change in any one will most probably result in compensatory (or retaliatory) change in others. In discussing organizational change, therefore, I shall assume that it is one or more of these variables that we seek to change. Sometimes we may aim to change one of these as an end in itself, sometimes as a mechanism for effecting some changes in one or more of the others.

Thus, for example, structural change toward, say, decentralization should change the performance of certain organizational tasks (indeed, even the selection of tasks); the technology that is brought to bear (e.g., changes in accounting procedures); and the nature, numbers, and/or motivation and attitudes of people in the organization. Any of these changes could presumably be consciously intended; or they could occur as unforeseen and often troublesome outcomes of efforts to change only one or two of the variables.

Similarly, the introduction of new technological tools—computers, for example—may effect changes in structure (e.g., in the communication system or decision map of the organization), changes in people (their numbers, skills, attitudes, and activities), and changes in task performance or even task definition, since some tasks may now become feasible of accomplishment for the first time.

Changes in the people and task variables could presumably branch out through the system to cause similar changes in other variables.

We can turn now to the central focus of this chapter, namely, a categorization and evaluation of several approaches to organizational change—approaches that differ markedly in their degree of emphasis and their ordering of these four variables.

Clearly most efforts to effect change, whether they take off from people, technology, structure, or task, soon must deal with the others. Human relators must invent technical devices for implementing their ideas, and they must evaluate alternative structures, classing some as consonant and some as dissonant with their views of the world. Structuralists must take stands on the kinds of human interaction that are supportive of their position, and the kinds that threaten to undermine it, etc.

Although I differentiate structural from technical from human approaches to organizational tasks, the differentiation is in points of origin, relative weightings, and underlying conceptions and values, not in the exclusion of all other variables.

This categorization must be further complicated by the fact that the objectives of the several approaches to organizational change are not uniform. All of them do share a considerable interest in improved solutions to tasks. But while some of the technical approaches focus almost exclusively on task solutions, that is, on the *quality* of decisions, some of the people approaches are at least as interested in performance of task subsequent to decisions. Although improved task solution serves as a common goal for all of these approaches, several carry other associated objectives that weigh almost as heavily in the eyes of their proponents. Thus some of the early structural approaches were almost as concerned with maintaining a power status quo as with improving task performance, and some of the current people approaches are at least as interested in providing organizations that fulfill human needs as they are in efficacious performance of tasks.

The several approaches are still further complicated by variations in the causal chains by which they are supposed to bring about their intended changes. Some of the structural approaches, for example, are not aimed directly at task but at people as mediating intervening variables. In these approaches, one changes structure to change people to improve task performance. Similarly, some of the people approaches seek to change people in order to change structure and tools, to change task performance, and also to make life more fulfilling for people. We can turn now to the several varieties of efforts themselves.

THE STRUCTURAL APPROACHES

Applied efforts to change organizations by changing structure seem to fall into four classes. First, structural change has been the major mechanism of the "classical" organization theorist. Out of the deductive, logical, largely military-based thinking of early nonempirical organization theory, there evolved the whole set of now familiar "principles" for optimizing organizational performance by optimizing structure. These are deductive approaches carrying out their analyses from task backwards to appropriate divisions of labor and appropriate systems of authority. These early structural approaches almost always mediated their activities through people to task. One improves task performance by clarifying and defining the jobs of people and setting up appropriate relationships among these jobs. Operationally one worried about modifying spans of control, defining nonoverlapping areas of responsibility and authority, and logically defining necessary functions.

In retrospect, most of us think of these early approaches as abstractions, formal and legalistic, and poorly anchored in empirical data. They were also almost incredibly naive in their assumptions about human behavior. In fact, almost the only assumptions that were made were legalistic and moralistic ones: that people, having contracted to work, would then carry out the terms of their contract; that people assigned responsibility would necessarily accept that responsibility; that people when informed of the organization's goals would strive wholeheartedly to achieve those goals.

The values underlying these early approaches were thus probably more authoritarian and puritanical than anything else. Order, discipline, system, and acceptance of authority seemed to be dominant values. The objective, of course, was optimal task performance, but within the constraints imposed by the hierarchy of authority.

In one variation or another, such structural approaches are still widely applied. It is still commonplace for consultants or organization planning departments to try to solve organizational problems by redefining areas of responsibility and authority, enforcing the chain of command, and so on.

A second widespread approach to structural change, allied to the first, somewhat more modern and sophisticated and somewhat narrower, too, is the idea of decentralization. The idea of changing organizations by decentralizing their structure was probably more an invention of the accounting profession than anyone else, though it has been widely endorsed by structuralists and by human relators too. Almost nobody is against it. Not too long ago, I heard the senior officer of one of the nation's largest consulting firms remind his large staff of young consultants that their firm was founded on the "bedrock principle of decentralization."

Decentralization affects the performance of tasks partially through its intervening effects on people. By creating profit centers, one presumably increases the motivation and goal-oriented behavior of local managers. One also adds flexibility so that variations in technology appropriate to the different tasks of different decentralized units now become more possible; so do sub-variations in structure, and local variations in the use of people. Decentralization can be thought of as a mechanism for changing organizations at a meta level, providing local autonomy for further change. Thus, within limits, decentralized units may further change themselves through the use of any one of the many alternatives available, and perhaps for this reason no group has questioned it, at least until the last couple of years.

Recently, two other structural approaches have shown up, but they have not yet reached a widespread level of application. One of them is best represented by Chapple and Sayles. Theirs is a form of social engineering aimed at task, but via people. They seek to modify the behavior of people in order to improve task performance, but they do it by modifying structure, in this case, the flow of work. Out of the tradition of applied anthropology, they argue that planning of work flows and groupings of specialities will directly affect the morale, behavior, and output of employees. One of the failings of earlier structural models, in their view, is that the design of work was almost entirely determined by task and technical variables, and failed to take account of human social variables. They provide illustrative cases to show that appropriate redesigning of work, in a social engineering sense, affects both human attitudes and output.

I cannot overlook in this discussion of structure the implications of a second approach—the research on communication networks. I know of no *direct* applications of this laboratory research to the real world, though it has had some indirect influence on structural planning. In that research, variations in communication nets affect both routine and novel task performance rather significantly. The results suggest that appropriate communication structures might vary considerably within a complex organization, depending upon the type of task that any subunit of the organization undertakes. Thus for highly programmed repetitive tasks, highly centralized communication structures seem to operate most efficiently, but with some human costs. For more novel, ill-structured tasks, more wide-open communication nets with larger numbers of channels and less differentiation among members seem to work more effectively.

TECHNOLOGICAL APPROACHES TO ORGANIZATIONAL CHANGE

My first entry in this technological category is Taylor's *Scientific Management.* Its birth date was around 1910, its father, Frederick W. Taylor. Its tools were work measurement tools. It bore none of the abstract deductive flavor of the structural approaches. From the classic programming of the labors of Schmidt, the immigrant pig-iron handler at Bethlehem, on to the more sophisticated forms of work measurement and analysis of succeeding decades, Taylorism has constituted a significant force in influencing task performance in American organizations.

Scientific Management, almost from its inception, took a position outside of the task, not of it. Taylor created a new technical skill—industrial engineering—and a new class of specialized practitioners—the industrial engineers. Theirs was a staff skill, a planning skill. They were the organizers and designers of work. The Schmidts were the doers.

Like the early structural approaches, Scientific Management was thus to a great extent ahuman, perhaps even inhuman. For in creating the separate planning specialist, it removed planning from its old location—the head of the doer of work. Many observers, both contemporary and subsequent, saw this phase of scientific management as downright demeaning of mankind. Taylor put his foot deeply into his mouth by saying things like this: "Now one of the very first requirements for a man who is fit to handle pig iron . . . is that he shall be so stupid and so phlegmatic that he more nearly resembles . . . the ox than any other type. . . . He must consequently be trained by a man more intelligent than himself."

But despite the flurry of congressional investigations and active counterattack by Taylor's contemporaries, Scientific Management grew and prospered, and radically changed structure, people, and the ways jobs got done. Indeed, it spread and flourished until no self-respecting manufacturing firm was without time-study men, methods engineers, work standards, piece rates, and job classification schemes.

The range of Scientific Management, however, was limited by its relatively simple tools largely to the programming of eye-hand and muscle jobs. Though Taylor and his fellows were ready to generalize their methods to almost any organizational problem, the methods themselves fell pretty short when applied to judgment and think-type jobs.

If one asks why Scientific Management flourished, several reasonable answers appear. The environment of the day, despite counterattacks by Upton Sinclair and others, was probably supportive. It was an environment of growth, expansiveness, and muscle flexing. Work in associated disciplines was supportive, too. Psychology, for example, was physiologically oriented, concerned with individual differences and anxious to be treated as a science. Hence it, too, was measurement happy.[1] Finger dexterity tests meshed neatly with Taylor's motion study.

But most of all, Taylorism, like many other ideas, seemed to be carried by its own operational gimmicks—by its cheap, workable, easily taught techniques and methods.

Scientific Management receded into a relatively stable and undramatic background in the late 1930's and 1940's and has never made a real comeback in its original form. But the technological approaches were by no means dead. The development of operations research and the more or less contemporaneous invention and exploitation of computers have more than revived them.

I submit that operational operations research methods for changing organizational problem solving can be reasonably placed in the same category with Scientific Management. They have both developed a body of technical methods for solving work problems. They both are usually *external* in their approach, essentially separating the planning of problem-solving programs from the routine acting out of solutions. Operations research, too, is quickly developing, in its operational form, a new class of hot-shot staff specialists, in many ways analogous to the earlier staff efficiency man. What is *clearly* different, of course, is the nature of the techniques, although there may be larger differences that are not yet so clear.

The operations research and information processing techniques are turning out to be, if not more general, at least applicable to large classes of tasks that Scientific Management could not touch. Now, armed with linear programming methods, one can approach a task like media selection in an advertising agency, though it would have been nonsense to time study it.

But note the overall similarity: change the setting of the movie from Bethlehem, Pa., to Madison Avenue; the time from 1910 to 1962; the costuming from overalls to gray flannel suits; and the tasks from simple muscular labor to complex judgmental decisions. Turn worried laborer Schmidt into worried media executive Jones. Then replace Taylor with Charnes and Cooper and supplant the stopwatch with the computer. It is the same old theme either way—the conflict between technology and humanity.

A distinction needs to be drawn, of course, between operational operations research and other computer-based information-processing approaches, although they are often closely allied. "Management Science" hopefully will mean more than highly operational applications of specific techniques, and organizations are also being changed by simulation techniques and by heuristic problem-solving methods. Their impact has not yet been felt in anything like full force; but tasks, people, and structures are already being rather radically modified by them. In fact, one wonders if these task-directed efforts will not end up having at least as radical an impact on structure and on the role of humans as on task solutions themselves. For out of new information-processing methods we now begin to reconsider the bedrock issue of decentralization and to reconsider the permanency and primacy of human judgments for making certain classes of decisions. All the way round the organization, visible changes are being generated out of technical innovations.

Without delving further into the substance of these more recent technological approaches, it may be worth pointing up one other characteristic that they share with many of their predecessors—a kind of faith in the ultimate victory of *better* problem solutions over less good ones. This faith is often perceived by people-oriented practitioners of change as sheer naïveté about the nature of man. They ascribe it to a pre-Freudian fixation on rationality; to a failure to realize that human acceptance of ideas is the real carrier of change, and that emotional human resistance is the real roadblock. They can point, in evidence, to a monotonously long list of cases in which technological innovations, methods changes, or operations research techniques have fallen short because they ignored the human side of the enterprise. It is not the logically better solutions that get adopted, this argument runs, but the more humanly acceptable, more feasible ones. Unless the new technologist wises up, he may end up a miserable social isolate, like his predecessor, the unhappy industrial engineer.

Often this argument fits the facts. Operations research people can be incredibly naïve in their insensitivity to human feelings. But in another, more gracious sense, one can say that the technological approaches have simply taken a more macroscopic, longer view of the world than the people approaches. Better solutions do get accepted in the long run, because deeper forces in the economy press them upon the individual organization—competitive forces, mainly. Macroscopically these ahuman or people-last approaches may encounter bumps and grinds in the microcosms of the individual firm; but sooner or later, in the aggregate, human resistances will be allayed or displaced or overcome, and the steam drill must inevitably defeat John Henry.

The technological approaches assume some communication among firms, and between firms and the world; and they assume further that the demonstration of more economic solutions will eventually result in their adoption, though the road may be rough.

The technological approaches seem not only to predict the victory of cleaner, more logical, and more parsimonious solutions but also to *value* them. Failure of human beings to search for or use more efficient solutions is a sign, from this perspective, of human weakness and inadequacy. People must be teased or educated into greater logic, greater rationality. Resistance to better solutions is proof only of the poverty of our educational system; certainly it is not in any way an indication that "optimal" solutions are less than optimal.

THE PEOPLE APPROACHES

The people approaches try to change the organizational world by changing the behavior of actors in the organization. By changing people, it is argued, one can cause the creative invention of new tools, or one can cause modifications in structure (especially power structure). By one or another of these means, changing people will cause changes in solutions to tasks and performance of tasks as well as changes in human growth and fulfillment.

In surveying the people approaches, one is immediately struck by the fact that the literature dealing directly with organizational change is almost all people-oriented. Just in the last four or five years, for example, several volumes specifically concerned with organizational change have been published. All of them are people-type books. They include Lippitt, Watson, and Westley's *The Dynamics of Planned Change;* Lawrence's *The Changing of Organizational Behavior Patterns;* Ginsberg and Reilly's *Effecting Change in Large Organizations,* Bennis, Benne, and Chin's *The Planning of Change;* and Guest's *Organizational Change.*

This tendency to focus on the process of change itself constitutes one of the major distinguishing features of the people approaches. The technological and structural approaches tend to focus on problem-solving, sliding past the microprocesses by which new problem-solving techniques are generated and adopted.

Historically, the people approaches have moved through at least two phases. The first was essentially manipulative, responsive to the primitive and seductive question, "How can we get people to do what we want them to do?"

Although most of us identify such questions with borderline workers like Dale Carnegie, much of the early work (immediately post-World War II) by social scientists on "overcoming resistance to change" dealt with the same issues.

Carnegie's *How to Win Friends and Influence People* was first published in 1936, a few years ahead of most of what we now regard as psychological work in the same area. Like the social scientists that followed, Carnegie's model for change focused on the relationship between changer and changee, pointing out that changes in feelings and attitudes were prerequisites to voluntary changes in overt behavior. Carnegie proposes that one changes others first by developing a valuable (to the other person) relationship, and then using that relationship as a lever for bringing about the change one seeks. One does not attack with logic and criticism and advice. *A* offers *B* support, approval, a permissive atmosphere; and having thus established warm, affective bonds (invariably "sincere" bonds, too), *A* then requests of *B* that he change in the way *A* wishes, while *A* holds the relationship as collateral.

Though social scientists have tended to reject it out of hand, current research on influence processes suggests that the Carnegie model is not technically foolish at all, although we have disavowed it as manipulative, slick, and of questionable honesty.

The Carnegie model, moreover, has some current social scientific parallels. Thus Martin and Sims, for example, directly attack the issue of how to be a successful power politician in industrial organizations. They argue that dramatic skill, capacity to withhold certain kinds of information, the appearance of decisiveness, and a variety of other calculatedly strategic behaviors, appear to be effective in influencing behavior in organizational hierarchies.

In fact, Carnegie-like interest in face-to-face influence has finally become a respectable area of social scientific research. Several works of Hovland *et al.* on influence and persuasion provide experimental support for the efficacy of certain behavioral techniques of influence over others.

But if we move over into the traditionally more "legitimate" spheres of social science, we find that much of the work after World War II on "overcoming resistance to change" was still responsive to the same manipulative question. Consider, for example, the now classic work by Kurt Lewin and his associates on changing food habits, or the later industrial work by Coch and French. In both cases, *A* sets out to bring about a predetermined change in the behavior of *B*. Lewin sets out to cause housewives to purchase and consume more variety meats—a selling problem. Coch and French set out to gain acceptance of a preplanned methods change by hourly workers in a factory. In both cases the methodology included large elements of indirection, with less than full information available to the changees.

But whereas Dale Carnegie built warm personal relationships and then bargained with them, neither Lewin nor Coch and French are centrally concerned about intimate relationships between changer and changee. Their concern is much more with warming up the interrelationships among changees.

Thus 32 percent of Lewin's tests housewives exposed to a group-decision method served new variety meats, as against only 3 percent of the women exposed to lectures. Lewin accounts for these results by calling upon two concepts: "involvement" and "group pressure." Lectures leave their audiences passive and unpressed by the group, whereas discussions are both active and pressing. Similarly, Coch and French, causing the girls in a pajama factory to accept a methods change, emphasize *group* methods, seeing resistance to change as partially a function of individual frustration, and partially of strong group-generated forces. Their methodology, therefore, is to provide opportunities for need satisfaction and quietly to corner the group forces and redirect them toward the desired change.

But it is this slight thread of stealth that was the soft spot (both ethically and methodologically) of these early people approaches to change, and this is the reason I classify them as manipulative. For surely no bright student has ever read the Coch and French piece without wondering a little bit about what *would* have happened if the change being urged by management just did not seem like a good idea to the "smaller, more intimate" work groups of Coch and French's "total participation" condition.

One might say that these early studies wrestled rather effectively with questions of affect and involvement, but ducked a key variable—power. Coch and French modified behavior by manipulating participation while trying to hold power constant. In so doing, the artistry of the "discussion leader" remained an important but only vaguely controlled variable, causing difficulties in replicating results and generating widespread discomfort among other social scientists.

Other contemporary and subsequent people approaches also avoided the power problem and encountered similar soft spots. The Western Electric counseling program that emerged out of the Hawthorne researches sought for change through catharsis, with a specific prohibition against any follow-up action by counselors—a "power-free" but eminently human approach. Later, users of morale and attitude surveys sought to effect change by feeding back anonymous aggregate data so that the power groups might then modify their own behavior. But the very anonymity of the process represented an acceptance of the power status quo.

It was to be expected, then, that the next moves in the development of people approaches would be toward working out the power variable. It was obvious, too, that the direction would be toward power equalization rather than toward power differentiation. The theoretical underpinnings, the prevalent values, and the initial research results all pointed that way.

But though this is what happened, it happened in a complicated and mostly implicit way. Most of the push has come from work on individuals and small groups, and has then been largely extrapolated to organizations. Client-centered therapy and applied group dynamics have been prime movers. In both of those cases, theory and technique explicitly aimed at allocating at least equal power to the changee(s), a fact of considerable importance in later development of dicta for organizational change.

Thus Carl Rogers describes his approach to counseling and therapy:

> This newer approach differs from the older one in that it has a genuinely different goal. It aims directly toward the greater independence and integration of the individual rather than hoping that such results will accrue if the counsellor assists in solving the problem. The individual and not the problem is the focus. The aim is not to solve one particular problem, but to assist the individual to grow.

At the group level, a comparable development was occurring, namely, the development of the *T* (for training) group (or sensitivity training or development group). The *T* group is the core tool of programs aimed at teaching people how to lead and change groups. It has also become a core tool for effecting organizational change. *T* group leaders try to bring about changes in their groups by taking extremely permissive, extremely nonauthoritarian, sometimes utterly nonparticipative roles, thus encouraging group members not only to solve their own problems but also to define them. The *T* group leader becomes, in the language of the profession, a "resource person," not consciously trying to cause a substantive set of changes but only changes in group processes, which would then, in turn, generate substantive changes.

Though the *T* group is a tool, a piece of technology, an invention, I include it in the people rather than the tool approaches, for it evolved out of those approaches as a mechanism specifically designed for effecting change in people.

In contrast to earlier group discussion tools, the *T* group deals with the power variable directly. Thus Bennis and Shepard comment:

> The core of the theory of group development is that the principle obstacles to the development of valid communication are to be found in the orientations toward authority and intimacy that members bring to the group. Rebelliousness, submissiveness or withdrawal as the characteristic responses to authority figures ... prevent consensual validation of experience. The behaviors determined by these orientations are directed toward enslavement of the other in the service of the self, enslavement of the self in the service of the other, or disintegration of the situation. Hence, they prevent the setting, clarification of, and movement toward, group shared goals.

I offer these quotes to show the extent to which the moral and methodological soft spots of the early manipulative models were being dealt with directly in group training situations. These are not wishy-washy positions. They deal directly with the power variable. Their objective is to transfer more power to the client or the group.

But these are both nonorganizational situations. For the therapist, the relationship with the individual client bounds the world. For the *T* group trainer, the group is the world. They can both deal more easily with the power variable than change agents working in a time-constrained and work-flow-constrained organizational setting.

At the organizational level, things therefore are a little more vague. The direction is there, in the form of movement toward power equalization, but roadblocks are many and maps are somewhat sketchy and undetailed. McGregor's development of participative Theory *Y* to replace authoritarian Theory *X* is a case in point. McGregor's whole conception of Theory *Y* very clearly implies a shift from an all-powerful superior dealing with impotent subordinates to something much more like a balance of power:

> People today are accustomed to being directed and manipulated and controlled in industrial organizations and to finding satisfaction for their social, egoistic and self-fullfillment needs away from the job. This is true of much of management as well as of workers. Genuine "industrial citizenship"—to borrow a term from Drucker—is a remote and unrealistic idea, the meaning of which has not even been considered by most members of industrial organizations.
>
> Another way of saying this is that Theory "X" places exclusive reliance upon external control of human behavior, while Theory "Y" [the theory McGregor exposits] relies heavily on self-control and self-direction. It is worth noting that this difference is the difference between treating people as children and treating them as mature adults.

Bennis, Benne and Chin specifically set out power equalization (PE) as one of the distinguishing features of the deliberate collaborative process they define as planned change: "A power distribution in which the client and change agent have equal, or almost equal, opportunities to influence" is part of their definition.

In any case, power equalization has become a key idea in the prevalent people approaches, a first step in the theoretical causal chain leading toward organizational change. It has served as an initial subgoal, a necessary predecessor to creative change in structure, technology, task solving, and task implementation. Although the distances are not marked, there is no unclarity about direction—a more egalitarian power distribution is better.

It is worth pointing out that the techniques for causing redistribution of power in these models are themselves power-equalization techniques—techniques like counseling and *T* group training. Thus both Lippitt *et al.* and Bennis *et al.* lay great emphasis on the need for collaboration between changer and changee in order for change to take place. But it is understandable that neither those writers nor most other workers in power equalization seriously investigate the possibility that power may be redistributed unilaterally or authoritatively (e.g., by the creation of profit centers in a large business firm or by coercion).

If we examine some of the major variables of organizational behavior, we will see rather quickly that the power-equalization approaches yields outcomes that are very different from those produced by the structural or technological approaches.

Thus in the PE models, *communication* is something to be maximized. The more channels the better, the less filtering the better, the more feedback the better. All these because power will be more equally distributed, validity of information greater, and commitment to organizational goals more intense.

Contrast these views with the earlier structural models which argued for clear but limited communication lines, never to be circumvented; and which disallowed the transmission of affective and therefore task-irrelevant information. They stand in sharp contrast, too, to some current technical views which search for optimal information flows that may be far less than maximum flows.

The PE models also focus much of their attention on issues of *group pressure, cohesiveness,* and *conformity.* The more cohesiveness the better, for cohesiveness causes commitment. The broader the group standards, the better. The more supportive the group, the freer the individual to express his individuality.

These, of course, are issues of much current popular debate. But as factors in effecting change, they are almost entirely ignored by the technical and most of the structural models. In their faith that best solutions will be recognized and in their more macroscopic outlook, until very recently at least, the technical and structural models did not concern themselves with questions of human emotionality and irrationality. If these were treated at all, they were treated as petty sources of interference with the emergence of Truth.

Evidence on this last question—the question of whether or not truth is obscured or enhanced by group pressures—is not yet perfectly clear. On the one hand, Asch has shown in his classic experiments that group pressures may indeed cause individuals to deny their own sense data. On the other hand, Asch himself has warned against interpreting this denial as an entirely emotional noncognitive process. When 10 good men and true announce that line *A* is longer than line *B,* and when the 11th man, still seeking truth, but himself seeing *B* as longer than *A,* still goes along with the group, he may do so not because he is overwhelmed by emotional pressure but because "rationally" he decides that 10 other good sets of eyes are more likely to be right than his own.

Moreover, some data from some recent experiments being conducted at Carnegie Tech and elsewhere[2] suggest that in-fighting and debate will cease rather rapidly within a group when a solution that is prominently better than other alternatives is put forth. This is to say that people use their heads as well as their guts; though at times in our history we have vociferously denied either one or the other.

Consider next the *decision-making* variable. Decision making, from the perspective of power equalization, is viewed not from a cognitive perspective, nor substantively, but as a problem in achieving committed agreement. The much discussed issues are commitment and consensual validation, and means for lowering and spreading decision-making opportunities.

Contrast this with the technical emphasis on working out optimal decision rules, and with the structuralist's emphasis on locating precise decision points and assigning decision-making responsibility always to individuals.

SUMMARY

If we view organizations as systems of interaction among task, structural, technical, and human variables, several different classes of efforts to change organizational behavior can be grossly mapped.

Such a view provides several entry points for efforts to effect change. One can try to change aspects of task solution, task definition, or task performance by introducing new tools, new structures, or new or modified people or machines. On occasion we have tried to manipulate only one of these variables and discovered that all the others move in unforeseen and often costly directions.

We have more than once been caught short by this failing. The Scientific Management movement, for example, enamored of its measurement techniques, worked out efficient task solutions only to have many of them backfire because the same methods were also evoking human resistance and hostility. The human relations movement, I submit, is only now bumping into some of the unforeseen costs of building a theory of organization exclusively of human bricks, only to find that technological advances may obviate large chunks of human relations problems by obviating large chunks of humans or by reducing the need for "consensual validation" by programming areas formerly reserved to uncheckable human judgment.

Approaches with strong structural foci have also on occasion fallen into the one-track trap, changing structure to facilitate task solution only then to find that humans do not fit the cubbyholes or technology does not adapt to the new structure.

On the positive side, however, one can put up a strong argument that there is progress in the world; that by pushing structural or human or technical buttons to see what lights up, we are beginning gropingly to understand some of the interdependencies among the several variables.

What we still lack is a good yardstick for comparing the relative costs and advantages of one kind of effort or another. We need, as Likert has suggested, an economics of organizational change.

If we had one, we could more effectively evaluate the costs of movement in one direction or another. Likert urges an economics of change because he believes the presently unmeasured costs of human resistance, if measured, would demonstrate the economic utility of organizational designs based on PE models. But such an economics might also pinpoint some of the as yet unmeasured costs of PE-based models. For the present state of unaccountability provides a protective jungle that offers quick cover to the proponents of any current approach to organizational change.

If I may conclude with a speculation, I will bet long odds that, as we develop such an economics, as we learn to weigh costs and advantages, and to predict second and third order changes, we will not move uniformly toward one of these approaches or another, even within the firm. We will move instead toward a mélange, toward differentiated organizations in which the nature of changes becomes largely dependent on the nature of task. We have progressed, I submit; we have not just oscillated. We have learned about people, about structure, about technology; and we will learn to use what we know about all three to change the shape of future organizations.

Notes

1. See for example Bendix's account of the early enthusiasm of industrial psychologists. He quotes Hugo Munsterberg appraising the promise of industrial psychology in 1913: ". . . Still more important than the valued commercial profit on both sides is the cultural gain which will come to the total economic life of the nation, as soon as everyone can be brought to the place where his best energies may be unfolded and his greatest personal satisfaction secured. The economic experimental psychology offers no more inspiring idea than this adjustment of work and psyche by which mental dissatisfaction with the work, mental depression and discouragement, may be replaced in our social community by overflowing joy and perfect inner harmony."

2. As reported in a personal communication from T. C. Schelling, 1961.

Introduction to the
Structural Design of Organizations
Jay W. Lorsch

Our purpose is to introduce you to a useful way of thinking about the structural design of organizations, and to make you aware that the structure of an organization is not an immutable given, but rather a set of complex variables about which managers can exercise considerable choice.

DEFINITION OF STRUCTURAL DESIGN

It is useful to make a distinction between the basic structure and the operating mechanisms which implement and reinforce this basic structure.[1] Design of the *basic structure* involves such central issues as how the work of the organization will be divided and assigned among positions, groups, departments, divisions, etc., and how the coordination necessary to accomplish total organizational objectives will be achieved. Choices made about these issues are usually publicized in organization charts and job descriptions. If we recognize that behavior in an organization is influenced by a system of variables (technical, individual, social and organizational inputs), it is obvious that such formal documents are only one method of signaling to individuals what behavior is expected of them. Nevertheless, this method is important because it is so widely used by managers to define and communicate their expectations of other organization members.

Managers also can reinforce the intent of their basic structural design through what we call *operating mechanisms.* Operating mechanisms include such factors as control procedures, information systems, reward and appraisal systems, standardized rules and procedures, and even spatial arrangements. These structural variables can be used to more clearly signal to organizational members what is expected of them, to motivate them toward their assigned part of the organization's goal, and, as necessary, to encourage them to undertake collaborative activity. While our central focus is on the basic structure, we shall have more to say about these operating mechanisms later.

Reprinted with permission from Gene W. Dalton, Paul R. Lawrence, and Jay W. Lorsch, *Organizational Structure and Design,* Homewood, Ill.: Richard D. Irwin, Inc., 1970 ©, pp. 1–16.

CONVENTIONAL APPROACHES TO STRUCTURAL DESIGN

In the past, the most widely used ideas about structural design were those developed by a group of organization theorists who have been labeled the *classicists.*[2] Fayol, Gulick, Urwick, Mooney and their colleagues and successors drew heavily on their own experience in early twentieth century organizations and on the industrial engineering ideas of Frederick J. Taylor. While a detailed review of these ideas is beyond our scope, we can briefly summarize the central features of their "principles of organization."

With regard to the division of work, most of the authors recommended dividing up the work by function (i.e., sales, manufacturing, engineering, etc.). The one exception was Gulick, who suggested that the work of an organization could be divided on several bases: by function; by product; by territory; by time. In any case these writers emphasized economic and technical efficiency. The only human variable given major attention was the limited intellectual capacity of the individual. To cope with this limitation, division of labor was advocated. Each individual would have a narrow task which, given his limited capacity, he could accomplish in the most technically efficient manner. While these ideas are based on the simplistic assumption that man is motivated only by money and will do as he is directed, they still persist and are widely used as a basis for making decisions about organization structure.

According to these writers, coordination was not a major problem. Work was to be divided so that the subgoals of various units would add up to the overall organizational goals. Any remaining coordinating issues would be handled through the management hierarchy. Since people followed the direction of their superiors, the management hierarchy was the only coordinating device necessary.

While this approach has been widely used, it has severe limitations. First, it provides little help in designing a task with intrinsic motivation. Second, it is of limited value in dealing with the multiple levels of division of work in most large organizations. Third, managers have become more aware that the management hierarchy is not sufficient as a mechanism to achieve the coordination required in an organization. The goals of individuals and units do not automatically add up to the total goals of the organization.

Because of these shortcomings, other organizational theorists, most of whom were psychologists or social psychologists, began conducting research into these issues and have more recently come up with a second set of prescriptions which, while less widely applied, are sufficiently used to be worthy of mention. Perhaps the most concise statement of these ideas is offered by Likert.[3] This approach considers the motivational and collaborative issues left unattended by the classical theorists. While these behavioral scientists do not deal explicitly with the issue of division of labor, they do implicitly suggest that jobs should be divided to give the individual meaningful work over which he can have some feeling of control and influence. According to this view, the individual is motivated by self-actualization, and it follows that he will seek more complicated and engaging jobs. This must be taken into account in the division of work. The individual is also motivated by social needs and it is therefore important, according to Likert, to structure the organization so that each individual belongs to a cohesive work group in which participation in decision making is the accepted norm.

While this approach offers no explicit recommendation about how to divide up the work of an organization to provide self-actualizing work and group membership, it is very explicit about how to achieve collaboration or coordinated effort. This is done by linking work groups together by members who hold overlapping membership in two or more groups. This "linking pin" individual is a key figure in the organization, since it is through him that information about group objectives and decisions is transmitted and conflicting viewpoints are resolved.

One shortcoming of this approach is the implicit assumption that all individuals are motivated by similar needs. No attention is focused on the important differences in individual needs. A second problem is, because of either the needs of organization members or the nature of the task, linking pin and participative decision-making practices are often impractical. For example, some managers find it difficult because of their own predispositions to involve subordinates in all decisions. Similarly, some tasks require decisions for which the information is not available to all the members of the work group.

Both of these approaches described above are subject to a more general criticism. While each offers a particular prescription about how to design the basic structure of an organization, both approaches are offered as the one best way to organize. To the readers who have already been exposed to a systemic conceptual framework, it should be obvious that any blanket prescription is an oversimplification. As the recent title of a book on organization theory states, "It all depends."[4] Furthermore, recent research which utilizes the systemic approach suggests that the choices made in designing a basic structure depend on the task and human inputs involved.

A SYSTEMIC APPROACH TO THE DESIGN OF ORGANIZATION STRUCTURE

Two recent studies point to the validity of this conclusion. Burns and Stalker, in their pioneering study of firms in both a dynamic, changing industry and a more established, stable industry, report that there were important structural differences between the successful firms in each industry.[5] In the stable industry, successful organizations tended to be what the authors called "mechanistic." There was more reliance on formal rules and procedures. Decisions were made at the higher levels of the organization. The spans of supervisory control were narrow. In the more dynamic industry, the authors characterized the effective organizations as "organic." Spans of supervisory control were wider; less attention was paid to formal procedures; and more decisions were reached at the lower levels of the organization. The second study was conducted by Joan Woodward.[6] She found that economically successful organizations in industries with different production technologies were characterized by different organization structures. For example, successful firms in industries with a unit or jobshop technology had wider spans of supervisory control and fewer hierarchical levels than did successful firms with continuous process technologies.

While both of these studies consider the structure of an organization as one variable in a system affecting behavior in organizations, they do not provide a conceptual framework which is sufficiently comprehensive for analyzing and solving structural design problems. A more recent study by Lawrence and Lorsch builds on the basic idea of Woodward, Burns and Stalker, and others, and provides a more comprehensive analytic framework for working on structural design problems.[7]

DIFFERENTIATION AND INTEGRATION

Before describing the analytic framework which Lawrence and Lorsch have developed, it is important to emphasize three points.[8] First, this conceptual scheme is based on an empirical study of ten organizations with varying levels of economic performance in three different industrial environments (plastics, consumer foods, standardized containers) and these findings have been corroborated by research in several additional settings. Second, this conceptual model does not provide a prescription for the one best way to organize. Instead, it provides a framework for thinking about structural design issues based on the demands of the organization's particular market and technological environment. Third, this set of concepts can be used to analyze the structural design which seems to best fit an organization's environment. These concepts can also be used to understand the organization's current strengths and weaknesses and to help determine what design changes will move a particular organization toward a better fit with the demands of its specific environment.

As we begin this discussion, we must first define two of the central concepts in this framework. First, *differentiation* is defined as *the differences in cognitive and emotional orientations among managers in different functional departments, and the differences in formal structure among these departments.* Rather than thinking of division of work as only affecting the economies and efficiencies of task performance, as did the classicists, Lawrence and Lorsch recognized that each unit was itself a subsystem in which members would develop particular orientations and structural patterns, depending on their task and their predispositions. Since different units were working with different parts of the organization's environment [e.g., market, scientific techno-economic (manufacturing) variables], these units would develop differentiation to some degree or other, depending upon the specific environment.

The second concept which we want to define is *integration—the quality of the state of collaboration that exists among departments that are required to achieve unity of effort by the environment.*

As we have already indicated, different environments require varying degrees of differentiation among organizational units. Basically, the extent of organizational differentiation depends upon the *certainty or uncertainty of the environment* and *its diversity or homogeneity.* Rather than being concerned with the environment as a single entity, the authors recognized that complex organizations—those with more than one unit—actually segment their environments into parts. The authors then identified the relative certainty of the parts of any environment. For example, each of the ten organizations was dealing with a market subenvironment (the task of the sales organization), a techno-economic subenvironment (the task of the manufacturing unit) and a scientific subenvironment (the task of the research or design unit). Each of these subenvironments within any one industry had a different degree of certainty of information about what needed to be done. How similar or different these parts of any environment were on the certainty-uncertainty continuum determined whether that environment was relatively homogeneous or diverse. For example, in one of the environments studied, the container industry, all parts of the environment were relatively certain and the environment was characterized as homogeneous. On the other hand, in a second environment, the plastics industry, the parts of the environment ranged from a highly certain techno-economic sector to a very uncertain scientific subenvironment and the total environment was characterized as more diverse. As suggested above, the degree of differentiation in an effective organization was found to be related to the diversity of the environment. Thus, in the economically effective container industry there was less differentiation than in an effective plastic organization. The less effective organizations in these industries did not meet the environmental demand for differentiation so well.

We can now summarize the general relationship the authors found between the certainty of the subenvironment a unit is dealing with and three of the unit characteristics along which differentiation was measured (Figure 1).

The fourth characteristic of units along which differentiation was measured—goal orientation—was not related to the certainty of the environment, but instead to the goals inherent in each part of the environment—e.g., the market (customer service, competitive action, etc.); techno-economic (costs, quality, efficient schedules, etc); science (discovery of new knowledge; utilization of technical talent, etc.).

We can quote from the original study for a more detailed picture of how the varying degrees of differentiation manifest themselves in the high-performing organizations in two of the three industries studied.[9]

Figure 1

Uncertainty of environmental sector	High	Moderate	Low
Extent of formalized unit structure	Low	Medium	High
Interpersonal orientation*	Task	Social	Task
Time orientation	Long	Medium	Short

* This curvilinear relation between the members' interpersonal orientation in a task-oriented/ social-oriented continuum is consistent with the work of Fred E. Fiedler, *Technical Report No. 10* (Urbana, Ill.: Group Effectiveness Research Laboratory, Department of Psychology, University of Illinois, May 1962).

To illustrate the varying states of differentiation among these three organizations, we can use hypothetical encounters among managers in both the plastics and the container high-performing organizations. In the plastics organization we might find a sales manager discussing a potential new product with a fundamental research scientist and an integrator. In this discussion the sales manager is concerned with the needs of the customer. What performance characteristics must a new product have to perform in the customer's machinery? How much can the customer afford to pay? How long can the material be stored without deteriorating? Further, our sales manager, while talking about these matters, may be thinking about more pressing current problems. Should he lower the price on an existing product? Did the material shipped to another customer meet his specifications? Is he going to meet this quarter's sales target?

In contrast, our fundamental scientist is concerned about a different order of problems. Will this new project provide a scientific challenge? To get the desired result, could he change the molecular structure of a known material without affecting its stability? What difficulties will he encounter in solving these problems? Will this be a more interesting project to work on than another he heard about last week? Will he receive some professional recognition if he is successful in solving the problem? Thus our sales manager and our fundamental scientist not only have quite different goal orientations, but they are thinking about different time dimensions—the sales manager about what's going on today and in the next few months; the scientist, how he will spend the next few years.

But these are not the only ways in which these two specialists are different. The sales manager may be outgoing and concerned with maintaining a warm, friendly relationship with the scientist. He may be put off because the scientist seems withdrawn and disinclined to talk about anything other than the problems in which he is interested. He may also be annoyed that the scientist seems to have such freedom in choosing what he will work on. Furthermore, the scientist is probably often late for appointments, which, from the salesman's point of view, is no way to run a business. Our scientist, for his part, may feel uncomfortable because the salesman seems to be pressing for immediate answers to technical questions that will take a long time to investigate. All these discomforts are concrete manifestations of the relatively wide differences between these two men in respect to their working and thinking styles and the departmental structures to which each is accustomed.

Between these different points of view stands our integrator. If he is effective, he will understand, and to some extent share, the viewpoints of both specialists and will be working to help them communicate with each other. We do not want to dwell on his role at this point, but the mere fact that he is present is a result of the great differences among specialists in his organization.

In the high-performing container organization we might find a research scientist meeting with a plant manager to determine how to solve a quality problem. The plant manager talks about getting the problem solved as quickly as possible, in order to reduce the spoilage rate. He is probably thinking about how this problem will affect his ability to meet the current production schedule and to operate within cost constraints. The researcher is also seeking an immediate answer to the problem. He is concerned not with its theoretical niceties, but with how he can find an immediate applied solution. (Research in this industry tended to focus on short-term process development.) What adjustments in materials or machine procedures can he suggest to get the desired effect? In fact, these specialists may share a concern with finding the most feasible solution. They also operate in a similar, short-term time dimension. The differences in their interpersonal styles are also not too large. Both are primarily concerned with getting the job done, and neither finds the other's style of behavior strange. They are also accustomed to quite similar organizational practices. Both see that they are rewarded for quite specific short-run accomplishments, and both might be feeling similar pressures from their superiors to get the job done. In essence, these two specialists, while somewhat different in their thinking and behavior patterns, would not find it uncomfortable or difficult to work together in seeking a joint solution to a problem. Thus they would need no integrator.

The authors summarize this approach as follows: "These two hypothetical examples show clearly that the differentiation in the [effective] plastics organization is much greater than in the equally effective container concern. The high-performing food organization fell between the extremes of differentiation represented by the other two organizations."[10]

But the environment of an organization imposes requirements other than differentiation upon the organization. One of these is the *dominant competitive issue.* In the plastics and food environment, this was the issue of innovating new products and processes; for the container industry the dominant issue was the scheduling and allocation of production facilities to meet market demands.

The dominant competitive issue was also related to the final environmental characteristic of interest to the authors—the pattern and degree of integration required among units. In all three environments the tightness of integration required was found to be identical. However, there was an important difference in the pattern around which this integration was occurring. In plastics and foods, where innovative issues are dominant, the tight integration was required between sales and research and production and research.

Figure 2

In the container industry, the tight integration was required between production and sales and between production and research.

Figure 3

The authors report that in each industry the high-performing organizations achieved more effective integration around these critical interdependencies than their less effective competitor. Thus, the effective organization more satisfactorily met the demands of its environment for both differentiation and integration than did the less effective organization(s) in the same environment.

This finding is particularly interesting, because the authors found a strong inverse relationship between differentiation and integration within any one organization. When highly interdependent units are highly differentiated, it is more difficult to achieve integration among them than when members of the units have similar ways of thinking and behaving. This antagonistic relationship is illustrated by Figure 4, taken from the original study.[11]

Thus, we are presented with an interesting paradox: effective organizations in a given environment achieve more differentiation *and* more integration, but these two states are basically antagonistic. How does an organization get both? The authors found that two related factors made this possible.

First, when an organization is both highly differentiated and well integrated, it is necessary for the organization to develop more complicated mechanisms for achieving integration. Of course the basic organizational device for achieving integration is the management hierarchy. In an organization such as the effective container firm, with relatively low differentiation, the authors found that the hierarchy, along with formal plans and controls, was sufficient to achieve the required integration. However, the effective plastics and food organizations, faced with a requirement for both high differentiation and close integration, developed other supplemental integrating devices. These included individual coordinators (integrators), cross-unit teams, and even whole departments of integrators—individuals whose basic contribution is achieving inte-

Fig. 4. *Relationship between differentiation and integration**

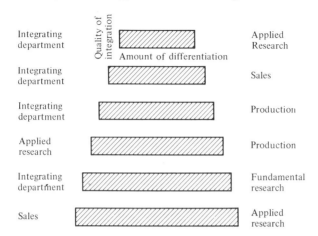

gration among units. The integrative devices present in the high-performing organization in each environment are summarized in Figure 5 on page 62.

The authors point out that while the effective organization always had integrative devices which were sufficient to handle both the differentiation and integration required, often the less effective firm also had appropriate integrative devices. Thus, the integrative devices alone do not explain why the more effective firms were able to achieve the required states of differentiation and integration while the less effective firms did not.

A second set of factors seems to account for this difference. This is the behavior pattern used within the organization to manage intergroup conflict. As individuals with different points of view attempt to attain unity of effort, conflicts inevitably arise. How well the organization does in achieving integration in the face of differentiation is very dependent upon how the individuals involved resolve their conflicts. Lawrence and Lorsch's findings indicate that the behavior which leads to effective conflict resolution in certain respects varies with environmental demands, but in other respects shows no such variations.

Those conflict management factors which vary with environmental influence include the pattern of power or influence among groups and at various levels of the management hierarchy of each group. In the high-performing organizations where conflict was managed effectively, influence was concentrated at the level within each group where the information relevant to the

---

*This is a schematic representation of the relationship among departments in one organization. The longer the bar, the more the differentiation; the wider the bar, the better the integration. This relationship held between pairs of units in all six organizations.

decision was also present. The exact level in any unit depended upon the certainty of information in its part of the particular environment. For example, in the research units of the effective plastics organization, because of the uncertainty of knowledge, influence was concentrated at the lowest management level. In the production unit of this same plastics organization, where environmental information was more certain, influence was concentrated at a higher level of the management hierarchy. Because of the diversity of this environment, the hierarchical influence in this organization was distributed differently among different levels in each function. The same was true of the effective food organization for similar reasons. However, in the container organization, dealing with more certain and more homogeneous environment, the information could be efficiently gathered by upper levels of management in all functions. Thus, hierarchical influence in this organization was concentrated at the top in all units.

The required pattern of influence among units also varied with environmental requirements. In the effective organization the unit(s) which had the central knowledge about environmental conditions related to the dominant strategic variable was the one with the most influence. For instance, in the effective plastics organization, where a separate integrating unit had been established, this group had the highest influence because it was in a position to have information about the various parts of the environment, all of which were important in achieving innovation. In the food organization, where the dominant issue was also innovation, the situation was slightly different. Here no integrating department had been established, because the differentiation required was not as high as in the plastics environment. Also, because of the consumer products involved, the dominant knowledge was in the market and scientific sectors of the environment. Therefore, the sales and research units had similar high levels of power in relation to the production unit. In the container industry the dominant issue of customer service meant that the sales unit must call the tune, and this unit did have the highest influence.

The two factors which led to effective resolution under all environmental conditions were the mode of conflict resolution, and the basis from which high influence was derived. In high-performing organizations in all environments, it was found that conflict was managed by involved individuals who dealt openly with the conflict and worked a problem until a resolution was reached which best met total organizational goals. In the effective organizations, there was more of a tendency to *confront* conflict instead of using raw power to *force* one party's compliance or instead of *smoothing* over the conflict by agreeing to disagree.

In all the high-performing organizations, the authors also found that the individuals primarily involved in resolving conflict, whether they were a common superior in the hierarchy or persons in special integrating positions, had influence based to a large extent on their perceived competence and knowledge.

This was in contrast to the less effective organizations where such persons usually drew their power solely from their position or from their control over scarce resources. The persons centrally involved in achieving integration in the high-performing organizations were followed not only because they had formal positional authority, but also because they were seen as knowledgeable about the issues which had to be resolved.

In those organizations where special integrators existed, Lawrence and Lorsch found one additional conflict management factor which seemed important. In the effective organizations, such integrators had orientations which were balanced between those of the groups whose efforts they were integrating. This made it possible for them to understand and communicate with each of the groups concerned. In the less effective organizations, these integrators tended to have one-sided orientations. They thought and acted like sales personnel or like researchers and this made it difficult for them to work with other groups.

All of these conflict management variables taken together suggest why the effective organizations in each environment were able to achieve the differentiation and integration required by the particular environment when less effective firms were not able to do so. These conflict management practices were the glue which held the differentiated units together as they worked toward integrated goals.

To summarize, then, the Lawrence and Lorsch study provides a set of research findings and concepts which enable us to understand what characteristics an organization must have to be effective in a particular set of environmental circumstances. This study directs our attention to the environmental demands placed on the organization in terms of the degree of differentiation, the pattern and degree of integration, integrative mechanisms, and conflict management behaviors. Those factors in the study which varied among high-performing organizations in the three environments studied are summarized in Figure 5.

With this summary of the findings of this study, we now want to examine briefly how these ideas can be put to use to work on the issues of structural design.

APPLYING DIFFERENTIATION AND INTEGRATION CONCEPTS TO STRUCTURAL DESIGN

As we consider these concepts as they apply to structural design decisions, we will also suggest the sequence of structural subproblems. While these subproblems are stated as discrete issues, the reader should be aware that in practice it is necessary to move back and forth among them as one thinks about the whole problem of structural design in a given organization. We will look first at the design of the basic structure and then at the necessary operating mechanisms.

Fig. 5 *Introduction to the structural design of organizations (environmental factors and organizational characteristics of effective organizations)*

Industry	Environment diversity	Actual differentiation	Actual integration	Integrative devices		Conflict management variables	
				Type of integrative devices	Special integrating personnel as % of total management	Hierarchical influence	Unit having high influence
Plastics	High	High	High	Teams, roles, departments, hierarchy, plans and procedures	22%*	Evenly distributed	Integrating unit
Foods	Moderate	Moderate	High	Roles, plans, hierarchy, procedures	17%*	Evenly distributed	Sales and research
Container	Low	Low	High	Hierarchy, plans and procedures	0%*	Top high, bottom low	Sales

* This proportion was constant for the high and low performer within these industries.

Grouping activities into units is the logical first step in designing a basic structure. The differentiation and integration concepts focus our attention on two criteria for making decisions about grouping activity. First, units which will have similar orientations and tasks should be grouped together, both because they can reinforce each other's common concerns to achieve the needed differentiation and because this will simplify the coordinating task of the common boss. Second, units which are required to integrate their activities closely should be grouped together, because the common superior can then work to achieve the required integration through the management hierarchy. Therefore units which have a requirement for both low differentiation and tight integration, should be grouped together. However, when some units are low in differentiation but are not highly interdependent, or conversely, high in differentiation but also highly interdependent, the choice about grouping becomes more complex. In these cases, we must use our judgment to determine which criterion—low differentiation or high integration—we want to optimize in grouping activities.

Designing integrative devices is the second step in determining the basic structure. As we suggested above, the grouping of activities itself has an effect upon the design of integrative devices. A primary integrative device in any organization is the management hierarchy. In grouping activities, we are essentially making choices about which units we want to integrate through the hierarchy. However, as the Lawrence and Lorsch findings suggest, even after the units are grouped and decisions have been made about where the heirarchy can be used to achieve integration, we are still left with the question of what other integrating devices are desirable and necessary. Their findings suggest that as the environment requires more differentiation and tighter integration it is necessary to build supplemental integrating mechanisms such as integrating departments or cross-functional teams into the organization. This study also suggests that these special devices should be built into the organization in such a way that they facilitate the interaction of integrators with functional specialists who have the relevant knowledge to contribute to joint decisions. Alternatively, they may also need to facilitate the direct interaction among functional specialists who have the necessary knowledge to contribute to these joint decisions.

Structuring the individual units is a third step in the design process. Here the emphasis is on operating mechanisms, which will be consistent with the unit task and the needs of its members. Issues of individual motivation are particularly relevant here.[12] In addition, the Lawrence and Lorsch findings underline the importance of designing measurement and reward prodecures to encourage orientations which are appropriate to the unit task. Similarly, reliance on formal rules and standardized procedures should be consistent with the task. Finally, the unit hierarchy and spans of control should be designed not only to provide the intra-unit coordination required by the task, but also to encourage involvement in decision making at the level where the relevant information is available.

Other Operating Mechanisms

In addition to the operating mechanisms within each unit, it is necessary to consider operating mechanisms which are applied across the whole organization. Do rewards and measurements encourage collaboration around the critical integrative issues? Do they demand consistency and conformity among units where more differentiation is required? Again, issues of individual rewards and motivation should be helpful here, but we must also realize that some operating mechanisms must be built to encourage differentiation, while others are necessary to encourage integration. We must understand the environmental demands on the organization so that reward and measurement systems can be designed to encourage both the differentiated and integrated behavior required.

Factors Affecting Conflict Management

Finally, we should consider the effect of the basic structure and the operating mechanisms on conflict resolution. The basic structure should assign responsibility for cross-functional liaison to individuals who have the relevant knowledge. If individuals who have such knowledge are formally assigned the responsibility for joint decision making, there is the highest probability they will develop the power necessary to resolve conflict effectively. A second issue is related to operating mechanisms. Do they induce unnecessary conflict? Do they cause organization members to see conflicts as win-lose rather than integrative? If so, can they be altered to encourage more integrative problem solving?

Finally, there is the issue of training and its impact on conflict-resolving behavior. While this topic could lead into a long discussion of organizational change, it is useful to mention here that some forms of laboratory training and education may be helpful to encourage the confrontation of conflict.[13] The ideas we have been discussing may be helpful in identifying which organization members are so involved in conflict management that such training might be useful.

SUMMARY

In this introduction we have explored the approaches available to solving structural design problems. In concluding, we offer a word of caution. Our understanding of organizations as systems is new and it is growing rapidly. The ideas which are presented here will certainly be modified and improved. But as crude as they are, they represent better tools than the principles which have been relied on in the past. These ideas clearly move us in a new and promising direction—that of tailoring the organization to its environment and to the complex needs of its members.

Notes

1. I am indebted to my colleague, Larry E. Greiner, for suggesting this conceptual distinction.

2. Henri Fayol, *Industrial and General Administration,* Part II, Chapter I, " General Principles of Organization"; Chapter II, "Elements of Administration." (Paris: Dunod, 1925); Luther Gulick, "Notes on the Theory of Organization," in Luther Gulick and Lyndall F. Urwick, (eds.), *Papers on the Science of Administration* (New York: Institute of Public Administration, Columbia University, 1937); Lyndall F. Urwick, "Organization as a Technical Problem," *ibid.*; James D. Mooney, "The Principles of Organization," *ibid.*

3. Rensis Likert, *The Human Organization* (New York: McGraw-Hill, 1968). See also Douglas McGregor, *The Human Side of Enterprise* (New York: McGraw-Hill, 1960).

4. Harvey Sherman, *It All Depends: A Pragmatic Approach to Organization* (Tuscaloosa: University of Alabama Press, 1966).

5. T. Burns and G. M. Stalker, *The Management of Innovation* (London: Tavistock Publications, 1961).

6. Joan Woodward, *Industrial Organization: Theory and Practice* (Oxford: Oxford University Press, 1965).

7. P. R. Lawrence and J. W. Lorsch, *Organization and Environment: Managing Differentiation and Integration* (Boston: Division of Research, Harvard Graduate School of Business Administration, 1967).

8. A more complete statement of their findings can be found in *Organization and Environment.*

9. *Ibid.,* p. 134–136.

10. *Ibid.,* p. 137.

11. *Ibid.,* Figure II–2, p. 48.

12. See G. W. Dalton and P. R. Lawrence, *Organizational Motivation and Control* (Homewood, Illinois: Irwin, 1970).

13. See G. W. Dalton and P. R. Lawrence, *Organizational Change and Development* (Homewood, Illinois: Irwin, 1970).

PART II

The introduction to Part I stressed the importance of looking at an organization from multiple perspectives. The need for a multiple-perspectives view derives from the fact that organizations are complex; they are made up of many kinds of component parts. An organization cannot be understood unless its parts are understood.

The selections in this section examine, first, the most basic building block of an organization—the individual person—an important starting point, since the organization's missions can be fulfilled only when and if individuals are motivated to work toward them. Two-person relationships, and the nature of communication within them, are examined next, followed by selections on the small group and on intergroup relationships. Part II concludes with four selections that deal with the role of the manager.

MOTIVATION

The first article, a short selection from *Business Week,* gives examples of several instances in which "reinforcement" methods have been successful in increasing employees' motivation to work efficiently. Reinforcement theory provides one model of individual motivation which you may wish to evaluate in the context of the more systematic review of motivation theories and research results presented in the second article by Chris Argyris.

PERCEPTION AND COMMUNICATION

The brief and tragic story by Joseph F. Dinneen illustrates that people can and do perceive their surroundings in incomplete and distorted ways. This human characteristic is important in understanding organizations, where people with differing points of view are often trying to communicate with one another in order to do a job or solve a problem. William F. Buckley's article

S(
a

be seen as having both positive and negativ
there is no single managerial style that i
situations.
The article by George Strauss b
wide choice of strategies that are a
applicable in certain kinds of c
from a perceptive study of the
which must be dealt with b
tional role, that of purch
Dalmar Fisher describes
managers have availab
and then suggests a

R. Rog
communication
nizational roles or oth
perceptions. The selection on
Dorothy Jongeward presents a simple,
and understanding the kind of communicatio
between two persons. It is a model that has helped ma
tions and in other settings to improve their communication s

THE GROUP IN THE ORGANIZATION

The article by Rensis Likert provides criteria for judging the effectiveness of a work group of any kind. Likert's section on leadership functions can be especially useful as an aid to identifying patterns of behavior occurring in a decision-making group, such as a committee, task force, or project team. Edgar Schein's article on intergroup problems looks at the effects that conflict or competition between groups have on the groups involved and suggests ways of reducing the adverse consequences of intergroup competition.

LEADERSHIP AND THE MANAGER

Leadership and management can be exercised in many ways. Charles R. Wilson describes two management styles, which he refers to as "homesteader" and "astronaut." The selection by Richard Tanner Johnson, from his recent book *Managing the White House,* identifies three approaches to management —"formalistic," "competitive," and "congenial"—which have been used by American Presidents. Each of the styles discussed in these two articles may

consequences, which suggests that
appropriate across the board in all

uilds on this insight, by defining a rather
ailable to a manager, each of which seems
cumstances. Strauss draws his conclusions
rganizational politics and conflicting demands
managers who occupy an interesting organiza-
sing agent. The selection by David Moment and
managerial life in three organizations, concludes that
e a wider range of style choices than they often realize,
approach to managerial career development.

MOTIVATION

Where Skinner's Theories Work

Giving praise and recognition to an employee for a task well done seems so fundamental that it appears a bit pretentious to label the act a management technique. But at a time when business is battling a cost squeeze, high rates of employee absenteeism and turnover, and low productivity, sometimes the first step toward finding a solution is to get back to basics.

That is precisely what managers from such diverse companies as Allis-Chalmers, Bethlehem Steel, Chase Manhattan Bank, Ford, IBM, ITT, Procter & Gamble, PPG Industries, Standard Oil of Ohio, and Westinghouse did last week. Along with managers from some 50 other companies, educational institutions, and government agencies, they paid $75 to attend a one-day conference in Pittsburgh on "Changing Employee Behavior," sponsored by the University of Pittsburgh's Graduate School of Business.

The conference's primary aim: to discuss how employers can apply the controversial theories of Harvard psychologist B. F. Skinner to improve worker performance. Skinner's theories—known as "behavior modification" or "positive reinforcement"—hold that an individual's behavior can be influenced by changing his environment and praising his performance.

ACCENTUATE THE POSITIVE
In essence, Skinner's disciples use praise, recognition, and a regular feedback system to tell an employee how he is doing. They avoid psychoanalyzing the worker. Instead, they analyze the work situation itself, focusing on what causes a worker to act the way he does.

In contrast, the non-Skinner behaviorists tend to concentrate more on the subconscious causes of behavior to determine why a person behaves in a given way. This fosters such techniques as sensitivity sessions and efforts to probe into personal motivations.

Critics complain that Skinner's theories smack of manipulation. But proponents such as E. Daniel Grady, division traffic manager for Michigan Bell Telephone Co., dismiss the charges. "There is no more manipulation involved in this than there is in the management task of directing people where to go and what to do," Grady told the conference.

Indeed, the examples Grady and Edward J. Feeney, vice-president of systems performance at Emery Air Freight Corp., offered of how they apply the Skinner theories bore little resemblance to manipulation in a sinister sense and, in fact, seemed deceptively simple. They involve designing methods to let employees know how well they are meeting specific goals and rewarding improvements by praise and recognition. Both Grady and Feeney stressed that to make the formula succeed, the necessary ingredient was to accentuate the positive. This, of course, is in line with Skinner's belief that punishment for poor performance produces negative results.

The insistence that a manager always has to find something positive in a worker's performance causes skeptics to say that Skinner's theories lead to mollycoddling and that happy workers are not necessarily the most productive workers. But Grady and Feeney say the approach works, and they cite cases to reinforce their contention.

CUTTING ABSENTEEISM

Grady, for example, faced an absenteeism problem with telephone operators in Detroit. He started off with a pilot program—which he recommends for managers using the Skinner techniques for the first time. He worked with 38 operators who as a group had an 11% absenteeism rate. First, he studied how attendance records were kept and found that the tally was made on a monthly basis.

Previous attempts to discourage absenteeism among various operator groups by setting up attendance recognition plans had not dented the rate. By digging further, Grady found that the operators felt that if they had missed a day early in the month, they had already messed up their own monthly attendance record as well as their group's chance for any positive recognition. Thus, it made little difference if they took a day off later in the month.

Grady decided to put the attendance records on a weekly basis. With the rules of the game changed, the operators' absentee rate declined. They no longer had the rationale for missing a day later in the month. Supervisors were encouraged to make positive comments to the operators on their attendance records. Within six weeks, the absenteeism rate in the pilot group dropped from 11% to 6.5%. Now, some 1,000 Detroit operators are on the weekly system, and absenteeism has decreased from 7½% in the first quarter of the year to 4½%.

Feeney reported on how Emery has applied the reinforcement tactic in a case that illustrates a significant point for managers trying the concept for the first time.

"You have to realize that both the managers and workers will think they are performing to a standard of performance that has been set," he said. "They usually aren't, but because they have no real measurements and feedbacks, they don't realize it."

This was what happened with Emery's use of large containers to forward small packages as a means of cutting handling and delivery times to airlines. Since container usage had been pushed, managers and dock workers assumed that containers were being used 90% of the time when possible.

Feeney was skeptical. He and his five-man staff made on-the-job analyses of container use. They found that instead of 90% container utilization, the figure was closer to 45%. Since most of the workers knew how and when to use containers, Feeney reasoned that an educational program would have little impact. He concluded that the answer was to tell the workers how much they were falling short of the 90% utilization rate and how profits would be increased if containers were used at an optimum level.

Feeney set up a checklist for the dock worker to mark each time he used a container. At the end of each shift, the worker totaled his own results to see whether he had hit the 90% goal. Feeney also encouraged supervisors and regional managers to apply "positive reinforcement" by praising any improvement in performance. If a worker's improvement was minimal, he was not criticized. Instead, he was lauded for keeping an honest record of his use of containers.

RESULTS

The results were impressive. In 80% of the offices where the technique was tried, the use of containers went from 45% to 95% in a single day. The increase was matched throughout the company and meant a savings of $44,000 a month and $520,000 a year. Equally important, said Feeney, this performance level has been maintained for almost three years.

When repeatedly pressed by a research psychologist on the psychological aspects of the technique, Feeney replied: "We do what works . . . what gets a payoff. For us, this behavioral approach got results."

Indeed, many conferees said they were at the conference because of curiosity about Emery's success. R. J. Stox, ITT's manager of training education, said that though the basic Skinner principles are not new and though "we and a lot of other people have used them in training, Feeney has applied them on the job." Edward Connelley, Bethlehem Steel's director of management development, also was intrigued by Emery's success and sent a staff member to the conference. "The more exposure to such processes we can get, the better," says Connelley.

Wheeling-Pittsburgh Steel Corp., represented by 14 staff and line managers—by far the largest delegation from any one company—wanted to know how the technique could be applied to a current drive to boost productivity among its 17,000 employees. The program is based on what a company official calls "a face-to-face commitment" to get each employee to increase efficiency. "Feedback is important," says the official, "and it has to be positive or the idea will backfire."

While no one at Wheeling-Pittsburgh considers the program an effort in "behavior modification," the company is getting results. Crews in a basic oxygen steelmaking shop, for example, took up a challenge to increase output. Working as a team, they cut scrap loss enough to boost the yield from the furnace by 3% a month, which amounts to a $200,000 savings.

HIGHER WAGES?

Clifford Mrazek, manager of organization development for Belden Corp., a Chicago-based copper fabricating company, raised a question often asked when success stories about positive reinforcement are cited: How long is it before the workers want more pay? "The whole idea of reinforcement or behavior modification seems something like cream chicken on toast," said Mrazek. "It looks good and tastes good, but it doesn't last long. Isn't money the real key?"

For any approach to be effective in boosting performance, responded Michigan Bell's Grady, the wage rate has to be reasonably close to the going rate in the area where the company operates. If the pay scale is high enough that people will work for you, added Grady, "you assume that other incentives are needed to boost performance." Grady's answer was supported by John LeCheminant, a Sun Life of Canada sales training officer. LeCheminant said that his experience with sales managers consistently showed that job satisfaction and feedback were crucial elements in an effective sales organization. "It isn't only money," contended LeCheminant.

One caveat on behavior modification and positive reinforcement was stressed during the session by Feeney and Grady as well as two other conference speakers, psychologist Karen Brethower and consultant Geary A. Rummler. "Don't oversell the idea," warned Rummler. "It's not this year's new technology that should cause a manager to drop everything else in favor of it." There is always the danger, added Feeney, that business will treat the technique as a solution in search of a problem. If that happens, a high failure rate is almost a certainty.

Personality and Organization Theory Revisited
Chris Argyris

I

Approximately every seven years this author develops an itch to examine the literature relevant to personality and organization theory (P and O theory) to determine the degree to which predictions from this framework can be identified, confirmed, or disproved by the literature.[1] The literature to be examined is limited to publications that have not appeared in two earlier reviews (Argyris, 1957, 1964).

The second purpose of the article is to build upon the assumption found in P and O theory that organizational theory requires an explicit model of man and to show that without such a model major difficulties arise in predicting important organizational events and processes. Finally, it will be noted that descriptive research is normative and that more explicit attention should be paid to normative factors for the designing of new organizations.

Model Development
The following steps indicate how the models of man and of formal organizations are developed.

1. Organizations come into being when goals to be achieved are too complex for any one individual. The sequence of events necessary to achieve these goals have to be divided into units manageable by individuals.

2. Individuals are themselves complex organizations. They produce the energy for an organization if there is some gain for them. The gain individuals seek can be understood by understanding their needs.

3. The intellectual history of the concept of needs is replete with lists, arguments, and differing views on the degree of depth to which they exist. An attempt was made previously by the author to bypass that morass by focussing on identifying relatively reliably and validly inferred predispositions that are highly influenced by the situation, yet also highly potent to the individuals (Argyris, 1960, 1964). This means that the individual seeks to fulfill these predispositions, yet their exact nature, potency, and degree to which they have to be fulfilled are influenced by the organizational context (for instance, job content or context).

Administrative Science Quarterly, **18,** 2 (June 1973), pp. 141–167. Reprinted by permission of the author and publisher.

4. Meaningful *a priori* statements about the predispositions of human beings can be developed by understanding the logic of their psycho-socio-genetic development. In examining the literature it becomes clear that there is significant agreement that humans are programmed, biologically and socially, to grow and become acculturated in certain directions. In their attempt to live, grow competently, and to seek a sense of self-acceptance, individuals tend to be programmed according to the following developmental continua (Argyris, 1957).

These continua together represent a developmental logic which is difficult for people to ignore or suppress. The degree of difficulty to suppress or alter depends upon the culture, the context, as well as the individual's interactions with key figures in his or her life. The model assumes that the thrust of this developmental program is from left to right, but nothing is said about the location of any given individual along these continua. The position of a given individual can vary from situation to situation and over time.

One of the central themes of P and O theory has been to study individual differences and to suggest new work worlds where individual differences may flourish. It is difficult to understand how some scholars, most recently Lichtman and Hunt (1971), can conclude that P and O theory has not been concerned with individual differences. Perhaps the confusion has arisen because P and O theory has been used to make generalizations about aggregate trends (for example, the higher one goes up the hierarchy, the greater the opportunity for expression of adult needs, or the lower one goes down the hierarchy, the higher the probability for employees to express frustration).

The theory does not limit itself to such generalizations, however. First, the personality model consists of continua along which individuals can be ordered, through empirical research, in terms of the kinds of needs and where they are located on each continuum. The variance of need expression can be studied among individuals as well as within individuals depending on the situation in which they exist, the particular stage of their personal development, or the history of need fulfillment.

The author published four such studies where the social environment and the needs, or predispositions as they were called, to highlight an individual's interrelationship with the work context were studied in detail. A separate analysis was made for each individual that included (1) the predispositions that he or she desired to express, (2) the potency of each predisposition, (3) the inferred probability that each would be expressed, and (4) a final score which indicated the degree to which the individual was able to express his or her predispositions, given the work content and context in which he or she functioned (Argyris, 1954, 1956, 1960).

Specific predictions were made and largely confirmed about individual reactions to the organization depending upon a personal expression score. Individuals with low scores, for example, would be expected to be judged as

Infants begin as	Adults strive toward
1) being dependent and submissive to parents (or other significant adult)	1) relative independence, autonomy, relative control over their immediate world
2) having few abilities	2) developing many abilities
3) having skin-surfaced or shallow abilities	3) developing a few abilities in depth
4) having a short time perspective	4) developing a longer time perspective

being, or should state that they were, frustrated, should have poorer attendance records, or should exhibit higher turnover. Finally, analyses were made to show how individual differences in predispositions were differentially rewarded in different types of departments. People with needs for mistrusting and controlling others, for example, sought out jobs in the internal audit department of the bank (Argyris, 1954).

Knowing something about an individual's needs was only part of the picture. Organizations have a life of their own, in the sense that they have goals that may be orthogonal or antagonistic with individual needs. The next step, therefore, was to ask if organizations had an organizational genetic logic with which they were programmed. If this program could be identified, it could be used to order the complex data about organizations.

An inspection of the literature suggested that an overwhelming number of organizations manifested organizational structures that looked like pyramids (of different shapes). The logical purpose of these pyramidal structures was (1) to centralize information and power (at the upper levels of the structure) and (2) to specialize work. This logic was described in detail in these studies by the principles of scientific management or Weberian concepts of bureaucracy. The logic explicitly stated that management should be in control over the key organizational activities. Thus, management should be high on the six organizational activities outlined below.

These continua together represented a logic which was difficult for designers of organizations to ignore, if the organizations were to have pyramidal structures. The model assumed that the more an organization approximated the right ends of the continua, the more it reproduced the ideal of formal organization. The model, however, said nothing a priori about where any given empirical organization would be along these continua.

Another major characteristic of the P and O theory model is that it requires scholars to cross disciplines, especially between psychology and sociology. One could focus on organizational structure, technology, managerial controls, reward and penalty systems, evaluation systems, leadership roles and styles, and job or role requirements, for example. The model suggests that no matter which one or which set of variables a person selects, it is important to

Designing specialized and fractionized work

low	high

Designing production rates and controlling speed of work

low	high

Giving orders

low	high

Evaluating performance

low	high

Rewarding and punishing

low	high

Perpetuating membership

low	high

measure each of the variables in terms of both sets of continua. If one selects structural variables, such as technology and managerial controls, one should ascertain the degree to which they fractionize work, give power to management, produce dependencies, and so forth. The same is true for such process variables as leadership and interpersonal relationships.

Interaction of Personality and Organization

If one has two models, each with several dimensions, it follows that the interaction between these two variables could occur at any point on any one or combinations of these dimensions. The possible combinations of points on the two models is very great, if not overwhelming.

   The author has previously developed a methodology by which to determine the needs or predisposition that employees desire to express in their work situation, the potency of each predisposition, the demands made on the individual by the organization, the probability that each predisposition will be expressed, and an overall score of the degree of self and organizational expressions as wholes (Argyris, 1954, 1956, 1965).

   To limit oneself to such research would produce a theory that would not generate *a priori* predictions about human behavior in organizations. Thus, the following step was taken. Predictions were generated about the consequences of the interaction between the individual and the organization under four conditions. They were:

If the individual aspired toward	And the organization (through its jobs, technology, controls, leadership, and so forth) required that the individual aspire toward
1) adulthood dimensions	1) infancy dimensions
2) infancy dimensions	2) adulthood dimensions
3) adulthood dimensions	3) adulthood dimensions
4) infancy dimensions	4) infancy dimensions

From the organizational model above, it was possible to hypothesize that the more the organization approximates the properties of a formal organization, the more individuals will be required to seek expression of needs that approximated the infant ends of the continua. What if (still at the level of a conceptualized exercise) the individuals aspired toward the adult ends of the continua? What would be the consequences?

To the extent that there is an incongruency between the needs of individuals and the requirements of a formal organization, the individuals will tend to experience (1) frustration, (2) psychological failure, (3) short time perspective, and (4) conflict.

The predictions can be made more specific by defining the possible formal organizational factors that influence the extent to which the incongruency may exist. They are (1) the lower one goes down the choice of command, the less the control and the fewer the abilities that may be used by an employee; (2) the more that leadership is directive, the more dependence or the less control the employee will tend to experience; and (3) the more managerial controls are unilateral, the more dependence or the less control the employee will tend to experience.

This means that the general tendency will be for lower-level employees to react to try to overcome frustration or conflict. How may individuals adapt or cope with such conditions? The alternatives are (1) to fight the organization by trying to redesign it and gain more control by, for example, creating a union; (2) to leave the organization permanently or periodically; (3) to remain in the organization but leave psychologically; to become uninvolved, apathetic, indifferent; to reduce the intrinsic importance of work; or (4) to increase the pay-offs from meaningless work; to become more market-oriented or instrumentally-oriented (Argyris, 1957).

These adaptive activities become part of the informal organization and through time become so inexorably woven into the formal organization that it is difficult for an individual to separate the two.

Several points need to be emphasized about these propositions.

1. The thrust of the model is that explanations can be developed and predictions made by ascertaining the impact of any organizational variable upon the individual and that the relevant dimensions to ascertain the impact are found in the personality model. One can understand, for example, the

impact of organizational structure, hierarchy, job content, leadership style, group norms, budgets, reward and penalty processes, and evaluation processes upon individuals and predict the consequences of their impact upon other individuals, groups, or aspects of organizational effectiveness by plotting the influence they will have along the adulthood-infancy dimensions.

2. Most attention in the literature has been paid to the first condition described above, probably because it tends to encompass most of the variance in actual life. As far as the comprehensiveness of the theory is concerned, however, the other three conditions should not be ignored.

A study, for example, was made of two organizations where the technology, job content, leadership style, and managerial controls combined to require (a) individuals in the high-skilled world to manifest needs toward the adult ends of the scales and (b) individuals in the low-skilled world to manifest needs toward the infancy ends of the scales.

In the case of the former, organization condition three, as predicted, was associated with little informal behavior (no union, almost no turnover or absenteeism, little withdrawal, high emphasis on quality of work, and so forth). In the case of the latter the same was found because the workers aspired proportionately more toward the infancy ends of the continua (conditions of paternalism). Thus, again there was a congruence (Argyris, 1960).

It is interesting to note that because of a major financial crisis the organization decided to tighten up. It dropped the level of skill required for many jobs and increased control through budgets, time study, and the like. The result was that the most frustrated were the highly skilled employees whose world had been switched from condition three to condition one. The predicted informal activities of absenteeism, turnover, and so on significantly increased. This was less true for the low-skilled employees who felt little change in their world.

3. The theoretical framework should apply to understanding individual-organizational behavior in societies regardless of political ideologies. Thus, the prediction would be made that the relationships being described will tend to hold for any organization (fitting the models below) regardless of whether it exists in the United States, England, Sweden, Yugoslavia, Russia, or Cuba (cf. Argyris, in press; Halmost, 1972).

II

There are three kinds of literature to be reviewed in this next section. First is the research that was designed directly to test aspects of P and O theory. Second is research that was not designed to test P and O theory directly but whose conclusions are predictable by and consonent with P and O theory. Third is the literature that does not test or illustrate P and O theory but where the P and O theory can provide a parsimonious explanation for the empirical data.

Research Designed to Test the Theory

Bonjean and Vance (1968) developed a questionnaire to measure self-expression at work (as defined by our model). In addition to showing that the instrument was more reliable than the author's more time-consuming interview method and that it possessed adequate concurrent validity and reliability, the writers were able to test aspects of the theory. In a random sample of 332 salaried managers, hourly-paid workers, and independent businessmen, they found that the adaptive behaviors predicted by personality and organization theory to be more frequent at the lower levels and less frequent at the upper levels were confirmed. They discovered, for example, that the lower the self-actualization (namely, expression along the adult ends of the continua defined above), the more likely employees are to (1) daydream, (2) have aggressive feelings toward their superiors, (3) have aggressive feelings toward their co-workers, (4) restrict output, (5) make mistakes or errors in their work, (6) postpone difficult tasks or decisions, (7) be concerned with the material rewards of work, (8) have thought about doing work other than that which they are currently engaged in; and the less likely employees are to (9) show interest in their work, and (10) indicate they are well satisfied with their jobs.

In another research supervised by Bonjean, Holtz (1969) studied 350 persons at seven socioeconomic levels. Using a multiple discriminant analysis, she found that different occupational status groups do have different rewards from their jobs and that "the higher the occupational status, the more the desire for 'maturity'-directed job characteristics and the higher the occupational status the greater the actual provision of maturity-directed demands and rewards (Holtz, 1969: 50–51)."

Grimes (1967), working with Bonjean, interviewed 332 respondents (104 businessmen, 108 managers, and 120 workers), as well as using the instruments described above. He found less strong support for the propositions stated. Although almost all were in the predicted direction, less than 25 percent were statistically significant. Three of the eighteen possible relationships were significant, for example, and the remaining fifteen were all in the predicted direction to support the proposition that respondents perceiving their work situation as highly bureaucratic will experience greater alienation than those without such perceptions. Similar results were obtained for propositions that respondents perceiving their work situations as highly bureaucratic will experience greater normlessness, powerlessness, and isolation.

Farris and Butterfield (1971) have conducted a study of 189 employees in thirteen Brazilian financial institutions. All but one of the organizations were in the public sector. They reported that 86 percent of the participants reported a lack of congruence between individual needs and organizational goals as predicted by the theory. Next, they compared the findings according to hierarchical positions. Sixteen top managers, forty-five middle managers, and 122 first-level technical men did not differ in the importance they attached to the goals. "However, goal congruence is higher for people at higher levels in these Brazilian organizations (1971: 6)." Moreover, "a low, but statistically significant, relationship between involvement and goal congruence [was found] in several areas. Strongest relationships occur for self-actualization and status (1971: 6–7)."

Maurer (1972) has conducted a study whose objective was to test the hypothesis that job content made a significant difference in the meaning of work, a hypothesis he correctly identifies with P and O theory. The study involved 231 males, full-time employees, going to night school. The sample was extremely heterogeneous. Only twenty-two occupations involved more than one individual. The maximum was an occupation with five occupants.

Among the findings reported was the fact that the Turner-Lawrence Perceived Task Attribute instrument was moderately correlated with job involvement (Pearson, r .45; Spearman, rho .46; Kendall, tau .34). The items that correlated most strongly were opportunity to learn, opportunity to advance, time needed to learn the job, and variety on the job. These factors are consonant with the adult ends of our continua. Opportunity to learn and variety on the job, for example, are related to utilizing one's abilities. Opportunity to advance is related to increasing the probability of control over one's work life and the enlargement of the abilities being used on the job. The relationships held with a regular multiple regression analysis which used the test unweighted job content variables as the independent variables and the six-item Lodahl-Kejner instrument as the dependent variable. A nonparameter statistic, X^2, was also used to determine if job content and job involvement were statistically significant as predicted.

Results of Research Predictable by the Theory

Herrick's recent study of a national sample of 1,533 employees confirmed that dissatisfaction increases as jobs become less challenging (1972: 57). Moreover, employees still valued work that approximates the mature ends of our personality model. When asked to rank various aspects of work, the first six factors, in order of importance, were (1) interesting work, (2) enough equipment to get the job done, (3) adequate information to get the job done, (4) enough authority and self-control related to the job, (5) pay, and (6) the use of one's abilities (1972: 68). Finally, the labor force as a whole considered job content characteristics to be more important than the economic benefits that derive from the job. The top-ranking item among all age groups was interesting work (1972: 277).

Gardell (1971) has published a systematic study relating production technology to alienation and mental health. The central independent variable inferred from an instrument designed to obtain ratings from technical experts, corporate staff members, and trade union leaders was discretion and skill level. This variable is related to the P and O theory in terms of the degree of control the individual has over his work, the degree of dependence and submissiveness, and the number of abilities used on the job. The second instrument included five scales intended to measure alienation as well as scales to measure job satisfaction and satisfaction with aspects of the work environment. The third instrument measured general life satisfaction, self-esteem and feelings of competence, and self-esteem and feelings of prestige and anxiety. The population was taken from four plants representing mass production and process industries.

Some of the findings reported were (1) the better the objective determinants of a discretionary and skilled relationship to work, the more meaningful and interesting the work is perceived to be; this finding holds for both mass and process production, (2) the more skilled tasks with their concomitant of more self-determination are also felt to be less mentally strenuous, more independent, and less socially isolating, (3) wide variations are found with some people finding jobs with low discretion as interesting; this finding, which is contrary to the prediction made by the P and O theory model (when assuming that the population aspires toward the adult ends of the continua), is relevant to 8 percent of the total population and only 25 percent of the comparison is confined within the group having low discretion jobs, and (4) various income groups do not differ from one another along the alienation scales (Gardell, 1971).

Gardell concludes:

> Severe restrictions in worker freedom and control and in skill level required are found to be related to increased work alienation and lowered level of mental health even after control is made for age, sex, income, type of leadership and satisfaction with pay. The relation between task organization and mental health is valid, however, only after allowance is made for work alienation. In both industries certain people regard jobs of low discretion and skill level as interesting and free from constraint and these groups do not tend to score low on different indices of mental health. However, these groups amount only to 8 percent in each industry and are strongly over-represented as to workers above fifty years of age.
>
> Within mass-production industry, restrictions in discretion and skill level are found to go together with increased feelings of psychological stress and social isolation. People working under piece-rate systems—compared to hourly paid workers—find their work more monotonous, constrained and socially isolating as well as having lower social status even when job content, skill level, income, and age are controlled for.
>
> High self-determination and job involvement are found to be related to high demands for increased worker influence on work and company decisions in the process industries while in the mass production industries demands for increased worker influence is greatest among those who feel their work to be monotonous and constrained. Perceptions of strong worker influence by collective arrangements are accompanied by increased demands for individual decision-power as well as increased job satisfaction and decreased alienation (Gardell, 1971).

Fullan (1970) studied oil workers, printers, and auto workers. In terms of our framework, the auto workers would have jobs that are closest to the right ends of the continua of formal organization, the printers would rank next, and the oil workers would least approximate the right ends of the continua. Fullan reported that the outstanding finding was that oil workers were much more integrated than printers and auto workers. Shepard (1969) also studied craftsmen, monitors, and assemblers (with the latter having the most specialized and fractionized jobs). Job satisfaction was lowest among the assemblers (14 percent), the next were monitors (52 percent), and finally came the craftsmen (87 percent), (Shepard, 1969: 190). He also found a strong relationship between job specialization and perceived powerlessness on the job. Thus, 19 percent of the craftsmen, 57 percent of the monitors, and 93 percent of the assemblers experienced a lack of freedom and control. Similar relationships were found for autonomy and responsibility.

Aiken and Hage (1966) reported that organizations that conform more to the formal bureaucratic arrangements are likely to have more work alienation and alienation from expressive relations. Moreover, there was greater dissatisfaction with work in those organizations in which jobs were fractionized and rigidly structured. Lichtman (1970) in a study of managers (fifteen), supervisors (twenty-six), and workers (fifty-four) found that the job satisfaction differed significantly among the means of each group and in the direction predicted by the theory; there was highest satisfaction for the managers, then for the supervisors, and last for the workers. Herzberg (1965) reported on a study by Russian social scientists of 2,665 Leningrad workers under thirty years of age. Again, the higher the job level, the higher the satisfaction with the job. In a partial confirmation, Pelz and Andrews (1966) reported that tightly controlled situations in scientific organizations resembled the conflict between the needs of mature individuals for independence and the requirements of a typical bureaucracy. Under these conditions low to moderate motivation for performance was functional; a highly motivated researcher in tight situations was, as predicted by P and O theory, extremely frustrated.

Next is reported a series of studies that suggest that employees (be they at the upper or lower levels) who have jobs that require behavior that approximated the adult ends of the personality continua reported greater satisfaction, more positive attitudes, and less frustration than those employees whose jobs required behavior that approximated the infant ends of the continua. Blankenship and Miles (1968), for example, found that higher-level managers reported greater freedom of action and less control than lower-level managers. Walton, Dutton, and Fitch (1966) reported that in six plants, as the control from above increased, the attitudes of people were more negative. As the degree of freedom and control increased, the attitudes were more positive. Pym (1963) found in a study of 310 men working in offices and factories of eight different organizations that frustration with work was dependent on job difference and on the degree of education largely because better educated people obtained jobs at higher levels in the hierarchy. Factory workers with jobs approximating the left ends of the personality continua scored significantly higher on the measure of frustration than did office workers with jobs approximating the right ends of the continua (Pym, 1963: 178).

Paine, Carroll, and Leete (1966) reported that where jobs were less structured and where there was greater opportunity for independent thought, action, growth, and feelings of accomplishment, there was a higher degree of satisfaction. Porter and Lawler (1965), in a comprehensive review of the literature, found a systematic tendency that the higher the positions the individuals held, the more positive their attitude tended to be. Margulies (1969) reported that organizations founded on classical principles of management tended to inhibit individual growth. In one department designed by more organic and flexible principles, there was significantly higher degree of satisfaction and involvement.

Carpenter (1971) found that the greater the teacher autonomy and opportunity to use professional authority (in our terms, less dependence and more use of their ability), the higher the satisfaction. Wicker studied undermanned and overmanned situations in schools (1968) and churches (1969). An undermanned situation means that there are fewer people than needed to perform according to some measure of the requirements of the situation. The deficiency is made up by participants taking on more responsibility and performing more tasks. Their work has become enriched. Overmanned situations have properties of the formal organization that are consonant with the infant ends of the continua because roles are molecularized to give every participant a piece of the action. Undermanned situations are consonant with the adult ends because participants are required to perform multiple roles. In both types of organizations Wicker found that the overmanned settings were more likely to have participants who reported less sense of responsibility, less opportunity to have control or take leadership positions, and a less rich array of tasks to perform.

Is it possible to reduce the negative consequences of fractionized work upon individuals? Can automation, for example, be of help? In a review article Susman (1972a) suggested three strategies to reduce powerlessness at work, a factor which is heavily associated with work alienation. They are (1) employees allocate tasks by themselves thereby reducing the need for close supervision, (2) crews should be permitted to select themselves through sociometric procedures, and (3) the leader of the group be elected by the group members. The first strategy would, in terms of the P and O model, encourage the use of the employees' more important abilities and decrease their sense of dependency upon the supervisor. The second would tend to increase the employees' control over membership in the work world. The third would increase employee control over work activities and reduce dependence upon the supervisor. In another article Susman (1972b) presented empirical evidence that automation may decrease meaningfulness and discretion for production work but the same factors may be increased for manual jobs.

How long does the dissatisfaction and frustration remain? Lodahl's (1964) research suggested that employees do not become habituated to work conditions. In an interesting analysis of a new and an old assembly plant, he found that the assembly-line worker in the old plant was even more dissatisfied. After fourteen years the habituated employees exhibited greater dissatisfaction with extrinsic features of their work than their younger brethren, as well as lower involvement in the product and the company. Although dissatisfaction does not decrease (it is already low), aggression toward the company and alienation from the company and product increased. Herrick (1972: 56) reported in a recent national sample that it was the first time that there was a major drop in Americans expressing job satisfaction.

Results Explained by the Theory

If individuals are predisposed toward greater autonomy and if formal organizations are designed to reduce autonomy, one should predict that individuals in organizations should seek more control over their own area. Moreover, if control at the top is greatest and least at the bottom, this should also be reflected in findings that the gap between desired and actual control is greatest at the lowest levels. Smith and Tannenbaum (1963) studied 200 geographically separate systems that were parts of larger organizations (for example, delivery companies, automotive dealers, clerical organizations, manufacturing plants, and power plants).

In the great majority of the organizational units there was a negatively sloped control curve (the lower the level of position in the hierarchy, the less the control). The ideal or preferred distribution of control was more positively sloped than the actual (that is, the workers wanted to have more control than they perceived they had). While members desired a more positively sloped distribution of control than they perceived, they did not wish to achieve this by reducing the control exercised by other levels. Ninety-nine percent of the rank-and-file groups reported that they wanted more control over their own immediate area. It was at the level of the rank-and-file member that the greatest discrepancy between actual and ideal control occurred. Interestingly, Zupanov and Tannenbaum (1968) confirmed the conclusion in a study of Yugoslavian employees and supervisors. Halter (1965) also reported that a study of 1,128 nonsupervisory employees in eighteen establishments in Oslo suggested that employees desire to enhance their degree of control over their immediate work world.

Baumgartel and Goldstein (1961) found that employees became more dissatisfied after moving to a newer, more efficient plant because the degree of control over their own work processes was greatly reduced. Bachman, Smith, and Slesinger (1966) reported that the more effective branch offices (of a sample of thirty-six employees, 656 salesmen) were characterized by high control by both management and salesmen.

Turning to the studies of preferences toward intrinsic and extrinsic factors, if we hypothesize that employees tend to be aware of and adapt to reality, it follows that they will tend to seek out those satisfactions that are possible, even though they may prefer others. Goldthorpe *et al.* (1968), for example, reported that even though employees had an instrumental orientation, they valued intrinsically satisfying work but doubted that they would be able to obtain it. Centers and Bugental (1966) reported that the individuals in lower-level occupations were more likely to seek out and be motivated by extrinsic needs, while white-collar workers sought out and were motivated by intrinsic needs.

Friedlander (1966: 44) found that medium- and high-status white-collar workers placed primary importance on the work-content factors, composed of job characteristics which might potentially fulfill growth needs. This was significantly less true for blue-collar workers and low-status white-collar workers. One reason that may be advanced is that the upper-level white-collar jobs offered more opportunity to fulfill growth needs. Blai (1964) reported that the needs for self-actualization, advancement, and interesting duties and leadership were all selected least often at the trades level and increased in frequency with employment at the higher occupations.

The hypothesis that the preference of intrinsic over extrinsic factors is related to the kind of job one has is supported by a study by Friedlander and Waltons (1964). They reported that "to the extent that the job involves functions intrinsic to the work process and content, it will appeal to positive motivation, serve as a potential satisfier, and may well influence the worker to remain in the organization (1964: 200)." Friedlander (1966: 441) also reported that work and the work environment provide greater opportunity for satisfying interaction than do nonwork factors. The combined values of the work content and work context, for example, exceeded, to a significant degree, that of church-related activities and educational factors.

Wilensky (1964) has concluded that investigators are unanimous that the lower one goes down on the social scale, the less satisfaction in work. In an attempt to explore beyond this finding, he conducted a study to ascertain what type of work people would select if they could start over again. First, Wilensky found that the general level of job satisfaction was fairly low. The proportion of satisfied employees ranged from nine in ten for professors and mathematicians to 16 percent for unskilled auto workers. Second, he found that the percentage of people who would go into similar type of work if they could start over again varied systematically with the degree of autonomy, control, and use of abilities that would be permitted by the job presently held.

Another prediction related to a derivation from the theory, namely that employees may choose to leave when they experience too much control by the organization or its representative. Farris and Butterfield (1971) found that turnover was associated with lower-goal congruence. Ley (1966) found that the major factor in labor turnover was the degree of authoritarianism of the foremen of the employees. Telly, French, and Scott (1971) showed that there was a strong relationship among hourly workers between feelings of inequity and turnover. The feelings of inequity were caused by the supervisors' inequitable treatment. The supervisors could not be influenced, did not support the workers, and did not attempt to correct employee complaints. Such conditions would, in our terms, increase the employees' feelings of dependence and submissiveness. Cooper (1967) reanalyzed the Turner-Lawrence data and developed a general factor entitled variety. The central features of this factor were highly related to workers' absence rates.

In summary it was noted that relationships have been found between the impact of technology, structure, formalization of rules, specialization of tasks, and authoritarian leadership upon individuals. In whatever language one uses the impact of these factors can be summarized as decreasing the individual's experience of control over his immediate work area, decreasing his use of the number of abilities, and increasing his dependence and submissiveness. To the extent that the individuals seek to use their more central abilities and to be autonomous, they may adapt by reactions ranging from absenteeism to withdrawal and noninvolvement, aggression, an increased emphasis on instrumental rewards, and a decreasing emphasis on intrinsic rewards. These conditions tend to increase in frequency and scope as one goes down the hierarchy. The lower-level worker is in a psychologically deprived condition. As Pym (1965) has shown, organizations are unintentionally designed to discourage the versatile and involved worker.

Job Enlargement or Enrichment

One way to define job enlargement or enrichment is to conceive of it as enlarging the job in such a way that it permits more opportunity for employees to experience jobs that approximate the right ends of the personality continua. Thus, increasing the variety increases the number of abilities used (usually motor or doing abilities). A richer enlargement is to redesign the work so that it enhances opportunity for the employee to experience greater autonomy and control over factors in job content and job context, lengthens the time perspective, and decreases dependence and submissiveness upon the superior. The former is usually called horizontal and the latter vertical enlargement.

Herzberg (1966), Davis (1966), Davis and Valfer (1965, 1966), and Emery, Thorsrud, and Lange (1966) represent the groups which have worked longest on horizontal and vertical job enlargement. All, together with Ford (1969), Sorcher (1967), and Paul, Robertson, and Herzberg (1969), have concluded that through the design of jobs that permit increased self-regulation, self-evaluation, self-adjustment, and participation to set goals, increases have been produced in productivity and positive attitudes. Thorsrud (1972a, 1972b) has recently related the concept of autonomous groups to all levels of organization, to staff as well as production employees. He conceives of autonomous groups as a basis for organizational redesign and development.

One of the more thorough correlational studies related to job enlargement has been reported by Hackman and Lawler (1971). They hypothesized that if employees are desirous of higher-order need satisfaction, there should be a positive relationship between the dimensions of jobs and motivation, satisfaction, performance, and attendance.

What are higher-order needs and are they relatable to the personality model described above? If one examines the actual items, there are "5 items related to the first dimension of degree of submissiveness, dependence or control, and autonomy; 3 items related to the second dimension of variety; 1 or perhaps 2 items related to the third dimension of abilities the individual values highly (Hackman and Lawler, 1971: 269)."

There are no items dealing with time perspective. The remaining two items seek to assess the individual's global desire for personal growth and feelings of worthwhile accomplishment on the job.

It seems legitimate, therefore, to correlate the Hackman-Lawler hypothesis with our model as follows. The more individuals seek to satisfy needs that are toward the adult ends of the continua, the higher the probability that they will report greater satisfaction, perform better, and be absent less if jobs also mirror these adult continua.

What are the characteristics jobs must have to provide the correlation predicted? Hackman and Lawler identified six job characteristics, although later they only used four (and the two they and their data rejected provide an important indirect test of one aspect of the personality and organization model). Hackman and Lawler defined six dimensions of jobs. They are variety, autonomy, task identity, feedback, dealing with others, and friendship opportunities (1971: 265). They identified the first four as core dimensions. These core dimensions are the higher order need items reconceptualized in terms of job characteristics. We may do the same. The first three core dimensions are consonant with the first three items in the personality development model, only now reconceptualized as task properties. The fourth core dimension of feedback was never included explicitly in the personality model when discussing the lower-level world, but was a central dimension in understanding the managerial world.

Nor were the dimensions of working with others and friendship opportunities included as core job characteristics because one of the derivations of the personality and organization model is that these two dimensions decrease in probability of existence and in importance to employees as one goes down the chain of command and/or as work becomes more fractionized. Thus, Hackman and Lawler's finding that these two job dimensions were not as potent would be consonant with the personality and organization model.

The primary results of the Hackman and Lawler study are:

1. The higher jobs are on the core dimensions, the more employees tend to report feeling internal pressures to take personal responsibility and do high-quality work. And, in fact, when jobs are described as being higher on variety, autonomy, and task identity, employees are rated as doing higher-quality work and as being more effective performers on the job (1971: 273).

2. When jobs are high on the core dimensions, employees report having higher intrinsic motivation to perform well.

3. The core job dimensions are strongly and positively related to job satisfaction and involvement (1971: 274).

4. The job satisfaction items that are strongly correlated with the job core dimension are related to control over one's own work, feeling of worthwhile accomplishment, personal growth, and self-esteem. These items strongly correlate with the Herrick (1972) and Seashore and Barnowe (1972) studies. They are the items that personality and organization theory would predict should be the strongest.

5. The strength of the relationships described above increases for those employees who seek more expression of higher-order needs (especially along the job dimensions of variety, autonomy, and to a lesser degree feedback) (1971: 278). This finding is of especial interest for it examines individual differences in a way rarely found in the literature. The finding is also relevant to this review because it illustrates a prediction of the theory described in condition three (1971: 12).

Finally, Hackman and Lawler differentiated between horizontal enlargement (namely, increasing the number of different things an employee does) from vertical enlargement (that is, increasing the degree to which an employee is responsible for making most major decisions about his work). Their research supports Lawler's earlier view (1969) that a combination of both types of enlargement is probably optimal. These conclusions are in line with the personality and organization model. Horizontal enlargement is related to dimensions 2 and 3 (number and depth of abilities used) while vertical enlargement is related to dimensions 1 and 4 (control and time perspective). As predicted by the model, the combination (called role enlargement by the present writer, 1957) will tend to increase the sense of personal responsibility and involvement.

Walton (1972) described an important attempt to design an entire plant using horizontal and vertical enlargement of work. The key features of the design are (1) autonomous work groups which include the team members performing different jobs, developing their own production schedule, managing production problems, screening and selecting new members, and maintaining self-policing activities; (2) integrated support functions (the team performs the maintenance, quality control, and industrial engineering functions), plus challenging job assignments; (3) job mobility and rewards for learning; and (4) self-government for the plant community.

Walton reported that the transition from a work environment that is consonant with the infant ends of our continua to one that approximates the adult ends was not an easy one for the personnel. The results to date, however, are impressive. Typically, the plant should be manned by 110 participants; the new plant was manned by seventy participants. Production has met or exceeded goals. Employees reported greater opportunities for learning and self-actualization. There were indications that the team leaders and plant managers were more involved in community affairs than foremen and managers of comparable plants.

Experiments in significant job enlargement are being conducted at Volvo. Gyllenhammar, the new and innovative president of Volvo, was directly involved in the design of a new assembly plant. The work of assembling the cars has been given to teams. Each team has responsibility for its special section of the car (for example, the electrical system, brakes and wheels, and so forth). Within a work team, the members decide the distribution and pace of work. Employees are permitted and encouraged to learn many different engineering skills in order to contribute to their team's effectiveness as well as maintain control over their work environment. It is estimated that the new plant will be more expensive (about 19,000,000 kroner) than the conventional car assembly. The top management decided that the expenditure was worth it because they valued increasing the quality of life within the plants and because they believed that it would lead to a work force with less turnover and absenteeism (Volvo, 1972).

III

Two important issues found in the literature that are relevant to P and O theory are (1) the relationship between sociological variables such as social class and the behavior of employees within the organization and (2) the relationship of leisure to the employees' work world.

Social Class and Employee Behavior

Although social class factors are seen as interacting with and influencing the factors found at the work place, P and O theory suggests that the work content and context are more potent than the relevant social class variables. The work content and context factors are assumed to have first causality in a circular process of interdependence between the former factors and social class factors. In speaking of first causality, focus is placed upon the variable that initially created the other variable(s), the variable one has to focus upon if change is to be brought about. It is contended here that the human behavioral variables produced the social class variables and other variables such as leisure. Once having produced them, they switched into an interdependent relationship where each variable influenced the other. An analogy would be that people create streets. Once streets are built, they coerce people to ride on them and not on sidewalks. People can create new streets and alter old ones; streets cannot create new streets.

This view was supported by the data cited in an earlier publication (Argyris, 1964). If individuals remain in a given social class and if they change their jobs, they take on the attitudes related to their new jobs (whether it is satisfying or not) and not those related to environmental factors such as social class. Workers, before their jobs were enlarged, for example, expressed typical lower social-class attitudes toward work (apathy, indifference, market-orientation). When their jobs were enlarged, however, the same workers first became tense and unhappy, and after becoming accustomed to more challenging and meaningful work, took on middle-class values (involvement, interest in intrinsic factors, and so forth). From a sociological view, however, their social class had not changed.

The data cited above (Goldthorpe *et al.,* 1968) in which it was found that workers can value intrinsic satisfactions and yet aspire toward an instrumental orientation (usually associated with the working class) raises questions as to whether social class variables can explain as much of the variance as can psychological and organizational variables. How can working-class people hold working-class and middle-class values?

Faunce and Clelland (1967) supported the view that the inside factors probably cause the external ones (although once both are in operation, they feed back to reinforce each other). They reported that class, status, and power arrangements in the community are in large part a function of the organizational structure, production technology, and division of labor. Mackonin (1970: 738) has reported that, "It was the bureaucratic type of organization that was playing a significant role in Czechoslovakian society. This was an obvious contradiction to the abolition of distinct inequality in all other spheres." Negandhi and Prasad (1971: 163–164), in a study of comparative management, have concluded that there has been an overemphasis on the environmental and cultural variables in understanding behavior within organizations (ranging from plants to bureaucracies to regional areas). Hrebiniak and Alutto (1972) reported that role-related factors were more important in explaining organizational commitment than father's occupation (a variable related to social class) and other nonorganizational factors such as sex and marital status.

Recently, Kohn (1969) and Kohn and Schooler (1969) have conducted studies that describe a more differentiated model as to why the internal variables will probably help to account for more of the nonrandom variance of human behavior within organizations than the approaches that focus on variables external to the organization. Their findings may be organized in the following outline form:

1. There is a linear relationship between values on conformity to externally imposed rules versus self-direction from the highest to the lowest socioeco-

nomic class. The relationship is essentially the same for whatever age and size of family (Kohn and Schooler, 1969: 664).

2. Consonant with greater valuation of self-direction, men of a higher class were found to take extrinsic aspects of jobs (pay and security) for granted and focus on opportunities jobs offer for self-expression and individual accomplishment.

The higher the men's social class, the more importance they attach to how interesting the work is, the amount of freedom, the opportunity to use their abilities, and the chance to help people. The lower their class position, the more importance they attach to pay, fringe benefits, hours of work, and so forth (Kohn and Schooler, 1969: 666).

3. The class relationships are predominantly linear, with virtually no significant curvilinear or higher-order relationships and no sharp breaks. It is profitable to think of a continuous hierarchy of positions, not of discrete social classes (Kohn and Schooler, 1969: 669).

4. Education and occupational position are each related, independently of the other, to almost all aspects of values and orientation and these relationships are essentially additive. Education and occupational position are important in understanding (a) self-direction versus conformity to externally imposed rules, (b) valuing intrinsic or extrinsic aspects of work and, less so, (c) self-confidence and self-deprecation (Kohn and Schooler, 1969: 669).

5. Income and class indentification are not very important for explaining the relationships of class to 4(a), (b), and (c) (Kohn and Schooler, 1969. 669).

Why is this so? What are the most potent variables influencing these relationships? After a careful statistical analysis of their data, the authors conclude that "only those conditions that vary continuously with education and with occupational position can be of great relevance to understanding such factors" as those in 4(a), (b), and (c).

Although educational experience is a potent variable, occupational position is more potent (Kohn and Schooler, 1969: 675). The aspect of occupational conditions that is more potent is occupational self-direction (Kohn and Schooler, 1969: 674–675).

If occupational position is crucial and if, within that, self-direction permitted on the job is most important, and if economic and class identification are not significantly related to self-direction, the direction to look for the potent variables is inside the organization. Kohn and Schooler (1969), for example, showed that: (a) closeness of supervision is significantly related to occupational self-direction and (b) the work requirements are also critical. Work with data or with people is more likely to require initiative and thought and judgment than is work with things. Work that is more complex and less routine is related to occupational self-direction.

Thus, we arrive at the point where the key factors identified with occupational position are those, on the job, that are related to providing opportunities for greater control over one's work, less dependence upon others, especially supervision, and more use of one's abilities.[2] These two sets of factors are congruent with the conditions represented as key developmental dimensions from infancy toward adulthood.

Leisure and Work Experiences

A question frequently asked of the P and O theory model is to what extent is it possible for employees to compensate for the impoverished life that they experience within the organization by designing and participating in leisure or other activities outside work that are more meaningful? The model of man used in P and O theory would require that the compensation hypothesis be rejected. The logic is as follows: if individuals tend to experience dependence, submission, frustration, conflict, and short time perspective at work and if they adapt to these conditions by psychological withdrawal, apathy, indifference, and a decrease in the importance of their worth as human beings, these adaptive activities become dominant in the person's life and they will guide his leisure behavior outside the work place. Individuals will seek leisure activities that are consonant with the adaptive activities.[3]

Two large research projects have been reported that bear directly on this hypothesis.

Meissner (1971) reported that the job probably influences the choice and quality of nonwork activities. The research results come from a sample of 206 industrial workers interviewed in a community with a population of about 20,000. They worked in a large wood-products manufacturing company.

Meissner (1971: 241) stated three options. (1) Workers compensate for the constraints and social isolation of the job in their free time. (2) The experience of constraint and isolation carries over into free time. (3) Life away from work is unaffected by the job.

The results that would support personality and organization theory would be those related to the carryover hypothesis.

Meissner reported that fifteen of the sixteen possible relations between indicators of work constraint and measures of organizational involvement clearly favored a carryover hypothesis; of the sixteen possible differences of participation roles in associations other than church, fourteen supported the carryover hypothesis. Meissner concluded that

> The results of the preceding analysis indicate strongly that neither the proposition of "compensation" nor the proposition of "no effect" are viable for participation in voluntary organizations other than church attendance. Instead, experience with work of little discretionary potential carries over into reduced participation in formally organized activities (1971: 253).

And later,

> When work is socially isolating, workers reduce their exposure to situations in which they have to talk and also spend less time in organized and purpose-

directed activities. They make up for it and spend a lot more time fishing on the week-end, and pushing the shopping cart through the supermarket on workdays. Lack of opportunity to talk on the job is associated with dramatically reduced rates of participation in associations, that is, in activity commonly believed to help integrate individuals into the community (1971: 260).

Torbert (1972), with the help of Malcolm Rogers, intensively interviewed 209 workers.[4] His basic hypothesis was that the more play (exploration and expression of oneself), the greater the commitment to the job; the more energetic the leisure; and the more proactive the political activity. Torbert developed several ratings. The first was a job rating of the degree of playful expression on the job (equivalent to our adult ends of the continua). Next, there was a rating of job involvement. Third was a rating of leisure involvement that included six dimensions, for example, discriminating about watching television, expansion and improvement of oneself or one's community, amount of activity, presence of a dominant interest, and absence of false expectations about the future. After a careful discussion of the operational and conceptual meaning of the various dimensions and their reliability, Torbert concluded, among other things, that (1) average leisure involvement increased as job ratings increased (significant at the .05 level and accounting for 46 percent of the nonrandom variance) and that this held true when one controlled for education, (2) the association between increasing job involvement and increasing leisure involvement is positive (and significant at the .05 level), (3) increasing job rating was positively associated with increasing political activity, even when controlling for education (at the .001 level of significance), and (4) there was evidence that the higher the job rating, the greater the probability that the political activity tended to be for the common good.

Torbert also reported that those who have work that has more variety and permits more proactivity should also tend to select such recreational pursuits. Those who have more routine work which requires them to be more passive should seek or select similar recreational activities. Parker (1971) also confirmed these findings. He reported a national recreation survey in England in which those with jobs in the higher occupational classes selected more active recreational pursuits while those in the lower occupational classes selected more passive recreational pursuits (Parker, 1971: 60). Another governmental study found that employers, managers, and professional people watched only half as much television, but participated nearly twice as often in physical recreation as semiskilled and unskilled manual workers (Parker, 1971: 60). After reviewing his own and others' work, Parker (1971: 114) concluded, "My view is that the causal influence is more likely to be *from* work experience and attitudes *to* leisure experiences and attitudes than the other way round, mainly because the work sphere is both more structured and more basic to life. . ."

Several studies have been reported whose conclusions are also in line with P and O theory. Cohen and Hodges (1963) found that lower-level employees participated least in voluntary organizations. They suggested that the cause was that severe social and work deprivation makes it difficult for lower-level employees to be concerned. Fisk (1964: 255) concluded that professionals are more often preoccupied with culture, cerebral skills, and group activities while blue-collar workmen are predisposed toward solitary pursuits and television viewing. Pope (1964) reported that the poor and less-educated workers belong to fewer formal voluntary associations (60 percent belonged to no formal organization). Langner (1963) found similar results. Van de Vall (1967) found that white-collar union members are more active and involved in their unions than are blue-collar employees.

IV
The Model of Man and the Organization

Organizations are designed to tap the energy and commitment of individuals who are to perform roles, produce work, and achieve goals of the organization. Many organizational variables are designed, therefore, on an explicit or implicit model of man. The concepts of centralization, decentralization, and span of control, for example, have developed around the problem of controlling and motivating human behavior. The design of work is heavily influenced by the model of man presented here. Taylor's molecularized jobs assumed one could hire a hand; the vertical and horizontal job enlargement adherents assumed that one hired a whole human being, and the concept of autonomous groups assumed that the whole human being was an intricate part of a group whose norms influenced human behavior.

There are several organizational theorists who reject the need to have an explicit model of man. Some theorists, such as Blau, Perrow, Dubin, Goldthorpe, and Lockwood, treat man as a black box. Elsewhere, it has been shown that such a strategy will lead to internal contradictions of the theory (Argyris, 1972). In Blau and Schoenherr's recent study (1971), for example, the model of man implicit in their theory suggests that human beings would report that they are experiencing decentralization if they are not supervised in their jobs even though the job is highly formalized with rigid rules that require strict compliance. Their theory does not differentiate between a state of decentralization in which the employee is free to perform his job with a minimum of rules and regulations and one in which the employee is free to perform his job under conditions of maximum rules and regulations (Argyris, 1972).

Crozier (1964: 23, 31, 33), though lacking an explicit model of man, also was able to conclude that the inhumanity of organization toward individuals was not confirmed by his data (how can one define inhumanity without a concept of man), yet, in the same work, he stated that nervous tension arises from monotonous and repetitive work, that apathy and social isolation is great, and that work loads produce pressure. Goldthorpe *et al.* (1968) asserted that employees are instrumentally oriented and do not seek intrinsically satisfying work, yet they reported psychological and physical stress among their subjects, that employees experienced their jobs as having little meaning, and that workers consciously chose to devalue their interest in intrinsically satisfying work because so little of it was available (Argyris, 1972). Perrow developed an insightful model positing a relationship between the nature of work and consequences on employee behavior. Without a concept of man to explain the hypothesized relationships, Perrow falls into the problem of developing a tautological theory (Argyris, 1972).

Rational Man Decision Theorists
Unlike the previous scholars quoted, Simon (1957) has always been centrally concerned with a model of man and of organization. Man is primarily a finite information processing system striving to be rational and to satisfice in his decision making (cf. Argyris, 1973). In terms of our model of man, Simon focuses primarily on cognitive dimensions and consequently has more to say about problem-solving activities than P and O theory. His model of man has little to say, however, about issues of dependence, submissiveness, the need for psychological success, confirmation, and feelings of essentiality.

Organization based on rational man administrative theory is similar in important respects to the organization of traditional administrative theory. In Simon's view organization and administration play a central and dominant role in designing and controlling human behavior. In Simon's organizations it is management which defines the objectives and the tasks and gives the orders downward. It trains—indeed indoctrinates—the employees and rewards and penalizes. The basic properties of formal pyramidal structures (specialization of tasks and centralization of power and information) are not altered. An analysis of the later work of Simon and his colleagues leads us to conclude that there were few changes (Argyris, 1973). The emphasis upon rationality and deemphasis of emotionality, and the implicit focus on formal organization and its dependence-producing qualities remained through the work described in *The New Science of Management Decision* (Simon, 1960).

If a major and subsequent work by two colleagues of Simon, Cyert and March's *A Behavioral Theory of the Firm* (1963), is examined, the same concepts of man and organization remain. The basic pyramidal system still applies. Management is still in control, still writing the major programs, and people are viewed as members of coalitions (departments) politicking against each other for scarce resources.

Cyert and March (1963: 21), however, do ask more questions about how an organization actually defines organizational goals, expectations, and choices and how one reduces the discrepancy between executive choice and how the decisions are implemented by those below the executives. Human beings are seen as influencing goals because, as new people enter the organization, they evoke new problems and develop different aspiration levels (Cyert and March, 1963: 116).

More important to understanding the intendedly rational view of the nature of organization is to focus on what Cyert and March describe as the "heart of their theory," that is, their relational concepts (1963: 116). Taking a behaviorally oriented view, they found (1) coalitions bargaining with each other in ways so that conflict was only quasi-resolved, (2) people searching within limits of the internal nature of the system, its goals, and norms, and (3) some organizational learning (Cyert and March, 1963: 116–127). With these concepts in their model, they were able to make more accurate predictions about such behavior as price determination.

The unintended consequence of this theorizing is to maintain the status quo. Not only does this view accept the power structure, the specialization of tasks, and managerial indoctrination, it also accepts as givens the dysfunctional consequences of the above, namely, quasi-resolution of conflict, uncertainty avoidance, and biased probabilistic search. P and O theory views these as variables to be altered because they tend to inhibit growth orientation and effective thinking (Argyris, 1973).

Recently, Allison has written a book (1971) which goes beyond the issues considered to date. Briefly, Allison suggested that decisions can be analyzed at three levels. Level I considers the decision makers as rational, attempting to maximize certain values where alternatives are carefully assessed and choices are made rationally. Although this provides insights into understanding decisions, Level I is a very limited view of reality and, at times, makes incorrect predictions. Level II views a decision as made by a working bureaucracy in the Simon tradition. Although Allison shows how this enlarges our understanding of decision making, he also shows how such a view is incomplete and could make incorrect predictions.

Level III goes beyond the formal organizational roles, rules and standard operating procedures, sequential attention to goals, and problem-directed search. Level III conceptualizes the actors as players in a central, competitive game whose name is politics: bargaining occurs along regularized circuits among players positioned hierarchically within the system in question. Moreover, the amount and nature of the responsibility men shoulder influences what they see, how they hear, and what actions they take (Allison, 1971: 144).

> The players are also people. The core of the bureaucratic politics mix is personality. How each man manages to stand the heat in his kitchen, each player's basic operating style, and the complimentarity or contradiction among personalities and styles in the inner circles are irreducible pieces of the policy blend. Moreover, each person comes to his position with baggage in tow, including sensitivities to certain issues, commitments to various programs . . . (Allison, 1969: 709).

Although Allison is careful to include new aspects of man's behavior, he does not include concepts (a model of man) to help us explain the behavior. Nor does Allison develop a theoretical framework of group and intergroup dynamics to help us understand that some of the causes of the new behavior are not limited to organizational factors. Man in our society, for example, may be programmed to create interpersonal relationships that are competitive (a win-lose proposition), in which there is little overt openness about, and concern over, interpersonal feelings, and where trust and a sense of individuality are low (Argyris, 1968). These are all behaviors that Allison relates to the model of organizational politics. But people behave this way even when they are placed in group settings that are designed to encourage the opposite behavior, even after they develop group commitment to such changes (Argyris, 1962, 1968).

This does not mean that it is wrong for Allison to relate such behavior as competitiveness to the organizational politics model. It may mean that the behavior is caused by more than one level of variable (a position that Allison accepts by developing three levels of causality). Thus, if we are to describe more fully the essence of a decision, we would need to develop a model of the human personality, interpersonal relations, and group dynamics that relates these variables to actual decision-making processes (which might be called Level IV). Unless these variables are included, there is serious question whether man will ever be offered a theory that would help him to change those aspects of organizational politics he wishes to change.

V
Inability to Predict Important Trends

The point has been made that the notion of the rational-satisficing man is a richer concept of man than the model found in most traditional organizational theories, as well as those found in some sociological theories. In terms of personality and organization, the issues of dependence, submissiveness, expression of feelings, and defenses and their relevance to problem solving and decision making have been ignored. Because of these omissions, these theories would have difficulty in predicting certain trends.

If man were primarily rational and effectively influenced by mechanisms of organizational influence, the pressures and uncertainty from the environment, or social trends and social class, there should be little need for participants to resist or to fight the development of management information systems, because they are rational modes designed to enhance organizational control, managing pressures and reducing uncertainty, and coping with the impact of certain social trends.

Recent research, however, suggests that managers may resist management information systems, even though it can be shown that they accomplish the desired objectives (for example, reducing uncertainty). The reasons for the resistance are related to the issue of a desire for control over the immediate work environment in order to survive, of the dislike of being dependent and submissive toward others, and the increased probability that when management information systems work best, the manager will tend to experience psychological failure (Argyris, 1971).

The second trend that would be difficult to predict by these theories is the hostility and aggression of an increasing number of young people toward the idea that organizations should be able to buy off people to be primarily rational, to submit to the mechanisms of organizational influence, and to suppress their feelings. Personality and organization theory predicts that the younger people (more oriented toward self-actualization) will find increasingly intolerable those organizations that do not encourage people to aspire toward relative independence, psychological success, and expression of their feelings and their abilities. This prediction is congruent with Maslow's, where he states that as a society progresses to the point that survival and security needs are fulfilled, then the desire will be to express more of the higher order needs (Maslow, 1970).

The third limitation flows from the combined action of the first two limitations. Given the inability to predict emotionality against rationality and the aggression against rational man and organizational mechanisms of influence and given the (unintended) support of the status quo and use of satisficing to rationalize incompetence, there is an interaction of forces that make change in organizations seem hopeless, if not impossible. How does one arrive at this conclusion? The argument is as follows.

1. To the extent man accepts inducements to behave rationally, he becomes a passive individual vis-à-vis the way power, information, and work are organized in the society and those who are responsible for such organization.

2. Over time such individuals resolve their self-actualizing tendencies by any one or a combination of approaches: suppressing them, denying them, or distorting them. They may soon come to see their legitimate role in the organization (in relation to the design of power, information, and tasks) as pawns rather than as origins. Their sense of being an origin and their feelings of personal causation will tend to be low.

3. Assuming that organizations survive, the members soon come to view themselves as being pawns, being passive (again to the issues discussed in this section), being controlled as good, natural, necessary. They may eventually define loyalty and a sense of responsibility and maturity in these terms (Argyris, 1960, 1971).

4. Individuals soon create managerial cultures in which the discussion of these possibilities is seen as inappropriate (Argyris, 1960, 1971).

5. The youth, who see the results within their families and who get their experiences confirmed in the literature and who, because of the very success of the system, are able to focus more on the self-actualizing needs, soon will attempt to change the situation. Given factors (1) to (4), however, they will be terribly frustrated.

6. The frustration will tend to lead to regression and one result of regression is to withdraw (communes) while another is to aggress (militancy).

7. Since little empirical research or tested experience is available to indicate

how self-actualizing activities and rational activities can be integrated, the hostility of youth may be seen as unfair by older people or their withdrawal as a cop-out.

The fourth and perhaps most important point is that none of the theories discussed above, with the exception of personality and organization theory and those similar to Likert's (1967) and McGregor's (1960), would predict the single most important trend about public and private organizations, namely, their increasing internal deterioration and lack of effectiveness in producing services or products (Benham, 1972; Bennis and Slater, 1968; Ewing, 1971; Gardner, 1968; Katz and Georgeopoulos, 1971; Kaufman, 1969; Long, 1971; Miner, 1971; Newman, 1971; Schon, 1971; and Smith, 1971). Twenty-five years ago 75 percent of the respondents in a national survey felt that public and private organizations performed well whereas only 25 percent believe the same today (Landau, 1972). It is ironic that during the same period that *Time* magazine published a special story about the deterioration of services in all types of organizations and called upon the public to complain and confront the increasing dry rot of organizations, Thompson gave a talk assuring the audience that organizations were doing quite well and that the pessimistic predictions about organizations were probably inaccurate (Thompson, 1972).

VI

Normative Theories About Human Behavior

The majority of the research reviewed attempts to describe, understand, and predict human behavior within organizations. Such research is typically described as descriptive and differentiated from normative which promulgates certain values (beyond those implicit in the scientific method). The more the differentiation between descriptive and normative is examined, the fuzzier it becomes. One contribution of the more humanistic researchers may be to point up that all research is normative because the social universe is not a given in the same sense as is the physical universe. The social universe is basically a convention; it is constructed and reconstructed by man.

The author recently illustrated this consequence by the concepts of dissonance and attribution. These two concepts are central in modern social psychology. Consequently, they occupy central positions in textbooks. One can show empirically that the interpersonal world of most people in ongoing organizations is characterized by much more mistrust, conformity, and closed-ness than trust, individuality, and openness. This world, called Pattern A, can be shown to be consonant with, if not derivable from, the values about effective human behavior endemic in the pyramidal structure, or in what Simon calls the mechanisms of organizational influence. The predictions from dissonance or attribution theories can be readily confirmed in this Pattern A world. Thus, findings based on descriptive research will tend to opt for the status quo.

If one creates a new pattern (Pattern B), which admittedly is very rare in the everyday world where trust, openness, and individuality are able to predominate, the same predictions are no longer readily confirmable. To put this another way, if our universe had been mostly Pattern B, dissonance and attribution theories would probably not be the central concepts they are today in descriptive social psychology. Thus, if students learn that it is natural to deal with postdecisional events by reducing dissonance, they will begin to behave in these ways. The concept of man implicit in such a theory becomes reinforced. It looks like it is natural because most people behave this way most of the time.

If it is possible, however, to take a sub-group of such people and significantly alter their behavior toward Pattern B within a period of two weeks, in a T group for example, then the natural characteristic of constancy seeking or dissonance reduction cannot be as basic as we thought.

Concepts created to explain various aspects of the theory will not have their limits tested because in order to do so, a nonconventional world would be required. But social scientists cannot produce a nonconventional (noncontrived) world without deviating from the present norm. If society is to permit scientists to conduct research on issues that deviate from and are designed to confront the foundations of present society, it will probably permit those deviations that are considered good. But research on good phenomena involves one in normative issues.

Are there concepts or ideas upon which a social scientist can base a normative theory? One possibility is to base the normative view upon the potentialities of man. Man should be studied in terms of what he is capable of, not only how he actually behaves. In the case of P and O theory, for example, the researcher could conduct research on worlds that would permit greater expression of the adult ends of the continua. Maslow would take the behavior that is characteristic of rare peak experiences and make them values toward which to aspire (Maslow, 1969).

If one replies that such behavior is rarely observed, we would agree and then ask for the systematic research to tell us how the behavior may be made more frequent. Twenty years ago no one had pole-vaulted higher than sixteen feet. Yet, no one took this as a given. Today the sixteen-foot mark is broken continually because people focused on enhancing the potentiality of man. To take an example from the field of health, individuals with no cavities were rare, yet scholars of dental health conducted research with this goal in mind.

Unless scholars are willing to develop new views of our society, the descriptive research that is conducted will tend to support the status quo. Thus, from a participant's point of view, the worlds implicit in Blau, Perrow, Thompson, Simon, Cyert, Allison, and so forth are not much different from the world in which they are involved.

Moreover, unless research on new worlds is conducted, there is the danger that scholars will tend to use data obtained in the present world as evidence that people do not seek a change. The question that these scholars seem to forget is how can human beings consider or desire worlds that they have learned, through experience, are not available, indeed, to date not realistic.

A recent publication by Gross (1970) illustrates the point. Gross suggested that concepts like individual dignity and self-development probably represent academic values more than employee desires because employees very rarely report the need to express such values. Even if we were to agree with Gross (and there is ample evidence in the history of the labor movement and its demands to question his view), the problem is whether this state of affairs implies that people ought to accept them and ought to be trained to adapt to them. Gross seems to suggest that this should be the case. He stated that there is little one could do to provide opportunities for self-actualization and that it might frighten some people if they were offered such opportunities. Moreover, he noted that assembly-line jobs do not require a worker who demonstrates initiative, who desires variety. "One wants him [the worker] simply to work according to an established pace. Creativity, then, is not always desirable (Gross, 1970: 103)."

Note the logic. Gross begins by stating that the personality and organizationists cannot state that one *should* (Gross' italics) provide workers with more challenge or autonomy in accordance with their values because to do so would be to rest their case not on a scientific theory (which describes what is—not what ought to be) but a program for organizations. Then he suggests that no one has proven how harmful dissatisfaction, anxiety, dependency, and conformity are to the individual (which is probably correct). He continues to say that a certain amount of these conditions is unavoidable and necessary and helpful (and he provides no empirical data for this assertion). Then he concludes that employees should be educated to live within this world.

> Perhaps the most general conclusion we can draw is that since organizations appear to be inevitable . . . a major type of socialization of the young ought to include methods for dealing with the organization. . . . [For example], an important consideration in the preparation of individuals for work should include training for the handling of or adjustment to authority (Gross, 1970: 104–105).

At this point Gross has taken a normative position.

Katz (1965) has argued that attention may not need to be paid to integrating the individual and the organization. He argued, as we do, that organizations offer few rewards and satisfactions, workers respond with informal activities (Katz cites Roy's example of banana time), these informal activities help to separate the worker from the organization, and this separation helps keep the employees sane and the organization operating effectively. Consequently, Katz raised the issue that organizations need not necessarily be redesigned to increase intrinsic rewards thereby reducing the gap and increasing the integration of the individual and the organization.

Katz's option is one that should be considered. But should not social scientists conduct research on other options? Moreover, there is the nagging possibility that workers can be brainwashed by their working conditions to accept primitive, steady-work conditions. In a factory administered by warm paternalism, for example, many employees were found who preferred the infant ends of the continua (and who also preferred the same conditions or isolation in their nonwork life) (Argyris, 1964). How can people be helped to consider other states of affairs if they prefer the ones in which they exist? One way to help employees realize how unidimensional they are would be to design new environments and then require them to experiment with such environments. If they find them dissatisfying, they can leave them and take assignments that require behavior closer to the infant ends of the continua.

The position that raises the most concern for the writer is exemplified by the work of Scott and Mitchell (1972). They take the position that job enlargement may not be necessary because workers in an automobile company have about the same favorable or unfavorable attitudes as do workers with jobs with greater freedom and job variety. That workers may state that they are satisfied in their jobs has been noted by the author in all three reviews of the literature. The question arises, however, as to what is the meaning of the response to a question such as "How satisfied would you say you are with your present job?" Relative deprivation theory would tell us that the individual will probably respond relative to other opportunities available to them. Most workers know, as has been reported above, that few opportunities exist for jobs that are significantly different and pay better and that, if found, would not require the painful experience of leaving one setting for a new one. Under these conditions dissonance theory would predict that one way to resolve the dissonance of deciding to remain in a job that is not what one prefers is to become satisfied with what one has. These two theories help provide explanations for the frequently observed fact that the greatest dissatisfaction on a routine job occurs during the first years. After three to five years, the individual becomes adapted and satisfied (Herrick, 1972).

In another example Scott and Mitchell agreed with MacKinney, Wernimont, and Galitz (1972) that specialization has not necessarily reduced job satisfaction. To these writers if a poor person fills out a life satisfaction questionnaire at the same point that it is filled out by a millionaire, these people are in the same psychological situation. Thus, their counter to job enlargement is counselling, scientific selection, and personnel development. The first two represent processes to maintain the system as it is. The third one is never defined. What kind of personnel development is possible for aggregates of workers (not few individuals) if there is little variance in work and, therefore, little opportunity to use new skills that may have been developed.

In another example Scott and Mitchell agreed with MacKinney, Wernimont, and Galitz that job enlargement does not take individual differences into account. The opposite is the case. Job enlargement increases the variance possible in work and therefore accommodates to a greater range of individual differences. MacKinney, Wernimont, and Galitz raised a straw man when they argued against forcing job enlargement upon everyone. Such a condition is unrealistic. There will be many jobs that cannot be enlarged and thus employees will have choice. There is a deeper question, however, that goes to the heart of the function of social science research; namely, what kind of a world do we help to design. Let us assume that all jobs could be enlarged. We now have two work worlds; the present with its high routine and the other with less routine. Either world would be coercive in the sense that it makes requirements on employees. If we had the choice, why not opt for the world that is psychologically richer? The authors suggest that employees can cope with this problem by fulfillment outside their jobs. It is ironic that scholars who argue against job enlargement because it has not been proven by a high degree of scientific rigor (Scott and Mitchell, 1972: 279) recommend an alternative for employees that has little empirical support. As has been shown above, the degree of deprivation on the job significantly influences the kind of fulfillment employees seek outside their job.

As shown elsewhere (Argyris, In press) industrial psychology of this type fundamentally opts for the status quo and creates a field whose causal variables reside in other disciplines, thereby relieving psychologists of the knotty issues of the design of a world whose quality of life options are greater than those presently available. It is interesting to note that Scott and Mitchell (1972: 371) acknowledged that the interest in humanistic factors is increasing and assign the cause to "social and technological forces beyond the comprehension, much less the control, of anyone."

Notes

1. The author wishes to thank Professors Clayton Alderfer, Lee Bolman, J. Richard Hackman, and William Torbert for their helpful comments.

2. It may also be that the relationships between self-direction and organizational experiences are partially explained by early life experiences and subsequent occupational choice. If so, then the impoverished work experiences may interact with early life experiences and occupational choice to produce the results described above.

3. In cases where the frustrations, conflict, and so forth are low because individuals aspire toward the adult ends of the continua and have jobs where such expression is realistic (and that the adaptive activities would be low), then one would predict that the employees would design their leisure activities to be consonant with the adult ends of the continua. Where the frustration, conflict, and so forth are low because people aspire to the infant ends of the continua (and that is what they are offered at work), then one would predict that they would design their leisure activities to be consonant with the infant ends of the continua.

4. Torbert is the first researcher, to the present author's knowledge, who develops a theory of man which he then uses to understand such basic concepts as play, leisure, recreation, free time, and self. He has done an excellent job in integrating an essentially humanistic approach with empirical research.

References

Aiken, Michael, and Jerald Hage. "Organizational alienation: a comparative analysis," *American Sociological Review,* 31 (1966): 497–507.

Allison, Graham T., "Conceptual models and the Cuban missile crisis," *American Political Science Review,* 14 (1969): 689–718.

_____. *Essence of Decision,* New York: Little, Brown, 1971.

Argyris, Chris. *Organization of a Bank,* New Haven: Yale University, Labor and Management Center, 1954.

_____. *Diagnosing Human Relations in Organizations,* New Haven: Yale University, Labor and Management Center, 1956.

_____. *Personality and Organization,* New York: Harper, 1957.

_____. *Understanding Organizational Behavior,* Homewood, Ill.: Dorsey Press, 1960.

_____. *Interpersonal Competence and Organizational Effectiveness,* Homewood, Ill.: Dorsey Press and Richard D. Irwin, 1962.

_____. *Integrating the Individual and the Organization,* New York: Wiley, 1964.

_____. *Organization and Innovation,* Homewood, Ill.: Irwin, 1965.

_____. "Some unintended consequences of rigorous research," *Psychological Bulletin,* 70 (1968): 185–197.

_____. *Management and Organizational Development,* New York: McGraw-Hill, 1971.

_____. *The Applicability of Organizational Sociology,* Cambridge: Cambridge University Press, 1972.

_____. "Organizations of the Future," Sage Professional Papers, 1973.

_____. "Some problems and new directions for industrial psychology," in Marvin Dunnette (ed.), *Handbook of Industrial and Organizational Psychology,* Chicago: Rand McNally, in press.

Bachman, Jerald G., Clagett G. Smith, and Jonathan A. Slesinger. "Control performance and satisfaction: an analysis of structural and individual effects," *Journal of Personality and Social Psychology,* 4 (1966): 127–136.

Baumgartel, Howard, and Gerald Goldstein. "Some human consequences of technical change," *Personnel Administration,* 24 (1961): 32–40.

Benham, Thomas W. "Trends in public attitudes toward business and the free enterprise system," Princeton: Opinion Research Corporation, 1972.

Bennis, Warren G., and Philip E. Slater. *The Temporary Society,* New York: Harper and Row, 1968.

Blai, Boris. "An occupational study of job satisfaction and need satisfaction," *Journal of Experimental Education,* 32 (1964): 383–388.

Blankenship, Vaughn, and Raymond E. Miles. "Organizational structure and managerial decision behavior," *Administrative Science quarterly,* 13 (1968): 106–121.

Blau, Peter M., and R. A. Schoenherr, with the collaboration of S. R. Klatzry. "The structure of organizations," processed, 1971.

Bonjean, Charles M., and Gary G. Vance. "A short-form measure of self-actualization," *Journal of Applied Behavioral Science,* 4 (1968): 297–312.

Carpenter, Harrell H. "Formal organizational structural factors and perceived job satisfaction of classroom teachers," *Administrative Science Quarterly,* 16 (1971): 460–466.

Centers, Richard, and Daphne E. Bugental. "Intrinsic and extrinsic job motivations among different segments of the working population," *Journal of Applied Psychology,* 50 (1966): 193–197.

Cohen, Albert K., and Harold M. Hodges, Jr. "Characteristics of the lower-blue-collar-class," *Social Problems,* 10 (1963): 303–334.

Cooper, Robert. "Alienation from work," *New Society,* (1967): 1–10.

Crozier, Michel. *The Bureaucratic Phenomenon,* London: Tavistock Publications, 1964.

Cyert, Richard M., and James G. March. *A Behavioral Theory of the Firm,* Englewood Cliffs: Prentice-Hall, 1963.

Davis, Louis E. "The design of jobs," *Industrial Relations,* 6 (1966): 21–45.

Davis, Louis E., and Ernest S. Valfer. "Intervening responses to change in supervisor job designs," *Occupational Psychology,* 39 (1965): 171–189.

————. "Studies in supervisory job designs," *Human Relations,* 19 (1966): 339–352.

Emery, Frederick E., Einar Thorsrud, and K. Lange. *Field Experiments at Christiana Spigerwerk,* London: Tavistock Institute of Human Relations, 1966.

Ewing, David W. "Who wants corporate democracy?" *Harvard Business Review,* 40 (1971): 2–28ff.

Farris, George F., and D. Anthony Butterfield. "Goal congruence in Brazilian organizations," Massachusetts Institute of Technology, Sloan Institute of Management, processed, 1971.

Faunce, William A., and Donald A. Clelland. "Professionalization and stratification patterns in an industrial community," *American Journal of Sociology,* 72 (1967): 341–350.

Fisk, George. "Personal disposable time: the psychology of occupational differences in the use of leisure," in George Fisk (ed.), *The Frontiers of Management Psychology,* New York: Harper and Row, 1964, 255–259.

Ford, Robert N. *Motivation Through the Work Staff,* New York: American Management Association, 1969.

Friedlander, Frank. "Importance of work versus nonwork among socially and occupationally stratified groups," *Journal of Applied Psychology*, 50 (1966): 437–441.

Friedlander, Frank, and Eugene Waltons. "Positive and negative motivations toward work," *Administrative Science Quarterly*, 9 (1964): 194–207.

Fullan, Michael. "Industrial technology and worker integration in the organization," *American Sociological Review*, 35 (1970): 1028–1039.

Gardell, Bertil. *Produktionsteknik och arbetsglädje; en socialpsykologisk studie av industriellt arbete*, Stockholm: (English summary of the entire book by the author, pp. 375–391), Swedish Council for Personnel Administration, 1971.

Gardner, John. "America in the twenty-third century." *The New York Times*, July 27, 1968.

Goldthorpe, J. H., D. L. Lockwood, F. Bechofer, and J. Platt. *The Affluent Worker: Industrial Attitudes and Behaviour*, Cambridge: Cambridge University Press, 1968.

Grimes, Michael G. "Bureaucracy and personality: the effect of perceived work environment on social integration and alienation," unpublished master's thesis, University of Texas, 1967.

Gross, E. "Work, organization, and stress," in S. Levine and N. Scotch (eds.), *Social Stress*, Chicago: Aldine, 1970, 54–110.

Hackman, Richard, and Edward E. Lawler, III. "Employee reactions to job characteristics," *Journal of Applied Psychology Monograph*, 55 (1971): 259–286.

Halmost, Paul (ed.). *Hungarian Sociological Studies*, The Sociological Monograph 17. Keele: University of Keele, 1972.

Halter, Harriet. "Attitudes towards employee participation in company decision-making processes," *Human Relations*, 18 (1965): 297–319.

Herrick, Neal Q. *Where Have All the Robots Gone?* Glencoe, Ill.: Free Press, 1972.

Herzberg, Fred. "Job attitudes in the Soviet Union," *Personnel Psychology*, 18 (1965): 245–252.

––––––. *Work and the Nature of Man*, New York: World Publishing, 1966.

Holtz, Winifred Lee. "Occupation and self-actualization: the expression of maturity-directed predispositions in the work situation," master's thesis, University of Texas, 1969.

Hrebiniak, Lawrence G., and Joseph A. Alutto. "Personal and role-related factors in the development of organizational commitment," *Administrative Science quarterly*, 17 (1972): 555–573.

Katz, Dan, and Basil S. Georgeopoulos. "Organizations in a changing world," *Journal of Applied Behavioral Science*, 7 (1971): 342–370.

Katz, Fred E. "Exploring informal groups in complex organizations," *Administrative Science Quarterly*, 10 (1965): 204–223.

Kaufman, Herbert. "Administrative decentralization and political power," *Public Administration Review*, 29 (1969): 3–15.

Kohn, Melvin L. *Class and Conformity: A Study of Values,* Homewood, Ill.: Dorsey Press, 1969.

Kohn, Melvin L., and C. Schooler. "Class occupation and orientation," *American Sociological Review,* 34 (1969): 659–758.

Landau, Martin. "On the concept of a self-correcting organization," paper prepared for the Albert Schweitzer Chair in the Humanities, Maxwell School, Syracuse University, 1972.

Langner, Thomas S. "Adult poor physical health and poor interpersonal affiliation," in Thomas S. Langner and Stanley T. Michael (eds.), *Life Stress and Mental Health,* Glencoe, Ill.: Free Press, 1963, 266–300.

Lawler, Edward E., III. "Job design and employee motivation," *Personnel Psychology,* 22 (1969): 426–435.

Ley, Ronald. "Labor turnover as a function of worker-differences, work environment, and authoritarianism of foremen," *Journal of Applied Psychology,* 50 (1966): 497–500.

Lichtman, Cary M. "Some intrapersonal response correlates of organizational rank," *Journal of Applied Psychology,* 54 (1970): 77–80.

Lichtman, Cary M., and Raymond G. Hunt. "Personality and organization theory: a review of some conceptual literature," *Psychological Bulletin,* 76 (1971): 271–294.

Likert, Rensis. *The Human Organizations,* New York: McGraw-Hill, 1967.

Lodahl, Thomas M. "Man on the assembly-line: job attitude at two and fourteen years," Cornell University, School of Business and Public Administration, processed, 1964.

Long, Norton E. "The city as a reservation," *Public Interest,* 1971, 22–38.

McGregor, Douglas. *The Human Side of Enterprise,* New York: McGraw-Hill, 1960.

MacKinney, A. C., P. F. Wernimont, and W. O. Galitz cited in William G. Scott and Terence Mitchell (eds.). *Organization Theory: A Behavioral Analysis for Management,* rev. ed., Homewood, Ill.: Richard D. Irwin, 1972.

Mackonin, Pavel. "Social stratification in contemporary Czechoslovakia," *American Journal of Sociology,* 75 (1970): 725–741.

Margulies, Newton. "Organizational culture and psychological growth," *Journal of Applied Behavioral Science,* 5 (1969): 491–508.

Maslow, Abraham H. "Toward a humanistic biology," *American Psychologist,* 24 (1969): 724–735.

———. *Motivation and Personality,* New York: Harper and Row, 1970.

Maurer, John G. "The relationship of perceived task attributes and opportunity to contribute to the meaning of work," paper presented at the 19th International Meeting of the Institute of Management Sciences (Maurer is located at the School of Business Administration, Wayne State University), 1972.

Meissner, Martin. "The long arm of the job: a study of work and leisure," *Industrial Relations,* 10 (1971): 239–260.

Miner, John E. "Changes in student attitudes toward bureaucratic role prescriptions during the 1960's," *Administrative Science Quarterly*, 16 (1971): 351–364.

Negandhi, Anant R., and S. Benjamin Prasad. *Comparative Management*, New York: Appleton-Century-Crofts, 1971.

Newman, Frank (ed.). *Report on Higher Education*, Washington: GPO, 1971.

Paine, Frank T., Stephen J. Carroll, Jr., and Burt A. Leete. "Need satisfactions of managerial level personnel in a government agency," *Journal of Applied Psychology*, 50 (1966): 247–249.

Parker, Stanley. *The Future of Work and Leisure*, New York: Praeger Press, 1971.

Paul, William T., Jr., Keith B. Robertson, and Fred Herzberg. "Job enrichment pays off," *Harvard Business Review*, 47 (1969): 61–78.

Pelz, Donald C., and Frank M. Andrews. "Autonomy, coordination, and stimulation in relation to scientific achievement," *Behavioral Science*, 11 (1966): 89–97.

Pope, Hallowell. "Economic deprivation and social participation in a group of 'middle class' factory workers," Reprint Series No. 9, Center for Research in Social Organization, Department of Sociology, University of Michigan, Ann Arbor, 1964, 290–300.

Porter, Lyman W., and Edward E. Lawler. "Properties of organizational structure in relation to job attitudes and job behavior," *Psychological Bulletin*, 64 (1965): 23–51.

Pym, Denis. "A study of frustration and aggression among factory and office workers," *Occupational Psychology*, 37 (1963): 165–179.

———. "Exploring characteristics of the versatile worker," *Occupational Psychology*, 39 (1965): 271–278.

Schon, Donald A. *Beyond the Stable State*, New York: Random House, 1971.

Scott, William G., and Terence Mitchell. *Organization Theory: A Behavioral Analysis for Management*, rev. ed., Homewood, Ill.: Richard D. Irwin, 1972.

Seashore, Stanley E., and J. Thad Barnowe. "Collar color doesn't count," *Psychology Today*, 6 (1972): 53–54ff.

Shepard, Jon M. "Functional specialization and work attitudes," *Industrial Relations*, 8 (1969): 185–194.

Simon, Herbert A. *Administrative Behavior*, 2d ed., Glencoe, Ill.: The Free Press, 1957.

———. *The New Science of Management Decision*, New York: Harper and Row, 1960.

Smith, Clagett G., and Arnold S. Tannenbaum. "Organizational control structure: a comparative analysis," *Human Relations*, 16 (1963): 299–316.

Smith, David H. "Voluntary organization activity and poverty," *Urban and Social Change Review*, 5 (1971): 2–7.

Sorcher, Melvin. "Motivating the hourly employee," General Electric, Personnel and Industrial Relations Services, 1967, 1–24.

Susman, Gerald I. "Automation, alienation, and work group autonomy," *Human Relations*, 25 (1972a): 171–180.

———. "Process design, automation, and worker alienation." Industrial Relations, 11 (1972b): 34–45.

Telly, Charles S., Wendell L. French, and William G. Scott. "The relationship of inequity to turnover among hourly workers," *Administrative Science Quarterly,* 16 (1971): 164–172.

Thompson, James D. "Society's frontiers for organizing activities," Department of Sociology, Vanderbilt University, mimeographed, 1972.

Thorsrud, Einar. "Job design and the wider context," in L. Davis and B. Taylor (eds.), *Design of Jobs,* London: Penguin, 1972a.

————. "The organization of industry and trade unions," in R. Mayne (ed.), *Europe Tomorrow.* London: Fontana/Collins, 1972b.

Torbert, William R. *Being for the Most Part Puppets. . . . ,* Cambridge, Mass.: Schenkman, 1972.

Van De Vall, Mark. "Voluntary Participation in Democratic Organizations, Buffalo Studies," *Studies in Sociology,* Vol. 3, No. 2, 1967.

Volvo. *Job Environment and Satisfaction: New Production Systems at Volvo,* Göteborg, Sweden, 1972.

Walton, Richard E. "How to counter alienation in the plant," *Harvard Business Review,* 50, 6 (1972): 70–81.

Walton, Richard E., J. M. Dutton, and H. G. Fitch. "A study of conflict in the process, structure, and attitudes of lateral relationships," in Albert H. Rubenstein and Chadwick J. Haberstroh, *Some Theories of Organization,* Homewood, Ill.: Richard D. Irwin, 1966, 444–465.

Wicker, Allan W. "Undermanning, performances, and students' subjective experiences in behavior settings of large and small high schools," *Journal of Personality and Social Psychology,* 10 (1968): 255–261.

————. "Size of church membership and members' support of church behavior settings," *Journal of Personality and Social Psychology,* 13 (1969): 278–288.

Wilensky, Harold. "Varieties of work experience," in Henry Borow (ed.), *Man in a World of Work,* Boston, Mass.: Houghton Mifflin, 1964, 124–154.

Zupanov, Josip, and Arnold S. Tannenbaum. "The distribution of control in some Yugoslav industrial organizations as perceived by members," in Arnold S. Tannenbaum (ed.), *Control in Organizations,* New York: McGraw-Hill, 1968, 91–109.

PERCEPTION AND COMMUNICATION

The Heartache of Parenthood
Joseph F. Dinneen

The heartache of being a parent was reflected deeply in a dramatic news photo in The Globe last week.

Anyone who saw the photograph could not help but be moved by the explanation that The Globe cameraman who photographed the body lying on the ground at an accident scene in Plymouth had unknowingly snapped a photo of his dead son.

Monitoring a police radio while on a day off at his Manomet home, photographer Bob Dean raced off like the proverbial fire-horse he is known to be after hearing around 9:30 P.M. of a five-car accident on Rte. 3 in nearby Plymouth.

With his usual professional diligence, Dean quickly banged a half-dozen shots, including the badly crumpled body of a teenage boy, and took off for The Globe to develop his photographs, as he had done many times through the years.

As Dean was racing to The Globe, Plymouth police found papers in the dead boy's pocket identifying him as Steven Dean. Attempts were made to reach Dean on a two-way radio but he was by then out of range.

Dean was making prints from negatives in the Globe photo department when Plymouth Det. Sgt. Larry Mansfield, the department photographer, whom Dean knows well from working together for years, sadly broke the news to him.

Mansfield at first had asked Dean to come to the police station, then finally told him, "Bob, the boy you photographed at the scene was Steven."

Boston Sunday Globe, September 9, 1973. Courtesy of the Boston Globe.

Dean studied his photographs. He made out the outline of the battered son that he had not been able to distinguish as he had worked feverishly at the accident scene. His son had been a passenger in a friend's car.

It was then that the heartache began to wash over him. Gone. In a twinkling. Ironically, he had captured it all on film. And Bob reflected on how the 17-year-old boy had worked hard in the Donut Hut in Plymouth and had been saving to purchase a car when he became 18. Now there would be no car and life had been snuffed out at a tender 17.

After turning in his pictures to the city desk, Dean returned to Plymouth, identified the body, and then returned to his Winthrop drive home in Manomet to comfort his wife Barbara.

Dean had been accompanied to the off-duty story by his son, Robert Jr., 20, a Plymouth firefighter. Another son, David, 15, also arrived at the death scene on a tow truck but, too, was unaware his brother was one of the two lifeless bodies there. Besides his parents and brothers, Steven is survived by a sister, Mrs. Sheryl Karklin.

At 9 A.M. on Wednesday, a bare 36 hours after Bob Dean had left to make the ironic, dramatic pictures, the Dean family sat in St. Bonaventure's Church, Manomet, for the Mass of Christian Burial. Burial followed in Manomet Cemetery.

The tragedy that struck the Dean family, the almost unbelievable irony that Bob Dean had unknowingly recorded the death of his own son, made a tremendous impact both within The Globe and among readers, some of whom were critical about using such an explicit photograph.

Why did The Globe use it when it could have been so easily discarded? A variety of reasons:

- It was an unusual news event and picture.
- The Globe prints a lot of grim pictures and its integrity might be challenged if it begins getting selective when it comes to using or not using a photograph because it involves a Globe employee.
- Urging by Dean himself, recently named Photographer of the Year by the Boston Press Photographers Assoc., who disclosed his creed as a photographer and a person when he said simply: "Use it. If it can save one life it's worth it."

And so the photograph was used and the heartache of being a parent was aroused and, perhaps, the fear of being one instilled, too.

Most of our young adult lives, after the children are born, parents impatiently wish the children would grow up. Parents weary of the problems of caring for the youngsters and look forward to the days when they reach some maturity, the teens.

What is it they say—never wish your life away?

And then, suddenly, they are grown, tasting the adventures of life, like fast-moving cars and the now older adults sit at home and wish the children were young again. On reflection, wasn't it so much easier to take care of them when they were youngsters underfoot, knowing where they were, rather than out on their own?

The tragedy that touched the Dean family is still another bitter reminder, recorded almost daily in the newspapers, that death walks beside us each day and none of us knows when it will beckon.

A Criminologist Learns the Hard Way
William F. Buckley, Jr.

Hugo Park of the Atlanta Journal has the good sense to read the FBI Law Enforcement Bulletin where recently he saw an account of the extraordinary experiences of one George L. Kirkham, assistant professor of criminology at Florida State University, from which account I put together the following . . .

Dr. Kirkham apparently decided that as a professor of criminology, he lacked something, namely police experience. Accordingly he took time off and attended the police academy. Having done so, he was assigned the regular work of a patrolman. By his own account, he will not be the same again.

"I had personally been of the opinion," writes Dr. Kirkham, "that police officers greatly exaggerate the amount of verbal disrespect and physical abuse to which they are subjected in the line of duty." Well, the police do not tend to exaggerate, Dr. Kirkham discovered. Notwithstanding that he approached his—clients? patients?—with exaggerated civility, he was seldom repaid in kind.

"Excuse me, sir," he said to a barroom brawler, "but I wonder if I could ask you to step outside and talk with me for a minute?" That was very nearly

Boston Globe, June 8, 1974. Courtesy of the Boston Globe.

the end of Dr. George L. Kirkham, whom the brawler turned on, intending mayhem.

Soon after his tour of duty began, he told someone double-parked in a crowded thoroughfare to move his car. He refused. So our hero told him he was under arrest. Whereupon the double-parker raised a Saturday night crowd by shouting and yelling that the police were harassing him.

"A hysterical woman unsnapped and tried to grab Kirkham's revolver and an angry mob converged on the two officers," Park writes. "Fearing for his life, Kirkham pressed the hidden release button on the shotgun rack."

Meditating on the incident, Kirkham later wrote, "How readily as a criminology professor I would have condemned the officer who was now myself (for) menacing an 'unarmed' assembly with an 'offensive' weapon."

A complaint was filed against the double-parker who very nearly caused a riot. "I felt bitter when I saw this individual . . . back on the streets the next night, laughing."

Dr. Kirkham discovered something we all know in the abstract, but take little into account. "As a criminology professor, I had always enjoyed great amounts of time in which to make difficult decisions. As a police officer however, I found myself forced to make the most critical choices in the time frame of seconds rather than days: to shoot or not to shoot, to arrest or not to arrest, to give chase or let go—always with the nagging certainty that others, those with great amounts of time in which to analyze and think, stood ready to judge and condemn me for whatever action I might take or fail to take."

Coming off duty one night, exhausted from a French Connection type car chase, Kirkham and another patrolman headed for a restaurant when they heard a sound of breaking glass at a nearby church.

"(We) spotted two longhaired teen-aged boys running from the area. . . . I asked for identification. He sneered at me, cursed, and turned to walk away. The next thing I knew I had grabbed the youth by the shirt and spun him around, shouting, 'I'm talking to you, punk!' "

Dr. Kirkham has the grace to recall one of his standard lectures back at Florida State U. It goes, "Any man who is not able to maintain absolute control of his emotions at all times has no business being a police officer."

It is curious that everyone in America who practices the profession of instructing everyone else on the subject of ghetto life advises us all that we should cross the tracks and see what conditions there are really like, which is good advice. It is not often that comparable advice is given to those whose knowledge of crime is circumscribed by poetic admiration for the decisions of the Warren Court. Dr. Kirkham may have discovered that he has choleric weaknesses, but he is an honor to his profession.

Active Listening
C. R. Rogers and R. E. Farson

THE MEANING OF ACTIVE LISTENING

One basic responsibility of the supervisor or executive is the development, adjustment, and integration of individual employees. He tries to develop employee potential, delegate responsibility, and achieve cooperation. To do so, he must have, among other abilities, the ability to listen intelligently and carefully to those with whom he works.

There are, however, many kinds of listening skills. The lawyer, for example, when questioning a witness, listens for contradictions, irrelevancies, errors, and weaknesses. But this is not the kind of listening skill we are concerned with in this booklet. The lawyer usually is not listening in order to help the witness adjust or cooperate or produce. On the other hand, we will be concerned with listening skills which *will help* employees gain a clearer understanding of their situations, take responsibility, and cooperate with each other.

Two Examples

The kind of listening we have in mind is called "active listening." It is called "active" because the listener has a very definite responsibility. He does not passively absorb the words which are spoken to him. He actively tries to grasp the facts and the feelings in what he hears, and he tries, by his listening, to help the speaker work out his own problems.

To get a fuller picture of what is meant by active listening, let us consider two different approaches to the same work problem.

Example no. 1

Foreman: Hey, Al, I don't get this production order. We can't handle this run today. What do they think we are?

Supervisor: But that's the order. So get it out as soon as you can. We're under terrific pressure this week.

Foreman: Don't they know we're behind schedule already because of that press breakdown?

Reprinted by permission of the Industrial Relations Center of the University of Chicago.

Supervisor: Look, Kelly, I don't decide what goes on upstairs. I just have to see that the work gets out and that's what I'm gonna do.

Foreman: The guys aren't gonna like this.

Supervisor: That's something you'll have to work out with them, not me.

Example no. 2

Foreman: Hey, Ross, I don't get this production order. We can't handle this run today. What do they think we are?

Supervisor: Sounds like you're pretty sore about it, Kelly.

Foreman: I sure am. We were just about getting back to schedule after that press breakdown. Now this comes along.

Supervisor: As if you didn't have enough work to do, huh?

Foreman: Yeah. I don't know how I'm gonna tell the guys about this.

Supervisor: Hate to face'em with it now, is that it?

Foreman: I really do. They're under a real strain today. Seems like everything we do around here is rush, rush.

Supervisor: I guess you feel like it's unfair to load anything more on them.

Foreman: Well, yeah. I know there must be plenty of pressure on everybody up the line, but—well, if that's the way it is . . . guess I'd better get the word to 'em.

There are obviously many differences between these two examples. The main one, however, is that Ross, the supervisor in the second example is using the active-listening approach. He is listening and responding in a way that makes it clear that he appreciates both the meaning and the feeling behind what Kelly is saying.

Active listening does not necessarily mean long sessions spent listening to grievances, personal or otherwise. It is simply a way of approaching those problems which arise out of the usual day-to-day events of any job.

To be effective, active listening must be firmly grounded in the basic attitudes of the user. We cannot employ it as a technique if our fundamental attitudes are in conflict with its basic concepts. If we try, our behavior will be empty and sterile and our associates will be quick to recognize this. Until we can demonstrate a spirit which genuinely respects the potential worth of the individual, which considers his rights and trusts his capacity for self-direction, we cannot begin to be effective listeners.

What We Achieve by Listening

Active listening is an important way to bring about changes in people. Despite the popular notion that listening is a passive approach, clinical and research evidence clearly shows that sensitive listening is a most effective agent for individual personality change and group development. Listening brings about changes in people's attitudes toward themselves and others, and also brings about changes in their basic values and personal philosophy. People who have been listened to in this new and special way become more emotionally mature, more open to their experiences, less defensive, more democratic, and less authoritarian.

When people are listened to sensitively, they tend to listen to themselves with more care and make clear exactly what they are feeling and thinking. Group members tend to listen more to each other, become less argumentative, more ready to incorporate other points of view. Because listening reduces the threat of having one's ideas criticized, the person is better able to see them for what they are, and is more likely to feel that his contributions are worthwhile.

Not the least important result of listening is the change that takes place within the listener himself. Besides the fact that listening provides more information than any other activity, it builds deep, positive relationships and tends to alter constructively the attitudes of the listener. Listening is a growth experience.

These, then, are some of the worthwhile results we can expect from active listening. But how do we go about this kind of listening? How do we become active listeners?

HOW TO LISTEN

Active listening aims to bring about changes in people. To achieve this end, it relies upon definite techniques—things to do and things to avoid doing. Before discussing these techniques, however, we should first understand why they are effective. To do so, we must understand how the individual personality develops.

The Growth of the Individual

Through all of our lives, from early childhood on, we have learned to think of ourselves in certain, very definite ways. We have built up pictures of ourselves. Sometimes these self-pictures are pretty realistic but at other times they are not. For example, an overage, overweight lady may fancy herself a youthful, ravishing siren, or an awkward teenager regard himself as a star athlete.

All of us have experiences which fit the way we need to think about ourselves. These we accept. But it is much harder to accept experiences which don't fit. And sometimes, if it is very important for us to hang on to this self-picture, we don't accept or admit these experiences at all.

These self-pictures are not necessarily attractive. A man, for example, may regard himself as incompetent and worthless. He may feel that he is doing his job poorly in spite of favorable appraisals by the company. As long as he has these feelings about himself he must deny any experiences which would seem not to fit this self-picture, in this case any that might indicate to him that he is competent. It is so necessary for him to maintain this self-picture that he is threatened by anything which would tend to change it. Thus, when the company raises his salary, it may seem to him only additional proof that he is a fraud. He must hold onto this self-picture, because, bad or good, it's the only thing he has by which he can identify himself.

This is why direct attempts to change this individual or change his self-picture are particularly threatening. He is forced to defend himself or to completely deny the experience. This denial of experience and defense of the self-picture tend to bring on rigidity of behavior and create difficulties in personal adjustment.

The active-listening approach, on the other hand, does not present a threat to the individual's self-picture. He does not have to defend it. He is able to explore it, see it for what it is, and make his own decision as to how realistic it is. And he is then in a position to change.

If I want to help a man reduce his defensiveness and become more adaptive, I must try to remove the threat of myself as his potential changer. As long as the atmosphere is threatening, there can be no effective communication. So I must create a climate which is neither critical, evaluative, nor moralizing. It must be an atmosphere of equality and freedom, permissivenss and understanding, acceptance and warmth. It is in this climate and this climate only that the individual feels safe enough to incorporate new experiences and new values into his concept of himself. Let's see how active listening helps to create this climate.

What To Avoid
When we encounter a person with a problem, our usual response is to try to change his way of looking at things—to get him to see his situation the way we see it, or would like him to see it. We plead, reason, scold, encourage, insult, prod—anything to bring about a change in the desired direction, that is, in the direction we want him to travel. What we seldom realize, however, is that, under these circumstances, we are usually responding to *our own* needs to see the world in certain ways. It is always difficult for us to tolerate and understand actions which are different from the ways in which *we* believe *we* should act. If, however, we can free ourselves from the need to influence and direct others in our own paths, we enable ourselves to listen with understanding, and thereby employ the most potent available agent of change.

One problem the listener faces is that of responding to demands for decisions, judgments, and evaluations. He is constantly called upon to agree or disagree with someone or something. Yet, as he well knows, the question or challenge frequently is a masked expression of feelings or needs which the speaker is far more anxious to communicate than he is to have the surface questions answered. Because he cannot speak these feelings openly, the speaker must disguise them to himself and to others in an acceptable form. To illustrate, let us examine some typical questions and the type of answers that might best elicit the feeling beneath it.

Employee's question	*Listener's answer*
Just whose responsibility is the tool room?	Do you feel that someone is challenging your authority in there?
Don't you think younger able people should be promoted before senior but less able ones?	It seems to you they should, I take it.
What does the super expect us to do about those broken-down machines?	You're pretty disgusted with those machines, aren't you?
Don't you think I've improved over the last review period?	Sounds as if you feel like you've really picked up over these last few months.

These responses recognize the questions but leave the way open for the employee to say what is really bothering him. They allow the listener to participate in the problem or situation without shouldering all responsibility for decision-making or actions. This is a process of thinking *with* people instead of *for* or *about* them.

Passing judgment, whether critical or favorable, makes free expression difficult. Similarly, advice and information are almost always seen as efforts to change a person and thus serve as barriers to his self-expression and the development of a creative relationship. Moreover, advice is seldom taken and information hardly ever utilized. The eager young trainee probably will not become patient just because he is advised that, "The road to success in business is a long, difficult one, and you must be patient." And it is no more helpful for him to learn that "only one out of a hundred trainees reach top management positions."

Interestingly, it is a difficult lesson to learn that positive *evaluations* are sometimes as blocking as negative ones. It is almost as destructive to the freedom of a relationship to tell a person that he is good or capable or right, as to tell him otherwise. To evaluate him positively may make it more difficult for him to tell of the faults that distress him or the ways in which he believes he is not competent.

Encouragement also may be seen as an attempt to motivate the speaker in certain directions or hold him off rather than as support. "I'm sure everything will work out O.K." is not a helpful response to the person who is deeply discouraged about a problem.

In other words, most of the techniques and devices common to human relationships are found to be of little use in establishing the type of relationship we are seeking here.

What To Do

Just what does active listening entail, then? Basically, it requires that we get inside the speaker, that we grasp, *from his point of view,* just what it is he is communicating to us. More than that, we must convey to the speaker that we are seeing things from his point of view. To listen actively, then, means that there are several things we must do.

Listen for total meaning. Any message a person tries to get across usually has two components: the *content* of the message and the *feeling* or attitude underlying this content. Both are important, both give the message *meaning.* It is this total meaning of the message that we try to understand. For example, a machinist comes to his foreman and says, "I've finished that lathe set-up." This message has obvious content and perhaps calls upon the foreman for another work assignment. Suppose, on the other hand, that he says, "Well, I'm finally finished with that damned lathe set-up." The content is the same but the total meaning of the message has changed—and changed in an important way for both the foreman and the worker. Here sensitive listening can facilitate the relationship. Suppose the foreman were to respond by simply giving another work assignment. Would the employee feel that he had gotten his total message across? Would he feel free to talk to his foreman? Will he feel better about his job, more anxious to do good work on the next assignment?

Now, on the other hand, suppose the foreman were to respond with, "Glad to have it over with, huh?" or "Had a pretty rough time of it?" or "Guess you don't feel like doing anything like that again," or anything else that tells the worker that he heard and understands. It doesn't necessarily mean that the next work assignment need be changed or that he must spend an hour listening to the worker complain about the set-up problems he encountered. He may do a number of things differently in the light of the new information he has from the worker—but not necessarily. It's just that extra sensitivity on the part of the foreman which can transform an average working climate into a good one.

Respond to feelings. In some instances the content is far less important than the feeling which underlies it. To catch the full flavor or meaning of the message one must respond particularly to the feeling component. If, for instance, our machinist had said "I'd like to melt this lathe down and make paper clips out of it," responding to content would be obviously absurd. But to respond to his disgust or anger in trying to work with his lathe recognizes the meaning of this message. There are various shadings of these components in the meaning of any message. Each time the listener must try to remain sensitive to the total meaning the message has to the speaker. What is he trying to tell me? What does this mean to him? How does he see this situation?

Note all cues. Not all communication is verbal. The speaker's words alone don't tell us everything he is communicating. And hence, truly sensitive listening requires that we become aware of several kinds of communication besides verbal. The way in which a speaker hesitates in his speech can tell us much about his feelings. So too can the inflection of his voice. He may stress certain points loudly and clearly, and may mumble others. We should also note such things as the person's facial expressions, body posture, hand movements, eye movements, and breathing. All of these help to convey his total message.

What We Communicate By Listening
The first reaction of most people when they consider listening as a possible method for dealing with human beings is that listening cannot be sufficient in itself. Because it is passive, they feel, listening does not communicate anything to the speaker. Actually, nothing could be farther from the truth.

By consistently listening to a speaker you are conveying the idea that: "I'm interested in you as a person, and I think that what you feel is important. I respect your thoughts, and even if I don't agree with them, I know that they are valid for you. I feel sure that you have a contribution to make. I'm not trying to change you or evaluate you. I just want to understand you. I think you're worth listening to, and I want you to know that I'm the kind of a person you can talk to."

The subtle but most important aspect of this is that it is the *demonstration* of the message that works. While it is most difficult to convince someone that you respect him by *telling* him so, you are much more likely to get this message across by really *behaving* that way—by actually *having* and *demonstrating* respect for this person. Listening does this most effectively.

Like other behavior, listening behavior is contagious. This has implications for all communications problems, whether between two people, or within a large organization. To insure good communication between associates up and down the line, one must first take the responsibility for setting a pattern of listening. Just as one learns that anger is usually met with anger, argument with argument, and deception with deception, one can learn that listening can be met with listening. Every person who feels responsibility in a situation can set the tone of the interaction, and the important lesson in this is that any behavior exhibited by one person will eventually be responded to with similar behavior in the other person.

It is far more difficult to stimulate constructive behavior in another person but far more profitable. Listening is one of these constructive behaviors, but if one's attitude is to "wait out" the speaker rather than really listen to him, it will fail. The one who consistently listens with understanding, however, is the one who eventually is most likely to be listened to. If you really want to be heard and understood by another, you can develop him as a potential listener, ready for new ideas, provided you can first develop yourself in these ways and sincerely listen with understanding and respect.

Testing for Understanding

Because understanding another person is actually far more difficult than it at first seems, it is important to test constantly your ability to see the world in the way the speaker sees it. You can do this by reflecting in your own words what the speaker seems to mean by his words and actions. His response to this will tell you whether or not he feels understood. A good rule of thumb is to assume that one never really understands until he can communicate this understanding to the other's satisfaction.

Here is an experiment to test your skill in listening. The next time you become involved in a lively or controversial discussion with another person, stop for a moment and suggest that you adopt this ground rule for continued discussion: Before either participant in the discussion can make a point or express an opinion of his own, he must first restate aloud the previous point or position of the other person. This restatement must be accurate enough to satisfy the speaker before the listener can be allowed to speak for himself.

This is something you could try in your own discussion group. Have someone express himself on some topic of emotional concern to the group. Then, before another member expresses his own feelings and thought, he must rephrase the *meaning* expressed by the previous speaker to that individual's satisfaction. Note the changes in the emotional climate and the quality of the discussion when you try this.

PROBLEMS IN ACTIVE LISTENING

Active listening is not an easy skill to acquire. It demands practice. Perhaps more important, it may require changes in our own basic attitudes. These changes come slowly and sometimes with considerable difficulty. Let us look at some of the major problems in active listening and what can be done to overcome them.

The Personal Risk

To be effective at all in active listening, one must have a sincere interest in the speaker. We all live in glass houses as far as our attitudes are concerned. They always show through. And if we are only making a pretense of interest in the speaker, he will quickly pick this up, either consciously or unconsciously. And once he does, he will no longer express himself freely.

Active listening carries a strong element of personal risk. If we manage to accomplish what we are describing here—to sense deeply the feelings of another person, to understand the meaning his experiences have for him, to see the world as he sees it—we risk being changed ourselves. For example, if we permit ourselves to listen our way into the psychological life of a labor leader or agitator—to get the meaning which life has for him—we risk coming to see the world as he sees it. It is threatening to give up, even momentarily, what we believe and start thinking in someone else's terms. It takes a great deal of inner security and courage to be able to risk one's self in understanding another.

For the supervisor, the courage to take another's point of view generally means that he must see *himself* through another's eyes—he must be able to see himself as others see him. To do this may sometimes be unpleasant, but it is far more *difficult* than unpleasant. We are so accustomed to viewing ourselves in certain ways—to seeing and hearing only what we want to see and hear—that it is extremely difficult for a person to free himself from his needs to see things these ways.

Developing an attitude of sincere interest in the speaker is thus no easy task. It can be developed only by being willing to risk seeing the world from the speaker's point of view. If we have a number of such experiences, however, they will shape an attitude which will allow us to be truly genuine in our interest in the speaker.

Hostile Expressions

The listener will often hear negative, hostile expressions directed at himself. Such expressions are always hard to listen to. No one likes to hear hostile action or words. And it is not easy to get to the point where one is strong enough to permit these attacks without finding it necessary to defend himself or retaliate.

Because we all fear that people will crumble under the attack of genuine negative feelings, we tend to perpetuate an attitude of pseudopeace. It is as if we cannot tolerate conflict at all for fear of the damage it could do to us, to the situation, to the others involved. But of course the real damage is done to all these by the denial and suppression of negative feelings.

Out-Of-Place Expressions

There is also the problem of out-of-place expressions, expressions dealing with behavior which is not usually acceptable in our society. In the extreme forms that present themselves before psychotherapists, expressions of sexual perversity or homicidal fantasies are often found blocking to the listener because of their obvious threatening quality. At less extreme levels, we all find unnatural or inappropriate behavior difficult to handle. That is, anything from an "off-color" story told in mixed company, to seeing a man weep is likely to produce a problem situation.

In any face-to-face situation, we will find instances of this type which will momentarily, if not permanently, block any communication. In business and industry any expressions of weakness or incompetency will generally be regarded as unacceptable and therefore will block good two-way communication. For example, it is difficult to listen to a supervisor tell of his feelings of failure in being able to "take charge" of a situation in his department because *all* administrators are supposed to be able to "take charge."

Accepting Positive Feelings

It is both interesting and perplexing to note that negative or hostile feelings or expressions are much easier to deal with in any face-to-face relationship than are truly and deeply positive feelings. This is especially true for the business man because the culture expects him to be independent, bold, clever, and aggressive and manifest no feelings of warmth, gentleness, and intimacy. He therefore comes to regard these feelings as soft and inappropriate. But no matter how they are regarded, they remain a human need. The denial of these feelings in himself and his associates does not get the executive out of the problem of dealing with them. They simply become veiled and confused. If recognized they would work for the total effort; unrecognized, they work against it.

Emotional Danger Signals

The listener's own emotions are sometimes a barrier to active listening. When emotions are at their height, when listening is most necessary, it is most difficult to set aside one's own concerns and be understanding. Our emotions are often our own worst enemies when we try to become listeners. The more involved and invested we are in a particular situation or problem, the less we are likely to be willing or able to listen to the feelings and attitudes of others. That is, the more we find it necessary to respond to our own needs, the less we are able to respond to the needs of another. Let us look at some of the main danger signals that warn us that our emotions may be interfering with our listening.

Defensiveness. The points about which one is most vocal and dogmatic, the points which one is most anxious to impose on others—these are always the points one is trying to talk oneself into believing. So one danger signal becomes apparent when you find yourself stressing a point or trying to convince another. It is at these times that you are likely to be less secure and consequently less able to listen.

Resentment of opposition. It is always easier to listen to an idea which is similar to one of your own than to an opposing view. Sometimes, in order to clear the air, it is helpful to pause for a moment when you feel your ideas and position being challenged, reflect on the situation, and express your concern to the speaker.

Clash of personalities. Here again, our experience has consistently shown us that the genuine expression of feelings on the part of the listener will be more helpful in developing a sound relationship than the suppression of them. This is so whether the feelings be resentment, hostility, threat, or admiration. A basically honest relationship, whatever the nature of it, is the most productive of all. The other party becomes secure when he learns that the listener can express his feelings honestly and openly to him. We should keep this in mind when we begin to fear a clash of personalities in the listening relationship. Otherwise, fear of our own emotions will choke off full expression of feelings.

Listening to Ourselves

To listen to oneself is a prerequisite to listening to others. And it is often an effective means of dealing with the problems we have outlined above. When we are most aroused, excited, and demanding, we are least able to understand our own feelings and attitudes. Yet, in dealing with the problems of others, it becomes most important to be sure of one's own position, values, and needs.

The ability to recognize and understand the meaning which a particular episode has for you, with all the feelings which it stimulates in you, and the ability to express this meaning when you find it getting in the way of active listening, will clear the air and enable you once again to be free to listen. That is, if some person or situation touches off feelings within you which tend to block your attempts to listen with understanding, begin listening to yourself. It is much more helpful in developing effective relationships to avoid suppressing these feelings. Speak them out as clearly as you can, and try to enlist the other person as a listener to your feelings. A person's listening ability is limited by his ability to listen to himself.

ACTIVE LISTENING AND COMPANY GOALS

"How can listening improve production?"

"We're in business, and it's a rugged, fast, competitive affair. How are we going to find time to counsel our employees?"

"We have to concern ourselves with organizational problems first."

"We can't afford to spend all day listening when there's a job to be done."

"What's morale got to do with production?"

"Sometimes we have to sacrifice an individual for the good of the rest of the people in the company."

Those of us who are trying to advance the listening approach in industry hear these comments frequently. And because they are so honest and legitimate, they pose a real problem. Unfortunately, the answers are not so clear-cut as the questions.

Individual Importance

One answer is based on an assumption that is central to the listening approach. That assumption is: the kind of behavior which helps the individual will eventually be the best thing that could be done for the group. Or saying it another way: the things that are best for the individual are best for the company. This is a conviction of ours, based on our experience in psychology and education. The research evidence from industry is only beginning to come in. We find that putting the group first, at the expense of the individual, besides being an uncomfortable individual experience, does *not* unify the group. In fact, it tends to make the group less a group. The members become anxious and suspicious.

We are not at all sure in just what ways the group does benefit from a concern demonstrated for an individual, but we have several strong leads. One is that the group feels more secure when an individual member is being listened to and provided for with concern and sensitivity. And we assume that a secure group will ultimately be a better group. When each individual feels that he need not fear exposing himself to the group, he is likely to contribute more freely and spontaneously. When the leader of a group responds to the individual, puts the individual first, the other members of the group will follow suit, and the group comes to act as a unit in recognizing and responding to the needs of a particular member. This positive, constructive action seems to be a much more satisfying experience for a group than the experience of dispensing with a member.

Listening and Production
As to whether or not listening or any other activity designed to better human relations in an industry actually raises production—whether morale has a definite relationship to production is not known for sure. There are some who frankly hold that there is no relationship to be expected between morale and production—that production often depends upon the social misfit, the eccentric, or the isolate. And there are some who simply choose to work in a climate of cooperation and harmony, in a high-morale group, quite aside from the question of increased production.

A report from the Survey Research Center[1] at the University of Michigan on research conducted at the Prudential Life Insurance Company lists seven findings relating to production and morale. First-line supervisors in high-production work groups were found to differ from those in low-production work groups in that they:

1. Are under less close supervision from their own supervisors.

2. Place less direct emphasis upon production as the goal.

3. Encourage employee participation in the making of decisions.

4. Are more employee-centered.

5. Spend more of their time in supervision and less in straight production work.

6. Have a greater feeling of confidence in their supervisory roles.

7. Feel that they know where they stand with the company.

After mentioning that other dimensions of morale, such as identification with the company, intrinsic job satisfaction, and satisfaction with job status, were not found significantly related to productivity, the report goes on to suggest the following psychological interpretation:

> People are more effectively motivated when they are given some degree of freedom in the way in which they do their work than when every action is prescribed in advance. They do better when some degree of decision-making about their jobs is possible than when all decisions are made for them. They respond more adequately when they are treated as personalities than as cogs in a machine. In short if the ego motivations of self-determination, of self-expression, of a sense of personal worth can be tapped, the individual can be more effectively energized. The use of external sanctions, or pressuring for production may work to some degree, but not to the extent that the more internalized motives do. When the individual comes to identify himself with his job and with the work of his group, human resources are much more fully utilized in the production process.

The Survey Research Center has also conducted studies among workers in other industries. In discussing the results of these studies, Robert L. Kahn writes:

> In the studies of clerical workers, railroad workers, and workers in heavy industry, the supervisors with the better production records gave a larger proportion of their time to supervisory functions, especially to the interpersonal aspects of their jobs. The supervisors of the lower-producing sections were more likely to spend their time in tasks which the men themselves were performing, or in the paper-work aspects of their jobs.[2]

Maximum Creativeness
There may never be enough research evidence to satisfy everyone on this question. But speaking from a business point of view, in terms of the problems of developing resources for production, the maximum creativeness and productive effort of the human beings in the organization are the richest untapped source of power still existing. The difference between the maximum productive capacity of people and that output which industry is now realizing is immense. We simply suggest that this maximum capacity might be closer to realization if we sought to release the motivation that already exists within people rather than try to stimulate them externally.

This releasing of the individual is made possible first of all by sensitive listening, with respect and understanding. Listening is a beginning toward making the individual feel himself worthy of making contributions, and this could result in a very dynamic and productive organization. Competitive business is never too rugged or too busy to take time to procure the most efficient technological advances or to develop rich raw material resources. But these in comparison to the resources that are already within the people in the plant are paltry. This is industry's major procurement problem.

G. L. Clements, president of Jewel Tea Co., Inc., in talking about the collaborative approach to management says:

> We feel that this type of approach recognizes that there is a secret ballot going on at all times among the people in any business. They vote for or against their supervisors. A favorable vote for the supervisor shows up in the cooperation, teamwork, understanding, and production of the group. To win this secret ballot, each supervisor must share the problems of his group and work for them.[3]

The decision to spend time listening to his employees is a decision each supervisor or executive has to make for himself. Executives seldom have much to do with products or processes. They have to deal with people who must in turn deal with people who will deal with products or processes. The higher one goes up the line the more he will be concerned with human relations problems, simply because people are all he has to work with. The minute we take a man from his bench and make him a foreman he is removed from the basic production of goods and now must begin relating to individuals instead of nuts and bolts. People are different from things, and our foreman is called upon for a different line of skills completely. His new tasks call upon him to be a special kind of a person. The development of himself as a listener is a first step in becoming this special person.

Notes

1. "Productivity, Supervision, and Employee Morale," *Human Relations,* Series 1, Report 1 (Ann Arbor, Mich.: Survey Research Center, University of Michigan).

2. Robert L. Kahn, "The Human Factors Underlying Industrial Productivity," *Michigan Business Review,* November, 1952.

3. G. L. Clements, "Time for 'Democracy in Action' at the Executive Level," an address given before the A.M.A. Personnel Conference, February 28, 1951.

An Overview of Transactional Analysis
Muriel James and Dorothy Jongeward

Many people come to a time in their lives when they are provoked to define themselves. At such a time transactional analysis offers a frame of reference that most people can understand and put to use in their own lives. This chapter provides a brief overview of TA theory and its applications. Subsequent chapters consider each phase in depth.

Transactional analysis is concerned with four kinds of analysis:

Structural Analysis: the analysis of individual personality.

Transactional Analysis: the analysis of what people do and say to one another.

Game Analysis: the analysis of ulterior transactions leading to a payoff.

Script Analysis: the analysis of specific life dramas that persons compulsively play out.

INTRODUCTION TO STRUCTURAL ANALYSIS

Structural analysis offers one way of answering the questions: Who am I? Why do I act the way I do? How did I get this way? It is a method of analyzing a person's thoughts, feelings, and behavior, based on the phenomena of ego states.[1]

Imagine a mother loudly scolding her noisy quarrelsome children. Her face wears a scowl. Her voice is shrill. Her arm is tense and held high in the air. Suddenly the phone rings and she hears a friend's voice. The mother's posture, tone, and expression begin to change. Her voice becomes well modulated. Her once tense arm lies quietly in her lap.

Imagine two factory workers angrily arguing with each other about a work problem. Their argument is animated and fierce. They look like two children fighting over a piece of candy. Suddenly, they hear a crash of steel followed by an agonized scream. Their entire demeanor changes. Their argument is dropped. Their angry expressions give way to concern. One hurries to see what's wrong; the other calls an ambulance. According to the theory of structural analysis, the workers, as well as the mother, changed ego states.

Berne defines an ego state as "A consistent pattern of feeling and experience directly related to a corresponding consistent pattern of behavior."[2] The findings of Dr. Wilder Penfield, neurosurgeon, support this definition. He found that an electrode applied to different parts of the brain evoked memories and feelings long forgotten by the person.[3] Berne writes:

> ... in this respect the brain functions like a tape recorder to preserve complete experiences in serial sequence, in a form recognizable as "ego states"—indicating that ego states comprise the natural way of experiencing and of recording experiences in their totality. Simultaneously, of course, experiences are recorded in fragmented forms ...[4]

The implications are that what happens to a person is recorded in his brain and nervous tissue. This includes everything a person experienced in his childhood, all that he incorporated from his parent figures, his perceptions of events, his feelings associated with these events, and the distortions that he brings to his memories. These recordings are stored as though on videotape. They can be replayed, and the event recalled and even reexperienced.

Each person has three ego states which are separate and distinct sources of behavior: the Parent ego state, the Adult ego state, and the Child ego state. These are not abstract concepts but realities. "Parent, Adult, and Child represent real people who now exist or who once existed, who have legal names and civic identities."[5]

The structure of personality is diagrammed below.

Ego states are colloquially termed Parent, Adult, and Child. When capitalized in this book they will refer to ego states, not to actual parents, adults, or children.

The three ego states are defined as follows:

The *Parent ego state* contains the attitudes and behavior incorporated from external sources, primarily parents. Outwardly, it often is expressed toward others in prejudicial, critical, and nurturing behavior. Inwardly, it is

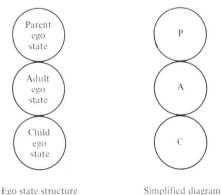

Ego state structure   Simplified diagram

experienced as old Parental messages which continue to influence the inner Child.

The *Adult ego state* is not related to a person's age. It is oriented to current reality and the objective gathering of information. It is organized, adaptable, intelligent, and functions by testing reality, estimating probabilities, and computing dispassionately.

The *Child ego state* contains all the impulses that come naturally to an infant. It also contains the recordings of his early experiences, how he responded to them, and the "positions" he took about himself and others. It is expressed as "old" (archaic) behavior from childhood.

When you are acting, thinking, feeling, as you observed your parents to be doing, you are in your Parent ego state.

When you are dealing with current reality, gathering facts, and computing objectively, you are in your Adult ego state.

When you are feeling and acting as you did when you were a child, you are in your Child ego state.

Case Illustration

A client was advised to investigate a private school for his son. When he reported his findings about the school where the teaching was informal and creativity encouraged, three distinct reactions were easily observable. First he scowled and said, "I can't see how anyone could learn anything at that school. There's dirt on the floor!" Leaning back in his chair, his forehead smoothed out as he reflected, "Before I decide, I think I should check with the school's scholastic rating and talk to some of the parents." The next minute, a broad grin crossed his face, and he said, "Gee, I'd love to have gone to a school like that!"

When queried about his responses, the client readily analyzed that his first was the way his father would have responded. His second was his Adult looking for more data. His third was his Child recalling his own unhappy school experience and imagining the fun he might have had at a school such as the one he visited.

Before making a final decision, he pursued his Adult questions. Subsequently, his son attended this school, is currently having a good time there, and is achieving well beyond his former level.

According to structural analysis, each person may respond to a specific stimulus in quite distinct ways from each of his ego states, sometimes these ego states are in concert, sometimes in conflict. Let's look at the following examples.

To a stimulus of a piece of modern art

Parent: Good grief! What's it supposed to be!
Adult: That costs $350 according to the price tag.
Child: Ooo, what pretty color!

To a request for an office report

Parent: Mr. Brown is not cut out to be a supervisor.
Adult: I know Mr. Brown needs these by five o'clock.
Child: No matter what I do I can't please Mr. Brown.

To an act of violence on the street

Parent: It serves that girl right for being out so late.
Adult: I'd better call the police.
Child: Say, is this ever exciting!

To being offered a piece of chocolate cake when dieting

Parent: Go ahead honey, it will keep up your energy.
Adult: That piece of cake must have at least 400 calories. I think I'll skip it.
Child: What yummy cake! I could eat the whole thing.

To a crash of rock music

Parent: That horrible stuff kids listen to today!
Adult: It's hard for me to think or talk when the music is so loud.
Child: That makes me want to dance.

To the late arrival of a young secretary

Parent: Poor thing looks as if she hasn't slept a wink.
Adult: If she doesn't make up her time, the other employees will be dissatisfied.
Child: I sure wish I could take time off for fun.

To a lecturer using four-letter words

Parent: Using such expletives only shows a weak vocabulary.
Adult: I wonder why he chooses those words to use and what their effect is on the audience.
Child: I wish I dared to talk like that.

To the smell of cabbage

Parent: Cabbage really keeps the family healthy.
Adult: Cabbage has high vitamin C content.
Child: Nobody's going to make me eat that stinky stuff.

To a new acquaintance putting his arm around you

Parent: Never let a stranger touch you.
Adult: I wonder why he's doing it?
Child: He scares me.

People can feel, smell, touch, speak, listen, look, and act from each ego state. Each ego state has its own programming. Some people respond from one ego state more than from the others. If, for example, a person tends to respond most often from his Parent ego state, his view of the world will be as he observed his parents viewing it. In this case his ability to sense the world for himself is diminished or distorted.

DEVELOPMENT OF EGO STATES

When first born, the infant's awareness is centered around his own needs and comforts. He seeks to avoid painful experiences and responds at the feeling level with whatever he has and is. Almost immediately his unique Child ego state emerges. (Prenatal influences on the Child ego state have not yet been determined.)

The Parent ego state develops next. It is often first observed when the young child plays at parenting, imitating his parents. Sometimes it's a shock for parents to see themselves being played back. Sometimes they are very pleased.

The Adult ego state develops as the child tries to make sense out of his world, and figures out he can manipulate others. He may ask, "Why do I have to eat when I'm not hungry?" and figures out he can manipulate others by faking a stomach ache when he doesn't want to eat.

Case Illustration

Sheri, aged twenty-two months, received a doll-stroller at Christmas. She tried to climb into it saying, "Me, baby." It was too small. She then tried putting her doll in. The doll fit. Sheri squealed, "Me, mommy," and started to push the stroller but soon grew tired of playing this part. Angrily she threw the doll out, pushed over the stroller, righted it, and tried to get in again. Still she could not fit. Frustrated, she put the doll in once more. She tried this switch four times. Then, apparently deciding she was too big, she settled for being mommy and acted toward her doll in ways her mother acted toward her.

Sheri's motherly behavior was an actual imitation of her mother from her Parent ego state. Although in her Child ego state Sheri wanted to be a baby, her emerging Adult ego state collected and processed objective data—that she couldn't fit into the stroller.

Any situation may activate a specific ego state and sometimes, as in the case of Sheri, different ego states within a person vie for control. Between two people, one "baby" confronted with another "baby" may try to be a parent to him or may try to be a "bigger" baby.

INTRODUCTION TO ANALYZING TRANSACTIONS

Anything that happens between people will involve a transaction between their ego states. When one person sends a message to another, he expects a response.

All transactions can be classified as (1) complementary, (2) crossed, or (3) ulterior.[6]

Complementary Transactions

A complementary transaction occurs when a message, sent from a specific ego state, gets the predicted response from a specific ego state in the other person. Berne describes a complementary transaction as one which is "appropriate and expected and follows the natural order of healthy human relationship."[7] For example, if a wife who is grieving for her lost friend is comforted by a sympathetic husband, her momentary dependency need is answered appropriately (see Fig. 2.1).

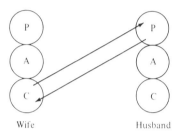

A complementary transaction can occur between any two ego states. For example, two people may transact Parent-Parent when lamenting their children's leaving home; Adult-Adult when solving a problem; Child-Child or Parent-Child when having fun together. A person from his Parent can transact with any of the ego states of another person. He can also do this with his Adult and Child. If the response is the expected one, the transaction is complementary. The lines of communication are *open,* and the people can continue transacting with one another.

Gestures, facial expressions, body posture, tone of voice, and so forth, all contribute to the meaning in every transaction. If a verbal message is to be completely understood, the receiver must take into consideration the nonverbal aspects as well as the spoken words.

To better understand the following illustrations, we must assume that the stimulus is straightforward and the verbal and nonverbal messages are congruent. Any illustration is, at best, an educated guess. To be totally accurate, the actual Parent, Adult, and Child ego states of each person would need to be known.

Fig. 2.2. *Data exchange in Adult/Adult transaction*

1. What is the yearly salary for this job?
2. It starts at $10,000.

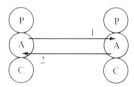

Fig. 2.3 *Sympathetic Parent/Parent transaction*

1. Those children really miss their father.
2. Yes, let's take them to the park for a little fun.

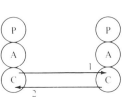

Fig. 2.4. *Playful Child/Child transaction*

1. I really like you.
2. I like you, too.

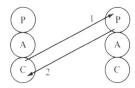

Fig. 2.5. *Child/Nurturing Parent transaction*

1. I'm so worried about my son I can't concentrate on this report.
2. You can leave work early to go by the hospital and see him.

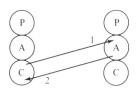

Fig. 2.6. *Angry Child/Listening Adult feedback transaction*

1. I'm so mad I could throw this darn typewriter out of the window.
2. Something made you so angry you'd like to throw the equipment around. Is that how it is?

In each of the above transactions communication is open because the responses given were expected responses and were appropriate to the stimulus. This does not always happen. Sometimes a stimulus receives an unexpected or inappropriate response, and the lines of communication become crossed.

Crossed Transactions
When two people stand glaring at each other, turn their backs on each other, are unwilling to continue transacting, or are puzzled by what has just occurred between them, it is likely that they have just experienced *a crossed transaction.* A crossed transaction occurs when an unexpected response is made to the stimulus. An inappropriate ego state is activated and the lines of transacting between the people are crossed. At this point, people tend to withdraw, turn away from each other, or switch the conversation in another direction. If a husband responds unsympathetically to his grieving wife, "Well, how do you think I feel!" he is likely to cause her to turn away from him (Fig. 2.7).

Crossed transactions are a frequent source of pain between people—parents and children, husband and wife, boss and employee, teacher and student, and so forth. The person who initiates a transaction, expecting a certain response, does not get it. He is crossed and often left feeling discounted.

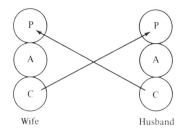

Wife   Husband

Figure 2.8

1. Boss: What time is it?
2. Secretary: You're always in such a hurry!

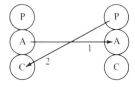

Figure 2.9

1. Husband: Can you take the car to be serviced this afternoon?
2. Wife: Today I iron. Johnny expects a birthday cake. The cat has to go to the vet, and now you want me to take the car in!

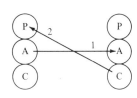

Figure 2.10

1. Boss: I need 25 copies of this report for the board meeting this afternoon. Can you get them for me?
2. Secretary: Aren't you lucky you've got me around to take care of you?

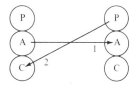

Figure 2.11

1. Scientist A: There may be some variables we haven't considered for this experiment.
2. Scientist B: So what, who cares around here?

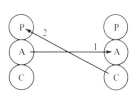

Figure 2.12

1. Wife: I'd like to use the car on Wednesday night and have a good visit with my sister.
2. Husband: Gee, you never want to talk to me.

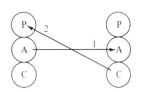

Figure 2.13

1. Supervisor: Have you seen the Willows contract, Miss Smith?
2. File clerk: If you ran this department the way you're supposed to, you wouldn't have to ask me where the Willows contract is.

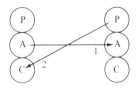

Figure 2.14

1. John: Let's have fun.
2. Marcia: Can't you ever be serious?

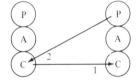

Transactions may be direct or indirect, straightforward or diluted, intense or weak. *Indirect transactions* are three-handed. One person speaks to another while hoping to influence the third who can overhear it. For example, a man may be too fearful to speak directly to his boss so says something to a co-worker hoping the boss will "get the message."

Diluted transactions are often half hostile, half affectionate. The message is buried in some form of kidding. For example, one student may say to another. "Hey genius, when are you going to finish that book? I want to read it." The other may toss it to him with "Here you are, butterfingers. Catch it if you can."

Weak transactions are those that are superficial, perfunctory, and lack feelings of intensity. Such is the case if a wife says to her husband, "I wonder if we should go out for dinner tonight," and he responds, "I don't care, dear. Whatever you say, dear."

In healthy relationships people transact directly, straightforwardly and, on occasion, intensely.[8] These transactions are complementary and free from ulterior motives.

Ulterior Transactions

Ulterior transactions are the most complex. They differ from complementary and crossed in that they always involve more than two ego states. When an ulterior message is sent, it is disguised under a socially acceptable transaction. Such is the purpose of the old cliché: "Wouldn't you like to come up to see my etchings?" In this instance the Adult is verbalizing one thing while the Child, with the use of innuendo, is sending a different message (Fig. 2.15).

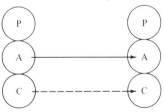

If a car salesman says to his customer with a leer, "This is our finest sports car, but it may be too racy for you," he is sending a message that can be heard either by the customer's Adult ego state or by his Child ego state (see Fig. 2.16). If the customer's Adult hears, he may respond, "Yes, you're right, considering the requirements of my job." If his Child responds, he may say, "I'll take it. It's just what I want."

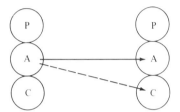

An ulterior message is also given when a secretary submits a letter to her boss with several typing errors. This invites him to give her a Parental put-down (see Fig. 2.17). The same happens when a student is continually late with assignments, absent from class, writes illegibly, or in some way provokes the equivalent of parental criticism.

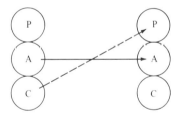

The same kind of ulterior transaction occurs if a man who has been a "reformed" alcoholic comes to work with a hangover but a glimmer in his eye, and boasts to his co-worker, "Boy, I really blew it last night and drank myself under the table. What a head I've got today!" On the surface he is giving factual information. However, at the ulterior level, the alcoholic's Child ego state is looking for the Parent in the other to smile indulgently and thus condone his drinking.

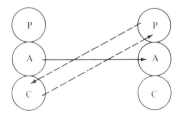

Instead of a Parent response he may activate his co-worker's Child ego state, and he may respond by laughing at the tragedy. If the co-worker laughs, either from his Parent or his Child ego state, he reinforces the (parental) injunction usually given nonverbally to the alcoholic (as a child), "Get lost, you bum." This inappropriate laugh or smile is described by Claude Steiner as the *gallows transaction*.[9] The smile serves to tighten the noose and destructive behavior is reinforced.

Any smiling response to a person's misfortunes may serve as a gallows transaction. Such is the case when

a teacher acts amused at her pupil's "stupid behavior,"

a mother laughs at her accident-prone three-year-old.

a father beams over the risks his son takes.

These gallows transactions, like other transactions with ulterior motives, are common among losers. Losers use them to promote their psychological games.

Notes

1. Eric Berne, *Transactional Analysis in Psychotherapy,* New York: Grove Press, pp. 17–43.
   Cf. Paul McCormick and Leonard Campos, *Introduce Yourself to Transactional Analysis:* ATA *Handbook* Stockton, Calif.: San Joaquin TA Study Group, distributed by Transactional Pub., 3155 College Ave., Berkeley, Calif., 94705, 1969.
   Also see John M. Dusay, "Transactional Analysis," in *A Layman's Guide to Psychiatry and Psychoanalysis* by Eric Berne, New York: Simon and Schuster, 3rd ed., 1968, pp. 277–306.

2. Berne, *Principles of Group Treatment,* New York, Oxford University Press, 1964, p. 364.

3. W. Penfield, "Memory Mechanisms" A.M.A. *Archives of Neurology and Psychiatry,* Vol. 67 (1952), pp. 178–198.

4. Berne, *Principles of Group Treatment,* p. 281.

5. Berne, *Transactional Analysis in Psychotherapy,* p. 32.

6. Berne, *Games People Play,* New York: Grove Press, pp. 29–64.

7. *Ibid.,* p. 29.

8. *See* Eric Berne, *The Structure and Dynamics of Organizations and Groups,* Philadelphia: J. B. Lippincott, 1963.

9. *See* Claude M. Steiner, *Games Alcoholics Play: The Analysis of Life Scripts,* New York: Grove Press, 1971.
   Cf. David Steere, "Freud on the 'Gallows Transaction,' " *Transactional Analysis Bulletin,* Vol. 9, No. 1 (Jan. 1970), pp. 3–5.

THE GROUP IN THE ORGANIZATION

The Nature of Highly Effective Groups
Rensis Likert

We concluded in Chapter 8 that the form of organization which will make the greatest use of human capacity consists of highly effective work groups linked together in an overlapping pattern by other similarly effective groups. The highly effective work group is, consequently, an important component of the newer theory of management. It will be important to understand both its nature and its performance characteristics. We shall examine these in this chapter, but first a few words about groups in general.

Although we have stressed the great potential power of the group for building effective organizations, it is important to emphasize that this does *not* say that all groups and all committees are highly effective or are committed to desirable goals. Groups as groups can vary from poor to excellent. They can have desirable values and goals, or their objectives can be most destructive. They can accomplish much that is good, or they can do great harm. There is nothing *implicitly* good or bad, weak or strong, about a group.

The nature of the group determines the character of its impact upon the development of its members. The values of the group, the stability of these values, the group atmosphere, and the nature of the conformity demanded by the group determine whether a group is likely to have a positive or negative impact upon the growth and behavior of its members. If the values of the group are seen by the society as having merit, if the group is stable in its adherence to these values, and if the atmosphere of the group is warm, supportive, and full of understanding, the group's influence on the development of its members will be positive. A hostile atmosphere and socially undesirable or unstable values produce a negative impact upon the members' growth and behavior.

Loyalty to a group produces pressures toward conformity. A group may demand conformity to the idea of supporting, encouraging, and giving recognition for individual creativity, or it may value rigidity of behavior, with seriously narrowing and dwarfing consequences. This latter kind of pressure for conformity keeps the members from growing and robs the group of original ideas. Many writers have pointed to these deleterious effects of conformity. They often overlook the capacity of groups to stimulate individual creativeness by placing a high value on imaginative and original contributions by their members. As Pelz's findings, reported in Chapter 2, demonstrate, groups can contribute significantly to creativity by providing the stimulation of diverse points of view within a supportive atmosphere which encourages each individual member to pursue new and unorthodox concepts.

Some business executives are highly critical of groups—or committees —and the inability of committees to accomplish a great deal. Their criticisms are often well warranted. In many instances, committees are wasteful of time and unable to reach decisions. Sometimes the decisions, when reached, are mediocre. Moreover, some members of management at various hierarchical levels use committees as escape mechanisms—as a way to avoid the responsibility for a decision.

The surprising thing about committees is not that many or most are ineffective, but that they accomplish as much as they do when, relatively speaking, we know so little about how to use them. There has been a lack of systematic study of ways to make committees effective. Far more is known about time-and-motion study, cost accounting and similar aspects of management than is known about groups and group processes. Moreover, in spite of the demonstrated potentiality of groups, far less research is being devoted to learning the role of groups and group processes and how to make the most effective use of them in an organization than to most management practices. We know appreciably less about how to make groups and committees effective than we know about most matters of managing.

We do know that groups can be powerful. The newer theory takes this into account and tries to make constructive use of the group's potential strength for developing and mobilizing human resources.

In this and other chapters the use of the term "group" may give the impression that groups have the capacity to behave in ways other than through the behavior of their members. Thus, such expressions appear as the "group's goals," "the group decides," or the "group motivates." In many instances, these expressions are used to avoid endless repetition of the words, "the members of the group." In other instances, something more is meant. Thus, in speaking of "group values," the intent is to refer to those values which have been established by the group through a group-decision process involving consensus. Once a decision has been reached by consensus, there are strong motivational forces, developed within each individual as a result of his membership in the group and his relationship to the other members, to be guided by that decision. In this sense, the group has goals and values and makes decisions. It has properties which may not be present, as such, in any one individual. A group may be divided in opinion, for example, although this may not be true of any one member. Dorwin Cartwright puts it this way: "The relation between the individual members and the group is analogous to the distinction made in mathematics between the properties of a set of elements and the properties of the elements within a set. Every set is composed of elements, but sets have properties which are not identical with the properties of the elements of the set."

THE HIGHLY EFFECTIVE WORK GROUP

Much of the discussion of groups in this chapter will be in terms of an ideal organizational model which the work groups in an organization can approach as they develop skill in group processes. This model group, of course, is always part of a large organization. The description of its nature and performance characteristics is based on evidence from a variety of sources. Particularly important are the observational and experimental studies of small groups such as those conducted by the Research Center for Group Dynamics (Cartwright & Zander, 1960; Hare et al., 1955; Institute for Social Research, 1956; Institute for Social Research, 1960; Thibaut & Kelly, 1959). Extensive use is made of data from studies of large-scale organizations (see Chapters 2 to 4). Another important source is the material from the National Training Laboratories (Foundation for Research on Human Behavior, 1960d; National Training Laboratories, 1953; National Training Laboratories, 1960; Stock & Thelen, 1958). The NTL has focused on training in sensitivity to the reactions of others and in skills to perform the leadership and membership roles in groups.

In addition to drawing upon the above sources, the description of the ideal model is derived from theory. Some of the statements about the model for which there is little or limited experimental or observational data have been derived directly from the basic drive to achieve and maintain a sense of importance and personal worth. At several points in this chapter and Chapter 12 the author has gone appreciably beyond available specific research findings. The author feels, however, that the generalizations which are emerging based on research in organizations and on small groups, youth, and family life, personality development, consumer behavior, human motivation, and related fields lend strong support to the general theory and the derivations contained in this book.

It has been necessary to go beyond the data in order to spell out at this time in some detail the general pattern of the more complex but more effective form of organization being created by the higher-producing managers. The author hopes that the theory and model proposed will stimulate a substantial increase in basic and developmental research and that they will be tested and sharpened by that research.

The body of knowledge about small groups, while sufficiently large to make possible this description of the ideal model, is still relatively limited. Without question, as the importance of the work group as the basic building block of organizations becomes recognized, there will be a great increase in the research on groups and our knowledge about them. The over-all pattern of the model described here will be improved and clarified by such research. Our understanding of how to develop and use groups effectively will also be greatly advanced.

The following description of the ideal model defines what we mean by *a highly effective group*. The definition involves reference to several different variables. Each of them can be thought of as a continuum, i.e., as a characteristic which can vary from low to high, from unfavorable to favorable. For example, a group can vary from one in which there is hostility among the members to one in which the attitudes are warm and friendly. The ideal model is at the favorable end of each variable.

THE NATURE OF HIGHLY EFFECTIVE WORK GROUPS

The highly effective group, as we shall define it, is always conceived as being a part of a larger organization. A substantial proportion of persons in a company are members of more than one work group, especially when both line and staff are considered. As a consequence, in such groups there are always linking functions to be performed and relationships to other groups to be maintained. Our highly effective group is not an isolated entity.

All the persons in a company also belong to groups and organizations outside of the company. For most persons, membership in several groups both within and outside the company is the rule rather than the exception. This means, of course, that no single group, even the highly effective work group, dominates the life of any member. Each member of the organization feels pressures from membership in several different groups and is not influenced solely by loyalty to any one group.

Since the different groups to which a person belongs are apt to have somewhat different and often inconsistent goals and values, corresponding conflicts and pressures are created within him. To minimize these conflicts and tensions, the individual seeks to influence the values and goals of each of the different groups to which he belongs and which are important to him so as to minimize the inconsistencies and conflicts in values and goals. In striving for this reconciliation, he is likely to press for the acceptance of those values most important to him.

The properties and performance characteristics of the ideal highly effective group are as follows:

1. The members are skilled in all the various leadership and membership roles and functions required for interaction between leaders and members and between members and other members.

2. The group has been in existence sufficiently long to have developed a well-established, relaxed working relationship among all its members.

3. The members of the group are attracted to it and are loyal to its members, including the leader.

4. The members and leaders have a high degree of confidence and trust in each other.

5. The values and goals of the group are a satisfactory integration and expression of the relevant values and needs of its members. They have helped shape these values and goals and are satisfied with them.

6. In so far as members of the group are performing linking functions, they endeavor to have the values and goals of the groups which they link in harmony, one with the other.

7. The more important a value seems to the group, the greater the likelihood that the individual member will accept it.

8. The members of the group are highly motivated to abide by the major values and to achieve the important goals of the group. Each member will do all that he reasonably can—and at times all in his power—to help the group achieve its central objectives. He expects every other member to do the same. This high motivation springs, in part, from the basic motive to achieve and maintain a sense of personal worth and importance. Being valued by a group whose values he shares, and deriving a sense of significance and importance from this relationship, leads each member to do his best. He is eager not to let the other members down. He strives hard to do what he believes is expected of him.

9. All the interaction, problem-solving, decision-making activities of the group occur in a supportive atmosphere. Suggestions, comments, ideas, information, criticisms are all offered with a helpful orientation. Similarly, these contributions are received in the same spirit. Respect is shown for the point of view of others both in the way contributions are made and in the way they are received.

There are real and important differences of opinion, but the focus is on arriving at sound solutions and not on exacerbating and aggravating the conflict. Ego forces deriving from the desire to achieve and maintain a sense of personal worth and importance are channeled into constructive efforts. Care is taken not to let these ego forces disrupt important group tasks, such as problem-solving. Thus, for example, a statement of the problem, a condition which any solution must meet, a suggested solution, or an item of relevant fact are all treated as from the group as a whole. Care is taken so that one statement of the problem is not John's and another Bill's. A suggested solution is not referred to as Tom's and another as Dick's. All the material contributed is treated as *ours:* "One of our proposed solutions is *A,* another is *B."* In all situations involving actual or potential differences or conflict among the members of the group, procedures are used to separate the ego of each member from his contribution. In this way, ego forces do not stimulate conflict between members. Instead, they are channeled into supporting the activities and efforts of the group.

The group atmosphere is sufficiently supportive for the members to be able to accept readily any criticism which is offered and to make the most constructive use of it. The criticisms may deal with any relevant topic such as operational problems, decisions, supervisory problems, interpersonal relationships, or group processes, but whatever their content, the member feels sufficiently secure in the supportive atmosphere of the group to be able to accept, test, examine, and benefit from the criticism offered. Also, he is able to be frank and candid, irrespective of the content of the discussion: technical, managerial, factual, cognitive, or emotional. The supportive atmosphere of the group, with the feeling of security it provides, contributes to a cooperative relationship between the members. And this cooperation itself contributes to and reinforces the supportive atmosphere.

10. The superior of each work group exerts a major influence in establishing the tone and atmosphere of that work group by his leadership principles and practices. In the highly effective group, consequently, the leader adheres to those principles of leadership which create a supportive atmosphere in the group and a cooperative rather than a competitive relationship among the members. For example, he shares information fully with the group and creates an atmosphere where the members are stimulated to behave similarly.

11. The group is eager to help each member develop to his full potential. It sees, for example, that relevant technical knowledge and training in interpersonal and group skills are made available to each member.

12. Each member accepts willingly and without resentment the goals and expectations that he and his group establish for themselves. The anxieties, fears, and emotional stresses produced by direct pressure for high performance from a boss in a hierarchical situation is not present. Groups seem capable of setting high performance goals for the group as a whole and for each member. These goals are high enough to stimulate each member to do his best, but not so high as to create anxieties or fear of failure. In an effective group, each person can exert sufficient influence on the decisions of the group to prevent

the group from setting unattainable goals for any member while setting high goals for all. The goals are adapted to the member's capacity to perform.

13. The leader and the members believe that each group member can accomplish "the impossible." These expectations stretch each member to the maximum and accelerate his growth. When necessary, the group tempers the expectation level so that the member is not broken by a feeling of failure or rejection.

14. When necessary or advisable, other members of the group will give a member the help he needs to accomplish successfully the goals set for him. Mutual help is a characteristic of highly effective groups.

15. The supportive atmosphere of the highly effective group stimulates creativity. The group does not demand narrow conformity as do the work groups under authoritarian leaders. No one has to "yes the boss," nor is he rewarded for such an attempt. The group attaches high value to new, creative approaches and solutions to its problems and to the problems of the organization of which it is a part. The motivation to be creative is high when one's work group prizes creativity.

16. The group knows the value of "constructive" conformity and knows when to use it and for what purposes. Although it does not permit conformity to affect adversely the creative efforts of its members, it does expect conformity on mechanical and administrative matters to save the time of members and to facilitate the group's activities. The group agrees, for example, on administrative forms and procedures, and once they have been established, it expects its members to abide by them until there is good reason to change them.

17. There is strong motivation on the part of each member to communicate fully and frankly to the group all the information which is relevant and of value to the group's activity. This stems directly from the member's desire to be valued by the group and to get the job done. The more important to the group a member feels an item of information to be, the greater is his motivation to communicate it.

18. There is high motivation in the group to use the communication process so that it best serves the interests and goals of the group. Every item which a member feels is important, but which for some reason is being ignored, will be repeated until it receives the attention that it deserves. Members strive also to avoid communicating unimportant information so as not to waste the group's time.

19. Just as there is high motivation to communicate, there is correspondingly strong motivation to receive communications. Each member is genuinely interested in any information on any relevant matter that any member of the group can provide. This information is welcomed and trusted as being honestly and sincerely given. Members do not look "behind" the information item and attempt to interpret it in ways opposite to its purported intent. This interest

of group members in information items and the treatment of such items as valid reinforces the motivation to communicate.

20. In the highly effective group, there are strong motivations to try to influence other members as well as to be receptive to influence by them. This applies to all the group's activities: technical matters, methods, organizational problems, interpersonal relationships, and group processes.

21. The group processes of the highly effective group enable the members to exert more influence on the leader and to communicate far more information to him, including suggestions as to what needs to be done and how he could do his job better, than is possible in a man-to-man relationship. By "tossing the ball" back and forth among its members, a group can communicate information to the leader which no single person on a man-to-man basis dare do. As a consequence, the boss receives all the information that the group possesses to help him perform his job effectively.

22. The ability of the members of a group to influence each other contributes to the flexibility and adaptability of the group. Ideas, goals, and attitudes do not become frozen if members are able to influence each other continuously.

Although the group is eager to examine any new ideas and methods which will help it do its job better and is willing to be influenced by its members, it is not easily shifted or swayed. Any change is undertaken only after rigorous examination of the evidence. This stability in the group's activities is due to the steadying influence of the common goals and values held by the group members.

23. In the highly effective group, individual members feel secure in making decisions which seem appropriate to them because the goals and philosophy of operation are clearly understood by each member and provide him with a solid base for his decisions. This unleashes initiative and pushes decisions down while still maintaining a coordinated and directed effort.

24. The leader of a highly effective group is selected carefully. His leadership ability is so evident that he would probably emerge as a leader in any unstructured situation. To increase the likelihood that persons of high leadership competence are selected, the organization is likely to use peer nominations and related methods in selecting group leaders.

An important aspect of the highly effective group is its extensive use of the principle of supportive relationships. An examination of the above material reveals that virtually every statement involves an application of this principle.

LEADERSHIP FUNCTIONS

Several different characteristics of highly effective groups have been briefly examined. The role of the leader in these groups is, as we have suggested, particularly important. Certain leadership functions can be shared with group members; others can be performed only by the designated leader. In an organization, for example, the leader of a unit is the person who has primary responsibility for linking his work group to the rest of the organization. Other members of the group may help perform the linking function by serving as linking pins in overlapping groups other than that provided by the line organization, but the major linking is necessarily through the line organization. The leader has full responsibility for the group's performance and for seeing that his group meets the demands and expectations placed upon it by the rest of the organization of which it is a part. Other members of the group may share this responsibility at times, but the leader can never avoid full responsibility for the adequate performance of his group.

Although the leader has full responsibility, he does not try to make all the decisions. He develops his group into a unit which, with his participation, makes better decisions than he can make alone. He helps the group develop efficient communication and influence processes which provide it with better information, more technical knowledge, more facts, and more experience for decision-making purposes than the leader alone can marshal.

Through group decision-making each member feels fully identified with each decision and highly motivated to execute it fully. The over-all performance of the group, as a consequence, is even better than the excellent quality of the decisions.

The leader knows that at times decisions must be made rapidly and cannot wait for group processes. He anticipates these emergencies and establishes procedures with his group for handling them so that action can be taken rapidly with group support.

The leader feels primarily responsible for establishing and maintaining at all times a thoroughly supportive atmosphere in the group. He encourages other members to share this responsibility, but never loses sight of the fact that as the leader of a work group which is part of a larger organization his behavior is likely to set the tone.

Although the leader accepts the responsibility associated with his role of leader of a group which is part of a larger organization, he seeks to minimize the influence of his hierarchical position. He is aware that trying to get results by "pulling rank" affects adversely the effectiveness of his group and his relationship to it. Thus, he endeavors to deemphasize status. He does this in a variety of ways that fit his personality and methods of leading, as for example by:

- Listening well and patiently
- Not being impatient with the progress being made by the group, particularly on difficult problems
- Accepting more blame than may be warranted for any failure or mistake

- Giving the group members ample opportunity to express their thoughts without being constrained by the leader pressing his own views
- Being careful never to impose a decision upon the group
- Putting his contributions often in the form of questions or stating them speculatively
- Arranging for others to help perform leadership functions which enhance their status

The leader strengthens the group and group processes by seeing that all problems *which involve the group* are dealt with by the group. He never handles such problems outside of the group nor with individual members of the group. While the leader is careful to see that all matters which involve and affect the whole group are handled by the whole group, he is equally alert not to undertake in a group-meeting agenda items or tasks which do not concern the group. Matters concerning one individual member and only that member are, of course, handled individually. Matters involving only a subgroup are handled by that subgroup. The total group is kept informed, however, of any subgroup action.

The leader fully reflects and effectively represents the views, goals, values, and decisions of his group in those other groups where he is performing the function of linking his group to the rest of the organization. He brings to the group of which he is the leader the views, goals, and decisions of those other groups. In this way, he provides a linkage whereby communication and the exercise of influence can be performed in both directions.

The leader has adequate competence to handle the technical problems faced by his group, or he sees that access to this technical knowledge is fully provided. This may involve bringing in, as needed, technical or resource persons. Or he may arrange to have technical training given to one or more members of his group so that the group can have available the necessary technical know-how when the group discusses a problem and arrives at a decision.

The leader is what might be called "group-centered," in a sense comparable with the "employee-centered" supervisor described in Chapter 2. He endeavors to build and maintain in his group a keen sense of responsibility for achieving its own goals and meeting its obligations to the larger organization.

The leader helps to provide the group with the stimulation arising from a restless dissatisfaction. He discourages complacency and passive acceptance of the present. He helps the members to become aware of new possibilities, more important values, and more significant goals.

The leader is an important source of enthusiasm for the significance of the mission and goals of the group. He sees that the tasks of the group are important and significant and difficult enough to be challenging.

As an over-all guide to his leadership behavior, the leader understands and uses with sensitivity and skill the principle of supportive relationships.

Many of these leadership functions, such as the linking function, can be performed only by the designated leader. This makes clear the great importance of selecting competent persons for leadership positions.

Roles of Membership and Leadership

In the highly effective group, many functions are performed either by the leader or by the members, depending upon the situation or the requirements of the moment. The leader and members, as part of their roles in the group, establish and maintain an atmosphere and relationships which enable the communication, influence, decision-making, and similar processes of the group to be performed effectively. This means not only creating positive conditions, such as a supportive atmosphere, but also eliminating any negative or blocking factors. Thus, for example, groups sometimes have to deal with members who are insensitive, who are hostile, who talk too much, or who otherwise behave in ways adversely affecting the capacity of the group to function. In handling such a problem, the group makes the member aware of his deficiency, but does this in a sensitive and considerate manner and in a way to assist the member to function more effectively in the group. The members of most ordinary groups stop listening to a member who expresses himself in a fuzzy or confused manner. In a highly effective group, the members feed back their reaction to the person involved with suggestions and assistance on how to make his contributions clear, important, and of the kind to which all will want to listen. Friendly assistance and coaching can help a member overcome excessive talking or help him to learn to think and express himself more clearly.

Benne and Sheats (1948) have prepared a description of the different roles played in well-functioning groups. These roles may at times be performed by one or more group members, at others times by the leader. The list, while prepared on the basis of roles in discussion and problem-solving groups, is useful in considering the functions to be performed in any work group which is part of a larger organization.

The following material is taken from the Benne and Sheats article (pp. 42–45) with slight modifications. Group roles are classified into two broad categories:

1. *Group task roles.* These roles are related to the task which the group is deciding to undertake or has undertaken. They are directly concerned with the group effort in the selection and definition of a common problem and in the solution of that problem.

2. *Group building and maintenance roles.* These roles concern the functioning of the group as a group. They deal with the group's efforts to strengthen, regulate, and perpetuate the group as a group.

Group Task Roles

The following analysis assumes that the task of the group is to select, define, and solve common problems. The roles are identified in relation to functions of facilitation and coordination of group problem-solving activities. Each member may, of course, enact more than one role in any given unit of participation and a wide range of roles in successive participations. Any or all of these roles may be performed, at times, by the group "leader" as well as by various members.

A. Initiating-contributing: suggesting or proposing to the group new ideas or a changed way of regarding the group problem or goal. The novelty proposed may take the form of suggestions of a new group goal or a new definition of the problem. It may take the form of a suggested solution or some way of handling a difficulty that the group has encountered. Or it may take the form of a proposed new procedure for the group, a new way of organizing the group for the task ahead.

B. Information seeking: asking for clarification of suggestions made in terms of their factual adequacy, for authoritative information and facts pertinent to the problems being discussed.

C. Opinion seeking: seeking information not primarily on the facts of the case, but for a clarification of the values pertinent to what the group is undertaking or of values involved in a suggestion made or in alternative suggestions.

D. Information giving: offering facts or generalizations which are "authoritative" or involve presenting an experience pertinent to the group problem.

E. Opinion giving: stating beliefs or opinions pertinent to a suggestion made or to alternative suggestions. The emphasis is on the proposal of what should become the group's view of pertinent values, not primarily upon relevant facts or information.

F. Elaborating: spelling out suggestions in terms of examples or developed meanings, offering a rationale for suggestions previously made, and trying to deduce how an idea or suggestion would work out if adopted by the group.

G. Coordinating: showing or clarifying the relationships among various ideas and suggestions, trying to pull ideas and suggestions together or trying to coordinate the activities of various members or sub-groups.

H. Orienting: defining the position of the group with respect to its goals by summarizing what has occurred, departures from agreed upon directions or goals are pointed to, or questions are raised about the direction the group discussion is taking.

I. Evaluating: subjecting the accomplishment of the group to some standard or set of standards of group functioning in the context of the group task. Thus, it may involve evaluating or questioning the "practicality," the "logic," or the "procedure" of a suggestion or of some unit of group discussion.

J. Energizing: prodding the group to action or decision, attempting to stimulate or arouse the group to "greater" activity or to activity of a "higher quality."

K. Assisting on procedure: expediting group movement by doing things for the group—performing routine tasks, e.g., distributing materials, or manipulating objects for the group, e.g., rearranging the seating or running the recording machine, etc.

L. Recording: writing down suggestions, making a record of group decisions, or writing down the product of discussion. The recorder role is the "group memory."

Group Building and Maintenance Roles

Here the analysis of member-functions is oriented to those activities which build group loyalty and increase the motivation and capacity of the group for candid and effective interaction and problem-solving. One or more members or the leader may perform each of these roles.

A. Encouraging: praising, showing interest in, agreeing with, and accepting the contributions of others; indicating warmth and solidarity in one's attitudes toward other group members, listening attentively and seriously to the contributions of group members, giving these contributions full and adequate consideration even though one may not fully agree with them; conveying to the others a feeling that—"that which you are about to say is of importance to me."

B. Harmonizing: mediating the differences between other members, attempting to reconcile disagreements, relieving tension in conflict situations through jesting or pouring oil on troubled waters, etc.

C. Compromising: operating from within a conflict in which one's ideas or position is involved. In this role one may offer a compromise by yielding status, admitting error, by disciplining oneself to maintain group harmony, or by "coming half-way" in moving along with the group.

D. Gate-keeping and expediting: attempting to keep communication channels open by encouraging or facilitating the participation of others or by proposing regulation of the flow of communication

E. Setting standards or ideals: expressing standards for the group or applying standards in evaluating the quality of group processes.

F. Observing: keeping records of various aspects of group process and feeding such data with proposed interpretations into the group's evaluation of its own procedures. The contribution of the person performing this role is usually best received or most fittingly received by the group when this particular role has been performed by this person at the request of the group and when the report to the group avoids expressing value judgments, approval, or disapproval.

G. Following: going along with the group, more or less passively accepting the ideas of others, serving as an audience in group discussion and decision.

The *group task roles* all deal with the intellectual aspects of the group's work. These roles are performed by members of the group during the problem-solving process, which usually involves such steps as:

1. Defining the problem

2. Listing the conditions or criteria which any satisfactory solution to the problem should meet

3. Listing possible alternative solutions

4. Obtaining the facts which bear on each possible solution

5. Evaluating the suggested solutions in terms of the conditions which a satisfactory solution should meet

6. Eliminating undesirable solutions and selecting the most desirable solution

The *group building and maintenance roles* are, as the label suggests, concerned with the emotional life of the group. These roles deal with the group's attractiveness to its members, its warmth and supportiveness, its motivation and capacity to handle intellectual problems without bias and emotion, and its capacity to function as a "mature" group.

The membership roles proposed by Benne and Sheats, while they are not definitive or complete, nevertheless point to the many complex functions performed in groups and dealt with by leader and members. The members of a highly effective group handle these roles with sensitivity and skill, and they see that the emotional life of the group contributes to the performance of the group's tasks rather than interfering with them.[1]

The highly effective group does not hesitate, for example, to look at and deal with friction between its members. By openly putting such problems on the table and sincerely examining them, they can be dealt with constructively. An effective group does not have values which frown upon criticism or which prevent bringing friction between members into the open. As a consequence, it does not put the lid on these emotional pressures, causing them to simmer below the surface and be a constant source of disruption to the performance of group tasks. The intellectual functions of any group can be performed without bias and disruption only when the internal emotional tensions and conflicts have been removed from the life of the group. Differences in ideas are stimulating and contribute to creativity, but emotional conflict immobilizes a group.

Group building and maintenance functions and group task functions are interdependent processes. In order to tackle difficult problems, to solve them creatively, and to achieve high performance, a group must be at a high level of group maintenance. Success in task processes, fortunately, also contributes to the maintenance of the group and to its emotional life, including its attraction to members and its supportive atmosphere.

In the midst of struggling with a very difficult task, a group occasionally may be faced with group maintenance problems. At such times, it may be necessary for the group to stop its intellectual activity and in one way or another to look at and deal with the disruptive emotional stresses. After this has been done, the group can then go forward with greater unity and will be more likely to solve its group task constructively.

The leader and the members in the highly effective group know that the building and maintenance of the group as well as the carrying out of tasks need to be done well. They are highly skilled in performing each of the different membership and leadership roles required. Each member feels responsible for assuming whatever role is necessary to keep the group operating in an efficient manner. In performing these required roles, the member may carry them out by himself or in cooperation with other group members. Each exercises initiative as called for by the situation. The group has a high capacity to mobilize fully all the skills and abilities of its members and focus these resources efficiently on the jobs to be done.

The larger the work group, the greater the difficulty in building it into a highly effective group. Seashore (1954) found that group cohesiveness, i.e., attraction of the members to the group, decreased steadily as work groups increased in size. This finding is supported also by other data (Indik, 1961; Revans, 1957).

To facilitate building work groups to high levels of effectiveness it will be desirable, consequently, to keep the groups as small as possible. This requirement, however, must be balanced against other demands on the organization, such as keeping the number of organizational levels to a minimum. This suggests the desirability of running tests and computing the relative efficiencies and costs of different-sized work groups. It is probable also that the optimum size for a group will vary with the kind of work the group is doing.

The highly effective group as described in this chapter, it will be recalled, is an "ideal model." It may sound completely unattainable. This does not appear to be the case. There is impressive evidence supporting the view that this ideal can be approximated, if not fully reached, in actual operations in any organization. This evidence is provided by the highest-producing managers and supervisors in American industry and government. If the measurements of their work groups and the reports of their work-group members are at all accurate, some of these managers have built and are operating work groups strikingly similar to our ideal model.

This chapter started by observing that groups can have constructive or destructive goals and can achieve these goals fully or partially, that there is nothing inherently good or bad about groups. If we reflect on the nature and functional characteristics of the highly effective group, however, some qualification of our initial comments may be warranted. In the highly effective group, the members can and do exercise substantial amounts of influence on the group's values and goals. As a consequence, these goals reflect the long-range as well as the short-range needs, desires, and values of its members. If we assume that the long-range desires and values will reflect, on the average, some of the more important long-range values and goals of the total society, we can draw some inferences about the highly effective group. These groups will, in terms of probability, reflect the constructive values and goals of their society. They are likely to be strong groups seeking "good" goals.

Notes

1. Although the Benne and Sheats list does not define each category unambiguously, it is useful in helping a group analyze and improve its processes. Another list has been prepared by Bales (1950) which has relatively precise definitions. The Bales list will be of interest to those who wish to do research on group processes or who wish to observe and analyze them systematically.

Intergroup Problems in Organizations
Edgar H. Schein

The first major problem of groups in organizations is how to make them effective in fulfilling both organizational goals and the needs of their members. The second major problem is how to establish conditions *between groups* which will enhance the productivity of each without destroying intergroup relations and coordination. This problem exists because as groups become more committed to their own goals and norms, they are likely to become competitive with one another and seek to undermine their rivals' activities, thereby becoming a liability to the organization as a whole. The over-all problem, then, is how to establish high-productive, *collaborative* intergroup relations.

SOME CONSEQUENCES OF INTERGROUP COMPETITION
The consequences of intergroup competition were first studied systematically by Sherif in an ingeniously designed setting. He organized a boys' camp in such

a way that two groups would form and would become competitive. Sherif then studied the effects of the competition and tried various devices for reestablishing collaborative relationships between the groups.[1] Since his original experiments, there have been many replications with adult groups; the phenomena are so constant that it has been possible to make a demonstration exercise out of the experiment.[2] The effects can be described in terms of the following categories:

A. What happens *within* each competing group?

1. Each group becomes more closely knit and elicits greater loyalty from its members; members close ranks and bury some of their internal differences.

2. Group climate changes from informal, casual, playful to work- and task-oriented; concern for members' psychological needs declines while concern for task accomplishment increases.

3. Leadership patterns tend to change from more democratic toward more autocratic; the group becomes more willing to tolerate autocratic leadership.

4. Each group becomes more highly structured and organized.

5. Each group demands more loyalty and conformity from its members in order to be able to present a "solid front."

B. What happens *between* the competing groups?

1. Each group begins to see the other groups as the enemy, rather than merely a neutral object.

2. Each group begins to experience distortions of perception—it tends to perceive only the best parts of itself, denying its weaknesses, and tends to perceive only the worst parts of the other group, denying its strengths; each group is likely to develop a negative stereotype of the other ("they don't play fair like we do").

3. Hostility toward the other group increases while interaction and communication with the other group decrease; thus it becomes easier to maintain negative stereotypes and more difficult to correct perceptual distortions.

4. If the groups are forced into interaction—for example, if they are forced to listen to representatives plead their own and the others' cause in reference to some task—each group is likely to listen more closely to their own representative and not to listen to the representative of the other group, except to find fault with his presentation; in other words, group members tend to listen only for that which supports their own position and stereotype.

Thus far, I have listed some consequences of the competition itself, without reference to the consequences if one group actually wins out over the other. Before listing those effects, I would like to draw attention to the generality of the above reactions. Whether one is talking about sports teams, or interfraternity competition, or labor-management disputes, or interdepartmental competition as between sales and production in an industrial organization, or about international relations and the competition between the Soviet Union and the United States, the same phenomena tend to occur. If you will give just a little thought to competing groups of which you have been a member, you will begin to recognize most of the psychological responses described. I want to stress that these responses can be very useful to the group in making it more effective and highly motivated in task accomplishment. However, the same factors which improve *intragroup* effectiveness may have negative consequences for *intergroup* effectiveness. For example, as we have seen in labor-management or international disputes, if the groups perceive themselves as competitors, they find it more difficult to resolve their differences.

Let us next look at the consequences of winning and losing, as in a situation where several groups are bidding to have their proposal accepted for a contract or as a solution to some problem. Many intra-organizational situations become win-or-lose affairs, hence it is of particular importance to examine their consequences.

C. What happens to the *winner?*

1. Winner retains its cohesion and may become even more cohesive.

2. Winner tends to release tension, lose its fighting spirit, become complacent, casual, and playful (the "fat and happy" state).

3. Winner tends toward high intragroup cooperation and concern for members' needs, and low concern for work and task accomplishment.

4. Winner tends to be complacent and to feel that winning has confirmed the positive stereotype of itself and the negative stereotype of the "enemy" group; there is little basis for reevaluating perceptions, or reexamining group operations in order to learn how to improve them.

D. What happens to the *loser?*

1. If the situation permits because of some ambiguity in the decision (say, if judges have rendered it or if the game was close), there is a strong tendency for the loser to deny or distort the reality of losing; instead, the loser will find psychological escapes like "the judges were biased," "the judges didn't really understand our solution," "the rules of the game were not clearly explained to us," "if luck had not been against us at the one key point, we would have won," and so on.

2. If loss is accepted, the losing group tends to splinter, unresolved conflicts come to the surface, fights break out, all in the effort to find a cause for the loss.

3. Loser is more tense, ready to work harder, and desperate to find someone or something to blame—the leader, itself, the judges who decided against them, the rules of the game (the "lean and hungry" state).

4. Loser tends toward low intragroup cooperation, low concern for members' needs, and high concern for recouping by working harder.

5. Loser tends to learn a lot about itself as a group because positive stereotype of itself and negative stereotype of the other group are upset by the loss, forcing a reevaluation of perceptions; as a consequence, loser is likely to reorganize and become more cohesive and effective, once the loss has been accepted realistically.

The net effect of the win-lose situation is often that the loser is not convinced that he lost, and that intergroup tension is higher than before the competition began.

REDUCING THE NEGATIVE CONSEQUENCES
OF INTERGROUP COMPETITION

The gains of intergroup competition may under some conditions outweigh the negative consequences. It may be desirable to have work groups pitted against one another or to have departments become cohesive loyal units, even if interdepartmental coordination suffers. Other times, however, the negative consequences outweigh the gains, and management seeks ways of reducing intergroup tension. Many of the ideas to be mentioned about how this might be accomplished also come from the basic researches of Sherif and Blake; they have been tested and found to be successful. As we will see, the problems derive not so much from being unable to think of ways for reducing intergroup conflict as from being *unable to implement some of the most effective ways.*

The fundamental problem of intergroup competition is the conflict of goals and the breakdown of interaction and communication between the groups; this breakdown in turn permits and stimulates perceptual distortion and mutual negative stereotyping. The basic strategy of reducing conflict, therefore, is to find goals upon which groups can agree and to reestablish valid communication between the groups. The tactics to employ in implementing this strategy can be any combination of the following:

Locating a common enemy. For example, the competing teams of each league can compose an all-star team to play the other league, or conflicts between sales and production can be reduced if both can harness their efforts to helping their company successfully compete against another company. The conflict here is merely shifted to a higher level.

Inventing a negotiation strategy which brings subgroups of the competing groups into interaction with each other. The isolated group representative cannot abandon his group position but a subgroup which is given some power can not only permit itself to be influenced by its counterpart negotiation team, but will have the strength to influence the remainder of the group.

Locating a superordinate goal. Such a goal can be a brand new task which requires the cooperative effort of the previously competing groups or can be a task like analyzing and reducing the intergroup conflict itself. For example, the previously competing sales and production departments can be given the task of developing a new product line that will be both cheap to produce and in great customer demand; or, with the help of an outside consultant, the competing groups can be invited to examine their own behavior and reevaluate the gains and losses from competition.

Reducing Intergroup Competition Through Laboratory Training Methods
The last procedure mentioned above has been tried by a number of psychologists, notably Blake, with considerable success.[3] Assuming the organization recognizes that it has a problem, and assuming it is ready to expose this problem to an outside consultant, the laboratory approach to reducing conflict might proceed as follows: (1) The competing groups are both brought into a training setting and the goals are stated to be an exploration of mutual perceptions and mutual relations. (2) Each group is then invited to discuss its perceptions of and attitudes toward itself and the other group. (3) In the presence of both groups, representatives publicly share the perceptions of self and other which the groups have generated, while the groups are obligated to remain silent (the objective is simply to report to the other group as accurately as possible the images that each group has developed in private). (4) Before any exchange has taken place, the groups return to private sessions to digest and analyze what they have heard; there is a great likelihood that the representative reports have revealed great discrepancies to each group between its self-image and the image that the other group holds of it; the private session is partly devoted to an analysis of the reasons for the discrepancies, which forces each group to review its actual behavior toward the other group and the possible consequences of that behavior, regardless of its intentions. (5) In public session, again working through representatives, each group shares with the other what discrepancies they have uncovered and their analysis of the possible reasons for them, with the focus on the actual behavior exhibited. (6) Following this mutual exposure, a more open exploration is then permitted between the two groups on the *now-shared goal* of identifying further reasons for perceptual distortions.

Interspersed with these steps are short lectures and reading assignments on the psychology of intergroup conflict, the bases for perceptual distortion, psychological defense mechanisms, and so on. The goal is to bring the psychological dynamics of the situation into conscious awareness and to refocus the groups on the common goal of exploring jointly the problem they share. In order to do this, they must have valid data about each other, which is provided through the artifice of the representative reports.

The Blake model described above deals with the entire group. Various other approaches have been tried which start with members. For example, groups A and B can be divided into pairs composed of an A and B member. Each pair can be given the assignment of developing a joint product which uses the best ideas from the A product and the B product. Or, in each pair, members may be asked to argue for the product of the opposing group. It has been shown in a number of experiments that one way of changing attitudes is to ask a person to play the role of an advocate of the new attitude to be learned.[4] The very act of arguing for another product, even if it is purely an exercise, exposes the person to some of its virtues which he had previously denied. A practical application of these points might be to have some members of the sales department spend time in the production department and be asked to represent the production point of view to some third party, or to have some production people join sales teams to learn the sales point of view.

Most of the approaches cited depend on a recognition of some problem by the organization and a willingness on the part of the competing groups to participate in some training effort to reduce negative consequences. The reality, however, is that most organizations neither recognize the problem nor are willing to invest time and energy in resolving it. Some of the unwillingness also arises from each competing group's recognition that in becoming more cooperative it may lose some of its own identity and integrity as a group. Rather than risk this, the group may prefer to continue the competition. This may well be the reason why, in international relations, nations refuse to engage in what seem like perfectly simple ways of resolving their differences. They resist partly in order to protect their integrity. Consequently, the *implementation* of strategies and tactics for reducing the negative consequences of intergroup competition is often a greater problem than the development of such strategies and tactics.

PREVENTING INTERGROUP CONFLICT

Because of the great difficulties of reducing intergroup conflict once it has developed, it may be desirable to prevent its occurrence in the first place. How can this be done? Paradoxically, a strategy of prevention must bring into question the fundamental premise upon which organization through division of labor rests. Once it has been decided by a superordinate authority to divide up functions among different departments or groups, a bias has already been introduced toward intergroup competition; for in doing its own job well, each group must to some degree compete for scarce resources and rewards from the superordinate authority. The very concept of division of labor implies a reduction of communication and interaction between groups, thus making it possible for perceptual distortions to occur.

The organization planner who wishes to avoid intergroup competition need not abandon the concept of division of labor, but he should follow some of the steps listed below in creating and handling his different functional groups.

1. Relatively greater emphasis given to *total organizational effectiveness* and the role of departments in contributing to it; departments measured and rewarded on the basis of their *contribution* to the total effort rather than their individual effectiveness.

2. *High interaction* and *frequent communication* stimulated between groups to work on problems of intergroup coordination and help; organizational *rewards given partly on the basis of help* which groups give to each other.

3. Frequent *rotation of members* among groups or departments to stimulate high degree of mutual understanding and empathy for one another's problems.

4. *Avoidance of any win-lose situation;* groups never put into the position of competing for some organizational reward; emphasis always placed on pooling resources to maximize organizational effectiveness; rewards shared equally with all the groups or departments.

Most managers find the last of the above points particularly difficult to accept because of the strong belief that performance can be improved by pitting people or groups against one another in a competitive situation. This may indeed be true in the short run, and in some cases may work in the long run, but the negative consequences we have described are undeniably a product of a competitive win-lose situation. Consequently, if a manager wishes to prevent such consequences, he must face the possibility that he may have to abandon competitive relationships altogether and seek to substitute intergroup collaboration toward organizational goals. Implementing such a preventive strategy is often more difficult, partly because most people are inexperienced in stimulating and managing collaborative relationships. Yet it is clear from observing organizations such as those using the Scanlon Plan not only that it is possible to establish collaborative relationships, even between labor and management, but also that where this has been done, organizational and group effectiveness have been as high as or higher than under competitive conditions.

THE PROBLEM OF INTEGRATION IN PERSPECTIVE

I have discussed two basic issues in this chapter, both dealing with psychological groups: (1) the development of groups within organizations which can fulfill both the needs of the organization and the psychological needs of its members; and (2) the problems of intergroup competition and conflict. To achieve maximum integration, the organization should be able to create conditions that will facilitate a balance between organizational goals and member needs and minimize disintegrative competition between the subunits of the total organization.

Groups are highly complex sets of relationships. There are no easy generalizations about the conditions under which they will be effective, but with suitable training, many kinds of groups can become more effective than they have been. Consequently, group-dynamics training by laboratory methods may be a more promising approach to effectiveness than attempting *a priori* to determine the right membership, type of leadership, and organization. All the factors must be taken into account, with training perhaps weighted more heavily than it has been, though the training itself must be carefully undertaken.

The creation of psychologically meaningful and effective groups does not solve all of the organization's problems if such groups compete and conflict with each other. We examined some of the consequences of competition under win-lose conditions and outlined two basic approaches for dealing with the problem: (1) reducing conflict by increasing communication and locating superordinate goals, and (2) preventing conflict by establishing from the outset organizational conditions which stimulate collaboration rather than competition.

The prevention of intergroup conflict is especially crucial if the groups involved are highly interdependent. The greater the interdependence, the greater the potential loss to the total organization of negative stereotyping, withholding of information, efforts to make the other group look bad in the eyes of the superior, and so on.

It is important to recognize that the preventive strategy does not imply absence of disagreement and artificial "sweetness and light" within or between groups. Conflict and disagreement at the level of the group or organizational *task* is not only desirable but essential for the achievement of the best solutions to problems. What is harmful is *interpersonal* or *intergroup* conflict in which the task is not as important as gaining advantage over the other person or group. The negative consequences we described, such as mutual negative stereotyping, fall into this latter category and undermine rather than aid overall task performance. And it is these kinds of conflicts which can be reduced by establishing collaborative relationships. Interestingly enough, observations of cases would suggest that task-relevant conflict which improves overall effectiveness is greater under collaborative conditions because groups and members trust each other enough to be frank and open in sharing information and opinions. In the competitive situation, each group is committed to hiding its special resources from the other groups, thus preventing effective integration of all resources in the organization.

Notes

1. M. Sherif, O. J. Harvey, B. J. White, W. R. Hood, and Carolyn Sherif, *Intergroup Conflict and Cooperation: The Robbers Cave Experiment* (Norman, Okla.: University Book Exchange, 1961).

2. R. R. Blake and Jane S. Mouton. "Reactions to Intergroup Competition under Win-Lose Conditions," *Management Science* 7 (1961): 420–35.

3. R. R. Blake, and Jane S. Mouton, "Headquarters—field team training for organizational improvements," *Journal of the American Society of Training Directors* 16 (1962).

4. I. L. Janis and B. T. King, "The Influence of Role Playing on Opinion Change," *Journal of Abnormal and Social Psychology* 69 (1954): 211–18.

LEADERSHIP AND THE MANAGER

Turf vs. Systems: Two Management Styles
Charles R. Wilson

I. TURF VS. SYSTEMS: TWO MANAGEMENT STYLES

Two Models

Imagine a leader faced with many organizational problems or inadequacies
. . . what might be called a "mess" or a "can of worms." Let us call it
organizational chaos. Using the word "chaos" will help us maintain some
theological perspective. The job has to do with creating order, form or struc
ture expressing meaning and purpose. So imagine this leader . . . it could be
an executive taking over a leadership position in some enterprize that has been
torn with strife and demoralized . . . a university perhaps. Or it could be you
looking at your organization.

Let us also suppose that the leader is approaching the situation with a
positive attitude. No doubt there are many "problems" to be solved in the
corporate chaos in which he finds himself. But there are opportunities. In
many situations it is merely a matter of individual perspective, but the person
who "sees" opportunities instead of problems is already well on the way to
getting the energies focused and to developing a swinging outfit.

So there is the picture, and a kind of attitude about it. Now let's see how
the person is going to tackle the job at hand . . .

1. *The Homesteader*

One model of action is the homesteader. A couple generations ago the homesteader faced thousands of square miles of undeveloped land. He scanned the

A Working Paper in Church Management by the Reverend Charles R. Wilson, President, SALT Associates—Lebanon, New Jersey and Kent, Washington. pp. 1–9.

horizon, picked out one little hundred and sixty acre piece and literally staked out its boundaries and registered his claim. Perhaps he even fenced it.

It was thus established, before the rest of the world, that this was indeed his place. He then proceeded to organize that which lay inside with little concern for that which was outside. He built a house, subdivided the land for grain, pasture, row crops and so on. Once organized, he could apply himself to a piece at a time; do what was required in each part season by season and thus manage his turf.

Let's underline a few key points about this model of management: There is a strong emphasis on defining boundaries; a clear sense of what is in and what is out. The manager is the "owner" . . . he is possessive . . . it is *his* claim. Finally, what he is managing is a place. There is a kind of *space-things* basic orientation to his whole style.

2. *The Astronaut*

Another model of action is the astronaut. Like the fish that is not preoccupied with water, the space man is not particularly concerned with space. What is important to him are centers of gravity: how much pull each center has and what else is circling around it. He orbits around one center for awhile, then kicks free of its gravity and swings into orbit around another.

(We can stretch the image a bit in order to develop our model.) Note the similarity of the space man to the person who wants to promote a cause. There is no need to define boundaries or build fences. Rather, the person with a cause looks for centers of ferment or of action or of disaffection. He psychs out the nature of each, sees what kind of stuff orbits around each; what kind of leadership there is. He then decides which centers to relate to, and sets about strengthening them. He provides for linkage between them, strives to make common cause with them and in this manner builds his network.

Now to underline some key points in this model of management: Instead of concern with boundaries there is a primary focus on centers, a search for handles. To the extent that there are boundaries, they are open. The manager is not possessive; ownership is not particularly important to him. Finally, he is watching the dynamic interconnectedness of events . . . sequences, movements, influences . . . what he is managing is a process. Basic to this style is a kind of time/purpose rather than space/things orientation.

The Two Styles and Resultant Organizations

We now return to our person confronted with chaos. The theme is creation. He intends, deliberately and systematically, to bring about structure, form, order and meaning. If he is basically a homesteader, he will approach it this way:

1. *The Homesteader*

"You don't do everything, so identify the boundaries of what you want to do, divide up what is inside and begin to assign responsibilities and resources to people for the parts."

As he gets the thing in shape, here is what it will look like:

It will be a closed system. You will probably see organization charts showing each person's turf, and the chain of command indicating how each person is to relate to those "above" or those "below." Lines of authority, chain of command, who administers which budget will all be matters of great importance.

Decisions will tend to get pushed "up" in the organization where there is more authority to decide. A person's job description will probably define his "box" on the organization chart, his place in the authority structure and the things he is supposed to do daily, weekly and/or monthly. Considerable loyalty to the organization is expected of him.

This man's organization will probably be pretty rigid. However, there are some advantages. For one thing, he does not have to organize the whole universe. He just carves out a small piece and gets it in shape. Things will probably look pretty neat and people who are a part of it probably have a pretty good idea of what is expected of them. The organization avoids what Tillich calls "the anxiety of annihilating openness" and the accompanying nightmares of falling endlessly through infinite, formless space.

2. *The Spaceman*

On the other hand, our man (confronted with chaos) might be something of a spaceman. If so, his approach will go like this:

"You can't do everything (but we are not really going to rule out the possibility) so wade into the mess looking for centers of power, activity or interest. See what is swinging around each. How can they be strengthened? What are the clusters or patterns of action? How can the range of influence of healthy action be increased? Where are the handles where one might take hold; what can be managed from each?"

As he gets things in shape, here is what the organization will look like:

It will be an open system with ideas, people and resources flowing in and out. You will probably see flow charts showing how things are processed through the system. There will be considerable lateral activity and information flow, and no great concern with the formalities of the chain of command.

Decisions will tend to get pushed "down" in the organization where there is more information on which to base decisions. A person's position description will register the areas in which he has agreed to apply himself and the results expected. It will be assumed that he is loyal to the cause and will keep faith with his own integrity, but loyalty to the organization as organization is no big deal. People will change hats frequently in this organization, getting involved in all kinds of ad hoc agendas and temporary assignments.

The organization will be flexible; difficult to conceptualize mechanistically (organization charts and clearly defined roles).

With this approach to organization, we have the advantage of not limiting the size or scope of the effort and our organization avoids what Tillich calls "the anxiety of annihilating narrowness" and the accompanying nightmares of being boxed in . . . trapped . . . no escape.

How People Fit

So we have two organizational models drawn. Now let's take a look at the people who might want to be a part of them.

1. *Two kinds of employees*

First man:

> "I want to sell some of my time (as little as possible) for some money, so I can use the rest of my time doing what I really want to do. Therefore, I am interested in salary, fringe benefits and job security. Also, it will help if the things that you want me to do are pretty clearly spelled out because I really don't want to bother thinking about your long-range aims and where I fit in. Oh yes, I'd like to work for a boss who is a nice guy."

Second man:

> "There are some things I'd like to get done in this world and I want a chance to take a crack at them. Therefore, I'll use this organization as my base. I think there is sufficient compatability between what the organization stands for and what I am after. I can probably help shape its goals and I am willing to have the organization influence mine . . . well, to some extent! I enter with my own agenda, values, outside contacts and even (perhaps) power base. I'll be loyal to our corporate effort but don't expect me to be pious about institutional loyalty, its mythology, or about values from on high. I'll recognize the authority of those with personal integrity and professional competency but don't try to impress me with the chain of command or titles. I need a salary and benefits if I'm going to be able to stay here and such should be in line with my own self-esteem."

Obviously, the first man is looking for a job in a homestead; the second for an opportunity in a space station. Both will probably find what they are looking for. The questions are: (1) What kind of organization do *you* have? and (2) Which of these two men do you *want* to attract?

My impression is that there are many organizations that would like to function as a space station rather than a homestead but their personnel practices seem to assume that the first man described is really the only kind of person available. The result is more chaos. The rhetoric of the organization attracts some of the second type persons but the practices encourage only the first type to stay. The others move on.

There are so many subtleties in this whole area. It is not easy to develop an appropriate style in an organization. For example, there is considerable talk among managers these days about how to keep the innovative kind of person. He is unpredictable, a bit eccentric, unimpressed with the organization's history or values . . . not that he is against them . . . he just hasn't noticed them. So how do you keep him and his idea generating capacity in your organization?

Let's see how the homestead type organization would approach him: First of all it is assumed that money is power and that it can motivate the man. So an attempt is made to buy his time. The organization will try very hard to put up with his oddities and hope that the price they pay will produce some ideas. "The basic reality is money, and with money we can buy ideas and make more money."

In the space station type of organization it is assumed that ideas have their own value and power. This organization will have quite a different approach to the man and his cause. The idea is the more basic reality. There is no shortage of capital if you have ideas, but there *is* a shortage of ideas. So: "we can use the idea to generate capital and then use the capital to develop the idea."

Again it is obvious that the innovator will feel relatively at home in this type of organization. He will probably feel boxed in in the first.

2. *Choosing a style*

Yet apart from what kind of organization you *want* to have, what about this question: "What kind of people are more generally available?" In response to this, I feel that it is quite clear that we are living in the space age. It is not just that we live in an age in which space (incidentally) is beginning to get explored, but rather that we are the kind of people who have decided to explore space instead of (for example) the bottom of the sea. There is a deep psychological reality here. I believe, for instance, that the average modern man experiences more anxiety in the thought of being trapped in a wrecked submarine, never to return to the surface; than in the thought of being lost in a damaged space ship with no possibility of returning to earth.

He is just as dead in either case but, for modern man, "the anxiety of annihilating openness" is much more tolerable than "the anxiety of annihilating narrowness." We are space men not cave men.

With that my bias is clear. I feel that church organizations and probably most other organizations must be open systems deliberately designed to attract self-motivating people. So from this point on I shall assume that that is the kind of organization we want and forget the homestead.

Presidential Style
Richard Tanner Johnson

The orbits of advisers and agencies that revolve around the President do not, like the heavenly bodies, follow a strict and invariant course. To some extent their paths are determined by Constitution and custom; but, to an important degree, the President himself, as central occupant of the Executive galaxy, shapes the pattern of government.

This book examines the way in which successive Presidents, whether by intent or default, have left their imprint on government. Some, like Dwight D. Eisenhower, may have tried to rationalize the workload by establishing an elaborate staff system, but at the risk of becoming a prisoner of the staff machinery over which they preside. Others, like Franklin D. Roosevelt, may have striven to remain informed by playing aides off against one another, but at the price of exacerbated conflict and at the risk that aides might establish outside alliances to further their interests.

Since the time of George Washington political analysts have speculated about how well the President is managing. This reflects a general belief that the way a President organizes and relates to his close circle of advisers—and through them to the Executive branch—influences policy significantly.

This book will focus on the *process* of management and its *output,* that is, how six Presidents—Franklin D. Roosevelt, Harry S. Truman, Dwight D. Eisenhower, John F. Kennedy, Lyndon B. Johnson, and Richard M. Nixon —have organized their office and how their approaches have affected results.[1]

In weighing the consequences of Presidential style, it is convenient to label the different patterns of management that Presidents have used—*formalistic, competitive,* and *collegial.* Each of these patterns of management endeavors, in different ways, to resolve the four fundamental dilemmas of decision making. The first has to do with the trade-off between optimality and "doability"—how far can one go in the direction of doing "best" without being "impractical"? The second stems from the mechanisms that screen out or embrace conflicting viewpoints and personalities—how much conflict can a workable decision process tolerate? The third concerns the distortion of information—how much desirable screening can occur in the staffing process without incurring undesirable distortion? The fourth involves the constraint of time —how elaborate can the decision process be without sacrificing responsiveness? The choice of one managerial pattern over another depends upon how the manager resolves these trade-offs.

The point of this undertaking is not just to label a particular approach but to explain why it worked in some instances and failed in others. To the extent that it worked, what were the subtle factors in a President's style that kept his system in balance? How did his staff system reflect and complement his personal preferences and values? Truman's staff funneled in the facts; he made the decision—an aspect of the job he relished. Johnson, on the other hand, sought consensus and struggled mightily to establish agreement among his advisers. Both Presidents sought to make good policy decisions, yet each shaped his decisional machinery differently, rewarded his aides differently— and got different results. In evaluating these results we shall discover that associated with each pattern of management are costs and benefits that predictably surface when a given approach is used. In other words, given a particular style of management, we can anticipate the likely consequences of that style on the quality of decision making and implementation.

It should be stated at the outset that while each President may adopt a dominant pattern of management, his approach may vary from situation to situation. In addition, he must relate to subordinates of widely differing character, and this also may cause him to vary his managerial approach. He must deal with his own staff and personal advisers, and he must devise a way of working with important advisory groups that work closely with his office, like the Cabinet, the National Security Council, and the Council of Economic Advisors. Finally, he must strive to find some way to manage the giant Executive agencies like the Department of Defense (DOD) and Health, Education and Welfare (HEW). From these sources he must gather information and weigh it, make decisions, and pass his choices out again for implementation.

Each President distributes his energies differently, and like most people, he tries to use his experience and draws on what has worked for him before. While each President's approach is to some extent unique, there are striking similarities too.

THE FORMALISTIC APPROACH
Consider the similarities between the Eisenhower and Nixon Administrations. Common to both was an emphasis on order. Both Presidents installed a procedural system of decision making; both tended to underplay their political role—the stress was on finding the best solution to national problems rather than on working out "compromise settlements" among conflicting views. This emphasis on order and analysis was reflected in their choice of advisers: figures like Sherman Adams and Henry A. Kissinger emerged as predominant—the stereotype was analytical and dispassionate. Eisenhower and Nixon tended to

discourage staff conflict; open expressions of interpersonal conflict such as competition, bargaining, and hostility were taboo. They sought to preserve substantive conflict by having both sides of an issue presented on paper. Because they had these preferences, each devised a structured decision process that centered upon the reasoned discussion of prepared briefs rather than upon the heat of debate. A formalized staff system collected information and funneled it to the top; complex problems were analyzed into their pros and cons.[2] Ultimately, the President weighed his decision on the merits.

It is noteworthy that the formalized approach, at least in its idealized form, aspires to make "the best" decision. Decisions are expected to stand on their merits; implementation is not stressed in the decision-making process. In this respect, the assumptions underlying this approach bear some resemblance to "decision making" in the economic context: the decision maker is seen as a single agent striving to optimize his goals in the face of given costs.[3] This approach assumes that an optimal solution exists and that it can be identified and implemented; decisions are made and action is taken with complete information on all the alternatives and their consequences.

Clearly, decision making in this rarefied atmosphere bears little resemblance to the Presidency. But the differences, in terms of the basic assumptions of the formalistic approach, are more in degree than in kind. Agreed, Presidential decisions are rarely, if ever, made on the criterion of technical rationality alone. But an interesting feature of this approach is the tendency for technical considerations to be emphasized and political considerations deemphasized. Eisenhower steadfastly urged his Cabinet members to "not compromise on principle."[4] The Nixon invasion of Cambodia may or may not have been justified in terms of technical military criteria, but there is general agreement that he underestimated the political reaction that followed. A later section on the Nixon White House will provide fuller opportunity to examine the assumptions and consequences of the formalistic approach.

THE COMPETITIVE APPROACH

Against any standard of ordered decision making, the managerial approach of Franklin Roosevelt stands as the polar extreme. In passion, as well as administrative persuasion, Roosevelt sought involvement and controversy. He not only tolerated a great deal of conflict, he thrived on it. He sought aggressive advisers of divergent opinions—such as Harry L. Hopkins, Henry Morgenthau, Jr., and Harold L. Ickes—and pitted them against one another.[5] He delegated responsibility and authority in overlapping segments. The resulting clash generated heat, but also information. Roosevelt, pragmatic and opportunistic, sought above all to stay informed and to exploit prevailing political currents. His decision process, forged in the heat of debate, was preconditioned to withstand debate in Congress and the test of public exposure. Roosevelt may have overly sacrificed what was "best" for what was "doable"; but if the acceptance of his proposals was his criterion for success, acceptance is what he got to a greater extent than any President before or since.

Roosevelt exemplifies what will be termed the *competitive* pattern of management. His method of delegation left jurisdictional boundaries to be mapped out by conquest among his subordinates. It promoted conflict which often landed in his lap. He fully recognized the inherent conflicts of interest that surround the Presidency and assumed that, in most instances, the quarrels among his subordinates could not be resolved to the satisfaction of all disputants. Roosevelt thus sought to position himself as the arbitrator, as the "swing vote" in the decision-making process. In many respects his approach was well suited to the White House. The President must live with conflict; it is woven into the fabric of the Presidency. Roosevelt sought to sharpen this conflict as a means of staying informed, promoting creativity, and providing a healthy, renewing jolt to the system. But competition also exacted its price. Intense conflict among his subordinates at times drove them toward extreme and intransigent positions; aides were driven underground—withholding information or leaking tidbits to Congress or to the press in order to weaken adversaries or to limit the President's options.[6] The overlapping assignments which promoted conflict also fostered duplication of effort. A lesser President than Roosevelt might have become more the victim rather than the patron of power politics.

THE COLLEGIAL APPROACH

The two patterns of management, formalistic and competitive, describe the extremes of a range of possibilities. The principal strength of the formalized approach is its emphasis on thorough staff work and its stress on finding the best possible solution to a problem. The risk of this approach is that it may insulate the decision maker. Staff members working in specialized assignments become parochial, "the funneling of information" is ofttimes accompanied by the distortion of information. The more staff layers information has to filter through, the greater the risks of such distortion. There is also a tendency for the formalistic pattern of management to react too slowly or to generate solutions that seem utopian and hard to implement. In contrast, as often employed, the competitive pattern of management focuses attention on the power dimensions of a problem—at times sacrificing its substantive merits. Result: more attention is given to the bargaining than to the analysis. Under such circumstances, there is a tendency toward short-run solutions that are strongly influenced by the immediate political climate.

The collegial pattern of management strives to avoid these pitfalls. The managerial thrust is toward building a team of colleagues who work together to staff out problems and generate solutions which, ideally, fuse the strongest elements of divergent points of view. By virtue of encouraging subordinates to work together, this approach recognizes the existence, and in fact the merit, of conflict. The emphasis, however, is not on the win-lose interplay among competing individuals or ideas but rather on treating conflicting viewpoints as a resource. The collegial approach has as its principal strength the potential of forging solutions that are both substantively sound and politically doable, having taken the strongest arguments of all sides into account. Its greatest limitation stems from its dependence on people working together. Considerable managerial skill and attention is required to build an effective team. Collective endeavor requires patience and takes time.

Of all recent Presidents, perhaps John Kennedy went the furthest on some occasions toward adopting the collegial pattern of management. In the Cuban missile crisis, Kennedy incorporated conflict into his Executive Committee: he included representatives from the Department of Defense known for their commitment to "military solutions," as well as members who favored a diplomatic settlement. Unlike his mismanagement of the policy-making discussions leading to the Bay of Pigs, this time Kennedy did not attempt to stifle the expression of disagreement and debate among his advisers—in fact, he absented himself on several occasions so that it would be fully voiced.[7] He stressed solving the problem and emphasized the group's collective responsibility for coming up with sound recommendations. The resulting solution did not ignore conflict, but neither was it imprisoned by it. From the divergent views of Ex Comm's members, a composite plan was formulated which built upon the strengths of conflicting proposals and which in sum was better than any of the original plans.

These three managerial patterns—formalistic, competitive, and collegial —describe a range of approaches a President might employ. Clearly the patterns are highly simplified; but each provides a net of a different mesh, so to speak, which we might cast into the murky waters of Presidential performance. These nets will permit us to consider different managerial approaches that have been used in the White House, and their consequences.

Notes

1. James D. Barber, *The Presidential Character* (Englewood Cliffs, N.J.: Prentice-Hall, 1972).

2. For example, see Juan Cameron, "Richard Nixon's Very Personal White House," *Fortune,* July 1970, pp. 104–108.

3. Alfred Marshall, *The Economics of Industry* (London: Macmillan, 1885), p. 231.

4. See Ezra Taft Benson, *Cross Fire* (Garden City, N.Y.: Doubleday, 1962), pp. 36, 194, 206, 511; also Emmet John Hughes, *The Ordeal of Power* (New York: Atheneum, 1963).

5. For example, see Henry Morgenthau, Jr., "The Struggle for a Program," in James N. Rosenau, *The Roosevelt Treasury* (Garden City, N.Y.: Doubleday, 1951), pp. 310–321.

6. Robert E. Sherwood, *Roosevelt and Hopkins* (New York: Harper, 1948), pp. 71, 756; also see John Gunther, *Roosevelt in Retrospect,* (New York: Harper, 1960), pp. 133–134; also see Rexford G. Tugwell, *The Democratic Roosevelt* (Garden City, N.Y.: Doubleday, 1957), p. 547.

7. Arthur M. Schlesinger, Jr., *A Thousand Days* (Boston: Houghton Mifflin, 1965), p. 807; also see Robert F. Kennedy, *Thirteen Days* (New York, Norton, 1969), p. 33.

Tactics of Lateral Relationship:
The Purchasing Agent
George Strauss

This is a study of the tactics used by one functional group in an organization —purchasing—to influence the behavior of other functional departments of relatively equal status. It deals in part with "office politics" and "bureaucratic gamesmanship."

Most studies of human relations in management have dealt with *vertical* relations between superiors and subordinates or between line and staff.[1] Yet the purchasing agent's[2] internal relationships (as opposed to his external relationships with salesmen) are almost entirely *lateral;* they are with other functional departments of about the same rank in the organizational hierarchy— departments such as production scheduling, quality control, engineering, and the like. Most agents receive relatively little attention from their superiors; they must act on their own, with support being given by higher management only in exceptional cases. They are given broad freedom to define their own roles and are "controlled" chiefly by the client departments with which they deal.

Administrative Science Quarterly, 7, 2 (Sept. 1962), pp. 161–186. Reprinted by permission of *Administrative Science Quarterly* and the author.

Although purchasing is technically a staff department, its relations with other departments can best be analyzed in terms of work flow rather than according to the typical staff-line concept. At the beginning of the typical work flow the sales department receives an order; on the basis of this the engineering department prepares a blueprint; next the production scheduling department initiates a work order for manufacturing and a requisition for purchasing; with this requisition the purchasing department buys the needed parts.

But this process does not always work smoothly. Each department has its specialized point of view which it seeks to impose on others, and each department is struggling for greater authority and status. The purpose of this exploratory study is to illustrate the range of tactics available in the interdepartmental conflict which almost always results.

RESEARCH METHOD

The research methodology included a considerable number of informal contacts with agents, observation of them at work for periods of up to one week, twenty-five formal interviews, a written questionnaire, a review of purchasing journals, and an analysis of how agents, both individually and in groups, handled specially prepared case problems.[3] In the selection of firms to be studied there was a strong bias in favor of those with large engineering staffs, since agents in these firms face the most complex problems.

The discussion which follows will be largely impressionistic and will deal with broad aspects of tactics used by purchasing agents, since their problems vary greatly and various means are used to solve them. It should also be noted that the examples illustrate extreme cases, which, being extreme, illustrate some of the basic dilemmas which most agents face, though often in an attenuated form. This study is primarily concerned with the agent himself, the man who heads the purchasing office. It does not directly concern the buyers and expediters under him or the added complications that occur when divisions or plant agents have a staff relationship with a corporation-wide purchasing office.

CAUSES OF FRICTION

The agent originally had two primary functions: (1) to negotiate and place orders at the best possible terms—but only in accordance with specifications set by others—and (2) to expedite orders, that is, to check with suppliers to make sure that deliveries are made on time. This arrangement gave the agent broad power in dealing with salesmen but made him little more than an order clerk in terms of power or status within the company.

The ambitious agent feels that placing orders and expediting deliveries are but the bare bones of his responsibilities. He looks upon his most important function as that of keeping management posted about market developments: new materials, new sources of supply, price trends, and so forth. And to make this information more useful, he seeks to be consulted before the requisition is drawn up, while the product is still in the planning stage. He feels that his technical knowledge of the market should be accorded recognition equal to the technical knowledge of the engineer and accountant.

Specifically, the ambitious agent would like to suggest (1) alternative materials or parts to use, (2) changes in specifications or redesign of components which will save money or result in higher quality or quicker delivery, and (3) more economical lot sizes, and to influence (4) "make or buy" decisions. The agent calls these functions "value analysis."

One way of looking at the agent's desire to expand his influence is in terms of interaction. Normally orders flow in one direction only, from engineering through scheduling to purchasing. But the agent is dissatisfied with being at the end of the line and seeks to reverse the flow. Value analysis permits him to initiate for others. Such behavior may, however, result in ill feeling on the part of other departments, particularly engineering and production scheduling.

Conflicts with Engineering

Engineers write up the *specifications* for the products which the agents buy. If the specifications are too tight or, what is worse, if they call for one brand only, agents have little or no freedom to choose among suppliers, thus reducing their social status internally and their economic bargaining power externally. Yet engineers find it much easier to write down a well-known brand name than to draw up a lengthy functional specification which lists all the characteristics of the desired item. Disagreements also arise because, by training and job function, engineers look first for quality and reliability and thus, agents charge, are indifferent to low cost and quick delivery, qualities of primary interest to purchasing.

All these problems are aggravated by the "completion barrier." Usually the agent seeks to change specifications only after the engineer has already committed his plans to blueprints and feels he has completed his work—in fact, he may be starting another project; the agent's interference inevitably threatens the engineer's feeling of accomplishment and completion. In any case engineers are jealous of their professional status and often resent the efforts of the agent to suggest new techniques or materials. These are areas in which the engineer feels that he is uniquely competent. Finally, agents are particularly anxious to prevent "backdoor selling" which occurs when a salesman bypasses them and seeks to influence someone else in the organization (usually an engineer) to requisition the salesman's product by name or—more subtly—to list specifications which only this product can meet. Back-door selling threatens the agent's status in two ways: (1) it encourages specification by brand and (2) it makes both salesmen and engineers less dependent on him.

Conflicts with Production Scheduling

The size of the order and the date on which it is to be delivered are typically determined by production scheduling. The agent's chief complaint against scheduling is that delivery is often requested on excessively short notice—that schedulers engage in sloppy planning or "cry wolf" by claiming they need orders earlier than they really do—and thus force the agent to choose from a limited number of suppliers, to pay premium prices, and to ask favors of salesmen (thus creating obligations which the agent must later repay). Schedulers, on the other hand, claim that "short lead times" are not their fault, but the fault of departments farther up the line, such as engineering (which delays its blueprints) or sales (which accepts rush orders). In addition agents claim that schedulers order in uneconomic lot sizes and fail to consider inventory costs or the savings from quantity discounts. In some instances, as we shall see, the purchasing agent seeks to solve these problems through combining production scheduling, inventory control, and purchasing into one "materials handling" department, which he hopes he will head.

TECHNIQUES FOR DEALING WITH OTHER DEPARTMENTS

Normally the agent attempts to fill requisitions as instructed. The majority of interdepartmental contacts are handled routinely and without friction in accordance with standard operating procedures. Yet many difficult problems cannot be easily programmed. Other departments are constantly placing pressures on the agent, who must take countermeasures, if only to preserve the *status quo.* And if the purchasing agent wishes to expand his power aggressively, as many do, he will inevitably run into conflict.

Understandably, then, successful agents have developed a variety of techniques for dealing with other departments, particularly when they wish to influence the terms of the requisitions received. These techniques will first be summarized briefly under five general headings and then be discussed in greater detail.

1. *Rule-oriented tactics*
   a) Appeal to some common authority to direct that the requisition be revised or withdrawn.
   b) Refer to some rule (assuming one exists) which provides for longer lead times.
   c) Require the scheduling department to state in writing why quick delivery is required.
   d) Require the requisitioning department to consent to having its budget charged with the extra cost (such as air freight) required to get quick delivery.

2. *Rule-evading tactics*
   a) Go through the motions of complying with the request, but with no expectation of getting delivery on time.

   b) Exceed formal authority and ignore the requisitions altogether.

3. *Personal-political tactics*
   a) Rely on friendships to induce the scheduling department to modify the requisition.
   b) Rely on favors, past and future, to accomplish the same result.
   c) Work through political allies in other departments.

4. *Educational tactics*
   a) Use direct persuasion, that is, try to persuade scheduling that its requisition is unreasonable.
   b) Use what might be called indirect persuasion to help scheduling see the problem from the purchasing department's point of view (in this case it might ask the scheduler to sit in and observe the agent's difficulty in trying to get the vendor to agree to quick delivery).

5. *Organizational-interactional tactics*
   a) Seek to change the interaction pattern, for example, have the scheduling department check with the purchasing department as to the possibility of getting quick delivery *before* it makes a requisition.
   b) Seek to take over other departments, for example, to subordinate scheduling to purchasing in an integrated materials department.

Note that neither the over-all categories nor the tactics listed under them are all-exclusive and that there is a great deal of over-lapping. They are proposed not as comprehensive tools of analysis, but merely as fairly common examples of bureaucratic gamesmanship.

Each agent interviewed in the study was evaluated in terms of his reported success (in terms of specific accomplishments) in getting other departments to accept a wider role for purchasing. Although this measure was crude and subjective,[4] there seemed to be quite clear differences between the tactics used by those who looked upon their job description as a defensive bastion and those who sought to expand their power beyond it. (Note that success is measured here in terms of expansion of power, rather than money saved for the company.)

RULE-ORIENTED TACTICS

The tactics listed below are rule-oriented in the sense that the agent's approach is perfectly legitimate under the formal rules of the organization. Agents who emphasize these tactics seem to fit into Melville Dalton's category of "systematizers."

Appealing to the Boss

According to traditional organizational theory, whenever two executives on about the same level cannot agree, they should take the problem to their common superior for solution. Yet, most agents looked upon this as a drastic step, to be taken only when other means failed.

Only five of the agents interviewed mentioned appealing to their superior as a reasonably common means of dealing with interdepartmental problems. In three cases low status seemed to be largely responsible for their inability to handle problems on their own.

Two of these agents were new to the job. For example, one was a man in his early twenties, who had only a few months' experience and who commented that his chief problems were his age and his inability to understand what engineers were talking about. This man met daily to review his problems with his boss and commented that his boss ran interference for him, at least in big problems.

The purchasing agent of a large scientific laboratory was very successful in extending his authority. In dealing with research departments, however, he used the laboratory manager "as a buffer between me and the department heads." But in regard to equipment-maintenance departments, whose heads had much lower status than did the scientists, he commented that "if there were differences, I would discuss them with them. If we didn't agree the laboratory manager would have to arbitrate. But this has never happened here." Significantly, this agent did not have a college degree, while many of the scientists were Ph.D's.

The other two agents who frequently worked through their superiors came from branch plants of nation-wide firms, which placed strong emphasis on individual responsibility to live within rigid rules.

The more expansionist agents rarely relied on their superiors to help them in interdepartmental disputes (in part because they had little success in doing this). They often explained that they would take problems to a man's superior if necessary but that they rarely found it necessary. Many repeated versions of the following:

> We have a policy against engineers having lunch with salesmen. Since the engineer is on my level I couldn't *tell* him to stop it. But in a nice way I could talk to him. If this didn't work, I'd see the plant manager.
> *Q:* Have you ever done this [appealed to the boss]?
> *A:* No.

The general feeling, particularly among stronger agents, was that too frequent reference to the superior would weaken their relations both with the superior and with their fellow employees. ("After all you've got to live with them.") To bring in top management too often would, in effect, be an admission that the agent could not handle his own problems. Moreover, there is a myth in many corporations of being "one great big happy family," and, as a consequence, it is difficult to bring conflicts out in the open. Furthermore, since the agent is usually the aggressor, in the sense that he is seeking to expand his power beyond its formal limits, he is unlikely to go to the boss unless his case is unusually good.

On the other hand, the threat of going to the boss loses its effectiveness as a weapon if the threat is *never* carried out. The following quotation summarizes a common position:

> It depends on how much fuss you want to make. If it is really important, you can tell him you will discuss it with his boss. But, I don't want you to get the wrong impression. If you have to resort to this, you are probably falling down on the job. By and large, we have a good relationship with our engineers. However, there are times when you have to take a tough position. You aren't doing your job if you always go along with them in a wishy-washy fashion.

One agent explained how he "educated" engineers to accept substitute products instead of insisting on one brand.

> We prepared our evidence and we were all set to take it to the top—and then, at the last minute, we backed down and told them it was too late in the game. But we indicated that in the future we would take similar issues to the top and they knew we would. So there has been much more understanding. . . . You have to risk making a few enemies once in a while.

Use of Rules

A second traditional bureaucratic means of dealing with other departments is to cite applicable rules or to rely on a formal statement of authority (such as a job description). For instance, an agent may circumvent pressure to place an order with a given company by referring to company rules requiring competitive bidding on all purchases in excess of $10,000. Most agents agreed, in theory, that rules of this sort are useful weapons, but they varied greatly in the extent to which they relied upon them in practice.

Some agents went very much "by the book," day in and day out. In general, these were men without college training, and they worked for larger, rule-oriented companies that were not changing rapidly. In answer to questions, these men often said, "This matter is governed by corporate policy" or made references to manuals and procedures. They also had a tendency to draw the lines of responsibility quite tightly, so that there were few areas of joint decision making; for example, "Engineering has the final word as far as specs are concerned. But we decide from whom to buy, provided they meet the specs." On the other hand, many agents operated very effectively without any formal written statement of their authority; their authority was understood by everybody in the organization and there was no need to put it in writing.

The evidence suggests that the most successful expansionists preferred to operate informally until there was an open conflict with another department. When this happened, they were very glad to refer to rules to bolster their position. Thus, paradoxically, we found strong agents who worked hard to introduce purchasing manuals and then paid relatively no attention to them in daily practice. In effect these agents take the position of "speak softly and carry a big stick." Indeed, the use of rules involves an implicit threat to appeal to higher management if the rules are not obeyed. ("When everyone in the organization knows what your responsibility is—and that you are backed up —then there is no need to mention it constantly.")

If flexibly used, procedure manuals provide the agent with an added bargaining weapon in dealing with other departments. Even though he may permit rules in the manual to be ignored most of the time, he can always do this as a favor in return for which he may ask favors. And the rules put a legal stamp on his efforts whenever he decides to ensnarl another department in a mass of red tape. But the expansionist agent must be careful not to become too rule-oriented. After all, his goal is to expand his influence beyond the areas over which the rules give him definite authority—not to retreat behind them.

Requiring Written Acceptance of Responsibility

Another bureaucratic technique used by many agents is to require others to justify their decisions in writing. For example, if a production scheduler orders a part for delivery with very short lead time, the agent can ask him to explain in writing why there is such a rush. He hopes the scheduler will be embarrassed unless he has a good excuse—and in any case, the effort will make him reluctant to make such last-minute requests in the future. Certainly this helps expose the scheduler who constantly cries "wolf."

Agents may ask for written explanations to clear themselves. Just as often, however, this is done to make others hesitate or to have evidence against them later. In insisting that such reports be written, the purchasing agent can refer to company rules or to possible audits. Thus in asking for such a statement, agents often say, "I need it to document my records."

Again, it is the weaker, noncollege agent who makes the most persistent use of such tactics. Many seem to feel that an approach of this sort is cowardly and defeatist. As one put it, "If you are trying to get a man to say 'yes,' I don't see any value in forcing him to put his 'no' in writing. Then he will never move." And another said, "I suppose you do punish an engineer by forcing him to give you a long written explanation, but that's hardly the way to win friends or advance your point of view." Furthermore, "You can always ask an engineer to give you a formal test result, but if he wishes he can always make the test fail."

Financial Charges
Cost-accounting procedures may also be used as a lever. A number of agents made comments like this:

> Whenever I get a request for a rush delivery, I ask the department which wants it whether they are willing to authorize overtime[5] or air freight. Since this gets charged against their budget, they usually hesitate a bit. If they go along I know they really need it. And if they have too many extra charges the auditor starts asking questions.

This tactic resembles the one previously discussed, particularly when the agent enters a statement into his records that the product would have been cheaper had the requisition been received on time. (Some companies charge inbound freight to the budget of the purchasing or traffic department; in such cases purchasing's leverage is somewhat less effective.)

Some companies have what is often called an efficiency (or profit) improvement plan. According to such a plan each department (and sometimes each executive) receives credit[6] for the cost savings which can be attributed to the department's activities. Agents in two companies reported that engineers showed little enthusiasm for value analysis because the purchasing department got all the credit, even though part of the work was done by the engineering department. The situation greatly improved in one of these companies when "primary" credit was transferred to engineering, with purchasing retaining "participating" credit.

RULE-EVADING TACTICS

Literal Compliance
In dealing with pressures from other departments the agent can always adopt a policy of passive resistance—that is, he can go through the motions in hopes of satisfying the demands. This tactic of feigned acceptance[7] is often used with production scheduling. For instance, after completing a lengthy phone call in which he half-heartedly tried to persuade a vendor to make a very quick delivery, an agent commented, "My buyer tried already and I knew that they just weren't going to be able to deliver that soon. Still production scheduling was screaming and they threatened to go to the plant manager. So I tried to handle it in such a way as not to hurt my relations with the vendor. They knew why I had to call."

This game of passive resistance can be skillfully played in such a way as to set a trap for the other department.

Example. One agent told how he dealt with an engineer who had placed a requisition for one company's products after having been lavishly entertained by its salesman. The agent wrote a long memo explaining why he felt this to be a poor choice and presented it to the engineer in a fashion which he knew the engineer would reject. The agent then placed the order. As he had predicted, the products arrived late and were totally inappropriate. The subsequent investigation led both to this engineer's transfer and demotion and to the other engineers having greater respect for the agent's advice.[8]

It should be noted, however, that these tactics were reported by only a minority of agents. In almost every case the agent was "weak" (in terms of expansionism) or worked in large companies where there was considerable emphasis on following formal rule books. Instead of passively seeming to accept unreasonable requests, the stronger agents actively oppose them.

Exceeding Authority
Occasionally agents may revise the terms of requisitions on their own initiative, even though they have no formal authority to do so. For instance, an agent may extend a lead time if he knows the production scheduler has set the delivery date much earlier than is really required. Where a requisition calls for a given brand, he may purchase a substitute which he feels sure is an equivalent. Or, he may buy a larger quantity than requested in order to take advantage of quantity discounts.

When an agent revises requisitions in this manner, he may or may not tell the requisitioning department what he is doing. In either case he is exceeding his formal authority. In effect, he is daring the requisitioniong department to make an issue of it. This requires considerable courage. No sensible agent will expose himself in this way unless (1) his over-all political position is secure and (2) he feels the terms of the original requisition were clearly so unreasonable that the requisitioning department will hesitate to raise the issue and expose its mistake.

Most agents were reluctant to use this tactic. Even if they could safely change orders in a given case, continual flouting of the requisitioning department's desires would create too much antagonism in the long run.

PERSONAL-POLITICAL TACTICS
Friendships and exchange of favors are used in almost every organization to get things done and to oil the wheels of formal bureaucracy. The agent is no exception to this rule; yet the author found to his surprise that informal relations played a less important role than he had expected. Agents, on the whole, seemed oriented to doing things "through channels."

None of the tactics which follow are contemplated by the company's formal scheme; all involve the use of personal relations. It would seem that Dalton's "adapters" would make greatest use of these tactics.

Friendships

Most agents prefer to deal with friends. Friendships help reduce the kinds of tensions to which agents are commonly subject. Even where friendship is not involved, it is easier to deal with people when you know their idiosyncrasies and special interests. Not surprisingly, comments like this were common: "[In handling problems] friendships count a lot. Many of the people here started when I did twenty-five years ago. We are all at about the same level and most of them are pretty good friends of mine. A lot is a matter of trust and confidence."

Agents seem to rely on friendship contacts as a means of communication and of getting quick acceptance of proposals that could be justified on their merits in any case. Rarely do agents rely on friendship alone. As one put it, "You can accomplish some things on the basis of friendship, but you can't do too much or you will strain your friendship."

Exchange of Favors

To some extent agents operate on the principle of "reward your friends, punish your enemies." and are involved in a network of exchange of favors—and sometimes even reprisals. Favors of various sorts may be given. Most agents are under pressure to make personal purchases, for example, to help someone in management buy a set of tires at wholesale rates. Since there are usually no formal rules as to such extracurricular purchasing, the agent has a strong incentive to help those who help him most. Similarly an agent is in a position to suggest to a salesman that it might be strategic to take a "co-operative" engineer to lunch. And there are always people in management who would like him to do a favor for a friend or relative who is a salesman or who owns a small business.

Other favors are more work-related. An agent may expedite delivery for a production scheduler who normally gives plenty of lead time for his orders but who now has a real emergency on his hands. Or he may rush parts for an engineer who is building a prototype model. "If a man is reasonable with me," one agent commented. "I'll kill myself to get him what he wants." The agent is less likely to exert himself for the man who has been uncooperative in the past. Yet, in general, agents seem to play down the exchange of favors, perhaps because they have relatively few favors to offer, other than trivial ones such as personal purchases or lunches for salesmen.[9]

The use of reprisals can be seen most clearly in dealing with salesmen. As one agent put it, "I play ball with those who play ball with me. If a salesman operates behind my back, he's going to have a hell of a time getting me to give him an order." Reprisals are more risky in dealing with management.

Example.   One assistant agent, for example, told how he "delayed" getting catalogues for "uncooperative" engineers and gave "slow service" to engineers who habitually cried wolf. However, both this man's supervisor and his personnel director expressed concern over his poor human relations and his tendency to antagonize others.

The typical agent, however, seemed to feel that if he used such techniques he ran the risk of permanently impairing his relations with others. Furthermore, these techniques might always backfire; for example, if production were delayed because components were delivered late, he would be blamed.

Interdepartmental Politics

In addition to their personal relations with people, agents inevitably get involved in interdepartmental power struggles. Indeed, as the following quotation suggests, the agent is often a man in the middle, subject to conflicting pressures from all sides:

Production scheduling wants quick delivery, engineering wants quality, manufacturing wants something easy-to-make, accounting wants to save money, quality control has their own interests. And then you've got to deal with the supplier—and present the supplier's position back to your own organization (sometimes you think you are wearing two hats, you represent both the supplier and the company). Everybody has his own point of view and only the agent sees the over-all picture.

Much of the agent's time is spent seeking informal resolution of such problems[10]—and in these meetings he often acts as a mediator. The following is a common situation:

Example. Production scheduling has been pushing hard to get early delivery of a particular component (perhaps because the sales department has been pressing for increased production). In response to this pressure the vendor puts new, inexperienced men on the job. But when the components are delivered, quality control declares the work is sloppy, rejects it *in toto,* and wants to disqualify the vendor from doing further work for the company. Production scheduling and the vendor are naturally upset; the vendor insists that the defects are trivial and can be easily remedied; and purchasing is placed in the difficult position of trying to mediate the issue.

If the agent is not careful in situations like this, he may become a scapegoat; everyone may turn on him and blame him for the unhappy turn of events. On the other hand, the successful agent is able to play one pressure off against another and free himself—or he may enlist the support of a powerful department to back him. If he is shrewd, he can get both sides to appeal to him to make the final decision and thus gain prestige as well as bestow favors which he may later ask returned.

Like it or not, agents of necessity engage in power politics. In doing this, they necessarily develop allies and opponents. Each department presents a special problem.

1. *Engineering.* Unless the relationship with engineering is handled with great tact, engineering tends to become an opponent, since value analysis

invades an area which engineers feel is exclusively their own. Purchasing is at a disadvantage here. Engineers have the prestige of being college-trained experts, and engineering is much more strongly represented than purchasing in the ranks of higher management.

2. *Manufacturing.* There is often a tug of war between purchasing and manufacturing over who should have the greatest influence with production scheduling. These struggles are particularly sharp where purchasing is trying to absorb either inventory control or all of production scheduling.

3. *Comptroller.* The comptroller is rarely involved in the day-to-day struggles over specifications or delivery dates. But when purchasing seeks to introduce an organizational change which will increase its power—for example, absorbing inventory control—then the comptroller can be a most effective ally. But the agent must present evidence that the proposed innovation will save money.

4. *Sales.* Sales normally has great political power, and purchasing is anxious to maintain good relations with it. Sales is interested above all in being able to make fast delivery and shows less concern with cost, quality, or manufacturing ease. In general, it supports or opposes purchasing in accordance with this criteria. But sales is also interested in reciprocity—in persuading purchasing "to buy from those firms which buy from us."

5. *Production scheduling.* Relations with production scheduling are often complex. Purchasing normally has closer relations with production scheduling than any other department, and conflicts are quite common. Yet these departments are jointly responsible for having parts available when needed and, in several companies at least, they presented a common front to the outside world. Unfortunately, however, production scheduling has little political influence, particularly when it reports relatively low down in the administrative hierarchy.

The shrewd agent knows how to use departmental interests for his own ends. Two quotations illustrate this:

Engineering says we can't use these parts. But I've asked manufacturing to test a sample under actual operating conditions—they are easy to use. Even if engineering won't accept manufacturing's data, I can go to the boss with manufacturing backing me. On something like this, manufacturing is tremendously powerful.

[To get acceptance of new products] I may use methods and standards. Or I might go to engineering first and then to methods and standards if engineering shows no interest. If I go to methods and standards I got to emphasize the cost-saving aspect [as contrasted to engineering's interest in quality].

EDUCATIONAL TACTICS

Next we come to a set of tactics designed to persuade others to think in purchasing terms.

Direct Persuasion

Direct persuasion—the frank attempt to sell a point of view—is, of course the agent's typical means of influencing others. Successful persuasion means "knowing your products backwards and forwards . . . building your case so that it can't be answered . . . knowing what you are talking about."

Most agents feel it essential that they have complete command of the facts particularly if they are to bridge the status gap and meet engineers on equal terms. As one of them said, "The engineer thinks he is the expert; the only way you can impress him is to know more than he does." Thus many agents go to considerable lengths to acquire expertise; they spend a great deal of time learning production processes or reading technical journals.

Yet some of the stronger agents pointed out that too much expertise can be dangerous in that it threatens the other man's status. "Never put a man in a corner. Never prove that he is wrong. This is a fundamental in value analysis. It doesn't pay to be a know-it-all." Thus some agents look upon themselves primarily as catalysts who try to educate others to think in purchasing terms:

> Actually it is an asset not to be an engineer. Not having the [engineering] ability myself, I've had to work backwards. I can't tell them what to do but I can ask questions. They know that I'm not trying to design their instrument. . . . You have to give the engineer recognition. The less formal you are in dealing with them the better. It doesn't get their dander up.

Indirect Persuasion

Recognizing the danger of the frontal approach, agents often try forms of indirection—manipulation, if you like—which are designed to induce the other departments to arrive at conclusions similar to those of the agent but seemingly on their own. For example:

> We were paying $45.50 a unit, but I found a vendor who was producing a unit for $30 which I felt would meet our needs just as well. There was a lot of reluctance in engineering to accept it, but I knew the engineer in charge of the test was susceptible to flattery. So I wrote a letter for general distribution telling what a good job of investigating he was doing and how much money we'd save if his investigation was successful. . . . That gave him the motivation to figure out how it *could* work rather than how it *could not* work.

Indirect persuasion often involves presenting the facts and then letting the other person draw his own conclusions. The agent may ask the engineer to run a test on a product or even simply attach a sample of the product to an interoffice buck slip, asking, "Can we use this?" Similarly, choosing which salesmen may see engineers, he can indirectly influence the specification process. (In fact, once an agent decides that a product should be introduced, he and the salesman will often co-ordinate their strategies closely in order to get it accepted by others in management.)

Most agents feel engineers should have no part in negotiating prices; they feel this would be encroaching on purchasing's jurisdiction. But one successful agent encourages engineers to help out in the bargaining because "that's the best way I know to make these engineers cost conscious." Another arranges to have foremen and production schedulers sit in while he negotiates delivery dates with salesmen. "In that way they will know what I'm up against when they give me lead times which are too short for normal delivery."

ORGANIZATIONAL-INTERACTIONAL TECHNIQUES

Organizational factors play an important part in determining (1) whether the agent's relations with other departments will be formal or informal (for example, whether most contacts will be face-to-face, by phone, or in writing), (2) whether it will be easy or hard for other departments to initiate for purchasing, and (3) whether purchasing can make its point of view felt while decisions are being considered—or can intervene only after other departments have already taken a position. All these involve interaction patterns. We shall consider here only two types of organizational changes: informal measures which make it easier for other departments to initiate change in the usual flow of orders and formal changes involving grants of additional authority.

Inducing Others to Initiate Action

In most of the examples discussed here, the agent seeks to initiate change in the behavior of other departments. He is the one who is trying to change the engineer's specifications, the production scheduler's delivery schedules, and so forth. The other departments are always at the receiving (or resisting) end of these initiations. As might be expected, hard feelings are likely to develop if the initiations move only one way.[11]

Recognizing this, many of the stronger agents seem to be trying to rearrange their relations with other departments so that others might initiate changes in the usual work flow more often for them. Specifically they hope to induce the other departments to turn instinctively to purchasing for help whenever they have a problem—and at the earliest possible stage. Thus one agent explained that his chief reason for attending production planning meetings, where new products were laid out, was to make it easier for others to ask him questions. He hoped to encourage engineers, for example, to inquire about available components before they drew up their blueprints. Another agent commented, "I try to get production scheduling to ask us what the lead times for the various products are. That's a lot easier than our telling them that their lead times are unreasonable after they have made commitments based on these."

Some purchasing departments send out what are, in effect, ambassadors to other departments. They may appoint purchase engineers, men with engineering background (perhaps from the company's own engineering group) who report administratively to purchasing but spend most of their time in the engineering department. Their job is to be instantly available to provide information to engineers whenever they need help in choosing components. They assist in writing specifications (thus making them more realistic and readable) and help expedite delivery of laboratory supplies and material for prototype models. Through making themselves useful, purchase engineers acquire influence and are able to introduce the purchasing point of view before the "completion barrier" makes this difficult. Similar approaches may be used for quality control.

Work assignments with purchasing are normally arranged so that each buyer can become an expert on one group of commodities bought. Under this arrangement the buyer deals with a relatively small number of salesmen, but with a relatively large number of "client" departments within the organization. A few agents have experimented with assigning men on the basis of the departments with which they work rather than on the basis of the products they buy. In one case work assignments in both purchasing and scheduling were so rearranged that each production scheduler had an exact counterpart in purchasing and dealt only with him. In this way closer personal relations developed than would have occurred if the scheduler had no specific individual in purchasing to contact.

Even the physical location of the agent's office makes a difference. It is much easier for the agent to have informal daily contacts with other departments if his office is conveniently located. Some companies place their agents away from the main office, to make it easier for salesmen to see them. Although this facilitates the agents' external communications, it makes their internal communications more difficult. Of course, those companies that have centralized purchasing offices and a widespread network of plants experience this problem in an exaggerated form. Centralized purchasing offers many economic advantages, but the agent must tour the plants if he is not to lose all contact with his client departments.

Value analysis techniques sharply highlight the agent's organizational philosophy. Some agents feel that value analysis should be handled as part of the buyer's everyday activities. If he comes across a new product which might be profitably substituted for one currently used, he should initiate engineering feasibility studies and promote the idea ("nag it" in one agent's words) until it is accepted. Presumably purchasing then gets the credit for the savings, but resistance from other departments may be high. Other agents, particularly those with college training, reject this approach as unnecessarily divisive; they prefer to operate through committees, usually consisting of engineers, purchasing men and production men. Though committees are time consuming, communications are facilitated, more people are involved, more ideas are forthcoming—and in addition, the purchasing department no longer has the sole responsibility for value analysis.

To the extent that he allows others to take the initiative, the agent himself must take a passive role. Not all agents are emotionally prepared to do this.[12] Some feel that it smacks too much of the "order clerk." A number commented, in effect, "I don't want to be everyone's door mat." Many asked questions like, "How far do you go in cost estimating, in getting quotes for hypothetical orders? . . . What do you do if a man throws a label at you and says get me some of this? After all, our time is limited."

Formal Organizational Change
The final approach is for the agent to seek to expand the formal grant of authority given his department (which might mean a larger budget too), as, for example, to place other functions such as traffic, stores, or even inventory control and production scheduling in one combined materials department. Agents who exert their energies in this direction generally reject the "human relations" or "participative" approach to management. They like to resolve problems through memoranda ("it helps keep emotions down") and are not particularly optimistic about the possibilities of converting other departments to think in purchasing terms ("after all every department has its own point of view—that's natural"). They spend considerable time developing statistical means of measuring their own efficiency and that of their subordinates, and they are more likely to be in companies that have similar philosophies. For example, one agent explained why value analysis in his organization was concentrated in the purchasing department, "[Our company] doesn't believe in joint assignments or committees. If a man isn't competent to do the job himself, then we find another man. We don't want weak sisters." And another argued, "The responsibility must be concentrated in one department or another. It can't fall between two stools."[13]

CHOICE OF TECHNIQUES
The foregoing list of tactics are presented not as a formal typology but merely to illustrate the *range* of techniques available to the agent. Most agents use all of these techniques at one time or another, depending on the problem. A different technique might well be used in introducing a major policy change

than in handling routine orders. In trying to promote changes, one agent observed:

> You have to choose your weapons. I vary them on purpose. ... I ask myself, who has the final decision? How does the Chief Engineer operate? What does he delegate? What does he keep for himself? It all involves psychological warfare. Who are the people to be sold? Who will have the final say?

And even in dealing with one problem, a mixture of tactics will generally be used. Nevertheless, the over-all strategies used by various agents seem to vary greatly in terms of which tactics receive the greatest emphasis.

1. Some agents seek formal grants of power (for example, to get inventory placed under purchasing); others merely seek influence (for example, to persuade inventory control to order in more economic lot sizes).

2. Some agents want to influence decisions *before* they are made (for example, through encouraging engineers to turn instinctively to purchasing for help whenever they are even considering the use of a new component); others *after* (for example, through having their decisions upheld often enough for engineering to hesitate to make an issue of a request whenever purchasing questions a specification).

3. Some agents think in terms of their long-run position and thus seek to improve procedures; whereas others are interested chiefly in exerting their influence in each conflict as it comes along.

We have already noted a difference between successful expansionists and those content with their roles as they are. On the whole, expansionists seemed to be more likely to choose informal tactics such as indirect persuasion, inducing others to make changes in the work flow, and interdepartmental politics. They had long-run strategies and sought to influence decisions before they were made. Those who were successful in achieving more formal power were also well aware of the value of informal influence; those who merely *talked* about formal power seemed to be relatively unsuccessful even in informal influence. In fact, one of the most noticeable characteristics of successful expansionists was their flexibility. Most were equally adept at using both formal and informal tactics and were not averse to turning the formal organization against itself.

Differences in success in expansionism seem to be due to a number of factors.

1. *Technology.* Obviously the agent cannot expand very much in a service industry or one where only raw materials are bought. He has his greatest

chance for power in companies which make goods to order and in which there is a great deal of subcontracting.

2. *Management philosophy.* Where lines of authority are sharply drawn, the agent has little chance to extend his influence—except through direct seizure of another department's power, which is not easy. Note the comments of one agent in a highly rule-oriented company:

> We are a service department . . . We must see that parts are here at the proper time. . . . I usually let engineering pretty much make its own decisions. I may try to persuade an engineer to accept a new product. But if he says "no" all I can do is wait till he gets transferred and try to persuade his successor.

Of the agents interviewed, the most successful was one in a company which had just introduced a new management and in which all relationships were in flux.

3. *Education.* Purchasing agents who were college graduates seemed to be more expansionist than those who were not. This may be due to their higher level of aspiration. Moreover, any company that appoints a college graduate may well expect to grant him greater influence. The college-trained man may feel more as an equal of the engineer and therefore more willing to come into conflict with him.

Furthermore, the more educated men (and particularly those with a business school background) seemed more prone to rely on techniques that were informal and not rule-oriented. Specifically, they were less likely to rely on formal statements of authority, to require others to take formal responsibilities for decisions, or to insist that an agent should "yell loudly whenever his rights are violated"; and they were more willing to work through committees.[14]

CONCLUSION

Traditional organization theory emphasizes authority and responsibility; it deals largely with two types of relationships: (1) those between superiors and subordinates, which it conceives as being primarily authoritarian (though perhaps modifiable by participation, general supervision, and the like) and (2) those of staff and line, which are nonauthoritarian. Though the purchasing department is traditionally classified as a staff department, my own feeling is that the staff-line dichotomy in this case (as perhaps for most other purposes) tends to obscure more problems than it illuminates. As we have seen, the purchasing department's relations with other departments cannot be explained by any one simple phrase, such as "areas of responsibility," "exchange of favors," "advice," "control," or the like. Instead the skillful agent blends all these approaches and makes use of authoritarian and persuasive tactics as the situation requires. His effectiveness is largely dependent on the political power he is able to develop.

Recent authors have suggested that the study of organization should begin first with "the work to be done and resources and techniques available to do it."[15] The emphasis is on the technology of the job ("technology" being defined broadly to include marketing problems and the like as well as external environment) and the relationships between people which this technology demands. "Organizations should be constructed from the *bottom up,* rather than from the *top down.* In establishing work-group boundaries and supervisory units, management should start with the actual work to the performed, an awareness of who must co-ordinate his job with whom, when, and where."[16]

Some of us who are interested in this area are groping toward a concept of *work flow,* meaning the communications or interactions required by the job and including the flow of raw materials and products on the assembly line, the flow of paper work when a requisition moves through engineering, scheduling, and purchasing, as well as the flow of instruction, which may move down the chain of command from president to janitor.

This has been an exploratory study of the interrelationship between power struggles and lateral work flow. Of particular interest in this study, are: (1) the agent's strong desire for increased status, which upsets the stability of his relationship with other departments, (2) his attempts to raise his status through influencing the terms of the requisitions he receives and thus make interactions flow both ways, (3) the relatively limited interference on the part of higher management, which makes the lateral relationship especially important for the agent, (4) the "completion barrier," which requires the agent to contact an engineer before a blueprint is finished if the agent is to be successful in influencing the terms of the requisition, and (5) the differing vested interests or terms of reference of the various departments, which make agreement more difficult.

Finer mapping and more intensive research into interdepartmental relations is required; interactions should be precisely counted[17] and work should be done with specialties other than purchasing.

Notes

1. There have been many studies of lateral relations within or among primary work groups, but such studies have been concerned primarily with rank-and-file workers, not management. Three notable studies of horizontal relations within management are Melville Dalton, *Men Who Manage* (New York, 1959); Elliot R. Chapple and Leonard Sayles, *The Measure of Management* (New York, 1961); and Henry

A. Landsberger, "The Horizontal Dimension in a Bureaucracy," *Administrative Science Quarterly,* 6 (1961), 298–332.

2. Henceforth, I shall refer to the purchasing agent as the "agent."

3. I am indebted for assistance to the Buffalo and Northern California Association of Purchasing Agents and to the chairmen of their respective Committees for Professional Development, Messrs. Roger Josslyn and M. J. McMahon. Helpful criticism was provided by Profs. Delbert Duncan, E. T. Malm, and Lyman Porter at the University of California, Berkeley; Prof. John Gullahorn of Michigan State College; Prof. Leonard Sayles at Columbia University; and Dean Arthur Butler and Prof. Perry Bliss at the University of Buffalo. Part of the research was done while the author was a research associate at the Institute of Industrial Relations, University of California, Berkeley.

4. *Reported* success obviously involves a fair amount of wishful thinking—aspiration rather than accomplishment—but for the general character of this study this limitation was not too serious. It should be emphasized, however, that whether an agent was a successful expansionist depended not only on his own personality and his choice of techniques but also on the institutional characteristics of the organization in which he worked.

5. That is, the vendor is authorized to make an extra charge for having his men work overtime.

6. Though there is no direct pay-off, performance under the plan is often taken into account in determining bonuses or promotions.

7. Dalton, *op. cit.,* p. 232.

8. A tactic like this can always backfire. The agent himself may be blamed for the failure.

9. Reciprocity in the broader sense, as suggested by Gouldner and others, is, of course, inherent in the entire framework of relations discussed here. Cf. Alvin W. Gouldner, "The Norm of Reciprocity: A Preliminary Statement," *American Sociological Review,* 25 (1960). 161–177.

10. Dalton (*op. cit.,* pp. 227–228) points out the function of meetings in short-circuiting formal means of handling problems.

11. Actually, of course, initiations do occur in both directions. The production schedulers initiate for the agent when they file requisitions and the engineers initiate when they determine specifications. This normal form of programmed, routine initiation is felt to be quite different from the agent's abnormal attempts to introduce innovation. This distinction is quite important.

12. After all, a certain type of active, initiating sort of personality is required if the agent is to bargain successfully with suppliers; it is hard for the same individual to adopt a passive role within the organization.

13. Yet it could be argued that the committee system does not itself divide responsibility; it merely recognizes the fact that responsibility for value analysis is of necessity divided among departments.

14. These conclusions are consistent with the findings of the questionnaire sample (N = 142). The results are in the direction indicated for both degree of education and business school background (each taken separately) although only three out of eight relationships are significant at the .05 level. The questionnaire data are somewhat suspect, however, since the values which agents report are not always consistent with their observed behavior: in answering questionnaires many agents seem to place greater emphasis on formal techniques than they do in practice.

15. Wilfred Brown, *Explorations in Management* (London, 1960), p. 18. See Chapple and Sayles, *op. cit.;* William F. Whyte, *Men at Work* (Homewood, Ill., 1961).

16. George Strauss and Leonard R. Sayles, *Personnel: The Human Problems of Management* (Englewood Cliffs, N.J., 1960), p. 392. The sentence is Sayles's.

17. Albert H. Rubenstein of Northwestern University has completed an unpublished quantitative study of communications within a purchasing department.

Managerial Career Development and the Generational Confrontation
David Moment and Dalmar Fisher

There is no objective way to assess the amount of human ineffectiveness and waste at the managerial levels of organizations. However, most managers keenly sense a wide discrepancy between what they and what other managers feel they *could* accomplish in their work, and their actual results. From the organizational point of view, this kind of waste may be necessary—an inevitable consequence of highly complex organizational structures and processes. However, the social consequences are borne directly by the men and women in organizations whose personal values, attitudes, hopes, aspirations, and, above all, feelings of personal integrity and self-worth, suffer.

The dilemmas of personal integrity for the manager are severely heightened by the current cultural unrest of the various youth movements. Self-questioning which may arise from the managers' private and organizational lives is now demanded by news reports, contemporary cinema, music, theater, and literature all seemingly converging in their attacks on Mr. Businessman and the Establishment. Paradoxically, the very value system on which the manager relied in his own career provided the standard of living, with its value on higher education, which made youth what it is today: critical, questioning, searching for meaning, and rejecting the values which supported the successful managerial or professional career. Nevertheless, youth's insistence on finding meaning in the present offers today's manager a potentially important and useful approach to revitalizing his own life and career.

From our own experiences as teachers, management development trainers and researchers, we see some clear implications of this critical focus for the management of managers' careers, as practiced by themselves and by their organizations. First, let us explain how we look at managerial careers and the problems that managers report in them.

ORGANIZATIONAL AND PERSONAL PROBLEMS

Many managers, successful by the organizational and social standards of wealth, income, and status, report that they experience their working careers as living within "fur-lined traps"; the office environment, expense account, fringe benefits, income, status, and various luxury trappings pad their jobs, but they feel trapped within them. Their personal values, goals, senses of meaningful contribution and accomplishment, and desires to improve their organizations' performance fall by the wayside as they learn not to make waves. Whatever personally meaningful work they do in the organization is concealed, beneath or outside the formal definition and constraints of their jobs. Many give up even this activity and find whatever challenge and new experiences they can outside of their work, in community affairs, hobby and vacation interests, and other areas of personal activity.

Younger, middle-level managers report that they are kept busy "fighting the system," either warding off or starting to participate in company politics, engaging more energy in personal and departmental defense work than in their primary tasks. The middle-managerial ranks in many organizations are manned by young men and women who will stay and do competent work only until the point where they realize "how it really is" in the organization.[1]

Many of these personal career problems for managers can be viewed as organizational problems; individual dissatisfaction and motivation loss can be caused by poor job design, inappropriate organizational structures, and interpersonal and intergroup in-fighting. However, even under the best of organizational conditions, the organization's particular missions, tasks, specializations, and coordination needs limit the amount of the "total man" which can be effectively engaged with his work. The career development problem (in contrast to organizational development problems) is how to help the individual continually and congenially redefine the patterns and meanings of his work activities among his total life activities so that growth, and the motivational energies which accompany it, is not seriously abated as organizational and other environmental constraints are encountered in his work.[2]

CAREER DEVELOPMENT REDEFINED

The career development image stated above is very different from the "square pegs in square holes, round pegs in round holes" philosophy of the vocational guidance movement begun in the early twentieth century. The old view is still somewhat applicable to lower level work in organizations; however, the primitive "match the man with the job" philosophy is in itself a major cause of ineffective career development at the managerial and professional levels. There, neither the work nor the people can be described easily in terms of job stereotypes or personality stereotypes.

Managerial level careers and the actual work within them are more aptly described as *constrained opportunity systems* for the individual. The only parts of the work which are concretely describable are the least important clerical components, involving prescribed ways of handling certain paper work and routine organizational problems. Abstract job functions, labeled in terms of missions rather than job content, cover the most important aspects of the work which the individual can accomplish any way he chooses.

Furthermore, especially in industries featuring rapidly changing technologies, markets, and financial structures, managerial missions and specializations are likewise subject to change, characterized as overlapping sequences of relatively temporary projects. Most successful managers find themselves repeatedly stepping off into areas of work in which they have never before been engaged and, in many cases, which no one has ever done before. To restate the Peter Principle,[3] successful managers are continually doing things they have never done before.

We suggest, therefore, that effective managerial career development is not a case of the individual fitting into a clearly definable niche in a stable environment. Rather, it is an ongoing process of continual change in personal work activities and meanings, engaging with continually changing environmental conditions. With this picture in mind, we see ineffective careers as ones in which the individual persists in stereotyped activities and thinking stereotyped thoughts while the world of work changes around him. Part of the problem has to do with the need to keep up with new knowledge and technologies, but this kind of development can be relatively easily specified and remedied through adult educational technologies. The other part of the problem, which is our major concern here, is less accessible to existing developmental technologies—it is focused on the need for the continual revision of personal attitudes, motives, strivings, and meanings as the individual develops a comfortable style of working and living in perpetually new and unfamiliar situations. Style choice, style change, and deeper meaning in work can be difficult to achieve but are clearly possible.

CONSTRAINED OPPORTUNITY SYSTEMS

Although choice and change are possible for the developing manager, he faces substantial constraints placed on him by the particular mission requirements and behavior expectations that go with his specialized role in the organization. In measuring managers' adaptations to their roles' constraints, our research has disclosed substantial differences in personal style between managers in different managerial roles in the same organization.

We measured two major style components, Proaction (initiative) and Toward People, with a questionnaire where each manager described his behavior in particular situations. For example, one of the Proaction items asked the managers what percentage of the time they actively influenced work discussions or committee meetings in which they were involved and about what percentage of the time they let such discussions proceed without intervening. A Toward People item asked approximately what proportion of their time was spent alone and what proportion was spent talking with others, either in person or on the telephone. When we compared the style scores of managers in seven roles in a bank and a department store, we found some predictable differences. The buyers in the store, a role requiring a comparatively high degree of innovativeness and negotiatory ability, scored slightly higher on the average on both Proaction and Toward People than did trust officers in the bank.

We found that the buyers were more individually assertive and directive and less oriented toward building close cooperative relationships than were the operations managers or the managers in staff functions such as control, credit and personnel in the department store. In the bank, we found that the loan officers tended to be distant and skeptical of their clients, while the trust officers were sympathetic and authoritarian. The cashier officers, whose duties involved more routine dealings with large numbers of customers, were more bureaucratic than the other officers. Thus, while bank officers' and department store managers' work are often seen as describing two different kinds of managerial careers, there are in fact wide differences in performance requirements depending on the manager's specialized role within his organization.

Given the requirements of particular roles, it is not difficult to understand how a manager could come to see his surroundings as almost totally constraining, and thus develop a stereotyped style. Loan and trust officers in the bank and buyers in the department store were particularly susceptible to adopting role stereotypes. On the other hand, there were managers in the same roles in these organizations who saw their roles as opportunities rather than as constraints. These less constrained managers felt that choices of behavior style were possible within their roles, and were not compelled to conform to a behavioral stereotype of their role. Our research results strongly suggested in several ways that in managerial career development, choice and change are not only possible but are essential to the manager's job effectiveness and personal growth.

ALTERNATIVES WITHIN ROLE

We found that even within rather specialized managerial roles there is a wide range of personal style options, in spite of the tendency for stereotyped role behavior. Furthermore, effectiveness in role was, in most cases, associated with *non*-stereotypical behavior styles.

To obtain an independent measure of individual effectiveness in the bank and store organizations, we asked senior executives to rank their subordinate managers' performances. We found that among the highest performers in each role grouping, the range of acceptable style variations was somewhat narrower than for the role grouping as a whole; the most effective managers' styles did tend to be different from others' in their role group. However, there was wide enough variation, even among their styles, to indicate the possibility of choice.

In a large food products firm, our study focused on the product managers in the firm's marketing division and developed a somewhat different measure of effectiveness, spurred by the suggestions of our earlier findings in the bank and department store studies. This time, we distinguished between those who were seen as effective by a wide cross section of the other individuals with whom they worked and those who were not. The former we called Versatile product managers, while we referred to the others as Limited product managers. We found that the behavior of the Versatile managers tended to be seen differently by colleagues from different parts of the organization to a greater extent than was true of the Limited managers. For example, manufacturing managers, whose concerns centered on cost control and internal stability within the organization, saw the Versatile product managers as relatively conservative, while product research managers, who were concerned with innovation saw the same men as relatively innovative.[4] Thus, the effective manager's behavior choices were *not* stereotyped, but depended on his developing skill at reading the demands of the particular relationships in which he was involved. The overall breadth of his behavior style derived from variations that were chosen purposefully, not randomly.

While we focused primarily on the managers' situational adaptations to current role requirements in our studies, we noted that those managers who seemed to be "choosers" in their current work situations also reported to have been choosers in the earlier stages of their careers. In making both kinds of adaptations, situation and career, the less constrained managers made choices among behavioral alternatives, while the constrained managers were not aware that there were alternatives and that they could make choices among them.

ROLE TRANSITIONS OVER TIME

No matter how skillful a manager becomes in handling the demands of his current role, he will inevitably be faced with a further demand: the need for transition into new roles. In our data from the bank and department store, this requisite was revealed when we compared between different age groups the performance components associated with overall effectiveness. Our findings indicated that the higher executives weighted the importance of certain behavioral components differently for different age groups. Two executive-rated performance components, technical and interpersonal, were about equally related to effectiveness among the younger managers. Within the middle age group, however, technical performance showed a substantial increase, and interpersonal performance a decrease in importance. Between the middle and older age groups, the emphasis again shifted direction on both performance components, with technical decreasing in importance, according to the top executives, and interpersonal increasing. These results suggest that different performances are expected of the manager, and presumably rewarded, at different phases of his career and life. As a manager grows older, his organizational superiors' criteria for evaluating his performance change.

Unfortunately, top managers are not always as willing to facilitate their subordinates' career development as they are to judge it. Several obstacles to effective career development typically reside in the interpersonal relationship that forms between a superior and a subordinate.[5] The following conversation took place between one of the authors and a senior executive in the department store organization:

Executive: People change when they change jobs. You can take a buyer and put him in operations and he becomes uncommunicative and expresses the same gripes as the other operating people. If you take an operating person and make him a buyer, as we have sometimes done, he may open up and become creative.

Researcher: This is interesting. In other words, you can put a man in a buyer's job and develop his creativity.

Executive: Of course. But that's not what we're interested in. We are here to make a profit.

Despite the various constraints and complexities, including superiors' insensitivity or lack of concern, our data have indicated that it is possible for a manager to further his own development through the process of choosing among style alternatives. The way this process can be conceived and acted upon by the individual is illustrated in the following comments by a young branch store manager in the department store firm who described the style alternatives he faced as well as his own pattern of adjustment over time:

I'm changing as far as the allocation of my time. When I first came here I spent my time on paperwork. My second period was one where I would take a more cursory look at the papers and spend more time changing the physical layout of the store. Then I got an assistant, but I found it more difficult to teach and delegate than to do the work myself. Now my assistant has gotten to the point where he's able to *operate* the store, take care of adjustments, schedule employees, etc. So now I am doing more of what is the function of a manager, seeing what's moving, getting merchandise in that we need and knowing what we have . . . I thought it was automatic before. Now I'd say I can affect ten percent of the business of the store. We have no basement stock here, but I called a while back and asked for some basement suits and ended up selling plenty. This never would have happened if I hadn't done it myself.

This manager's development involved *learning through testing the limits of his constraints.* He was able to fashion appropriate behavioral goals out of the ambiguous opportunities which confronted him. His testimony, along with our other research results, implies that the developing manager is one who combines a willingness to engage the unfamiliar with an awareness of his existing and potential competences.

CONTEMPORARY APPROACHES TO MANAGERIAL CAREER DEVELOPMENT

Our work has led us to see the opportunity structure of managerial careers as consisting of sets of middle-range behavior alternatives for the individual, encountered sequentially over time. Some of the choice points are systematically predictable, while others appear in a more random manner. While we see the possibilities for personal choosing in managerial careers, many individuals do *not* often see alternatives for themselves and therefore do not see themselves as having made choices—in these cases, the individuals' careers "happen to them."

Individuals do tend to be thoughtful in considering major decisions such as job changes, changes in residence, choice of a spouse, choice of a college, making vacation plans, and so forth. Frequently, however, the middle-level decisions are not consciously experienced as choice situations. For example, most of the department store managers we studied did not deliberately allocate where they spent their time. Rather, they created a "style"—like the woman in the department store firm who called herself an "earthy buyer," spending time on the floor, handling the merchandise, interacting with clerks and customers, being where this kind of action was. Similarly, many did not choose to interact: they answered the phone when it rang and talked with people when they were approached, but with little thought to whom they were talking with (among alternatives) or what they were talking about (also among alternatives). Thus, these important middle-range behaviors, including where and when to be doing what with whom, just happened to them, as a result of the random reaction of their spontaneous personality characteristics with the impinging events around them.

Most of the contemporary theory and practices of managerial career development widely miss this important middle-range of behavior alternatives which directly determine work and career effectiveness. At one extreme, which we call managerial and organizational psychoanalysis, the gross behavioral, emotional, and attitudinal characteristics of the individual are probed in depth and his global organizational work alternatives are similarly analyzed in terms of his power, control, achievement, and affection needs on the one hand, and organizational opportunities for satisfying them on the other.[6] This approach can lead to improved understanding on the part of the individual and to his choosing situations in which he can work most effectively. It can help the organization and the individual deal with "big" behavior choices, but gives little guidance for handling of organizational situations once the individual is already in them.

The other extreme approach to managerial career development deals with relatively minor behaviors and technical decisions within the closed system of the organization's existing constraints and climate. Programs of management by objectives and performance appraisal can help the individual and his superiors set goals and measure their attainment strictly within the organization's purposes.[7] Goals are set in organizational terms and alternative means are specified in technical terms. The kinds of goals dealt with in this approach would normally include cost reductions, sales quotas, and other organizationally measurable indices, the attainment of which calls for changes in the relatively technical aspects of the manager's job.

The organizational development and sensitivity training approaches to improving individual and group work effectiveness aim more toward the middle-level behaviors with which we are concerned. However, just as the "technical" goal setting and performance appraisal approaches tend to overlook the non-technical relationship and initiative aspects of the manager's career, the interpersonal relations approaches tend to overlook alternatives in the technical job content aspects of his work. Furthermore, when sensitivity training approaches are used within an organizational program, they tend to limit concern to the individual's behavioral alternatives within the particular organization's system, rather than his lifetime career alternatives.

We believe that positive efforts in managerial career development need to be concerned with the individual's attitudes, behaviors, and alternatives within his total life, including organizational, community, family, and personal interest activities.[8] Many successful managers, for example, would do well for themselves and their orginizations by thinking of their organizational work commitment as part-time rather than full-time, thus not overburdening their technical work and their relationships with colleagues with personally compulsive, organizationally unnecessary, and possibly disruptive busy work. Much managerial work involves preparing and waiting for events such as meetings, and waiting for their results. We know of managers who cannot tolerate temporary idleness, who cannot wait graciously, overburdening their staffs with preparation, detail work, double, triple, and quadruple checking. Under these conditions, the individual, his staff, and the rest of the organization would be better off if the manager would do something else with his time and effort, engaging in activities that are broadly career and development related, though not narrowly and conventionally accepted as organizational career work.

On the other hand, managers who feel a relatively part-time commitment to their organizational work could, under the right conditions, find that more of their total lives could become involved usefully for the individual and the organization in organizational activities. One manager, for example, was highly educated in Slavic languages; he found that he could teach language in a company-sponsored adult education program. In another situation, an American manager working with other managers in a European city, found a way to integrate more of his life into work by having his wife work at getting the other lonely, displaced, highly educated management wives involved in socially useful activities of value both to the community and to the organization.

Marital, extra-marital, and family relationships are known to have important influences on the individual's working and community careers, as well as vice versa. Business trips and expenses are often planned with extra-marital interests in mind. Some men are over-involved in work because their work and their relationships with colleagues are more pleasant and rewarding than their home lives. Older superiors often overburden their relationships with subordinates with the residues of the problems with their growing children at home. These areas of personal concern are seldom dealt with as important elements of the individual's total career life; they are joked about, covered up by taboos, or dealt with as part of the superficial "organization wives" chatter in the popular media. Any serious study or improvement program addressed to managerial career development needs to include concern with the individual's *total* life and the relationships among the various interdependent parts of his life. The creative generativity of managerial careers draws its human energy from the same sources that affect the nature of all of his interpersonal relations, social involvements, and substantive personal interest patterns.

We conclude, therefore, that the several contemporary approaches to the study and improvement of managerial career development tend to deal in isolation with artificially disconnected parts of the total career life of the individual, and that they tend to deal with either macro-behavioral alternatives or micro-behavioral alternatives, either major career alternatives or relatively trivial technical alternatives. We suggest that effective research and action programs in managerial career development need to concentrate on the total life of the individual and on the middle-level, day-to-day behavior alternatives available within that total life process.

A DYNAMIC APPROACH

We have noted the kinds of problems that men and women in managerial careers express, and with which their superiors and their organizations' planners are concerned. Although those concerned with meaning, contribution, and using one's human resources effectively are extreme in managerial careers, they are not limited to them. To the contrary, *any* professional whose career success and satisfaction is dependent on organizational processes as well as on his own professional competence within his specialty, inevitably encounters the same problems. The problems are more extreme and more typical of managerial careers because the nature of the work involved is more ambiguous and susceptible to change, and because managers do not yet have the strong professional identification that can both provide independent standards of conduct and success and provide a strong supportive reference group of colleagues.

We attribute a large part of the manager's career development problems to his lack of sensitivity to middle-level behavior alternatives and their importance for work and life fulfillment, and to his lack of training and guided experience in practicing and evaluating choice among behavior alternatives. These deficiencies are generally reinforced by the prevalent human tendency *not* to see one's behavior as an independent variable in the scheme of living. Rather, we predominantly learn to adjust, as dependent variables, to the patterns of events and opportunities that impinge upon us. Under these conditions, our active seeking tends to be confined to finding comfortable niches in our work and life environments and avoiding uncomfortable situations. We hold our personalities to be sacred and our behaviors, when we are at all aware of them, to be sacred parts of the "real us." As long as these assumptions prevail, so will the life-attitude of "nichemanship," exemplified by the "square pegs in square holes" philosophy of person/environment matching. Because of the rapid and continuing changes in the nature and structure of our work and living environments, as well as in our own value systems, this quaint mechanistic metaphor is doomed to lead to failure when taken completely seriously by individuals, educators, counselors, and managers of others' careers.

ELEMENTS OF EFFECTIVE CAREER DEVELOPMENT PROGRAMS

Any effective plans for helping people develop increasing effectiveness in managerial careers must (1) deal with the total life space of the individual, (2) concentrate on the middle-level behavior alternatives which can be controlled by the individual and which can make differences in his external results and his personal feelings, and (3) must involve him in interactive communication with other people, preferably a combination of group work, two person discussions, and even written communications.

Total Life Space

A whole person reports to work, greets his spouse at home, interacts with his family, and lives in his community; but each of these areas of his life engages only part of him. We would ask men and women first to become aware of their work and life styles with the help of suitable concepts, and with special attention to the relationships among the various areas of living in their lives. Then we would ask them to become aware of changes in these patterns of relationships in their past lives and in the projected future. Next we would ask them to discuss their own patterns with other people, and thus vividly encounter alternatives while exposing their own patterns as alternatives to others. In addition to enabling some degree of self-discovery, this process helps the individual see differences among people, and as a consequence of this, some alternatives for himself.

For example, and in terms of middle-level behavior styles and alternatives, we have seen managers in face-to-face conversation with another person interrupt that conversation to answer a ringing telephone, unwittingly assuming and communicating that an unknown stranger at the other end of the line was more important than the person at hand. We are reasonably sure that most people who do this do not see the alternative of letting the phone ring or taking it off the hook while maintaining attention to the person present. However, some people give such rapt attention to the person they are talking with that they ignore *all* intrusions. Out of context this example sounds trivial; in the real organizational context it represents a concrete manifestation of the individual's frequently inadvertent means of assigning priorities, which have very important consequences for the individual and for the organization. Similar comparative analysis of personal stylistic behaviors can highlight not only the fact of alternatives, but also encourage consideration of their personal and organizational consequences.

Middle-Level Behavior Alternatives
Men and women tend to label themselves and each other in terms of character and personality traits, and much of "performance appraisal" and coaching consists of this activity. However, it is the *behavior* of the person, rather than his "traits" which directly cause results, for better and for worse. People can change certain of their behaviors more easily than they can alter their traits. For any program of self-help or counseling to be effective, the individual must see and experiment with those aspects of himself which he can control. It is easier, and more possible, to speak more quietly (behavior) than to become less aggressive (trait).

Clearly, concentration on behavior alternatives to the exclusion of understanding causes within the individual's personality can lead to superficial charm school behaviors, and an aura of manipulative phoniness. However, in the seriousness and depth of the approach we are prescribing, the consideration of behavior alternatives includes the anticipation of consequences, both for relationships with others and with one's self. The limits of behavioral experimentation lie in the individual's own feelings of integrity, and the outer world's capacity to adapt to his behavior.

We have found a useful method of helping people describe, analyze, and contemplate change experiments in their middle-level behavior patterns. We call the method "Role Network and Activity Analysis." In addition to the description and explanation of the network of interpersonal relationships and social memberships surrounding and including the individual in his total life, we would ask him to describe his relationships with ideas and things, his personal interests in hobbies, scholarly reading projects, and gratifying objects such as tools, boats, paintings, and music which strongly attract and occupy many people.

This process of role network and activity analysis would help people become aware of their existing and changing relationships with specific people and groups as well as with objects and interests. The meanings of these relationships and activities to them, to people with whom they are involved, to their work, to their families, and to their communities would be explored.

Stressful as well as comfortable and gratifying relationships would be identified. The personal, interpersonal, social, organizational, and community consequences of these patterns would be examined. Through comparison of one person's role network and activity pattern with others', some mutual exposure to behavioral alternatives would result, from which people could plan, experiment with, and evaluate behavior changes.

Focused Interaction on Mutual Career Development
We suggest small group discussions of mutual career development problems as the third important element in a dynamic approach to career development. Focused interaction with others provides several functions necessary to plan, support, and facilitate individual development. First, many people really do not know how they think or feel until they are required to express themselves openly. Writing also serves to clarify thought. Furthermore, the focused discussion process, including focused listening (for which deliberate training may be necessary in some groups), exposes individuals to alternatives for themselves. It is surprising how many mature, and even highly educated people, are not aware that other people, even of the same social class, educational background, and occupation, live and work by means of behavior pattern and relationship qualities very much different from their own.

The well-developed group can provide important support for the individual members. One kind of support is reflected in the "we're all in the same boat" reaction to discussions. Since acting "cool" and unemotional is part of the role expectation of managers in many organizations, they are often surprised and relieved to learn that other people are just as doubtful and concerned about their own effectiveness and satisfaction as they are. Another kind of support in well-developed groups provides safety for experimentation. In the everyday organizational world a man is often afraid to express his inevitable concerns and doubts about himself and his performance for fear of being ridiculed and punished by his colleagues and superiors.

A well-developed support group allows free expression of individuals' doubts and concerns about themselves, and through supportive relationships with each other encourage experimentation with the assurance to the individual that they will be with him and not ridicule and punish him for "failures." Since much developmental learning consists of experimental trials, errors, and successes, it is vital to create for the individual a setting in which trial and error is encouraged and supported, in marked contrast to the usual organizational climate which discourages experimentation.

A final function of a well-developed group for individual development is reinforcement, related closely to the support functions described above. When a person does experiment and finds an effective new behavior, especially if it tends to upset others as many effective behaviors inevitably must do, it will quickly be extinguished in day-to-day organizational, family, and community life by the disturbances or lack of immediately gratifying response that it evokes. The support group provides positive reinforcement in the form of encouragement and discussion with the individual that enables him to go out into the relatively hostile and non-rewarding "outside world" with the mission of enhancing his personal effectiveness even in the absence of immediate gratifications from that world.

We believe strongly that for *career* development, in contrast to *organizational* development, which can also use parts of the approach we are describing, the support group should consist of members of different organizations, rather than managers and other professionals from one particular organization. This is because the process we advocate, if it proceeds in depth and integrity, must include in its open considerations for the individual not only the possibility of leaving his employing organization, but also the possibilities of adopting an entirely different occupational and life style. This is not because we believe managers and professionals would necessarily be happier in farming, joining hippie communes, working for volunteer social welfare organizations, or taking up art, but rather because we think that any honest consideration of alternative life styles must openly consider *all* alternatives.

To allow this open confrontation with extreme alternatives in career development, we believe cross-organizational, and even cross-occupational support groups, would be more effective than organizational groups. A possible exception to this would be in the few organizations we know of where open developmental climates exist at managerial and professional levels. Even in these situations, it is difficult to conceive of a superior listening supportively to a valued subordinate talking about the alternative of leaving the organization, or, conversely, listening openly to a subordinate whom he wishes would leave voluntarily, without pushing him out. While we would not want to discourage the developmental organization from trying an in-company career development program, we would caution that the membership of the group, especially the members' outside relationships with each other, should be such that no alternative considered by any one member should threaten directly the alternatives of other members.

TOWARD PERSONAL INTEGRATION IN CAREER
The dynamic approach which we have described is a means to increase individuals' awareness of the existence and meanings of their behavior patterns. It focuses primarily on work but is not limited to that area of life. People have more alternatives open to them than they usually realize and need to examine alternatives in the realm of the "middle-ranges" of behavior: what people do to and with each other. We can now see more clearly why youths view their elders as "plastic" people, and how "meaning" and "relevance," so actively sought by youth, have slipped out of the lives of their elders through lack of self-examination.

If one listens to youth, as we have done in our teaching roles, one hears self-examination, questioning, self-consciousness of relationships with others, and a tremendously strong desire to communicate with us about these concerns. In contrast, the stereotyped people, a few of whom we deal with in our work, are characterized by *avoidance* of self-examination until, under the stress of their work and education, they are forced to look at themselves consciously and systematically. The "gap" is closed for them.

We maintain that the more the adult individual can incorporate into his total life the positive aspects of youth's self-questioning, the more he sees alternatives and the opportunities for choice while mellowing this youthful zest with his accumulating life experiences, the more effective and integrated he will feel and be in his career and life.

References

1. See Eugene E. Jennings, *The Mobile Manager* (Ann Arbor, Michigan: Bureau of Industrial Relations, University of Michigan Graduate School of Business Administration, 1967).

2. See Eugene E. Jennings, *The Executive in Crisis* (East Lansing, Michigan: Division of Research, Graduate School of Business Administration, Michigan State University, 1965), especially chapter 8, entitled "Crisis of the Total Self."

3. Laurence F. Peter and Raymond Hull, *The Peter Principle* (New York: William Morrow and Company, 1969).

4. Dalmar Fisher, "Entrepreneurship and Moderation: The Role of the Integrator," in Jay W. Lorsch and Paul R. Lawrence, eds., *Studies in Organization Design* (Homewood, Illinois: Richard D. Irwin and the Dorsey Press, 1970), pp. 153–167.

5. See Harry Levinson, "A Psychologist Looks at Executive Development," *Harvard Business Review* (September–October, 1962), pp. 69–75.

6. See Abraham Zaleznik, "Power and Politics in Organizational Life," *Harvard Business Review* (May–June, 1970), pp. 47–60; also, Harry Levinson, *The Exceptional Executive* (Cambridge, Massachusetts: Harvard University Press, 1968).

7. See J. Sterling Livingston, "Pygmalion in Management," *Harvard Business Review* (July–August, 1969), pp. 81–89; also, Paul H. Thompson and Gene W. Dalton, "Performance Appraisal: Managers Beware," *Harvard Business Review* (January–February, 1970), pp. 149–157.

8. See Harry Levinson, "On Being a Middle-Aged Manager," *Harvard Business Review* (July–August, 1969), pp. 51–60.

PART III
Objectives and Control Systems;
Selection and Training

PART III

Part III examines some of the more traditional aspects of the management of people. As this book focuses on a systemic-contingency approach to the facets of management, the articles in this section show how the management of appraisal, selection, and training have built in, either consciously or unconsciously, various self-correcting mechanisms, which are characteristic of any subsystem.

OBJECTIVES AND CONTROL SYSTEMS

James L. Bowditch's brief article on long-range planning in a church organization outlines how goals may be set, plans made and carried out, and the whole process assessed for effectiveness over time. This assessment will help determine future goals and plans and how they should be carried out.

The second article, "Human Resource Accounting in Industry," by R. Lee Brummet, William C. Pyle, and Eric G. Flamholtz, describes the pioneering effort at feeding in personnel hiring and training costs as investments in an overall accounting system. Treating human resources as investments sharpens organizations' abilities to use personnel in order to maximize return on their investment in people.

The article by Edgar F. Huse on management development in the installation of a type of management-by-objectives (MBO) procedure echoes two themes of this book. Since MBO is specific to both a job and the person who holds it, the MBO process improves the feedback part of a communications subsystem and makes the planning and appraisal approach contingent on how the superiors' and subordinates' personal styles operate within an overall framework.

The article by Donald Roy, "Selections from Quota Restriction and Goldbricking in a Machine Shop," shows what can happen when powerful,

Objectives and Control Systems; Selection and Training

informal groups try to subvert a rigid, mechanized-control feedback system. Since the informal group is much more flexible than the institutionalized feedback system (in this case the Methods Department), since the workers seem to be working under the rubric of "a fair day's pay for a fair day's work," and since the rate of pay is fixed, the workers adjust their output to conform to what they deem is appropriate.

The section on objectives and control systems concludes with Lee Hansen's brief spoof outlining procedures for ". . . Subverting Management by Objectives." You will notice that these techniques are more general and can be used to subvert any organizational policy. The article does point up what are likely to be vulnerable points in any feedback system.

SELECTION AND TRAINING

The three articles about selection focus on current problems in this area. The first article, the government's executive order establishing the appropriate way to use tests, states that anything used as a test must: (1) not discriminate on the basis of ethicity, sex, race, or religion, and (2) be related to success on the job.

The second reading, "Validity of aptitude tests for the hardcore unemployed" by James F. Gavin and David L. Toole, demonstrates how aptitude tests may be used to predict turnover and various types of absenteeism for previously hardcore unemployed. Despite the relatively strong significance levels cited in the article, the correlations between predictor (test) and criteria (measures of turnover and other performance indices) are rather low.

The final article on selection, "The Unsettled DeFunis Case" by C. Robert Zelnick, shows that when the Supreme Court dismissed the case of a law school which had two different standards for admission—one for Caucasians, the other for minority groups—nothing was settled. The interesting implication to come from this article is that perhaps the worth of an attorney is better measured by his service as an attorney than by his grades in law school. This suggests that a longer-term criterion measurement may have to be developed and applied.

The one article on training, "Breakthrough in On-the-Job Training" by Earl R. Gomersall and M. Scott Myers, can be considered a "bridge" between Parts III and IV. The article cites impressive reductions in cost and gains in quality in an on-the-job training situation in which persons learning a job are asked for suggestions about the job as well as feelings as newcomers toward the job. Having begun to tap the creativity as well as the anxieties of people on the job allowed management to focus on problem areas rapidly.

For a more in-depth overview of the areas covered in Part III, see *Personnel Selection and Placement,* M. D. Dunnette, Belmont, Calif.: Wadsworth, 1966; *Training in Industry: the Management of Learning,* B. M. Bass, J. A. Vaughan, Belmont, Calif.: Wadsworth, 1966; and *Management by Objectives: A System of Managerial Leadership,* G. S. Odiorne, New York: Pitman, 1965.

OBJECTIVES AND CONTROL SYSTEMS

Long-Range Planning in the
Diocese of Massachusetts
James L. Bowditch

Does it take three race riots before there is a church policy to help promote understanding between races? What, if anything, should we be doing or saying regarding the energy crisis? What about the nine churches in a Boston suburb when perhaps four or five are viable? What about the five churches in a four-square-mile area of Boston, some of which are existing on their endowment and little else? What does long-range planning have to do with the resolution of these issues? In short, it helps groups of people make decisions which shape the future, rather than letting the future shape the people. Issues are identified prior to their becoming a crisis.

Long-range planning is a systematic way of developing important issues, setting priorities and goals, creating procedures for achieving the goals, and finally evaluating the results over a substantial period of time—usually two to five years. It is a proactive process which forces people to make conscious decisions about our future rather than "letting things happen."

THE BEGINNINGS IN EASTERN MASSACHUSETTS
In September 1972, the Diocesan Council, through the assistant bishop, agreed to establish a committee to study long-range planning procedures and to suggest a plan for the Diocese of Massachusetts. After visiting clusters of parishes, (districts) and congregations, talking with priests, sisters, and laypeople about problems faced by the Diocese, a process for planning was approved by the Bishop and the Diocesan Council.

Modified from an article appearing in *The Militant,* December 1973, p. 3. Reprinted by permission of Episcopal Diocese of Massachusetts.

The process of planning is relatively simple. It involves planning-doing-evaluating. At the outset, there must be a purpose statement for any organization. The Bishop issued a purpose statement for the Diocese of Massachusetts at the Annual Convention in October 1973. Future planning from any planning unit within the Diocese, such as parish, mission, specialized ministry, must integrate its goal with that of the Diocese.

In any planning process there are six steps which need to be done to complete the cycle. First, each planning unit must develop its own purpose statement, including what it determines to be its role and scope in the community within which it exists. Second, the planning unit should be examined to see what internal resources currently exist and what resources need to be developed. Besides its internal resources, a planning unit needs to examine the environment or community and make sure that local needs, desires, and resources are taken into account. If a district is confronting the issue of "more churches than people," for example, perhaps a group interested in architecture and sociology could make plans which would be consistent with canon law, effective physical plant utilization, and projected demographic shifts. Third, issues that are central to meeting these needs and that can be transformed into projects or programs are developed by the planning unit. Fourth, there is a resource development stage, such that the planning unit will be able to successfully reach its various goals. Fifth is the actual implementation of the plans, and finally there is a review and evaluation procedure for the plan over time. This allows all participants to check on the effectiveness of any particular planning unit. In order to guide the planning process for the Diocese, the Bishop and Diocesan Council has appointed a Long-Range Planning Committee to follow up on the Strategy Committee's recommendations. Additionally, a group of parish consultants have received professional training in helping districts, parishes, and missions go through the planning process in all phases of their ministry.

IMPACT ON THE DIOCESE, DISTRICT, AND PARISH
What is the likely outcome for planning units? For the Dioceses of Ohio and Bethlehem, two dioceses which have recently gone through the planning process, the results have been gratifying. The planning process has allowed the Dioceses of Ohio and Bethlehem to make some conscious, informed decisions about where they should place their emphases over a five-year period. For the parishes which participated, a course was charted, plans were implemented, and efforts to reach the goals became systematic. Putting it in financial terms, money was placed where it would do most good.

For the Diocese of Massachusetts, planning forces it to use its limited resources wisely. Parishes have to determine how and in what form they might minister most effectively to the community. Districts have to examine the extremely tough problems of parish placement and physical plant utilization.

Questions, such as "Does this district now need all of the parishes it now has?" have to be asked. If the answer is affirmative, what sorts of emphasis should there be for the various parishes within the district? If not, how should parishes be recombined to provide the area with a more effective witness?

Human Resource Accounting in Industry
R. Lee Brummet, William C. Pyle, and Eric G. Flamholtz

INVESTMENTS IN THE BUSINESS ENTERPRISE

Investments are expenditures made for the purpose of providing future benefits beyond the current accounting period. If a firm purchases a new plant with an expected useful life of fifty years, it is treated as an investment on the corporate balance sheet, and is depreciated over its useful life. If the structure should be destroyed or become obsolete, it would lose its service potential and be written off the books as a loss which would be reflected as an offset against earnings on the company's statement of income.

Firms also make investment in *human* assets. Costs are incurred in recruiting, hiring, training, and developing people as individual employees and as members of viable interacting organizational groups. Furthermore, investments are made in building favorable relationships with *external* human resources such as customers, suppliers, and creditors. Although such expenditures are made to develop future service potential, conventional accounting practice assigns such costs to the "expense" classification, which, by definition, assumes that they have no value to the firm beyond the current accounting year.

For this reason human assets neither appear on a corporate balance sheet, nor are changes in these assets reflected on the statement of corporate

Personnel Administration, **32**, 4, 1969, pp. 34–46. Reprinted by permission of the International Personnel Management Association.

income. Thus, conventional accounting statements may conceal significant changes in the condition of the firm's unrecognized human assets. In fact, conventional accounting statements may spuriously reflect *favorable* performance when human resources are actually being liquidated.[1] If people are treated abusively in an effort to generate more production, short term profits may be derived through liquidation of the firm's organizational assets. If product quality is reduced, immediate gains may be made at the expense of customer loyalty assets.

A need exists, therefore, to develop an organizational accounting or information system which will reflect the current condition of and changes in the firm's human assets. Some accountants have recognized such a need, but measurement difficulties pose problems for them. As early as 1922, William A. Paton observed:

> In the business enterprise, a well-organized and loyal personnel may be a more important "asset" than a stock of merchandise. . . . At present there seems to be no way of measuring such factors in terms of the dollar; hence, they cannot be recognized as specific economic assets. But let us, accordingly, admit the serious limitations of the conventional balance sheet as a statement of financial condition.[2]

IMPORTANCE OF HUMAN RESOURCES
Why have industry and the accounting profession steadfastly neglected accounting for human resources? Aside from the measurement difficulties, the answer may be found, partly, in the perpetuation of accounting practices which trace their origins to an early period in our industrial history when human resource investments were relatively low. In more recent years, however, those occupational classifications exhibiting the highest rates of growth, such as managerial and technical groupings, are those which require the greatest investment in human resources.[3] In addition, rising organizational complexity has created new demands for developing more sophisticated interaction capabilities and skills within industry.[4] These and other factors, coupled with persistent shortages in highly skilled occupational groupings increase the need for information relevant to the management of human resources.

RESOURCE MANAGEMENT NEEDS
Although oversimplified, management may be viewed as a process of *acquisition and development, maintenance,* and *utilization* of a "resource mix" to achieve organizational objectives, as suggested in Figure One. Accounting and information systems contribute to this process by identifying, measuring, and communicating economic information to permit informed judgments and decisions in the management of the resource mix. Management needs information

Fig. One.   *The process of resource management*

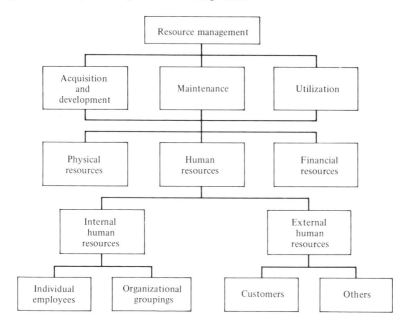

regarding: (1) resource acquisition and development, (2) resource maintenance or condition, and (3) resource utilization.

Resource Acquisition and Development Information Needs

Organizations acquire a wide variety of resources to achieve their purposes.
Investments are undertaken in those resources which offer the greatest potential returns to the enterprise given an acceptable degree of risk. Calculation of
resource acquisition and development costs is necessary, therefore, not only for
investment planning, but also as a base for determining differential returns
which accrue to those investments. The *resource acquisition and development
information needs* reflect themselves along two dimensions; (1) the need for
measurement of *outlay costs* when assets are actually acquired, and (2) the
need for estimating the *replacement cost* of these investments in the event they
should expire.

Resource Maintenance or Condition Information

Investments are undertaken in resources with the objective of creating new
capabilities, levels of competency, types of behavior, forms of organization,
and other conditions which will facilitate achieving organizational objectives.
An information need exists, therefore, to ascertain the degree to which invest-

ments in resources actually produce and sustain the desired new capabilities, levels of competency, types of behavior, and forms or organization.

Resource Utilization Information
Once new capabilities, levels of competency, and other "system states" are achieved, *resource utilization information* needs become more salient. Management should know the degree to which changes in resource conditions or "system states" are translated into organizational performance. The answer to this question is reflected in the rate of return on the investments which created the new "system state" or resource condition.

Conventional Accounting and Information Needs
Conventional accounting or information systems answer these three basic information needs for *non-human resources.* Measurement of investment in plant and equipment fulfills the "acquisition information need." Over time, these assets are depreciated, and new investments are recorded. The current "book values" of such investments reflect, at least in theory, the "resource condition" of the organization's physical assets. Finally, "utilization information needs" are supplied in the form of return on investment calculations.

Unfortunately, conventional accounting systems do not answer these three basic information needs for human assets. The objective of our research effort, therefore, is to develop a body of human resource accounting theory and techniques which will, at least in part, alleviate these information deficiencies.

HUMAN RESOURCE ACCOUNTING MODEL
The development of human resource accounting in the business enterprise derives from the pioneering work of Rensis Likert and his colleagues at the University of Michigan's Institute for Social Research. For more than two decades, their research studies have revealed that relationships exist between certain variable constructs and organizational performance. *"Causal variables,"* such as organizational structure and patterns of management behavior have been shown to affect *"intervening variables"* such as employee loyalties, attitudes, perceptions, and motivations, which in turn have been shown to affect *"end-result variables"* such as productivity, costs, and earnings.[5] Furthermore, research by Likert and Seashore indicates that time lags of two years or more often exist between changes in the "causal variables" and resultant changes in the "end-result variables."[6]

As seen in Figure Two, Likert's three variable models have been adopted into a human resource accounting model with the addition of two variable constructs—*"Investment variables"* and *"return on investment variables."* Why have these new variable classifications been added? All business firms wish to improve organizational performance. In doing so, however, a more crucial question is, *how much* will performance be improved and *what will it*

Fig. Two. *A human resource accounting model (with examples of variables)*

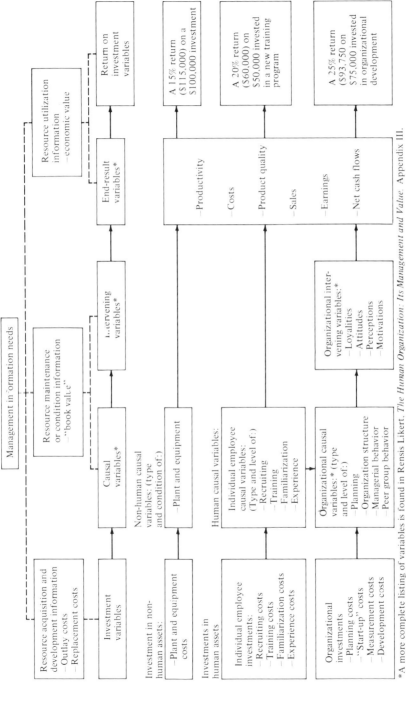

* A more complete listing of variables is found in Rensis Likert, *The Human Organization: Its Management and Value*. Appendix III.

an intermediate objective, we are concentrating on the development of an *internal human resource* accounting capability. This research effort divides itself into three functions: (1) *the development of a human resource accounting system oriented to basic managerial information needs,* (2) *the development and refinement of managerial applications of human resource accounting, and* (3) *the analysis of the behavioral impact of human resource accounting on people.* These objectives are being pursued in a five-year inter-company research program which has been initiated by the University of Michigan's Institute for Social Research and Graduate School of Business Administration in cooperation with several corporations.

Research at the R. G. Barry Corporation

Since October 1966, the University of Michigan has been engaged, along with the management of the R. G. Barry Corporation, in development of what is believed to be the first human resource accounting system. The Barry Corporation's 1,300 employees manufacture a variety of personal comfort items including foam-cushioned slippers, chair pads, robes, and other leisure wear, which are marketed in department stores and other retail outlets under brand names such as Angel Treds, Dearfoams, Kush-ons, and Gustave. The corporate headquarters and four production facilities are in Columbus, Ohio. Several other plants, warehouses, and sales offices are located across the country. The firm has expanded from a sales volume of about $5½ million in 1962 to approximately $20 million in 1968.

Implementation of a Human Resource Accounting System

The first phase of a human resource accounting system became operational at the R. G. Barry Corporation during January 1968. This system measures investments which are undertaken in the firm's some 96 members of management, on both *outlay cost* and *replacement cost* bases. An account structure applicable to organizational investments is now being developed. The Barry Corporation is now in the process of extending human resources accounting to other occupational classifications in the firm. In the future, a system will be developed for its customer resources. A model of an outlay cost measurement system for employees is presented in Figure Three.

HISTORICAL AND REPLACEMENT INVESTMENTS MEASURED

An Outlay Cost Measurement System

Investments in human resources may be measured in terms of outlay costs. *Outlay costs* are sacrifices incurred by the firm in the form of out-of-pocket expenditures associated with a particular human resource investment. These are measured in terms of *non-salary* and *salary* costs. Examples of the former include travel costs in support of recruiting or training, and tuition charges for

Fig. Three. *Model of an outlay cost measurement system*

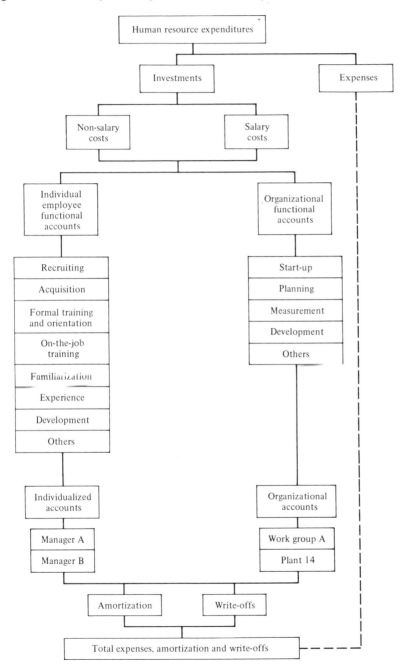

management development programs. The latter would include employee salary allocations during an investment period. For example, if an executive attends a two-week management seminar, his salary for this time period should be viewed as part of the investment, in addition to the tuition and travel costs. Similarly, if during the first year of tenure with a firm, 30 percent of a new manager's time is devoted to familiarization with company policy, precedents, organization structure, interaction patterns, and the like, 30 percent of his salary should be recorded as an outlay cost associated with the familiarization investment.

At the R. G. Barry Corporation, instruments have been designed to measure investments undertaken in *individual managers* for each of the functional accounts indicated in Figure Three. To qualify as assets, specific expenditures must meet the test of offering service potential beyond the current accounting period in relation to long term written corporate objectives. Charges to the functional accounts are also entered in "individualized accounts" for each manager. With a few modifications the individual manager account structure will also be applied to other occupational groupings within the firm. However, it is not contemplated that "individualized accounts" will be developed for factory and clerical personnel.

Procedures have also been designed to record investment expirations. Asset accounts are amortized on two bases: (1) *maximum life* and (2) *expected life.* Functional investments are separately identified in each manager's account and are amortized according to the *maximum life* of each investment type. For example, recruiting and acquisition costs provide benefits to the firm so long as an employee remains with the organization. The *maximum life* of this investment would be the mandatory retirement age less the employee's age when hired. If *maximum life* were relied on exclusively for amortization, asset accounts would be overstated since employees frequently leave the firm prior to the mandatory retirement age. To assure a more realistic statement of assets, maximum life amortization periods are adjusted to expected life by application of weighted probabilities which reflect a particular individual's likelihood of remaining until mandatory retirement based upon his age, tenure, organizational level, marital status, job satisfaction, and related factors. *Expected life* periods are employed in the amortization of the functional accounts.

The choice between these two bases is essentially a choice between relevance and verifiability. "Maximum life" provides a highly verifiable base, but it is less relevant than "expected life." "Expected life" may, to some degree, be influenced by job satisfaction as well as many other factors. For this reason, a firm may wish to obtain a range of estimates. To be more conservative, "expected life" is employed to calculate the investments shown on the firm's balance sheet and an adjustment to net income based upon changes occurring in those investments. Other estimates may be more useful for planning purposes.

Specific measurement instruments have been designed to record human asset losses resulting from turnover, obsolescence, and health deteriorations. Turnover is immediately identifiable; however, obsolescence is much more elusive. For this reason individual employee asset accounts are reviewed quarterly for obsolescence by each supervisor. Review also occurs when an employee is transferred to a new position. Accounts are also adjusted for known health deteriorations in proportion to the seriousness of the impairment as reflected in actuarial data.

As suggested in Figure Three, an outlay cost measurement system designed to record *organizational investments* is now being developed at the R. G. Barry Corporation. Investments are undertaken in human resources *over and above* those made in *individual employees as individuals.* Organizational "start-up" costs are reflected in heavy individual employee investments and in production below standard during the initial period when the organization is building and developing group interaction patterns for the first time. Additional investments are also made in the form of organizational planning. Furthermore, periodic measurement of organizational causal and intervening variables are in themselves investments in the organization when they lead to development activities which improve the functioning of the enterprise as an interacting system. Finally, investments are undertaken in the organization which cannot be readily traced to individual employees. A portion of the operating costs of the personnel department, company library, health service, safety department, and similar departments may be traced to activities which offer long term benefits to the organization.

Charges made to the "organizational functional accounts" will also be allocated to appropriate entities such as work groups, plants, divisions, or the enterprise as a whole. In addition, a capability is being developed to reflect expirations which occur in these accounts. Many "organizational investments" differ *in kind* from "individual employee investments" which lose their usefulness to the firm when a particular individual leaves the firm. For example, benefits could be derived indefinitely from costs incurred in molding the organization into a system of effective interacting groups despite a moderate level of individual employee turnover within the system. This suggests the possibility that some organizational investments may be non-depreciable.

This would not, however, preclude the possibility of expirations. If for example, an enterprise invests $50,000 in an organizational development program which succeeds in improving employee attitudes and motivations by a measurable amount, subsequent deterioration in those attitudes and motivations could justify a write-off of the original investment.

A Replacement Cost Measurement System
The outlay cost system described above is designed to record human resource investments, obsolescence, and losses as they are actually incurred. These data,

however, only partially fulfill the "resource information" needs of the organization. For planning purposes, the *positional replacement cost* of human resources becomes more salient. Positional replacement costs are the outlay costs (recruiting, training, etc.) which would be incurred if an incumbent should leave his position. The human resource accounting system which has been installed at the R. G. Barry Corporation has the capability of supplying average positional replacement cost data for each manager. These positional replacement cost data reflect annual adjustments for price level changes. The system also records "compositional" investment changes since some investments undertaken in the past will not be repeated and, conversely, others not made in the past will be undertaken in the future. For these and other reasons, positional replacement cost may be less than, equal to, or greater than historical outlay cost.

Appropriate Measurement Units

As noted above, "investment variables" are measured exclusively in dollar or socio-psychologically based units. However, "causal variables" may be measured in either dollars on socio-psychological terms. For example, the current condition of the firm's plant and equipment (a "causal variable") should be reflected at its current book value, although other indictors can also be employed. Similarly, the *current condition* of the company's "individual employee investments" (a "causal variable") should be reflected at the book values recorded in the functional asset accounts discussed above. However, other indicators are being developed as cross-checks. Socio-psychological survey questions are now being used to measure employee perceptions of the current condition of "individual employee causal variables" such as the quality of recruiting and training. Trends in these data are being compared with trends in the individual employee asset account balances. These socio-psychological data may suggest more realistic amortization procedures for individual employee investments." The current condition of "organizational causal variables" may also be reflected in the current book value of "organizational investments," recorded in dollar units. However, socio-psychological survey instruments may prove more valid since managerial behavior (a "causal variable") may be altered independently of cost outlays.

"Intervening variable" measurements have been undertaken at the R. G. Barry Corporation and additional surveys are planned. However, an accumulation of several years' data will be required before meaningful "return on investment variables" may be calculated.

HUMAN RESOURCE ACCOUNTING APPLIED

Human resource accounting system applications are oriented toward fulfilling the three basic organizational information needs: (1) resource acquisition and development information, (2) resource maintenance or condition information and (3) resource utilization information. Inasmuch as the human resource accounting system at the R. G. Barry Corporation is in an early stage of development, its potential applications can only be stated in tentative terms at this time.

It is contemplated that the system will generate two types of data: (1) information which is integrated with conventional accounting statements and (2) information which is presented independently of these statements.

Human Resource Data Integrated and Conventional Financial Reports

One of the first reports generated by the system is a *balance sheet* indicating the firm's investment in human resources. The corporate *income statement* is also affected to the degree that there is a net change in the firm's investment in human resources during the reporting period. This situation is illustrated in Figure Four. The two balance sheets indicate that a hypothetical company experienced a *net increase* in its investment in *individual employees* during the period. This change, taken by itself, would result in a positive adjustment to the firm's net income[9] of $100,000. However, this firm also experienced a *net decline* in its organizational investments during the period. (This could result, for example, from a plant being closed in one location with operations being moved to another state.) This change, taken by itself, would result in a negative net income adjustment of $200,000. When the two changes are taken together, a negative adjustment of $100,000 is reflected in the firm's net income.

Data generated by the human resource accounting system at the R. G. Barry Corporation indicate that the replacement investment of their some 96 managers is approximately $1,000,000, while the current "book value" is about $600,000. The firm invests around $3,000 in a first line supervisor and upwards of $30,000 in a member of top management.

Other Human Resource Accounting Reports

A variety of additional reports are now being generated by a human resource accounting system. Periodic comparative data for different work groups, plants, and divisions contrast human resource investment changes during reporting periods. Turnover losses are also being quantified and analyzed according to such factors as employee job satisfaction, age, occupation, tenure and the like. Special purpose reports are also being prepared to evaluate various organizational alternatives which require investments in human resources. To increase production capacity, for example, should a firm expand its existing plant or construct a new facility? For each alternative these reports indicate projected new investments, write-offs, and the effect on net cash flows. Once a particular alternative is chosen, actual investment, write-offs and cash flows may then be contrasted against projections. As patterns of return on investments in human resources become apparent, the firm will learn which

Figure Four

BALANCE SHEET

ASSETS	Dec. 31, 1967	Dec. 31, 1968
Current Assets (cash, etc.)	$1,000,000	$1,500,000
Plant and Equipment	8,000,000	8,000,000
Investment in Individual Employees (recruiting, training, development, etc.)	750,000	850,000
Organizational Investments (start-up, planning, development, etc.)	900,000	700,000
TOTAL ASSETS	$10,650,000	$11,050,000

EQUITIES		
Liabilities	$2,000,000	$2,000,000
Owner's Equity: Stock	6,000,000	6,000,000
Retained Earnings (including investment in human resources)	2,650,000	3,050,000
TOTAL EQUITIES	$10,650,000	$10,050,000

INCOME STATEMENT
Year Ending December 31, 1968

Sales		$2,000,000
Expenses		1,500,000
Net Income		$ 500,000
Adjustment for change in investment in human resources		
—Individual employee adjustment	+$100,000	
—Organizational adjustment	−$200,000	−100,000
Adjusted Net Income		$ 400,000

investment types should be increased, reduced, or maintained at their current level.

The ultimate success of any accounting system is determined by its impact on the behavior of people. Where the goals of employees and the organization are reasonably consistent, data may be employed as a problem solving tool to achieve organizational objectives. However, the social science literature is replete with evidence of the distortions which may be introduced into an information system when individual and organizational goals are not congruent.[10] For this reason, an integral part of human resource accounting research will focus on determining the behavioral impact of an operational human resource accounting system on employees. Socio-psychological survey instruments supplemented by personal interviews will be employed to assess the impact. These data will, in turn, be used to design organization development activities which will facilitate installation and sustained operation of the human resource accounting system.

CONCLUSIONS

Human resource accounting is now in an early stage, and a host of problems remain to be resolved before a fully developed system can become operational. However, the initial results are encouraging as many beneficial results are being derived prior to full scale operation. Investments in human resources may be determined at a relatively early stage. The techniques developed to measure these assets may also be employed in extended organizational and manpower planning which underlie and sustain corporate growth. Even before return on investment data become available, measurement of trends and rates of change in "causal" and "intervening" variable data may suggest new behaviors and investment routes which will improve organizational effectiveness.

Notes

1. Renis Likert, *The Human Organization: Its Management and Value,* New York: McGraw-Hill, 1967, pp. 101–115.

2. W. A. Paton, *Accounting Theory,* New York: The Ronald Press, 1922, pp. 486–87.

3. U. S. Bureau of the Census, Historical Statistics of the United States, Colonial Times to 1957, Washington, D.C. 1960, pp. 74–75; pp. 202–14.

4. Likert, *op. cit.,* pp. 156–160.

5. *Ibid.*

6. Likert, R. and Seashore, S., "Making Cost Control Work," *Harvard Business Review,* November–December 1963, pp. 96–108.

7. This research will be described in greater depth in a monograph now being prepared by the authors, and planned for publication in 1969.

8. Where relationships between the level of job satisfaction and expected tenure can be identified, turnover losses may be calculated in dollar terms and predicted for varying levels of job satisfaction, as a function of measured changes in causal and intervening variables.

9. The net income that would be indicated without a human resource accounting system.

10. Argyris, C., "Human Problems with Budgets," *Harvard Business Review,* January–February 1953, pp. 97–110; Whyte, W. F., *Money and Motivation,* New York: Harper & Row, 1955.

Putting in a Management Development Program that Works
Edgar F. Huse

One of the greatest challenges facing management today is to increase the skills of present and future managers. Two of the currently most popular approaches are formal management training programs and the installation of new performance appraisal systems—frequently described as management by objectives and appraisal by results. However, most of the follow-up studies on such programs have shown disappointing results; some have shown negative results.

A large, internationally famous company, an integrated organization engaged in the design, manufacturing, and marketing of complex systems for defense and civilian markets, decided to change its appraisal methods from a classic system to one best described as "management by objectives." Although the initial installation of the program did not succeed, the lessons learned allowed the company to install a subsequent program that showed gratifyingly positive and proven results at all levels of management. This corporation's experiences should be widely applicable.

Originally, the corporation considered that it had an outstanding classic performance appraisal program. Appraisals were completed annually by the immediate supervisor to provide subordinates with information and recommendations for developments and improvement and to provide bases for salary action. The appraisals were detailed, of three or four typed pages, together with

© 1966 by The Regents of the University of California. Reprinted from *California Management Review,* **9,** 2, pp. 73–80, by permission of The Regents.

a formal rating; they were reviewed by the next higher level of management and by the personnel department. After the immediate supervisor reviewed the appraisal with his subordinate, both signed the form. Completed appraisals were kept on permanent individual file. Elaborate procedures had been established and maintained to ensure that appraisals were completed properly and on time, and 98 per cent were.

A study was conducted to determine some of the effects of these performance appraisals. Performance appraisal discussions between worker and supervisor were observed *in situ*. Subordinates were interviewed before and after the appraisal discussions. In addition, a follow-up was made twelve to fourteen weeks after the discussions to determine the degree to which work had improved. The results have been described elsewhere,[1] but the conclusions will be briefly summarized here.

1. The appraisal discussion had no measurable influence on improvement of job performance as such.
2. Criticism of performance resulted in subordinate defensiveness.
3. The more the criticism, the more the defensiveness.
4. The more the defensiveness, the less the performance change noted in the subordinate.
5. Praise, in the discussion, had no measurable effect on the reaction to criticism or on later work performance.
6. Work improvement occurred only when specified goals, measurement of results, and deadlines were established and agreed upon separately from the appraisal discussion.

The findings of this study confirm the widespread criticism of performance appraisal and seemingly substantiate McGregor's comments that "the strategy of management by integration and self-control is more likely to be conducive to growth, learning and improved performance" than a performance appraisal system.[2] Company management studied these findings and decided that a new approach was necessary.

As a substitute for the performance appraisal system, it was decided to implement a modified form of Peter Drucker's "management by objectives and self-control." The program, called Work Planning and Review, can be described as a flexible process involving periodic sessions between the worker and his manager, with mutual planning of the work to be done, mutual review of progress, and mutual problem solving and assistance. The primary objective is to help the subordinate improve his work performance through a more effective working relationship with his supervisor.

Work Planning and Review (hereafter called WP&R) does not involve formal ratings. In their place, it provides an informal basis for the worker and his manager to discuss the job to be done in advance of doing it, to agree upon a plan of action and the measurement of results, and to review progress after completion of the task or project. Although there is no fixed time for such discussions, they typically take place at the beginning and end of projects, or monthly, or quarterly, depending on the job. The results of the discussions remain confidential; no copies or records go to the personnel department.

WP&R started as a pilot study. One-half of the organization continued with the classic performance appraisal, and the other half (approximately 125 managers) were "put on" WP&R. Forms were developed, and a brief booklet was prepared. The over-all principle of WP&R was explained to the managers in staff meetings. They were told that they should conduct work planning and review sessions with their subordinates rather than continuing the formal performance appraisal.

Three months later, the results were studied. The findings were largely negative. Almost universally, managers had stopped doing performance appraisals (with a great sense of relief). However, these managers had done very little of the "management by objectives" required by WP&R.

A number of factors were apparently involved in the initial failure of the program:

- The managers had been given insufficient background for, and understanding of, the program.
- The program was perceived as another kind of classical performance appraisal.
- The timing, forms, and techniques were regarded as rigid, inflexible, and unrelated to the job.
- The implementation violated some of the most important principles of the introduction of change.

At this point, I was made responsible for the implementation, acting as change agent, and the program was not abandoned, but a fresh start was made, working slowly and gradually, assisting managers in changing their behavior so that they could do a better job of assisting their subordinates in developing and improving their work performance. The focal point was shifted from the subordinate to manager, who had to change before the subordinate could.

IMPORTANT RELATIONSHIPS
Once these principles were followed, a highly successful program evolved.

The principles used to implement the successful program fall into three major dimensions.

- The first is the relationship of the manager to his own supervisor, and the necessity for executive support.
- The second is my relationship with the managers.
- The third is the worker-manager relationship.

Manager-Supervisor Relationship
The principle in this dimension relates to the method of using the executive hierarchy to gain support for the program. Industrial organizations are basically authoritarian, and expressed expectations of executives are more important forces for creating change than are the expectations of the subordinates.

Although change can be effective even if not started at the top, the tacit approval, if not the active support, of the top executives is extremely helpful. For this reason, the implementation of the process began at the top with heads of major departments. Individual meetings were first held with them to provide an understanding of the program and to obtain their approval, even if the support was not always wholehearted. Next, the results of the research showing the failings of the "classical" performance appraisal and the reasons for substituting WP&R were presented at the staff meetings of the department managers.

Follow-up individual coaching and counseling meetings were then held with each of the department head's immediate subordinates to obtain approval, understanding, and commitment. This combination of informational staff meetings, followed by individual coaching and counseling meetings, continued down the management hierarchy until each manager had had at least one individual meeting.

With few exceptions, changes in behavior did not occur as a result of the staff meetings. The staff meetings served to accomplish two objectives: to provide information to the staff about WP&R and to indicate to the staff that the "boss" had approved the program and expected his subordinates to implement it. The real changes in the supervisors came about as a result of the individual coaching and counseling meetings.

Relationship with Managers
Managers not only need to be involved but also need to see a "payoff" in what they are doing. As a change agent, my relationship with the managers involved three principles:

- The job-centered approach.
- The use of job-related material rather than abstract or theoretical material.
- Increased supervisory involvement and participation.

Job-centered coaching and counseling sessions are more effective in changing behavior than are either general exhortations or off-the-job training programs.

The first attempt at implementing WP&R consisted of general explanations and "exhortations" to one-half of the managers. This was not effective.

In the second attempt, two contrasting methods were used. One was individual coaching and counseling meetings with the supervisor. The other was a fourteen-week training program which I conducted for more than thirty managers, divided into two training sections.

Very little action was taken as a result of the training program. Although the principles and rationale of WP&R were carefully explained, together with the general principles of the motivation and development of subordinates, only one or two managers began using the work-planning approach. Follow-up questionnaires indicated that the managers regarded the training program as extremely helpful—but later interviews with the same managers showed that it had not resulted in implementing WP&R.

In contrast, the individual coaching and counseling sessions did result in behavior changes. The meetings centered around the manager's job, performance improvement needs of his subordinates, and ways in which he could assist his subordinates in improving their performances. I used an essentially nondirective approach in helping the manager to focus upon his job and the ways that WP&R could assist him in his work with his subordinates.

A group counseling approach was found to be successful after the managers had had an opportunity to experiment with the approach that best suited their needs and the demands of the job. These sessions were seminars conducted with small groups of supervisors who had similar jobs; they usually lasted approximately an hour and a half and were nondirective, but concentrated on the supervisors' successes and failures with work planning. The group shared experiences and picked up ideas that they could take back and try out on their jobs.

WP&R enhances the change process by giving the supervisor meaningful and relevant material rather than "theoretical" facts.

Changes in behavior presuppose prior changes in "attitudes." Changes in attitudes presuppose modifications of perceptual process. New facts must be presented or familiar facts reorganized in different ways. To the extent that the material is meaningful, relevant, and job-centered, the change in the perceptual process is made easier.

Change in subordinates presupposes change in supervisors. The individual coaching and counseling meetings were directed toward assisting the supervisor in improving the work performance of his subordinates, and the discussion remained within job-related areas, with little abstract or "theoretical" material presented.

In addition, the supervisors were provided with more specific and relevant material through the use of questionnaires which explored the way their subordinates perceived them as supervisors. The questionnaires were given anonymously to the immediate subordinates. After I analyzed them, the results were fed back only to the immediate supervisors. Because no one superior to the supervisor ever saw the results, his defensiveness was considerably reduced and he was able to take positive corrective actions rather than defending himself to higher management.

The change process needs to be tailored to the immediate situation and to provide for the increased involvement of the supervisor.

One's own facts are much more powerful instruments of change than facts or principles generated or presented by an outside "expert." A number of approaches were used to increase supervisory involvement and participation in the change-over.

No fixed form or technique was used in WP&R. A form was developed and provided, but the manager decided whether or not the form was used. This was contrary to the classic performance appraisal which has a fixed form and a fixed date. Managers were encouraged to develop their own forms or to use other approaches that appeared best to them in the job situation.

Managers were encouraged to experiment. Although I was in charge of implementing the program, I gave little direct advice to the managers. Rather, the coaching and counseling sessions, the feedback sessions after the administration of the questionnaires, and the small group seminars—these were all directed toward problem solving, with the individual manager being encouraged to work out his own solution within his unique situation.

Managers were encouraged to approach the change-over on a mutual problem-solving basis with their subordinates. This allowed some managers to remain fairly directive in their approach, while others were much more participative. Managers were not asked to make changes in their "managerial style." Instead, they were encouraged to experiment. One manager might start with only one of his subordinates, while another might shift his entire group to WP&R.

Man-Manager Relationship

The four principles in this area pertain to the man-manager relationship in the change-over from the classic performance appraisal system to WP&R:

- Preservation of the self-concept.
- Growth motives rather than deficit motives.
- Development through identification.
- Establishment of specific goals and criteria.

In a very real sense, it is line management and, more specifically, the immediate supervisor who has the responsibility for subordinate growth and development. Staff groups can assist but cannot assume the responsibility of the manager in this area.

Changes which enhance or, at least, do not disturb the self-concept are more easily accepted than changes which seek to modify or destroy it.

One of the most fundamental motives in human behavior is the preservation of the self-concept. Threats to the self-concept cause the individual to bring his defensive mechanisms into play. Actions which enhance or, at least, do not disturb the self-concept permit the individual to cooperate, to work with others, to avoid the win-lose dilemma so often seen in the classic performance appraisal discussions.

WP&R tends to reduce the win-lose dilemma. To the extent that the job requirements and criteria are discussed before it is done, both worker and manager have the opportunity to focus on the job rather than on the personality of the subordinate. WP&R seeks to change behavior, not to modify personality.

From the point of view of the manager, he sees as one of his duties and responsibilities that of "developing his subordinates." His self-concept is such that it is difficult for him to admit, even to himself, that he is not doing a good job in this area. At the same time, he is overburdened with more immediate and pressing tasks. He knew previously that the traditional performance appraisal method was not an effective tool for developing subordinates and resented the time it took. He conducted performance appraisal primarily because of the insistence of outside experts (the personnel department) and not because he had confidence in the method. At the same time, he felt a sense of guilt that the job pressures did not allow him to do as much as he wanted to do in the area of subordinate development. WP&R allows him to concentrate on getting the job done and, at the same time, provides a vehicle for subordinate development—a vehicle whose effectiveness he can easily see.

In addition, since work planning can be done differently by different managers, the manager's self-concept is enhanced. He is in control of the process, rather than the personnel department.

From the point of view of the subordinate, one of the most striking aspects of his self-concept is his desire to do a good job. But the subordinate's concept of "doing a good job" may not agree with his manager's. It may have mixtures of ego development and dependency needs; it may be distorted through projection, rationalization, and other defense structures. But he wants to do a good job as he sees it.

The criticism and "suggestions" received through the traditional performance appraisal procedures do not enhance or even coincide with the self-concept of the subordinate. Indeed, in many performance appraisal discussions, the manager is attempting, through such suggestions as, "Be more aggressive," to tear down defenses that the subordinate has spent years building up.

Conversely, the work planning approach, with the mutual involvement of manager and subordinate and the emphasis on doing the future job better rather than on criticism of past jobs, enhances rather than detracts from the self-concept. Such an approach builds on the desire of the subordinate to grow and develop on the job and to perform better in the service of his own need satisfaction.

Change processes which facilitate growth are more effective than deficit motivations.

The importance of the "ego" motives has been widely recognized. However, there is little research as to how these motives may be satisfied in industrial situations. Herzberg,[3] Huse,[4] and Myers,[5] among others, have pointed to the different roles played by "growth" and "hygienic" motives. In brief, the "growth" motives include feelings of achievement, recognition, and responsibility. These are conditions which must be present if productivity is to increase and work performance is to be improved. The deficit or hygienic motives, such as company policy, and administration, working conditions, and the like, are, of course, necessary pre-conditions, but "growth" motives are essential for improved work performance. The direct relationship between the "ego" motives of Maslow and McGregor and the "growth" motives are fairly obvious. To the extent that our needs for achievement, recognition, and responsibility are met, "ego" motives or reputation, self-confidence, and esteem are enhanced. WP&R is one of the most effective ways to develop and satisfy these growth motives.

As discussed earlier, it is a part of the manager's self-concept that he not only needs to get his job done and satisfy his boss, but he also needs to see himself fulfilling one of his additional responsibilities, that of assisting his subordinates in getting their job done better. To the extent that these two objectives are consonant, rather than conflicting, the manager's own feelings of achievement and recognition are enhanced. In the traditional performance appraisal approach, power and responsibility were shared—with the personnel department which drew up the forms and ensured, through appropriate police action, that procedures were complied with. In WP&R, power and responsibility are still shared but shared with a more appropriate source—the subordinate. As Blake[6] points out, the "best balance between power and distribution and the sense of responsibility" is when both supervisor and subordinate share as equally as possible.

WP&R facilitates communication between manager and subordinate. The subordinate has a much better idea of what it is that the manager wants. Perhaps, more importantly, he has the opportunity to influence his manager in the establishment of job goals and criteria. His ego involvement in the task is thereby enhanced. In addition, the establishment of relatively short-range goals, with clearly identified criteria, makes them more understandable and attainable. The subordinate's feelings of accomplishment and recognition are built into the program, particularly since he is put into a more active role. Goals are joint, not imposed; involvement is positive, not defensive; and the relationship with his supervisor is positive and man-to-man, rather than being that of judge and defendant. Responsibility is increased through participation and involvement in planning. Achievement is increased through clear, attainable goals. Recognition is increased through work review—in a nonpunitive approach. On the other hand, the classic performance appraisal process actually reduced the opportunity for growth motivators to operate, as the research shows.

A change process which fosters the development of identification is more effective than one which impedes the indentification process.

The process of identification, of incorporating into one's own personality the behavior and values of older and wiser persons, is a well-known psychological phenomenon. In addition, as Levinson has pointed out, it continues to be a mechanism for growth over a lifetime. As he puts it, "one of the significant differences between those who become executives and those who do not lies in the presence or absence of . . . identification models."[7]

The processes of mutually establishing job goals and criteria, mutually reviewing job progress, and mutually establishing a climate of reduced defensiveness—all these are provided in WP&R; they are also the processes that establish the best conditions for learning, growth, and development through identification.

CLIMATE FOR GROWTH

The manager has the opportunity to give the subordinate the benefit of his years of experience, and the subordinate has the opportunity to learn in an atmosphere that encourages rather than discourages the identification process. In WP&R sessions that I have observed, there appear to be four states:

1. The subordinate takes the lead in discussing his accomplishments since the last review period—as well as his failures. (However, it is vitally important to stress that these are handled in an objective, nondefensive fashion.) The manager interjects questions and comments, but it is the subordinate who is doing the appraisal, with the assistance of his manager.

2. The next state is subtly different. Plans for the next period are developed and here the manager takes the lead, although with the full participation of the subordinate.

3. In this state, the interplay between manager and subordinate is almost on an equalitarian basis, as both strive to develop fair and equitable criteria for the tasks outlined in the second stage. Communication is fully open—the manager relies on his years of experience and the subordinate relies on his more intimate knowledge of the job to develop jointly acceptable criteria and priorities.

4. The final stage is, again, subtly different. In this stage, the process of identification comes to full fruition. The subordinate tends to talk about his future job plans, and the manager gives him advice and counsel.

Throughout the entire interchange, the sense of mutual problem solving and of working toward common goals stands out in a far different fashion than one finds in the traditional performance appraisal discussion. The subordinate is exposed to the thinking, ideas, and values of his manager; perhaps just as importantly, he has an opportunity, in a nonhostile climate, to freely share his ideas with his superior—with acceptance of the good ideas, rejection of unworkable ones, and the supervisor's instructive analysis of both.

The process of identification is facilitated because the supervisor is operating much more as a "coach" or "counselor" than as a judge. In the latter role, the supervisor increased the defensiveness of his subordinate.

A learning process which specifies criteria of progress and furnishes adequate knowledge of results is more successful in creating and maintaining change than one which does not.

Learning is an active, rather than a passive, process which does not take place in a vacuum. The work planning process is built around the basic principles that better knowledge of what was expected and the results obtained would result in changed behavior on the part of both managers and subordinates.

The classic performance appraisal system gave the manager a broad, nonspecific criterion—improve subordinate performance. The necessity, however, for sticking with a rigid format and using broad, rather than individually tailored, goals reduced the manager's effectiveness. Furthermore, the managers could not see any results from their work, and they were certainly sensitive to the fact, later borne out by research, that subordinates became defensive rather than changing their behavior.

The classic appraisal program gave the subordinate vague, nonspecific criteria such as: "Be more aggressive," but little, if any, knowledge of results. The more specific goals established in work planning, the better knowledge of what was expected, and, perhaps most important, the opportunity to discuss and understand the criteria of a job in advance—these provided an opportunity for better knowledge of results.

As communications between worker and manager increased, both could see improved results. Managers found that their job was becoming easier; subordinates found their managers easier to approach. Additional contributing factors in this context were that the work planning and review processes were held on weekly, monthly or quarterly bases, thus allowing for much more immediate feedback of results than the classic annual performance appraisal.

PROGRAM RESULTS

The effectiveness of the program was examined in three different ways:

- The research conducted to determine the effectiveness of the program.
- A clinical "feel" based on observations and discussions with managers and subordinates.

- The results of a questionnaire completed on an anonymous basis, throughout the organization.

The research results have been reported previously in considerably greater detail,[8] but I will summarize them. Research was planned to find the actual changes in subordinates' behavior resulting from the program. The most important finding was that the work planning group, in specific actions taken to improve performance, showed a 72 per cent increase over the control group. (The control group cited specific actions to improve performance on 40 per cent of the items that they and their manager had discussed, while the work planning group had taken action on 70 per cent of the items.)

Both the work planning and performance appraisal groups completed "before" and "after" questionnaires. Both groups were equal in all respects in the "before" questionnaires but were quite different in their responses on the "after" questionnaires. The questionnaire measured five major areas:

1. Help received from manager in doing present job better.
2. Extent of mutual agreement on job goals.
3. Extent of improvement and development for the future.
4. Participation in job-related decisions.
5. Attitudes toward performance appraisal discussions.

On each of these, the performance appraisal control group showed no changes, but the work planning group showed positive and significant gains. (Significance, in this context, is at the statistical 5 per cent level or better.)

One measure of the low effectiveness of the classic performance appraisal system was that managers were forced by the personnel department to conduct appraisals on an annual basis. Unless they were continually reminded, the managers ignored the organization policy. Conversely, once managers became accustomed to the work planning process, they needed no policing. Instead, they kept it up on their own. In addition, they made a number of comments, such as: "I don't know how I managed without this," or, "This has really been a help to me," or, "At last, you people (personnel) are helping me rather than forcing me to do something I don't want to do."

Interviews with subordinates indicated that they now saw their supervisors more as helpers than as judges and that the subordinates' job goals were not only more clearly understood, but more important, far better accepted, primarily because they had greater participation in establishing the goals.

Limited experience in sitting in on work planning and review discussions indicated that there was much less defensiveness on the part of the subordinate and much greater self-measurement. Because of the research results, the decision was made to implement the program throughout the organization. Almost a year later, in late 1964, the compensation office asked all involved personnel in the organization to complete an anonymous questionnaire regarding salary practices. Because of the tightening of salary practices since 1961, all the questions regarding salary practices showed a drop from the previous questionnaire responses in 1961. One question, however, did not relate to salary practices. This question had to do with the extent to which "my manager encourages me to improve my job performance." In contrast to the rest of the questionnaire, this question showed almost 50 per cent improvement in the three years since 1961, indicating the effect of the work planning process.

SUMMARY

I have described the successful use of a management development program that works at all levels. Research on the classic performance appraisal system had demonstrated that it was not meeting its primary objective of improving work performance. As a result, it was decided to implement a modified management by objectives approach. Originally established on a pilot study basis, the program ultimately became successful (after an initial failure), when the implementation process was adapted to incorporate eight basic principles. Follow-up research indicated that there had been a 72 per cent increase over the control group in specific actions that the WP&R group had taken to improve performance. Other nonresearch data pointed to similar results.

Two major conclusions can be drawn:

- A change process needs to be carefully planned and implemented.
- WP&R is effective as a management development program at all levels of management in a wide variety of management positions.

References

1. E. F. Huse and E. Kay, "Improving Employee Productivity Through Work Planning," in *The Personnel Job in a Changing World,* ed. J. W. Blood (New York: American Management Association, 1964), pp. 298–315.

2. D. McGregor, "An Uneasy Look at Performance Appraisal," *Harvard Business Review,* May–June 1957, pp. 89–94.

3. F. Herzberg, *et al., The Motivation To Work* (New York: John Wiley and Sons, Inc., 1959).

4. E. F. Huse, "The Motivation of Engineers and Scientists" (unpublished study, 1962).

5. M. S. Myers, "Who Are Your Motivated Workers?" *Harvard Business Review,* Jan.–Feb. 1964, pp. 73–88.

6. R. R. Blake and J. S. Mouton, *The Managerial Grid* (Houston: Gulf Publishing Company, 1964).

7. H. Levinson, "A Psychologist Looks at Executive Development," *Harvard Business Review,* Sept.–Oct. 1962, pp. 69–74.

8. McGregor, *op. cit.,* pp. 89–94.

Selections from Quota Restriction and Goldbricking in a Machine Shop
Donald Roy

QUOTA RESTRICTION

It is "quota restriction" which has received the most attention. The Mayo researchers observed that the bank-wiring group at Western Electric limited output to a "quota" or "bogey."[1] Mayo inferred that this chopping-off of production was due to lack of understanding of the economic logics of management, using the following chain of reasoning: Insistence by management on purely economic logics, plus frequent changes in such logics in adaptation to technological change, results in lack of understanding on the part of the workers. Since the latter cannot understand the situation, they are unable to develop a nonlogical social code of a type that brought social cohesion to work groups prior to the Industrial Revolution. This inability to develop a Grade-A social code bring feelings of frustration. And, finally, frustration results in the development of a "lower social code" among the workers in opposition to the economic logics of management. And one of the symptoms of this "lower social code" is restriction of output.[2]

Mayo thus joins those who consider the economic man a fallacious conception. Now the operators in my shop made noises like economic men.

American Journal of Sociology, 1952, **57**, 5, pp. 430–432, 436–437. Reprinted by permission of the publisher, The University of Chicago Press, and the author; copyright 1952 by the University of Chicago Press.

Their talk indicated that they were canny calculators and that the dollar sign fluttered at the masthead of every machine. Their actions were not always consistent with their words; and such inconsistency calls for further probing. But it could be precisely because they were alert to their economic interests —at least to their immediate economic interests—that the operators did not exceed their quotas. It might be inferred from their talk that they did not turn in excess earnings because they felt that to do so would result in piecework price cuts; hence the consequences would be either reduced earnings from the same amount of effort expended or increased effort to maintain the take-home level.

When I was hired, a personnel department clerk assured me that the radial-drill operators were averaging $1.25 an hour on piecework. He was using a liberal definition of the term "averaging." Since I had had no previous machine-shop experience and since a machine would not be available for a few days, I was advised to spend some time watching Jack Starkey, a radial-drill man of high rank in seniority and skill.

One of Starkey's first questions was, "What have you been doing?" When I said I had worked in a Pacific Coast shipyard at a rate of pay over $1.00 an hour, Starkey exclaimed, "Then what are you doing in this place?" When I replied that averaging $1.25 an hour wasn't bad, he exploded:

"Averaging, you say! Averaging?"

"Yeah, on the average. I'm an average guy; so I ought to make my buck and a quarter. That is, after I get onto it."

"Don't you know," cried Starkey angrily, "that $1.25 an hour is the *most* we can make, even when we *can* make more! And most of the time we can't even make that! Have you ever worked on piecework before?"

"No."

"I can see that! Well, what do you suppose would happen if I turned in $1.25 an hour on these pump bodies?"

"Turned in? You mean if you actually did the work?"

"I mean if I actually did the work and turned it in!"

"They'd have to pay you, wouldn't they? Isn't that the agreement?"

"Yes! They'd pay me—once! Don't you know that if I turned in $1.50 an hour on these pump bodies tonight, the whole Goddamned Methods Department would be down here tomorrow? And they'd retime this job so quick it would make your head swim! And when they retimed it, they'd cut the price in half! And I'd be working for 85 cents an hour instead of $1.25!"

From this initial exposition of Starkey's to my last day at the plant I was subject to warnings and predictions concerning price cuts. Pressure was the heaviest from Joe Mucha, day man on my machine, who shared my job repertoire and kept a close eye on my production. On November 14, the day after my first attained quota, Mucha advised:

> Don't let it go over $1.25 an hour, or the time-study man will be right down here! And they don't waste time, either! They watch the records like a hawk! I got ahead, so I took it easy for a couple of hours."

> Joe told me that I had made $10.01 yesterday and warned me not to go over $1.25 an hour. He told me to figure the set-ups and the time on each operation very carefully so that I would not total over $10.25 in any one day.

Jack Starkey defined the quota carefully but forcefully when I turned in $10.50 for one day, or $1.31 an hour.

> Jack Starkey spoke to me after Joe left. "What's the matter? Are you trying to upset the apple cart?"

> Jack explained in a friendly manner that $10.50 was too much to turn in, even on an old job.

> "The turret-lathe men can turn in $1.35," said Jack, "but their rate is 90 cents, and ours 85 cents."

> Jack warned me that the Methods Department could lower their prices on any job, old or new, by changing the fixture slightly, or changing the size of drill. According to Jack, a couple of operators (first and second shift on the same drill) got to competing with each other to see how much they could turn in. They got up to $1.65 an hour, and the price was cut in half. And from then on they had to run that job themselves, as none of the other operators would accept the job.

> According to Jack, it would be all right for us to turn in $1.28 or $1.29 an hour, when it figured out that way, but it was not all right to turn in $1.30 an hour.

> Well, now I know where the maximum is—$1.29 an hour.

Starkey's beliefs concerning techniques of price-cutting were those of the shop. Leonard Bricker, an old-timer in the shop, and Willie, the stock-chaser, both affirmed that management, once bent on slashing a piecework price, would stop at nothing.

> "Take these $1.25 jobs. One guy will turn in $1.30 an hour one day. Then another fellow will turn in, say, $1.31 or $1.32. Then the first fellow will go up to $1.35. First thing you know they'll be up to $1.50, and bang! They'll tear a machine to pieces to change something to cut a price!"

> In the washroom, before I started work, Willie commented on my gravy job, the pedestals.

"The Methods Department is going to lower the price," he said. "There was some talk today about it."

"I hope they don't cut it too much," I said. "I suppose they'll make some change in the jigs?"

"They'll change the tooling some way. Don't worry, when they make up their minds to lower a price, they'll find a way to do it!"[3]

The association of quota behavior with such expressions about price-cutting does not prove a causal connection. Such a connection could be determined only by instituting changes in the work situation that would effect a substantial reduction of "price-cut fear" and by observing the results of such changes.

Even if it should be thus indicated that there is a causal relationship, testing of alternative hypotheses would still be necessary. It may be, but it is not yet known, that "economic determinism" may account for quota restriction in the shop investigated. It may also be, but it is not known, that factors such as Mayo's "failure to understand the economic logics of management" are influential. . . .

PIECEWORK GOLDBRICKING

On "gravy jobs" the operators earned a quota, then knocked off. On "stinkers" they put forth only minimal effort; either they did not try to achieve a turn-in equal to the base wage rate or they deliberately slowed down. Jobs were defined as "good" and "bad" jobs, not in terms of the effort or skill necessary to making out at a bare base-rate level, but of the felt attainability of a substantial premium, i.e., 15 cents an hour or more. Earnings of $1.00 an hour in relation to a $1.25 quota and an 85-cent base rate were considered worth the effort, while earnings of 95 cents an hour were not.

The attitude basic to the goldbricking type of restriction was expressed succinctly thus: "They're not going to get much work out of me for this pay!"

Complaints about low piecework prices were chronic and universal in this shop.

> The turret lathe men discussed the matter of making out, one man stating that only half the time could a man make 84 cents day rate on a machine. It was agreed: "What's the use of pushing when it's hard even to make day rate?"

His 50–50 estimate was almost equal to my own experience of 49.6–50.4. Pessimistic though it was, it was less so than usual statements on the subject:

> I asked Jackson if he was making out, and he gave me the usual answer, "No!"

> "They ask me how I'm making out, and I always say, 'O.K.' As far as

I'm concerned, I'm making out O.K. If they start asking me further, I'll tell them that this place stinks.

"The day man isn't making out either. We get a lot of little jobs, small lots. It's impossible to make out when you're getting small jobs all the time."

Joe was working on a new job, time study on some small pieces tonight. I asked him, "Something good?" and he replied, "Nothing is good any more!"

There seemed to be no relation between a man's ability to earn and his behavior on a "stinker." That the men who most frequently earned the quota goldbricked like the rest on poor jobs appears in the following extracts:

Al McCann (the man who made quota most often) said that he gives a job a trial, and if it is no good he takes his time. He didn't try to make out on the chucks tonight.

Joe Mucha, my day man, said of a certain job: "I did just one more than you did. If they don't like it they can do them themselves. To hell with them. I'm not going to bust my ass on stuff like this."

Old Peter, the multiple drill man, said "I ran some pieces for 25 minutes to see how many I could turn out. I turned out 20 at 1½ cents apiece (72 cents an hour). So I smoke and take it easy. I can't make out; so _____it."

I notice that when Ed Sokolsky, one of the better operators on the line, is working on an operation he cannot make out on, he does not go at his task with vigor. He either pokes around or leaves his machine for long periods of time; and Paul (set-up man) seems always to be looking for him. Steve (supt.) is always bellowing, "Where in hell is Ed?" or "Come on, Ed, let's have some production around here!" Tonight I heard him admonishing Ed again, "Now I want you to work at that machine 'til three o'clock, do you understand?"

Mike Koszyk, regarded as a crack operator: The price was a poor one (a few cents a hundred) and the job tough. Mike had turned out only 9 pieces in 3 hours. When Mike takes his time, he really takes his time!

According to Al, Jack Starkey turned in 40 cents an hour today on his chuck parts. Al laughed, saying, "I guess Jack didn't like this job."

Gus Schmidt, regarded as the best speed-drill operator on the second shift, was timed early in the evening on a job, and given a price of $1.00 per 100 for reaming one hole, chamfering both sides of three holes, and filing burrs on one end of one hole. All that for one cent!

"To hell with them," said Gus.

He did not try to make out.

The possibility of covering "day rate" was ordinarily no spur to the machine operator to bestir himself on a job. A remark of Mucha's was characteristic: "I could have made out," he said, "but why kill yourself for day rate?"

Average hourly earnings of less or even a little more than $1.00 an hour were usually thrown into the "day-rate" category.

Joe Mucha drilled 36 of the bases (at $8.80 per 100) today. "The most I'll ever do until they retime this job is 40," he said. "Do you know, they expect us to do 100? Why, I wouldn't bust my ass to do 50, for $8.00, when day rate is almost that!"

McCann was put to drilling some pieces at $6.50 per 100. I noticed him working furiously and walked over to see what he was doing. He asked me to figure out how many pieces at 6½ cents he had to turn out per hour to make $1.20. When I told him 18 or 19 he said, "I give up," and immediately slowed down.

A few minutes later I met him in the washroom, and he said, "I wouldn't work that hard for eight or ten hours even if I could make out. I thought I'd try it for an hour or so and see what I could do."

He figures he was making 95 cents an hour. At lunch time he said that he had averaged $1.00 an hour for the two hours and thought maybe he would try to make out.

Notes

1. Fritz Roethlisberger and J. Dickson, *Management and the Worker* (Cambridge: Harvard University Press, 1939).

2. Elton Mayo, *Human Problems of an Industrial Civilization* (New York: Macmillan Co., 1938), pp. 119–21.

3. John Mills, onetime research engineer in telephony and for five years engaged in personnel work for the Bell Telephone Company, has recently indicated the possibility that there were factors in the bank-wiring room situation that the Mayo group failed to detect: "Reward is supposed to be in direct proportion to production. Well, I remember the first time I ever got behind that fiction. I was visiting the Western Electric Company, which had a reputation of never cutting a piece rate. It never did; if some manufacturing process was found to pay more than seemed right for the class of labor employed on it—if, in other words, the rate-setters had misjudged—that particular part was referred to the engineers for redesign, and then a new rate was set on the new part. Workers, in other words, were paid as a class, supposed to make about so much a week with their best efforts and, of course, less for less competent efforts" (*The Engineer in Society* [New York: D. Van Nostrand & Co., 1946], p. 93).

A Model for Subverting Management by Objectives
Lee H. Hansen

A lot has been written recently about management by objectives (MBO), a process for supervising and integrating human behavior in an organization. The literature abounds with theoretical excursions, "do-it-yourself" instructions, expert critiques, and testimonials. What appears to be missing, however, is a plan for participant subversion: a design for rendering the concept harmless. Hopefully, these comments will rectify that omission.

Let me say at the outset that I am not an "official" MBO expert. I don't give talks on the subject, nor do I run workshops. What I offer is two years of experience observing an organization implement the concept. During those two years I have watched some of my colleagues unwittingly develop an MBO subversion model that is finally of sufficient quality to be exportable. In the remaining paragraphs I would like to describe that model.

The model operates in six phases: (1) lampoon-tation, (2) concept isolation, (3) Gandhian passive resistance, (4) overhead magnification, (5) feigned paranoia, and (6) prophetic self-fulfillment. Each phase includes a set of operations. All phases operate simultaneously. Now for the model:

1. *Lampoon-tation.* Lampoon-tation begins early in the subversion model, perhaps as early as the readiness and inservice phase of MBO. A likely beginning point is phrase substitution for the acronym "MBO." "Meandering by Objectives" or "Messing Before Operating" stresses its time-wasting qualities. "Missing by Objectives" points up its futility. "Muddling Between Opportunities" connotes its confusion-generating tendencies. These phrases should be used in gracious jest at every opportunity—in a phone call, as a "P.S." to a memo, and in conversation. It is a good rule of thumb, however, to disarm your audience first by noting in the sincerest tone your interest in MBO. These acronym substitutes also make good bulletin board graffiti.

Lampoon-tation can also be carried out effectively at meetings or luncheons. First, establish with your audience a "bland" level of support. Then make funny quips: "What are we going to have next year?" Kid the adminis-

Phi Delta Kappan, **55**, 4, December 1973, pp. 260–261. Reprinted by permission of Phi Delta Kappa.

trator who has been given the responsibility of implementing the concept, e.g., Frank's Folly or Joe's Road Show. Enveloping such quips in a statement of support diffuses your opposition.

2. *Concept isolation.* Isolating the MBO concept from the rest of the management process is a second phase of the subversion model. The quickest way to isolate the MBO process is extracurricularization, i.e., make it something else that you have to do in addition to your job. And gripe about that fact. Don't let on that you realize it can be a way of doing your job. Make it an extra burden. Plan to devote only 10% of your time to it (under protest).

A second isolation strategy is deification. Make MBO a legalistic religion. Develop ritual: all reviews the first week in October, all contracts in this form, all evaluation using this set of strategies. Demand that all MBO processes be written down and committed to official policy. Build out flexibility so that the MBO process cannot change as the needs of the organization change. It will soon become history.

A third isolation strategy is preoccupation. The intent of this strategy is to get MBO proponents so preoccupied with other issues that MBO implementation suffers. There are several ways of doing this. Stimulating crisis management situations causes MBO proponents not only to forget about the concept for the moment, it also causes them to model dysfunctional, anti-MBO behaviors themselves. And you know the power of behavior modification. Introducing attractive change substitutes like PPBS or MIS will often serve the same purpose, especially if a number of subversives group together to call for it. What top administrator can resist the thought of implementing an exciting new idea when he is not faced with resistance from below? Intellectualizing MBO also works. Don't challenge MBO directly. Talk it to death. Question if "we" have the right concept of MBO. Suggest that "you" have a view of the MBO process that is entirely different from the "official view." Put the MBO proponents on the defensive—explaining, clarifying, defending. Force them to behave like experts under attack. They will soon go away.

3. *Gandhian passive resistance.* Gandhian passive resistance is the safest yet effective phase of the six. It can be accomplished in a number of ways. First and foremost is the "broken wing" act. Make believe that you don't understand the MBO concept. Work hard at it but show little growth. Write a contract that is incomprehensible, eagerly accept help, then produce something equally incomprehensible. Such behavior is bound to wean proponents from the MBO concept.

"Mute discipleship" is a second passive resistance strategy. Its scenario is simple. Follow your supervisor blindly; ask him no questions; offer him no suggestions; give him no feedback. Convince him silently that he is an MBO expert. Let him wander about blindly until he is lost; then he too will join the subversive movement.

The simplest strategy is to "play it safe." Limit yourself to safe but innocuous MBO goals that you can't miss, but which offer little help for the organization. Above all, don't commit exciting and risky ideas to MBOs. Try to implement these outside the sphere of MBO; give the process a bland image.

Still another way to resist passively is through a well-planned review session. Don't come prepared; above all, don't help to structure the conference. Leave your supervisor with the impression that this is his responsibility. But bring in a lot of material—trivia, if possible. Don't sort it out; jump around. Assume your supervisor knows things he in fact does not. Bring an hour's worth of material to a half-hour conference. All the while, appear breathless and pleased with the MBO process. Such behavior will plunge a supervisor to the depths of frustration and have him on your side in no time.

4. *Overhead magnification.* This phase is easiest of all to implement, since MBO proponents themselves will unwittingly cause most of the overhead magnification. Overhead as used here refers quite simply to the organizational energy that is consumed in maintaining the MBO process. An easy way to subvert the MBO process is to so magnify the overhead that the cost exceeds the benefit. Several strategies will complete what MBO proponents have already started. An important one is to reduce everything to paper. Insist on documenting everything—in triplicate. Send "cc"s to as many as possible. Jam the communications network. It is particularly important to plague your immediate supervisor with memos, requests, reports, notes, and carbons. Add to the realism by labeling each communication "For Goal No. 3" or "With reference to Goal No. 1." Then he will have to look it up to know what you are talking about.

Encouraging your supervisor to make the process complex and pseudosophisticated is another ploy to increase overhead. Suggest various kinds of forms for gathering evidence: "telephone call" records, lengthy weekly progress reports, or meeting summaries. Get him to compile everyone's goals into a total book—to be printed. Demand complicated rating formulas. Above all, ritualize it.

5. *Feigned paranoia.* Feigning paranoia, phase five, may work, too. Remember, however, that such behavior is an expression of pain and as such may be confused by MBO proponents as healthy dissonance. The phase works best as a series of crises. A crisis can be stimulated by the "sacrificial lamb" act. Suddenly, act as though you are a lamb being led to the MBO slaughter. Blame your failures on it; give the concept breath—humanize it. Then appear defenseless before it. Flail about as though victimized. This is particularly effective after a review session.

A second crisis can be precipitated by demanding that the process build out supervisor judgment, particularly when it comes time for salary ratings. This is an ideal crisis because it poses an insoluble problem. Promote scientification and objectification of the process. Look suspicious; sound suspicious.

Point up all of the theory X behavior around. Note how everyone else is trying to steal your credit. Tell others that it is a plot to lower administrative salaries. Yell loud enough so it appears that the idea is tearing the organization apart.

6. *Prophetic self-fulfillment.* The final phase is among the strongest in the subversion model. It rests on two strong premises: (1) the power of negative thinking, and (2) the notion that saying it's so makes it so—especially if you say it often enough. Here there is a single overriding strategy. Keep the informal communication system filled with the powers of suggestion. Most subversives rely on rumor and incantation. Rumor is always quite effective. For example, suggest that "so-and-so" (who has much more status than I) hates MBO. Or, perhaps, start a rumor that teachers are next. An even better one is to suggest that the chief proponent and ramrod of MOBs will be leaving at the end of the year. Incantation also works. Mention as frequently as possible in acceptable circles that "MBO is sick" or "MBO is dying." Never blame MBO per se. Blame the implementation model or the inservice or the evaluation. If you can, get the members of your audience to repeat the words. A question like "Do you think MBO is just sick or is it dying?" seldom misses.

There you have it: a model for subverting the MBO process in any educational organization. It may not completely destroy an exciting idea; but it sure will slow it down.

SELECTION AND TRAINING

Title 41–
Public Contracts and Property Management:
Part 60–3–Employee Testing and
Other Selection Procedures
J. D. Hodgson

On April 21, 1971, notice of the proposed rule making was published in the *Federal Register* (36 F.R. 7532) with regard to amending Chapter 60 of Title 41 of the Code of Federal Regulations by adding a new Part 60–3, dealing with employee testing and other selection procedures. Interested persons were given 30 days in which to submit written comments, suggestions, or objections regarding the proposed amendments.

Having considered all relevant material submitted, I have decided to, and do hereby amend Chapter 60 of Title 41 of the Code of Federal Regulations by adding a new Part 60–3, reading as follows:

Sec.

The Federal Register, **36,** 192, p. 19307.

Authority: The provisions of this Part 60–3 are issued under secs. 201, 205, 206(a), 301, 303(a), 303(b), and 403(b) of Executive Order 11246, as amended, 30 F.R. 12319; 32 F.R. 14303; 34 F.R. 12986; § 60–1.2 of Part 60–1 of this chapter.

60–3.1 Purpose and Scope

a) This order is based on the belief that properly validated and standardized employee selection procedures can significantly contribute to the implementation of nondiscriminatory personal policies, as required by Executive Order 11246, as amended. It is also recognized that professionally developed tests, when used in conjunction with other tools of personnel assessment and complemented by sound programs of job design, may significantly aid in the development and maintenance of an efficient work force and, indeed, aid in the utilization and conservation of human resource generally.

b) 1. An examination of charges of discrimination filed with the Office of Federal Contract Compliance and an evaluation of the results of its compliance activities has revealed a decided increase in total test usage and a marked increase in testing practices which have discriminatory effects. In many cases, contractors have come to rely almost exclusively on tests as the basis for making the decision to hire, to promote, to transfer, to train, or to retain with the result that candidates are selected or rejected on the basis of test scores. Where tests are so used, minority candidates frequently experience disproportionately high rates of rejection by failing to attain score levels that have been established as minimum standards for qualification.

2. It has also become clear that in many instances contractors are using tests as the basis for employment decisions without evidence that they are valid predictors of employee job performance. Where evidence in support of presumed relationships between test performance and job behavior is lacking, the possibility of discrimination in the application of test results must be recognized. A test lacking demonstrated validity, i.e., having no known significant relationship to job behavior, and yielding lower scores for classes protected by Executive Order 11246, as amended, may result in the rejection of many who have necessary qualifications for successful work performance.

c) Section 202 of Executive Order 11246, as amended, requires each Government contractor and subcontractor to take affirmative action to insure that he will not discriminate against any employee or applicant for employment because of race, color, religion, sex, or national origin. This order is designed to serve as a set of standards for contractors and subcontractors subject to Executive Order 11246, as amended, in determining whether their use of tests conforms with the requirements of the Executive Order.[1]

60–3.2 Test Defined

For the purpose of this order, the term "test" is defined as any paper-and-pencil or performance measure used as a basis for any employment decision. This order applies, for example, to ability tests which are designed to measure eligibility for hire, transfer, promotion, training, or retention. This definition includes, but is not restricted to, measures of general intelligence, mental ability and learning ability; specific intellectual abilities; mechanical, clerical and other aptitudes; dexterity and coordination; knowledge and proficiency; occupational and other interests; and attitudes, personality or temperament. The term "test" also covers all other formal, scored, quantified or standardized techniques of assessing job suitability including, for example, personal history and background requirements which are specifically used as a basis for qualifying or disqualifying applicants or employees, specific educational or work history requirements, scored interviews, biographical information blanks, interviewers' rating scales and scored application forms. The term "test" shall not include other selection techniques discussed in § 60–3.13.

60–3.3 Violation of Executive Order

A contractor regularly using a test which has adversely affected the opportunities of minority persons or women for hire, transfer, promotion, training or retention violates Executive Order 11246, as amended, unless he can demonstrate that he has validated the test pursuant to the requirements of this part.

60–3.4 Evidence of Validity; Meaning of Technically Feasible

a) Each contractor using tests to select from among candidates for hire, transfer, promotion, training, or retention shall have available for inspection evidence that the test is being used in a manner which does not violate § 60–3.3.

b) Where technically feasible, a test should be validated for each minority group with which it is used; that is, any differential rejection rates that may exist, based on a test, must be relevant to performance on the jobs in question.

c) The term "technically feasible" as used in paragraph (b) of this section and elsewhere in this part means having or obtaining a sufficient number of minority individuals to achieve findings of statistical and practical significance, the opportunity to obtain unbiased job performance criteria, etc. It is the responsibility of the persons claiming absence of technical feasibility to demonstrate evidence of this absence.

1. Evidence of a test's validity should consist of empirical data demonstrating that the test is predictive or of significantly correlated with important elements of work behavior which comprise or are relevant to the job or jobs for which candidates are being evaluated.

2. If job progression structures and seniority provisions are so established that new employees will probably, within a reasonable period of time and in a great majority of cases, progress to a higher level, it may be considered that candidates are being evaluated for jobs at that higher level. However, where job progression is not so nearly automatic, or the time span is such that higher level jobs or employees' potential may be expected to change in significant ways, it shall be considered that candidates are being evaluated for a job at or near the entry level. This point is made to underscore the principle that attainment of or performance at a higher level job is a relevant criterion in validating employment tests only when there is a high probability that persons employed will in fact attain that higher level job within a reasonable period of time.

3. Where a test is to be used in different units of a multiunit organization and no significant differences exist between units, jobs, and applicant populations, evidence obtained in one unit may suffice for the others. Similarly, where the validation process requires the collection of data throughout a multiunit organization, evidence of validity specific to each unit may not be required. There may also be instances where evidence of validity is appropriately obtained from other companies in the same industry. Both in this instance and in the use of data collected throughout a multiunit organization, evidence of validity specific to each unit or company may not be required provided that no significant differences exist between companies units, jobs, and applicant populations.

60–3.5 Minimum Standards for Validation

a) For the purpose of satisfying the requirements of this part, empirical evidence in support of a test's validity must be based on studies employing generally accepted procedures for determining criterion-related validity, such as those described in "Standards for Educational and Psychological Tests and Manuals," published by the American Psychological Association, 1200 17th Street NW., Washington, DC 20036. Evidence of content or construct validity, as defined in that publication, may also be appropriate where criterion-related validity is not feasible. However, evidence for content or construct validity should be accompanied by sufficient information from job analyses to demonstrate the relevance of the content, in the case of job knowledge or proficiency tests, or the construct, in the case of trait measures. Evidence of content validity alone will be acceptable for well-developed tests that consist of suitable samples of the essential knowledge, skills or behaviors composing the job in question. The types of knowledge, skills or behaviors contemplated here do not include those which can be acquired in a brief orientation to the job. In the case of personal history, background, educational, and work history requirements which are specifically used as a basis for qualifying or disqualifying applicants (see § 60–3.2) evidence of content or construct validity may be sufficient.

b) Although any appropriate validation strategy may be used to develop such empirical evidence, the following minimum standards, as applicable, must be met in the research approach and in the presentation of results which constitute evidence of validity:

1. Where a validity study is conducted in which tests are administered to applicants, with criterion data collected later, the sample of subjects must be representative of the normal or typical candidates group for the job or jobs in question. This further assumes that the applicant sample is representative of the minority population available for the job or jobs in question in the local labor market. Where a validity study is conducted in which tests are administered to present employees, the sample must be representative of the minority groups currently included in the applicant population. If it is not technically feasible to include minority employees in validation studies conducted on the present work force, the conduct of a validation study without minority candidates does not relieve any contractor of his subsequent obligation for validation when inclusion of minority candidates becomes technically feasible.

2. Tests must be administered and scored under controlled and standardized conditions, with proper safeguards to protect the security of test scores and to insure that scores do not enter into any judgments of employee adequacy that are to be used as criterion measures.

3. The work behaviors or other criteria of employee adequacy which the test is intended to predict or identify must be fully described; and, additionally, in the case of rating techniques, the appraisal form(s) and instructions to the rater(s) must be included as a part of the validation evidence. Such criteria may include measures other than actual work proficiency, such as training time, supervisory ratings, regularity of attendance and tenure. Whatever criteria are used they must represent major or critical work behaviors as revealed by careful job analyses.

4. In view of the possibility of bias inherent in subjective evaluations, supervisory rating techniques should be carefully developed, and the ratings should be closely examined for evidence of bias. In addition, minorities or women might obtain unfairly low performance criterion scores for reasons other than supervisors' prejudice, as, when, as new employees, they have had less opportunity to learn job skills. In general, all criteria must be examined

to ensure freedom from factors which would unfairly depress the scores of minority groups or women.

5. Data must be generated and results separately reported for minority and nonminority groups wherever technically feasible. Where a minority group is sufficiently large to constitute an identifiable factor in the local labor market, but validation data have not been developed and presented separately for that group, evidence of satisfactory validity based on other groups will be regarded as only provisional compliance with this order pending separate validation of the test for the minority group in question (see § 60–3.9). A test which is differentially valid may be used in groups for which it is valid but not for those in which it is not valid. In this regard, where a test is valid for two groups but one group characteristically obtains higher test scores than the other without a corresponding difference in job performance, test results must be applied so as to predict the same probability of job success in both groups.

c) In assessing the utility of a test the following considerations will be applicable:

1. The relationship between the test and at least one relevant criterion must be statistically significant. This ordinarily means that the relationship should be sufficiently high as to have a probability of no more than 1 to 20 to have occurred by change. However, the use of a single test as the sole selection device, when that test is valid against only one component of job performance, will be scrutinized closely.

2. In addition to statistical significance, the practical significance of the relationship between the test and criterion should also be considered. The magnitude of the relationship needed for practical significance or usefulness is affected by several factors, including:

i) The larger the proportion of applicants who are hired for or placed on the job, the higher the relationship needs to be in order to be practically useful. Conversely, a relatively low relationship may prove useful when proportionately few job vacancies are available;

ii) The larger the proportion of applicants who become satisfactory employees when not selected on the basis of the test, the higher the relationship needs to be between the test and a criterion of job success for the test to be practically useful. Conversely, a relatively low relationship may prove useful when proportionately few applicants turn out to be satisfactory;

iii) The smaller the economic and human risks involved in hiring an unqualified applicant relative to the risks entailed in rejecting a qualified applicant, the greater the relationship needs to be in order to be practically useful. Conversely, a relatively low relationship may prove useful when the former risks are relatively high.

60–3.6 Presentation of Evidence of Validity

The presentation of the results of a validation study must include statistical and, where appropriate, graphic representations of the relationships between the test and the criteria, permitting judgments of the test's utility in making predictions of future work behavior. (See § 60–3.5(c), concerning assessing utility of a test.) Average scores for all tests and criteria must be reported for all relevant subgroups, including minority and nonminority groups where differential validation is required. Whenever statistical adjustments are made in validity results for less than perfect reliability or for restriction of score range in the test or the criterion, or both, the supporting evidence from the validation study must be presented in detail. Furthermore, for each test that is to be established or continued as an operational employee selection instrument, as a result of the validation study, the minimum acceptable cutoff (passing) score, if any, on the test must be reported. It is expected that each operational cutoff score will be reasonable and consistent with normal expectations of proficiency within the work force or group on which the study was conducted.

60–3.7 Use of Other Validity Studies

In cases where the validity of a test cannot be determined pursuant to §§ 60–3.4 and 60–3.5 (e.g., the number of subjects is less than that required for a technically adequate validation study, or an appropriate criterion measure cannot be developed), evidence from validity studies conducted in other organizations, such as that reported in test manuals and professional literature, may be considered acceptable when: (a) The studies pertain to jobs which are comparable (i.e., have basically the same task elements), and (b) there are no major differences in contextual variables or sample composition which are likely to affect significantly validity. Any contractor citing evidence from other validity studies as evidence of test validity for his own jobs must demonstrate that he meets requirements in paragraphs (a) and (b) of this section.

60–3.8 Assumption of Validity

a) Under no circumstances will the general reputation of a test, its author or its publisher, or casual reports of test utility be accepted in lieu of evidence of validity. Specifically ruled out are: Assumptions of validity based on test names or descriptive labels; all forms of promotional literature; data bearing on the frequency of a test's usage; testimonial statements of sellers, users, or consultants; and other nonempirical or anecdotal accounts of testing practices or testing outcomes.

b) Although professional supervision of testing activities may help greatly to insure technically sound and nondiscriminatory test usage, such involvement alone shall not be regarded as constituting satisfactory evidence of test validity.

60–3.9 Continued Use of Tests
Under certain conditions where validation is required by this order, a contractor may be permitted to continue the use of a test which is not at the moment fully supported by the required evidence of validity. If, for example, evidence of criterion-related validity in a specific setting is technically feasible and required but not yet obtained, the use of the test may continue: *Provided:* (a) The contractor can cite substantial evidence of validity as described in § 60–3.7 (a) and (b); and (b) he has in progress validation procedures which are designed to produce, within a reasonable time, the additional data required. It is expected also that the contractor may have to alter or suspend test cutoff scores so that score ranges broad enough to permit the identification of criterion-related validity will be obtained.

60–3.10 Employment Agencies and State Employment Services
A contractor utilizing the services of any private employment agency, state employment agency or any other person, agency or organization engaged in the selection or evaluation of personnel which makes its selections or evaluations of personnel wholly or partially on the basis of the results of any test shall have available evidence that any test used by such person, agency or organization is in conformance with the requirements of this order.

60–3.11 Disparate Treatment
The principle of disparate or unequal treatment must be distinguished from the concept of test validation. Disparate treatment, for example, occurs where members of a group protected by Executive Order 11246, as amended, have been denied the same opportunities for hire, transfer or promotion as have been made available to other employees or applicants. Those employees or applicants who can be shown to have been denied equal treatment because of prior discriminatory practices or policies must at least be afforded the same opportunities as had existed for other employees or applicants during the period of discrimination. Thus, no new test or other employee selection standard can be imposed upon an individual or class of individuals protected by Executive Order 11246, as amended, who, but for this prior discrimination, would have been granted the opportunity to qualify under less stringent selection standards previously in force.

60–3.12 Retesting
Contractors should provide an opportunity for retesting and reconsideration to earlier "failure" candidates who have availed themselves of more training

or experience. In particular, if any applicant or employee during the course of an interview or other employment procedure claims more education or experience, that individual should be retested.

60–3.13 Other Selection Techniques

Selection techniques other than tests, as defined in § 60–3.2, may be improperly used so as to have the effect of discriminating against minority groups or women. Such techniques include, but are not restricted to, unscored or casual interviews, unscored application forms and unscored personal history and background requirements not used uniformly as a basis for qualifying or disqualifying applicants. Where there are data suggesting employment discrimination, the contractor may be called upon to present evidence concerning the validity of his unscored procedures regardless of whether tests are also used, the evidence of validity being of the same types referred to in §§ 60–3.4 and 60–3.5. Data suggesting the possibility of discrimination exists, for example, when there are higher rates of rejection of minority candidates than of nonminority candidates for the same job or group of jobs or when there is an underutilization of minority group personnel among present employees in certain types of jobs. If the contractor is unable or unwilling to perform such validation studies, he has the option of adjusting employment procedures so as to eliminate the conditions suggestive of employment discrimination.

60–3.14 Affirmative Action

Nothing in this order shall be interpreted as diminishing a contractor's obligation under both title VII of the Civil Rights Act of 1964 and Executive Order 11246, as amended, to take affirmative action to ensure that applicants or employees are treated without regard to race, color, religion, sex, or national origin. Specifically, where substantially equally valid tests can be used for a given purpose, the contractor will be expected to use the test or battery of tests which will have the least adverse effect on the employment opportunities of minorities or women. Further, the use of tests which have been validated pursuant to this order does not relieve contractors of their obligation to take affirmative action to afford employment and training opportunities to members of classes protected by Executive Order 11246, as amended.

60–3.15 Recordkeeping

Each contractor shall maintain, and submit upon request, such records and documents relating to the nature and use of tests, the validation of tests, and test results, as may be required under the provisions of this chapter and under the orders and directives issued by the Office of Federal Contract Compliance.

60–3.16 Sanctions

    a)   The use of tests and other selection techniques by contractors as qualification standards for hire, transfer, promotion, training or retention shall be examined carefully for possible indications of noncompliance with the requirements of Executive Order 11246, as amended.

b) A determination of noncompliance pursuant to the provisions of this part shall be grounds for the imposition of sanctions under Executive Order 11246, as amended.

60–3.17 Exemptions

a) Requests for exemptions from this order or any part thereof must be made in writing to the Director, Office of Federal Contract Compliance, Washington, D.C., and must contain a statement of reasons supporting the request. Such request shall be forwarded through and shall contain the endorsement of the head of the contracting agency. Exemption may be granted for good cause.

b) The requirements of this part shall not apply to any contract when the head of the contracting agency determines that such contract is essential to the national security and that its award without complying with such requirements is necessary to the national security. Upon making such a determination, the agency head will notify the Director, in writing, within 30 days.

60–3.18 Effect of This Part on Other Rules and Regulations

a) All orders, instructions, regulations, and memoranda of the Secretary of Labor, other officials of the Department of Labor and contracting agencies are hereby superseded to the extent that they are inconsistent herewith.

b) Nothing in this part shall be interpreted to diminish the present contract compliance review and complaint investigation programs.

Effective date. This part shall become effective on the date of its publication in the *Federal Register* (10–2–71).

Signed at Washington, D.C., this 27th day of September 1971.

J. D. Hodgson,
Secretary of Labor.

[FR Doc. 71–14457 Filed 10–1–71; 8:46 a.m]

Notes

1. Except for the necessary differences in language arising from the different legal authority of the two agencies and for reasons of clarity, this order and the Guidelines on Employee Selection Procedures, issued earlier by the Equal Employment Opportunity Commission (35 F.R. 12333, Aug. 1, 1970) are intended to impose the same basic requirements on persons and contractors covered by each of them.

Validity of Aptitude Tests for the "Hardcore Unemployed"
James F. Gavin and David L. Toole

In response to former President Johnson's request to the American business community to develop better employment programs for hiring the "hardcore" unemployed (HCU), a number of corporations and businesses joined together to form the National Alliance of Businessmen (NAB). Since its inception, the NAB, a part of an overall government program known as JOBS (Job Opportunities in the Business Sector), has been responsible for returning large numbers of the HCU to productive employment. However, despite the overall success of the program, relatively high rates of turnover of the HCU in some corporations still cause concern among selection personnel.

While training programs to upgrade the basic skills of the HCU have been somewhat effective in reducing turnover, many corporations have purposely avoided the use of aptitude tests as an aid in the HCU selection process. Some justification for this practice can be found in recent publications discussing the problem of differential validity of selection tests for minority and nonminority employees (Bartlett and O'Leary, 1969; Campion and Freihoff, 1970; Einhorn and Bass, 1969; Kirkpatrick et al., 1968; Krug, 1966; Lopez, 1966). However, as a result of this, little information concerning the relationship of tests to job performance of the HCU has appeared in the literature (Kirkpatrick et al., 1968).

The purpose of this predictive validity study was to determine, for a sample of HCU, whether measures of verbal and arithmetic skills were related to measures of job behavior.

PROCEDURE

As part of an evaluation of an eight week "Basic Skills Training" program designed specifically for newly-hired, airline HC employees, a test battery was administered to all Basic Skills Training classes conducted between September 1968 and November 1969. A total of 35 training classes ranging in size from three to 16 individuals were held during this period at nine domestic airport locations.

The pre-test battery, consisting of a measure of verbal skills and a measure of arithmetic aptitude, was administered to each trainee prior to training.

Personal Psychology, **26,**1, 1973, pp. 139–146. Reprinted by permission of the publisher.

Following eight weeks of training, the post-test battery, alternate forms of the verbal and arithmetic tests given prior to training, was administered to all of the remaining trainees.

In 1970 absence and lateness data and supervisory ratings of job performance were collected, where possible, for all former trainees who were still employed by the airline. The employment status (i.e., employed vs. unemployed) of each trainee was also determined.

Sample Characteristics

The sample of HCU consisted of 295 male employees whose average age was 25. Sixty-three per cent did not have a high school diploma at the time of hire, and 45% had a previous criminal record. Approximately 76% of the sample were Blacks, 15% Puerto Rican, 8% Caucasian, and 1% were listed as "other." No aptitude tests were used in the selection process.

A majority of the sample was involved in servicing jet aircraft. Their job duties included such diverse activities as transporting cargo to and from aircraft, equipping airplane cabins for flight and operating air conditioning trucks and powered equipment on ramps and docks. Those employees not engaged in such activities were assigned to aircraft cleaning, building cleaning, and plant maintenance.

Predictor Instruments

Pre-tests. The following aptitude tests were administered prior to the Basic Skills training program:

A. Stanford Achievement Test—Word Meaning (Form W) Intermediate II Battery. (Stanford Achievement Test Manual, 1964)

B. Stanford Achievement Test—Arithmetic Computation Test (Form W) Intermediate II Battery.

Post-tests. The following aptitude tests were administered following the Basic Skills training program:

A. An alternate form of the Word Meaning (WM) pre-test (Form X or Y) Intermediate II Battery.

B. An alternate form of the Arithmetic Computation (AC) pretest (Form X or Y) Intermediate II Battery.

THE CRITERIA

Turnover

The June 1970 employment status of each of the 295 HC was determined from Company records. At this time, 54% of the total HCU sample were no longer employed by the airline. Since members of the HCU sample joined the company at different points in time within a 14-month period, "turnover" was defined in the following way: An employed person was anyone with tenure of 13 or more months. This group included three employees who had terminated after the first 12 months of service. An unemployed person was defined as any employee who terminated before completing 12 months of service. As a result of this procedure, 34 of the 295 HC in the sample were eliminated from the turnover analyses.

Absence and Lateness
The following 12 month "moving" records of four types of absence or lateness were obtained for HC still employed by the airline:

A. The number of times (SK-ID-times) and the number of hours (SK-ID-hours) an individual was absent due to illness or being injured-on-duty in the previous 12 months of service.

B. The number of times (NC-times) and the number of hours (NC-hours) an employee was absent or late during the previous 12 months when he did not call in to report he would be late or absent.

C. The total number of occurrences (Total-Times) and the total number of hours (Total-Hours) of lost time for any reason during the previous 12 months of employment.

D. The total number of times (RL-times) an employee reported late for work in the previous 12 months of employment.

Supervisory Ratings of Job Performance
Supervisory personnel rated each HC employee on 11 rating dimensions every six months. Each dimension had a 29-point graphic rating scale ranging from "unsatisfactory" at one to "excellent" at 29. The dimensions rated were quality of work, quantity of work, job knowledge, cooperation and general attitude, etc. The most recent supervisory performance rating was obtained for each of the HC employees.

RESULTS
Raw scores on the four Stanford Achievement Tests for 261 HC employees were converted to grade equivalent scores using the grade norms provided in the test manual. The mean grade equivalent scores for the pre-tests were 6.4 for Word Meaning and 5.8 for Arithmetic Computation. Post-test scores were 8.2 for Word Meaning and 8.5 for Arithmetic Computation. While these results suggest that the airline was not "skimming the cream" off the HC applicant population, it should be pointed out that the manual contains national grade norms, not "ghetto" school grade norms. The latter, which were

not available, might have been more appropriate for the HC sample. Results also indicate that the mean gains in scores on WM and AC were significant beyond the .01 level.

PREDICTOR RELIABILITY

Alternate form reliability for the Pre-Post WM test was fairly high ($r = .72$) for this sample. The Pre-Post AC test reliability was slightly lower ($r = .68$).

Turnover and Tenure

Correlations were computed between the four grade equivalent scores and the turnover criterion (coded $1 =$ employed; $2 =$ unemployed) described above. Also, the relationship between grade scores and company tenure was determined (Table 1). Statistically significant relationships were found between the two WM tests and employment status. Employees who scored high on the WM tests tend to be more termination-prone than those scoring low on the tests. The AC tests were not significantly related to the employment status criterion.

Both of the pre-tests showed significant relationships with company tenure. Those HC with longer tenure tended to have lower test scores than those employees with shorter tenure. The post-tests were unrelated to this criterion.

Absence and Lateness

Absence and lateness data for the 12 month period prior to data collection were available for 68% (93) of the employed sample. Unfortunately, data could not be obtained for those employees who had terminated and for those who had less than 12 months tenure.

The results of relating grade equivalent scores to the absence and lateness criteria are presented in Table 1. The WM pre-test and WM post-test were significantly related to a number of the same criteria. Considering the high correlation between these tests, this is not a surprising finding.

Additional analyses showed that age was also significantly related to the absence and lateness criteria. Part correlations were computed to control for age and the results indicated that, when age was partialled out, the pre- and post-WM tests were still significantly related to the criterion.

Supervisory Ratings of Job Performance

Ratings of on-the-job performance and other behavioral characteristics were obtained from supervisors for 82% (112) of the employed HC sample. The relationships between the Stanford Achievement tests and supervisory job performance ratings are not presented since only one of the 44 coefficients was significant at the .05 level.

Table 1 *Correlation coefficients for Stanford achievement test grade equivalent scores and absence, lateness, turnover, and tenure for HC employees*[a]

Stanford achievement test	Turnover	Tenure (months)	SK-ID (times)	SK-ID (hours)	NC (times)	NC (hours)	Total (times)	Total (hours)	RL (times)
Pre-test WM	.16†	-.13†	.21†	.20*	.22†	.21†	.27‡	.20	.24†
Pre-test AC	.10	-.13†	.00	-.02	-.07	-.06	.02	-.02	.14
Post-test WM	.12*	-.07	.20†	.12	.17	.17*	.27†	.13	.19*
Post-test AC	.02	.00	.01	-.05	.01	.01	.03	-.04	.0

[a] For turnover and tenure criteria, $N = 261$; for other criteria, $N = 93$.

* $p \leq .10$.
† $p \leq .05$.
‡ $p \leq .01$.

CHANGE SCORE

While not directly related to the principal focus of this study, crude gain scores were computed (post-test-pre-test) and correlated with the criteria. The hypothesis was that the magnitude of change would be related to the motivation of the employee during training and, subsequently, on the job. The results, however, provided no support for this hypothesis. Gain scores were uncorrelated with the criteria.

DISCUSSION

The authors' intention in this study was to determine whether verbal and arithmetic skills measures were related to indices of job behavior for a "hardcore" unemployed sample. The results, while not overly encouraging, do provide suggestions for future research. Also, an indirect product of this study was the finding that gains in verbal and arithmetic skills could be significantly affected by means of an 8-week training program.

Virtually all of the correlations between tests and performance ratings were found to be non-significant. On the other hand, a number of relationships between tests, particularly Word Meaning, and absenteeism, lateness and tenure criteria were significant. The correlations, however, tended to be in the negative direction, indicating that HC employees who scored high on the tests were more prone to be absent, late or to terminate. Some highly tentative interpretations of these results may be offered:

During the 8-week training program, HC employees tend to develop a sense of group identity and self-esteem (cf., Korman, 1970). Individuals with high test scores are often times singled out by instructors and company representatives. As a result, they are likely to experience situationally enhanced self-esteem. The transition from this ego-enhancing atmosphere to an on-the-job situation, where they are once again initiates and minority members, may lead to dissatisfaction with the job and avoidance behaviors on the part of the high scoring HC employees. A related hypothesis is that high scoring HC employees, whose self-esteem has been increased in the training program, may expect more frequent promotion and pay increases than is realizable. This could, in turn, result in termination or other "avoidance" behaviors.

In conclusion, the results from this study must be viewed with caution. The tests, which were designed as measures of academic progress, may well have been inappropriate to industrial applications and, therefore, lack of correlations with performance criteria would be misleading. Those correlations with attendance and turnover criteria, while suggestive of underlying causes, should not be taken as evidence that high scorers are poor employment risks. As mentioned at the outset, research in this area is lacking and more published reports would be necessary before even tentative conclusions can be drawn.

References

Bartlett, C. J. and O'Leary, B. S. A differential prediction model to moderate the effects of heterogeneous groups in personnel selection and classification. *Personnel Psychology,* 1969, 22, 1–17.

Campion, J. E. and Freihoff, E. C. Unintentional bias when using racially mixed samples for test validation. *Experimental Publication System,* October 1970, 8, Ms. #285–2.

Einhorn, H. J. and Bass, A. R. Discrimination in employment testing. *Experimental Publication System,* October 1969, 2, Ms. #048A.

Kirkpatrick, J. J., Ewen, R. B., Barrett, R. S., and Katzell, R. A. *Testing and fair employment.* New York: New York University Press, 1968.

Korman, A. K. Toward an hypothesis of work behavior. *Journal of Applied Psychology,* 1970, 54, 31–41.

Krug, R. E. Some suggested approaches for test development and measurement. *Personnel Psychology,* 1966, 19, 24–35.

Lopez, F. M. Current problems in test performance of job applicants. *Personnel Psychology,* 1966, 19, 10–17.

Stanford Achievement Tests. Manual of Administration. New York: Harcourt, Brace and World, 1964.

The Unsettled DeFunis Case
C. Robert Zelnick

The Supreme Court of the United States dismissed the case of Marco DeFunis against the University of Washington law school because he was in law school and about to graduate. He claimed he was rejected for the year beginning September, 1971, because arbitrary quotas established for racial minority students had used up all available places in his class.

The university was instructed to admit DeFunis by three separate courts in order that he suffer no irreparable injury while his case was pending. Those orders, in effect, permitted the Supreme Court to avoid determining DeFunis' case on its merits. But both the court majority and the dissenters agreed that the matter is certain not to remain dormant for very long.

To appreciate fully the complexity of the case it is necessary to examine the dissenting opinion of Associate Justice William O. Douglas. For while Justice Douglas alone purported to reach a decision on the core issue—voluntary racial quotas at state universities—he dodged it every bit as certainly as his brethren who made no similar pretense.

Justice Douglas began with a restatement of the undisputed facts: Thirty-eight blacks, Filipinos, Chicanos, and American Indians were accepted to the class from which DeFunis was rejected. Of these, 37 had lower academic credentials than he. Moreover, the applications of minority candidates were referred either to a black law student or an assistant dean and judged by a variety of standards. White applicants were, for the most part, subjected to rather rigid mathematical process that combined their last two years of college grades with scores on the standard law school admissions test.

Clearly, as Justice Douglas noted, "the school did not use one set of criteria but two, and then determined which to apply to a given applicant on the basis of his race."

True enough. Not even the University of Washington asserted its law school admissions policies were "racially neutral." State policies that create distinctions on the basis of race, creed, or national origin, while not illegal on their face, are viewed with deep suspicion by the courts. They must be justified by a compelling state interest, one that cannot adequately be served by a more

Christian Science Monitor, May 16, 1974. Reprinted by permission from the Christian Science Monitor. Copyright © 1974 The Christian Science Publishing Society. All rights reserved.

narrowly targeted approach. And not since the Korematsu case of 1944, when the court approved resettlement and curfews for Japanese Americans, has the nation's highest tribunal found any interest compelling enough to sanction racial or ethnic discrimination.

So one would have expected Justice Douglas to condemn out of hand Washington's law school admissions procedures. Instead he recommended that the matter be remanded for a new trial to determine whether law school admissions tests "should be eliminated so far as racial minorities are concerned."

But the question is not whether such tests are relevant to the cultural experience of minority candidates but whether they are helpful indicators as to whether a particular candidate for law school will do well in his studies. If they are, then eliminating them for minority applicants simply to increase minority enrollment at law schools runs afoul of the very constitutional principles Justice Douglas explains in his dissent:

> "The equal protection clause commands the elimination of racial barriers, not their creation in order to satisfy our theory as to how society ought to be organized. The purpose of the University of Washington cannot be to produce black lawyers for blacks. Polish lawyers for Poles, Jewish lawyers for Jews. It should be to produce good lawyers for Americans and not place First Amendment barriers against anyone."

Justice Douglas' dissent then was no more satisfying than the holding of the majority. Still one detected an almost audible sigh of relief from the nation's academic community that this issue was not decided on this set of facts. Racial quota systems simply cannot pass judicial muster. Yet the law school door can and ought to remain open to minority candidates, even those who may do less well in law school than certain of their white classmates.

The answer may well be for admissions offices simply to recognize that academic excellence is only one measure of an attorney's value to both the legal and lay communities. The demands upon a practicing attorney often run more to his character than his intellect.

Strength of character, then, is at least equally important. So is a commitment to decent causes, or a devotion to one's fellow man, or an unflinching sense of honor and integrity.

Unlike an ability to do well on multiple choice examinations or master a particular discipline or course of study, these attributes are never the monopoly of a single race or culture. They reside in varying degrees within each member of the family of man. And they must be discovered, nurtured, and rewarded by those in whom custody of our institutions is reposed, including our institutions of higher learning.

Breakthrough in On-The-Job Training
Earl R. Gomersall and M. Scott Myers

In this article we shall describe and analyze the results of an unusual study just completed at Texas Instruments Incorporated (TI). The study dealt with the relationship between organization climate and job performance. One of the objectives was to find out what would happen in a large manufacturing department if the causes of anxiety among new employees were reduced. The following gains were accomplished:

- Training time was shortened by one half.
- Training costs were lowered to one third of their previous levels.
- Absenteeism and tardiness dropped to one half of the previous normal.
- Waste and rejects were reduced to one fifth of their previous levels.
- Costs were cut as much as 15% to 30%!

We feel that similar gains can be realized in other organizations, in and out of manufacturing, if they use the approach to be described. If so, the TI study should lead to significant improvements in the efficiency of U.S. industry. Moreover, the gains are not limited to the categories just listed. In the TI manufacturing department, for instance, the results are stimulating managers to try other innovations which, in a circular fashion, are touching off chains of events leading to still more innovations and bringing about basic changes in the job and in the values of the supervisor.

SETTING OF THE STUDY

The study resulted from our cooperative efforts—one of us is a manufacturing manager and the other an industrial psychologist—in what was initially intended to be an application of motivational techniques through job enlargement (as defined in the box on page 272). Although job enlargement replicated from other TI experiments was successful, this article primarily describes innovations by line management to improve job performance through deliberate changes in the organizational climate of the manufacturing department.

The setting for the study was a rapidly growing TI department which, at the time of the experiment, included over 1,400 persons spread throughout three shifts. The department manufactured integrated circuits (microminia-

Harvard Business Review, **44**, 4, July–August 1966, pp. 62–72. Copyright © 1966 by the President and Fellows of Harvard College; all rights reserved.

Job Enlargement

Job enlargement is a means of countering trends toward regimentation, social stratification, technological displacement, and routinized work brought about by mass production methods. Industrial engineering has traditionally applied techniques to achieve organizational goals without thoughtful regard for, and sometimes at the *expense* of, individual goals. The manager's interest in job enlargement stems not from altruism, but rather from his observation that people are motivated by meaningful work which leads to the attainment of personal as well as organizational goals.

Job enlargement efforts follow several approaches. Earliest and best known at Texas Instruments is the work simplification process which equips individuals with knowledge, skills, and attitudes to apply industrial engineering techniques to their own jobs.* Through work simplification, individuals become the willing agents rather than the defensive targets of change. Because mass production operations have gradually limited independent action, a premium is placed on group effectiveness, and job enlargement is pursued through team approaches to problem solving and goal setting.

Jobs may be enlarged horizontally and/or vertically. If an operator's job is expanded so he is now *doing* a greater variety or number of operations, it is enlarged horizontally. If the operator is involved in the *planning, organizing, and inspection*—as well as the *doing* of his work, his job is enlarged vertically. Evidence from several companies indicates that most forms of job enlargement—horizontal or vertical, individual or group—result in improved performance or, at least, less job dissatisfaction. Manufacturing processes at TI appear to improve most through vertical enlargement involving groups united by common goals or processes.

One example of successful job enlargement at TI began with 10 assemblers and their supervisor in a conference for solving problems and setting production goals for the manufacture of complex radar equipment. Through their initiative and creativity, assemblers improved manufacturing processes and gradually reduced production time by more than 50% and exceeded labor standards (based on a previously approved method) by 100%.

This process ultimately embraced the entire group of 700 assemblers, and it led to substantial cost reductions in the division, less absenteeism and tardiness, and fewer complaints and personnel problems. This successful group process, which granted unprecedented freedom to assemblers in managing their own work (such as rearranging their own assembly lines), also caused supervisors to begin changing their traditional authoritarian self-image to one of coordination and support.

—The Authors

*See Auren Uris, "Mogy's Work Simplification Is Working New Miracles," *Factory,* September 1965, p. 112.

ture circuitry units). The subjects of the study were women operators who collectively performed approximately 1,850 different operations (the most numerously replicated of these operations having only 70 operators per shift). Approximately 57% of the operators worked with microscopes, and all jobs placed a premium on visual acuity, eye-hand coordination, and mechanical aptitude. Selection standards for operators included high school education and passing scores on the General Aptitude Test Battery of the Texas Employment Commission.

The work reported here commenced with a meeting of the authors to plan the application of job-enlargement programs as practiced by other areas of the corporation. Despite the fact that all first- and second-line supervisors had attended the TI motivation seminars and knew the principles of job enlargement, the department manager felt that, in practice, these principles were not being successfully implemented. Part of the answer seemed to lie in the fact that both the supervisors and the employees were in a continuous process of adapting to rapid expansion and technological change. For this and other reasons, as will be discussed later, supervisors and employees were experiencing anxiety. This anxiety appeared to have an effect on their work.

Operations were typified by a continuous training process—training new people hired for expansion and replacement purposes and retraining transferees and the technologically displaced. The consequences of this training program can be illustrated with the classical growth curve shown in Exhibit I. As this curve shows:

> The ball bonders required approximately three months to reach what we term the "competence" level. (The competence level is the stage at which assemblers can independently manufacture the product, but have not yet achieved the speed and accuracy ultimately expected of them to reach

Exhibit I. *Learning curve for ball bonders*

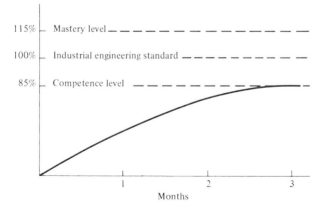

the labor standards set by industrial engineering. The competence level is about 85% of labor standards; a position about 115% of standard is termed the "mastery" level.)

The learning curve of ball bonders was fairly typical of production operations in the department (and, for that matter, of learning in many other companies and industries).

Competence & Creativity

A need was recognized to find out at what stage in the learning process assemblers could be meaningfully involved in the problem-solving, goal-setting process. Were they ready, for example, at one month, at which time they were halfway to the competence level? Or must they have fully reached the competence level before creative involvement in problem solving could be expected?

To answer this question, two experimental groups were selected, one comprised of individuals of one-month tenure, and the other of individuals who had been with the organization three or more months:

1. The one-month group, when involved in the problem-solving process, came up with maintenance-type suggestions such as:

- We need more coat racks.
- Standards not set right.
- We don't have enough time to eat.
- There aren't enough maintenance technicians around to fix machines.
- Too much confusion at shift breaks.

2. The more seasoned group came up with over two pages of specific, technically oriented suggestions to improve the quality of operations, many not previously considered from a management standpoint. Following are examples of suggestions from the seasoned group:

- Do not split manufacturing lots between operators.
- Assign the same quality inspector to a given group of operators to assure continuity.
- Print wiring diagrams on the backs of all lot travelers (operation sequence sheets).
- Give each girl a capillary punch for capillary repair.
- Technicians should always repair burnt-out electrical heaters, and girls should always change own capillaries.

This experiment corroborates earlier observations that minimal job competence is a requisite to creative problem solving. The finding seems to have quite general application. Not only do untrained employees impair the problem-solving efforts of skilled workers, but they themselves are frustrated by their inability to participate in the problem-solving activities. So there is added reason to seek ways to accelerate on-the-job learning.

EXPERIMENTS CONDUCTED

Why did the one-month group fail in the problem-solving experiment? The reason, we postulated, was not only lack of familiarity with hardware and processes, but also debilitating anxieties associated with lack of job competence during the early days of employment. These relationships were not mere conjecture. The department manager had, during the past year, followed a systematic program for interviewing individuals during the morning coffee break. The results of 135 interviews with 405 operators yielded the following facts:

- Their first days on the job were anxious and disturbing ones.
- "New employee initiation" practices by peers intensified anxiety.
- Anxiety interfered with the training process.
- Turnover of newly hired employees was caused primarily by anxiety.
- New operators were reluctant to discuss problems with their supervisors.
- Their supervisors had been unsuccessful in translating motivation theory into practice.

Similar interviews conducted with the supervisors and middle managers yielded these additional conclusions:

- They experienced as much anxiety as new assemblers.
- They felt inadequate with seasoned, competent subordinates.
- They cut off downward communication to conceal ignorance.
- Supervisory defensiveness discouraged upward communication.
- Motivation principles learned in the classroom were not being implemented on the assembly line.

Preliminary Analysis

Facts uncovered through these interviews underscored the importance of anxiety in inhibiting job effectiveness for both operators and supervisors. It seemed obvious that anxiety dropped as competence was achieved. The relationship between the learning curve and what was believed to be the anxiety curve of operators is illustrated in Exhibit II.

To supplement information obtained through personal interviews and to gain a better understanding of the characteristics of the anxiety to be reduced, we developed a 92-item questionnaire to measure the following possible causes of tension or anxiety: supervision; job knowledge and skill; social acceptance; physical condition; orientation; job pressure; regimentation; vocational adjustment; personal problems; financial worries; outside social factors; and opportunities for the satisfaction of growth, achievement, responsibility, and recognition needs.

Administration of this questionnaire to short-tenure and seasoned employees identified three types of tension in the job situation—the first two harmful and the third helpful:

1. One form of anxiety, mentioned previously, stemmed from the unpredictable and sometimes threatening new world of work and, as illustrated in Exhibit II, was higher among *new* trainees.

2. Another type of tension resulted from anxieties about non-job factors such as personal finances, domestic problems, professional status, and outside social relationships. This type existed in equal amounts in *both* groups.

3. The third type of tension was identified as a positive, inner-directed desire for constructive self-expression. This creative tension found con-

Exhibit II. *Relationship of anxiety to competence*

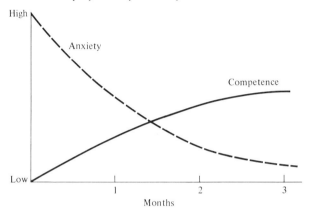

structive expression best in an atmosphere of approval and self-confidence after job competence was reached.

Anxiety vs. Performance

Assuming the validity of Exhibit II, we posed the following question: "Is it possible to accelerate achievement to the competence level by reducing anxiety at a faster rate?" In other words, we wanted to know if it were possible to achieve the relationships illustrated by the dotted lines in Exhibit III.

Anxiety on the job is characteristically assumed to be the dependent variable, gradually dropping as competence is acquired. Might not the reverse be true? Might not competence increase as a result of anxiety being decreased? With such questions in mind, we decided to design an orientation program to reduce the anxieties of experimental groups of new employees:

> The next group of ten girls hired for bonding work on the second shift was chosen as the first experimental group. A control group was selected from the first and third shifts. Precautions were taken to avoid the "Hawthorne effect" of influencing behavior through special attention. (The "Hawthorne effect" was first reported by Elton Mayo and F. J.

Roethlisberger in their experiments at Western Electric. They noticed that improvements in operators' performance often followed simply from outsiders' taking an interest in them.) The control group was oriented in the customary manner and the experimental group through a revised approach. Neither group was told of the experiment, and members of both groups had no reason to think they were being subjected to special treatment.

Exhibit III. *Postulated consequence of anxiety reduction*

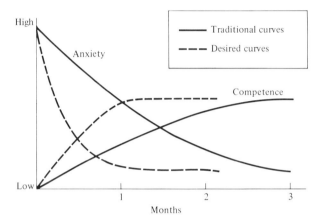

Months

Conventional Indoctrination

The control group went through the usual first-day orientation, which consisted of a two-hour briefing on hours of work, insurance, parking, work rules, and employee services. This session included warnings of the consequences of failure to conform to organization expectations and, though not intended as a threat, tended to raise rather than reduce anxieties.

Following this orientation, it was customary for a bonder to be introduced to her friendly but very busy supervisor, who gave her further orientation and job instruction. Unfortunately, the supervisor's detailed familiarity with the operations had desensitized him to the technological gap between them, and the following might be typical of what the operator heard him say:

> "Alice, I would like you to take the sixth yellow chair on this assembly line, which is in front of bonding machine #14. On the left side of your machine you will find a wiring diagram indicating where you should bond your units. On the right-hand side of your machine you will find a carrying tray full of 14-lead packages. Pick up the headers, one at a time, using your 3-C tweezers and place them on the hot substrate below the capillary head. Grasp the cam actuator on the right-hand side of the machine and lower the hot capillary over the first bonding pad indicated

by the diagram. Ball bond to the pad and, by moving the hot substrate, loop the wire to the pin indicated by the diagram. Stitch bond to this lead, raise the capillary, and check for pigtails. When you have completed all leads, put the unit back in the carrying tray.

"Your training operator will be around to help you with other details. Do you have any questions?"

Overwhelmed by these instructions and not wanting to offend this polite and friendly supervisor or look stupid by telling him she did not understand anything he said, the operator would go to her work station and try to learn by watching her peers on either side of her. But they, in pursuit of operating goals, had little time to assist her. Needless to say, her anxieties were increased and her learning ability was impaired. And the longer she remained unproductive, the more reluctant she was to disclose her wasted effort to her supervisor and the more difficult her job became.

Experimental Approach

The experimental group participated in a one-day program especially designed to overcome anxieties not eliminated by the usual process of job orientation. Following the two-hour orientation by Personnel, they were isolated in a conference room before they could be "initiated" by their peers. They were told there would be no work the first day, that they should relax, sit back, and have a coke or cigarette, and use this time to get acquainted with the organization and each other and to ask questions. Throughout this one-day anxiety-reduction session, questions were encouraged and answered. This orientation emphasized four points:

1. *"Your opportunity to succeed is very good."* Company records disclosed that 99.6% of all persons hired or transferred into this job were eventually successful in terms of their ability to learn the necessary skills. Trainees were shown learning curves illustrating the gradual buildup of competence over the learning period. They were told five or six times during the day that all members of this group could expect to be successful on the job.

2. *"Disregard 'hall talk.'"* Trainees were told of the hazing game that old employees played—scaring newcomers with exaggerated allegations about work rules, standards, disciplinary actions, and other job factors—to make the job as frightening to the newcomers as it had been for them. To prevent these distortions by peers, the trainees were given facts about both the good and the bad aspects of the job and exactly what was expected of them.

The basis for "hall talk" rumors was explained. For example, rumor stated that more than one half of the people who terminated had been fired for poor performance. The interviews mentioned earlier disclosed the fact that supervisors themselves unintentionally caused this rumor by intimating to operators that voluntary terminations (marriage, pregnancy, leaving town) were really performance terminations. Many supervisors felt this was a good negative incentive to pull up the low performers.

3. *"Take the initiative in communication."* The new operators were told of the natural reluctance of many supervisors to be talkative and that it was easier for the supervisor to do his job if they asked him questions. They were told that supervisors realized that trainees needed continuous instruction at first, that they would not understand technical terminology for a while, that they were expected to ask questions, and that supervisors would not consider them dumb for asking questions.

4. *"Get to know your supervisor."* The personality of the supervisor was described in detail. The absolute truth was the rule. A description might reveal that—

- the supervisor is strict, but friendly;
- his hobby is fishing and ham radio operation;
- he tends to be shy sometimes, but he really likes to talk to you if you want to;
- he would like you to check with him before you go on a personal break, just so he knows where you are.

Following this special day-long orientation session, members of the experimental group were introduced to their supervisor and their training operators in accordance with standard practice. Training commenced as usual, and eventually all operators went on production.

SIGNIFICANT GAINS
A difference in attitude and learning rate was apparent from the beginning in the progress of the two groups. By the end of four weeks, the experimental group was significantly outperforming the control group, as shown in Exhibit IV. Note that the experimental group excelled in production and job attendance as well as in learning time.

Exhibit V compares the learning curves of the two groups. It is interesting to note that when anxiety is minimized, learning appears to be almost a

Exhibit IV. *One-month performance levels of experimental and control groups*

	Experimental group	Control group
Units per hour	93	27
Absentee rate	0.5%	2.5%
Times tardy	2	8
Training hours required	225	381

Exhibit V. *Learning curves of experimental and control groups*

straight-line function of time, suggesting that the area between the experimental curve and the control curve represents learning time lag caused by anxiety.

When the experimental study began showing significant results, the anxiety-reduction process was used on additional groups. Exhibit VI shows performance curves reflecting similar results for more than 200 members of experimental and control groups for assembling, welding, and inspection; their absenteeism rates are also compared. It is interesting to note that the third week's methods change in the inspection department depressed the performance of the experimental group more than that of the control group, but the experimental group made a more rapid recovery.

Attaining Mastery

Now let us make a general observation: after an operator achieves an acceptable level of competence, further improvement depends on the nature of the incentive. The usual practice is to set labor standards somewhat in excess of the plateau which an operator can comfortably achieve in the short run. As noted earlier, standards traditionally impose an expectation about 15 percentage points above the competence plateau. However, there is more positive incentive for surpassing the competence plateau. This is the opportunity for self-initiated creative effort. Let us look at some aspects of the TI experiment which bear on this.

Exhibit VI. *Further comparisons of experimental and control groups*

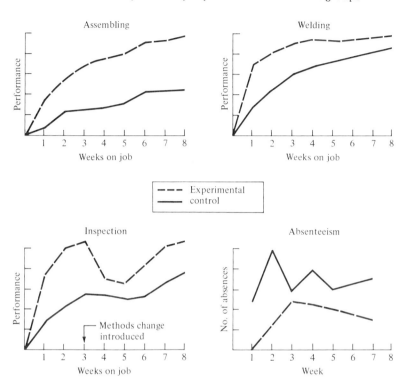

In the integrated circuits groups without methods improvement, the motivated assemblers exceeded labor standards by about 15% to achieve what we term the "mastery level." Since the mastery level is usually attained after plateauing at the competence level, members of the control group seldom reached the mastery level before the fifth month.

But in the experimental group, by contrast, the mastery level was achieved in two to three months.

As illustrated in the smoothed curves of Exhibit VII, the area between control group and experimental group curves represents an improvement in performance of approximately 50%. For 100 new hires in this department at TI, that gain was equivalent to net first-year savings of at least $50,000. On the basis of reduced turnover, absenteeism, and training time, additional annual savings of $35,000 were estimated.

Spread of Confidence

As trainees with less anxiety gradually became members of the regular work force, their attitudes began influencing the performance of the work groups

Exhibit VII. *Mastery attainment by experimental and control groups*

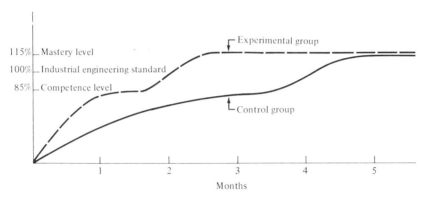

they joined. The greater confidence of the new members seemed to inspire greater confidence among their older peers; also, their higher performance established a new reference point for stimulating the natural competitiveness which existed among members of work groups. Old peers were sometimes hard pressed to maintain a superiority margin between themselves and the rapidly learning newcomers. There was evidence of improvements in quality and quantity, not only among immediate peer groups, but also among adjacent work groups who were influenced through the informal social system in the plant.

The performance of an entire shift was difficult to measure because of changing methods and standards, but Exhibit VIII shows the results of putting 10 operators trained under the system among 60 workers on the second shift. The second shift, which for the previous seven weeks had had the lowest productivity, became clearly the highest producer five weeks after the experiment began. Although transferring some of the 10 experimentally trained operators to the first shift in the thirteenth week dropped the performance level of the second shift, the transfusion appeared to raise the performance level of the first shift.

Quality Improvement

The new training system influenced performance in more ways than one. For example, in analyzing the causes of defects management noted that, contrary to common assumptions, the faster operators (by definition, master operators) were making fewer errors. The relationship of output to defects is shown in Exhibit IX; note that those trainees who exceeded the competence level within four weeks were usually making products with practically no defects.

It had been the practice to subject all units to 100% inspection for nine specific reject criteria. This required one inspector for every two assembly

Exhibit VIII. *Comparative performance of three shifts*

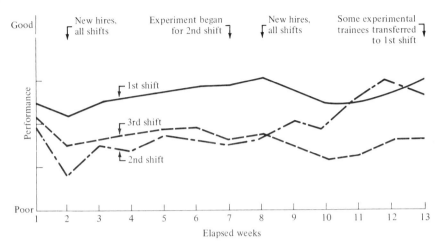

operators. Master operators, whose defects were close to zero, were now permitted to submit completed units to quality assurance inspectors for lot inspection, thus bypassing the normal 100% inspection. The pride which these operators felt because of their accomplishment and because of being identified with the master operator group actually improved their product quality over the standards achieved through 100% inspection. The lot rejection rate dropped by a factor of five, and labor costs were lowered by 30% Not only

Exhibit IX. *Quantity-quality relationships*

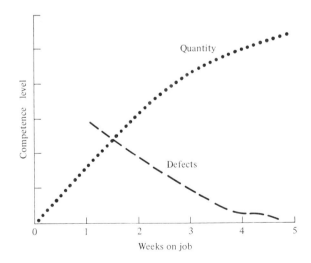

was pride in workmanship returned to the job, but an old manufacturers' axiom was validated: "Quality cannot be *inspected* into a product; it must be *built* into it."

BROADER IMPLICATIONS

The results of this experiment are significant to the operating manager in terms of the criteria most important to him—reduced costs, higher quality, satisfied customers, and increased profits. Without improvements in these measures, no matter how noble the other motives, experiments of this type generally have low priority.

At the same time, because this experiment has led to improvements in terms of these traditional management criteria at TI, managers have become enthusiastically involved in its implementation and, in the process, have become the agents for other changes. Now let us look at some of these effects.

New Understanding

As managers have gradually become more sensitive to the relationship between attitudes and behavior, they have begun to seek a better understanding of the causes of attitude change. Motivation theory, which they had learned as an intellectual process in a company motivation seminar, has become meaningful for them as they observe its implementation in the work situation. Job enlargement and increased motivation through the application of behavioral theory in other groups has become interesting to them; and systems for measuring attitudes, teaching problem solving, goal setting, and providing performance feedback are now seen in new perspective. These new perspectives constitute a foundation for greater managerial effectiveness at all levels and in all functions.

Improved Training

It is interesting to note that, as managers reviewed the results of anxiety reduction for production personnel, they would observe, "You know, managers have anxieties, too. . . . " And many would volunteer descriptions of their own debilitating anxieties.

Why do supervisors have anxieties about their competence as supervisors? Primarily because of mistaken concepts of the proper role of a supervisor. This error is understandable in the light of the typical man's background:

> Approximately 60% of the first-line supervisory positions are filled by new college graduates. They reach industry after a life of conditioning in "superior-subordinate" relationships. After a long background of parent-child, teacher-student, officer-enlisted man experiences, it is normal for them to come to their first supervisory job with the notion that a leader is someone who "can do everything his subordinates can, only better."

Because of this traditional image of infallibility of leaders, the new supervisor understandably feels inadequate in his new role of supervising large numbers of individuals, most of whom know the operations better than he does. He does not realize that the operators recognize and accept his limitations and that it is futile and self-defeating for him to try to conceal them.

To help new supervisors gain early acceptance of their limitations and a better understanding of their supervisory role, TI developed a plan for having operators train the supervisor! Working in pairs, operators (who have received trainer training) give the new or transferred supervisor his first orientation to the assembly line, acquainting him with the pitfalls traditionally encountered by new supervisors and defining his role as it is perceived by the operators. This innovative approach serves three basic purposes:

1. It provides a supervisor with valid information directly from the persons who have the greatest knowledge of the operations.

2. It provides assurance to the operators that the supervisor is properly qualified and acquainted with their problems. Because they get personally involved in his training, they will seek to make him successful.

3. Most importantly, this approach to training is significant because of its impact on the values of the supervisor. A supervisor who, in his first experience as a manager, learns to expect and seek information from subordinates, and discovers that they are creative and responsible, is conditioned or permanently "programmed" to look to, and rely on, subordinates for assistance in solving problems. And, as Douglas McGregor and many others have pointed out, people tend to rise to properly delegated expectations of supervision. Supervisors who are programmed to have high expectations of subordinates are ideally suited for pursuing job enlargement.

Fluid Communication

A significant effect of the new orientation program is the encouragement of upward communication. In the final analysis, communication depends upon the behavior of supervisors who, through the language of action, provide a climate conducive to natural and informal exchange of information. It was as a result of sensitizing supervisors to the importance of listening and maintaining fluid communication channels at all levels that the following incident took place:

An operator approached a manager during coffee break and casually struck up a conversation about the "units with little white specks on them that leaked after welding." The supervisor asked, "What little white specks?" The operator pointed out that almost all of the units that leaked after welding had little specks on them, a fact unnoted before. Verifying and investigating this fact revealed that units were placed in plastic trays while still hot from a previous process; their heat caused many of them to fuse to the plastic container. Pulling them from the container caused the units to pull away a small amount of plastic, thus insulating them during the welding process.

Once this was discovered, the problem was solved simply by delaying the placing of units in the plastic trays until they had cooled sufficiently. This single suggestion reduced rejects by a factor of four for this product—a projected cost prevention of hundreds of thousands of dollars.

The point we want to emphasize here is that casual questions and observations of the type described take place only in an atmosphere of approval, genuine respect, and interest.

CONCLUSION

As the principles of the new approach have been adopted and adapted by other departments at TI, we have been able to gain new appreciation of the respective roles of managers and behavioral scientists. The manager should look to behavioral scientists not to solve his problems, but only to provide needed information about them. To ask the scientists to do more robs the manager of his charter and violates the very principle which he is expected to implement through job enlargement.

However, the behavioral scientist is operating within his proper realm of responsibility if he serves as a change agent by assisting managers in planning the application of theories and principles and by giving visibility to their achievements. Incidentally, there should be broader recognition that, as the previous discussion indicates, behavioral science applications can be measured in traditional production indexes as well as in the more nebulous criteria of morale and attitudes.

Important Effects

The approach described in this article has had important effects on TI's manufacturing department:

1. It has made the department more effective by reducing costs and waste and by improving quality and profitability.

2. It has made the workplace more attractive for the employees by reducing anxiety and making work more challenging. This has resulted in less reactive behavior, better attendance, and better utilization of talent.

3. Supervisors are becoming more effective managers. As their involvement in anxiety reduction and job enlargement results in more responsible and creative behavior on the part of operators, supervisors learn to delegate with greater confidence. This in turn frees them from details which heretofore seemed oppressively inescapable so they can spend more time on higher level developmental work.

These gains do not, of course, happen independently but, rather, in a mutually reinforcing and circular way.

The new approach can, if applied broadly, reduce the costs of personnel administration. Outside their staffing responsibilities, personnel departments traditionally devote most of their efforts to administering supplemental benefits, working on collective bargaining, settling grievances, and, in general, dealing with causes of dissatisfaction. Dissatisfaction and preoccupation with so-called "maintenance" factors (that is, parking arrangements, fringe benefits, vacation schedules, and so on) are not usually a consequence of inadequacy of these factors but a symptom of thwarted motivation needs. People in jobs which offer opportunity for growth, for achievement, responsibility, and recognition, have little incentive to get sidetracked with peripheral issues and feel no need to seek the intervention of a labor union to "police" management. In fact, on a properly designed and delegated job in a suitable organizational climate, the employee is in a real sense a manager himself. His proprietary interest in managing his job gives him a sense of company identification that causes him to see unionism as a deterrent to his effectiveness. Hence, meaningful work eliminates the wastefulness of uninspired and reactive behavior and the cost of elaborate systems for dealing with dissatisfaction.

The rate of technological displacement—and hence the need for effective training—is increasing. This fact, in combination with the current labor shortage, the entry of more young people and minority groups into industrial employment, and the deployment of new plants domestically and internationally, means that management should place more emphasis on training and other personnel management innovations than ever before. Lessened turnover and accelerated learning curves constitute a significant advantage to companies that are able to achieve them.

U.S. business has been hard pressed to match international competition. Handicapped by the pay differential, American companies have met the challenge primarily through technical innovation and superior quality. They can also meet it with management innovation. A great deal can be accomplished in this way, as our experiences with accelerated learning and job enlargement demonstrate.

PART IV

In Part IV we examine some of the ways in which organizations can improve and develop. To help you understand this concept, we need to introduce two terms: organizational *effectiveness* and organizational *efficiency*. Organizational effectiveness is the degree to which an organization reaches its goals and objectives. Organization efficiency refers to the amount of resources the organization uses in attaining its goals. An organization may be highly effective in reaching its goals, but at the same time highly inefficient because it wastes its resources, particularly people. An illustration of this is given in Part III in the article "Human Resource Accounting in Industry."

Organization improvement and development is concerned with *both* effectiveness and efficiency, particulary regarding the growth and development of people. There are many different definitions of "Organization Development," but perhaps the simplest is that the process attempts to satisfy the needs of the organization *and* the needs of people *at the same time.*

STRUCTURE

In Part I of the text, we stressed the importance of considering an organization as a total system comprising a number of subsystems. The first two articles in Part IV examine the formal structure of the organization as a system. "Beyond Theory Y," by John J. Morse and Jay W. Lorsch, develops the concept that there is no one best way to design an organization; "Project Organization: Factors Affecting the Decision Environment," by Bruce N. Baker, Dalmar Fisher, and David C. Murphy, clears up a number of reasons why a very popular approach in many organizations ("Project Management") fails to achieve success.

Organization Improvement and Development

INFORMATION FLOW

The next two articles are concerned with flows *through* the system. "Cost Control, Production and People," by Chris Argyris, as well as "The Impact of Computerized Programs on Managers and Organization," by Edgar F. Huse, point up the harmful effects on both people and organization when flows through the system are not sufficiently integrated with both the structural approach and the feelings and needs of people.

ORGANIZATION DEVELOPMENT

The next five articles deal more directly with the human side of the enterprise, concentrating on what is now called Organization Development (OD). Because of space limitations, not all OD approaches could be covered. One of the most popular approaches to OD is the Managerial Grid, as developed by Robert R. Blake and Jane S. Mouton. One of the few research studies on the Grid is covered in the article by Michael Beer and Stephen W. Kleisath, "The Effects of the Managerial Grid Lab on Organizational and Leadership Dimensions." Another very popular approach is the use of questionnaires and the feedback of the data to the total system. This is covered in David G. Bowers' article "OD Techniques and Their Results in 23 Organizations," which also compares this approach to other OD techniques and interventions. "Flex time," which gives individual workers a choice about starting and quitting hours, is being used widely in Western Europe, and its use is steadily increasing in this country. This approach is described by David T. Cook in "Punching the Clock: When You Choose." Job enrichment and other approaches to OD are briefly described in Edgar F. Huse's article "Job Enrichment: A Valuable Tool for Company and Worker." Since the use of change agents or consultants employed by an organization is increasing rapidly, we have included Carol Weiss Heine's article "The Internal OD Consultant: Issues and Questions," which points up some of the problems of the "inside" change agent.

INTEGRATED APPROACHES

The next two articles cover some overall approaches to OD. The first, "OD Interventions—An Overview," by Wendell L. French and Cecil A. Bell, Jr., describes the general nature and process of OD, including the types of interventions commonly used. The second article Roger Harrison's "Choosing the Depths of Organizational Intervention," clearly spells out the types of OD interventions and makes suggestions about how and when they might be used. The final article by Michael Beer and Edgar F. Huse, describes a case study in which a number of different approaches to OD were used in a single plant from 1966–1969. The article also develops a number of "findings" about OD in general. In an eight-to-ten-year follow-up study, Suojannen (W. William Suojannen, "A Case Study of the Longitudinal Effects of A Job Enrichment Program," Ph.D. diss., Cambridge: Massachusetts Institute of Technology, June 1974) concluded that the initial program was held up well (under four different plant managers and a sizeable number of first-line production foremen).

If you would like to read further in this area, there are two excellent annotated bibliographies now in print. The first is by Jerome Franklin, *Organization Development: An Annotated Bibliography,* the Institute for Social Research, The University of Michigan, 1973. The second is by James C. Taylor, *"The Quality of Working Life: An Annotated Bibliography* 1957–1972, The Center for Organizational Studies, Graduate School of Management, University of California, Los Angeles.

STRUCTURE

Beyond Theory Y
John J. Morse and Jay W. Lorsch

An effective organization must be designed to fit its task and its people, not to satisfy some universal "theory"

FOREWORD

The concept of participative management, as symbolized by Douglas McGregor's "Theory Y," was an important insight into improving organizational effectiveness. But, many managers assume that Theory Y is the *only* correct approach. In this article, the authors go "beyond Theory Y" to propose that the most productive organization is one that fits the needs of its task and people in any particular situation. In some cases, this may well mean a more directive approach. Even more significant, the proper "fit" among task, organization, and people seems to develop strong "competence motivation" in individuals, regardless of the organizational style.

Mr. Morse is Assistant Professor of Behavioral Science at the Graduate School of Business Administration of the University of California at Los Angeles. Part of the research described in this article was done by Morse for his doctoral thesis at the Harvard Business School. Mr. Lorsch is Associate Professor of Organizational Behavior at the Harvard Business School.

During the past 30 years, managers have been bombarded with two competing approaches to the problems of human administration and organization. The first, usually called the classical school of organization, emphasizes the need for well-established lines of authority, clearly defined jobs, and au-

Harvard Business Review, May–June 1970, pp. 61–68. Copyright © 1970 by the President and Fellows of Harvard College; all rights reserved.

thority equal to responsibility. The second, often called the participative approach, focuses on the desirability of involving organization members in decision making so that they will be more highly motivated.

Douglas McGregor, through his well-known "Theory X and Theory Y," drew a distinction between the assumptions about human motivation which underlie these two approaches, to this effect:

- Theory X assumes that people dislike work and must be coerced, controlled, and directed toward organizational goals. Furthermore, most people prefer to be treated this way, so they can avoid responsibility.
- Theory Y—the integration of goals—emphasizes the average person's intrinsic interest in his work, his desire to be self-directing and to seek responsibility, and his capacity to be creative in solving business problems.

It is McGregor's conclusion, of course, that the latter approach to organization is the more desirable one for managers to follow.[1]

McGregor's position causes confusion for the managers who try to choose between these two conflicting approaches. The classical organizational approach that McGregor associated with Theory X does work well in some situations, although, as McGregor himself pointed out, there are also some situations where it does not work effectively. At the same time, the approach based on Theory Y, while it has produced good results in some situations, does not always do so. That is, each approach is effective in some cases but not in others. Why is this? How can managers resolve the confusion?

A NEW APPROACH

Recent work by a number of students of management and organization may help to answer such questions.[2] These studies indicate that there is not one best organizational approach; rather, the best approach depends on the nature of the work to be done. Enterprises with highly predictable tasks perform better with organizations characterized by the highly formalized procedures and management hierarchies of the classical approach. With highly uncertain tasks that require more extensive problem solving, on the other hand, organizations that are less formalized and emphasize self-control and member participation in decision making are more effective. In essence, according to these newer studies, managers must design and develop organizations so that the organizational characteristics *fit* the nature of the task to be done.

While the conclusions of this newer approach will make sense to most experienced managers and can alleviate much of the confusion about which approach to choose, there are still two important questions unanswered:

1. How does the more formalized and controlling organization affect the motivation of organization members? (McGregor's most telling criticism

of the classical approach was that it did not unleash the potential in an enterprise's human resources.)

2. Equally important, does a less formalized organization always provide a high level of motivation for its members? (This is the implication many managers have drawn from McGregor's work.)

We have recently been involved in a study that provides surprising answers to these questions and, when taken together with other recent work, suggests a new set of basic assumptions which move beyond Theory Y into what we call "Contingency Theory: the fit between task, organization, and people." These theoretical assumptions emphasize that the appropriate pattern of organization is *contingent* on the nature of the work to be done and on the particular needs of the people involved. We should emphasize that we have labeled these assumptions as a step beyond Theory Y because of McGregor's own recognition that the Theory Y assumptions would probably be supplanted by new knowledge within a short time.[3]

THE STUDY DESIGN

Our study was conducted in four organizational units. Two of these performed the relatively certain task of manufacturing standardized containers on high-speed, automated production lines. The other two performed the relatively uncertain work of research and development in communications technology. Each pair of units performing the same kind of task were in the same large company, and each pair had previously been evaluated by that company's management as containing one highly effective unit and a less effective one. The study design is summarized in Exhibit I.

The objective was to explore more fully how the fit between organization and task was related to successful performance. That is, does a good fit between organizational characteristics and task requirements increase the motivation of individuals and hence produce more effective individual and organizational performance?

An especially useful approach to answering this question is to recognize that an individual has a strong need to master the world around him, including the task that he faces as a member of a work organization.[4] The accumulated feelings of satisfaction that come from successfully mastering one's environ-

Exhibit I. *Study design in "fit" of organizational characteristics*

Characteristics	Company I (predictable manufacturing task)	Company II (unpredictable R&D task)
Effective performer	Akron containers plant	Stockton research lab
Less effective performer	Hartford containers plant	Carmel research lab

ment can be called a "sense of competence." We saw this sense of competence in performing a particular task as helpful in understanding how a fit between task and organizational characteristics could motivate people toward successful performance.

Organizational Dimensions

Because the four study sites had already been evaluated by the respective corporate managers as high and low performers of tasks, we expected that such differences in performance would be a preliminary clue to differences in the "fit" of the organizational characteristics to the job to be done. But, first, we had to define what kinds of organizational characteristics would determine how appropriate the organization was to the particular task.

We grouped these organizational characteristics into two sets of factors:

1. Formal characteristics, which could be used to judge the fit between the kind of task being worked on and the formal practices of the organization.

2. Climate characteristics, or the subjective perceptions and orientations that had developed among the individuals about their organizational setting. (These too must fit the task to be performed if the organization is to be effective.)

We measured these attributes through questionnaires and interviews with about 40 managers in each unit to determine the appropriateness of the organization to the kind of task being performed. We also measured the feelings of competence of the people in the organizations so that we could link the appropriateness of the organizational attributes with a sense of competence.

MAJOR FINDINGS

The principal findings of the survey are best highlighted by contrasting the highly successful Akron plant and the high-performing Stockton laboratory. Because each performed very different tasks (the former a relatively certain manufacturing task and the latter a relatively uncertain research task), we expected, as brought out earlier, that there would have to be major differences between them in organizational characteristics if they were to perform effectively. And this is what we did find. But we also found that each of these effective units had a better fit with its particular task than did its less effective counterpart.

While our major purpose in this article is to explore how the fit between task and organizational characteristics is related to motivation, we first want to explore more fully the organizational characteristics of these units, so the reader will better understand what we mean by a fit between task and organization and how it can lead to more effective behavior. To do this, we shall place the major emphasis on the contrast between the high-performing units (the Akron plant and Stockton laboratory), but we shall also compare each of these with its less effective mate (the Hartford plant and Carmel laboratory respectively).

Formal Characteristics

Beginning with differences in formal characteristics, we found that both the Akron and Stockton organizations fit their respective tasks much better than did their less successful counterparts. In the predictable manufacturing task environment, Akron had a pattern of formal relationships and duties that was highly structured and precisely defined. Stockton, with its unpredictable research task, had a low degree of structure and much less precision of definition (see Exhibit II)

Akron's pattern of formal rules, procedures, and control systems was so specific and comprehensive that it prompted one manager to remark:

> "We've got rules here for everything from how much powder to use in cleaning the toilet bowls to how to cart a dead body out of the plant."

In contrast, Stockton's formal rules were so minimal, loose, and flexible that one scientist, when asked whether he felt the rules ought to be tightened, said:

> "If a man puts a nut on a screw all day long, you may need more rules and a job definition for him. But we're not novices here. We're professionals and not the kind who need close supervision. People around here *do* produce, and produce under relaxed conditions. Why tamper with success?"

Exhibit II. *Differences in formal characteristics in high-performing organizations*

Characteristics	Akron	Stockton
1. Pattern of formal relationships and duties as signified by organization charts and job manuals	Highly structured, precisely defined	Low degree of structure, less well defined
2. Pattern of formal rules, procedures, control, and measurement systems	Pervasive, specific, uniform, comprehensive	Minimal, loose, flexible
3. Time dimensions incorporated in formal practices	Short-term	Long-term
4. Goal dimensions incorporated in formal practices	Manufacturing	Scientific

These differences in formal organizational characteristics were well suited to the differences in tasks of the two organizations. Thus:

- Akron's highly structured formal practices fit its predictable task because behavior had to be rigidly defined and controlled around the automated, high-speed production line. There was really only one way to accomplish the plant's very routine and programmable job; managers defined it precisely and insisted (through the plant's formal practices) that each man do what was expected of him.

    On the other hand, Stockton's highly unstructured formal practices made just as much sense because the required activities in the laboratory simply could not be rigidly defined in advance. With such an unpredictable, fast-changing task as communications technology research, there were numerous approaches to getting the job done well. As a consequence, Stockton managers used a less structured pattern of formal practices that left the scientists in the lab free to respond to the changing task situation.

- Akron's formal practices were very much geared to *short-term* and *manufacturing* concerns as its task demanded. For example, formal production reports and operating review sessions were daily occurrences, consistent with the fact that the through-put time for their products was typically only a few hours.

    By contrast, Stockton's formal practices were geared to *long-term* and *scientific* concerns, as its task demanded. Formal reports and reviews were made only quarterly, reflecting the fact that research often does not come to fruition for three to five years.

At the two less effective sites (i.e., the Hartford plant and the Carmel laboratory), the formal organizational characteristics did not fit their respective tasks nearly as well. For example, Hartford's formal practices were much less structured and controlling than were Akron's, while Carmel's were more restraining and restricting than were Stockton's. A scientist in Carmel commented:

> "There's something here that keeps you from being scientific. It's hard to put your finger on, but I guess I'd call it 'Mickey Mouse.' There are rules and things here that get in your way regarding doing your job as a researcher."

Climate Characteristics
As with formal practices, the climate in both high-performing Akron and Stockton suited the respective tasks much better than did the climates at the less successful Hartford and Carmel sites.

Perception of structure. The people in the Akron plant perceived a great deal of structure, with their behavior tightly controlled and defined. One manager in the plant said:

> "We can't let the lines run unattended. We lose money whenever they do. So we make sure each man knows his job, knows when he can take a break, knows how to handle a change in shifts, etc. It's all spelled out clearly for him the day he comes to work here."

In contrast, the scientists in the Stockton laboratory perceived very little structure, with their behavior only minimally controlled. Such perceptions encouraged the individualistic and creative behavior that the uncertain, rapidly changing research task needed. Scientists in the less successful Carmel laboratory perceived much more structure in their organization and voiced the feeling that this was "getting in their way" and making it difficult to do effective research.

Distribution of influence. The Akron plant and the Stockton laboratory also differed substantially in how influence was distributed and on the character of superior-subordinate and colleague relations. Akron personnel felt that they had much less influence over decisions in their plant than Stockton's scientists did in their laboratory. The task at Akron had already been clearly defined and that definition had, in a sense, been incorporated into the automated production flow itself. Therefore, there was less need for individuals to have a say in decisions concerning the work process.

Moreover, in Akron, influence was perceived to be concentrated in the upper levels of the formal structure (a hierarchical or "top-heavy" distribution), while in Stockton influence was perceived to be more evenly spread out among more levels of the formal structure (an egalitarian distribution).

Akron's members perceived themselves to have a low degree of freedom vis-à-vis superiors both in choosing the jobs they work on and in handling these jobs on their own. They also described the type of supervision in the plant as being relatively directive. Stockton's scientists, on the other hand, felt that they had a great deal of freedom vis-à-vis their superiors both in choosing the tasks and projects, and in handling them in the way that they wanted to. They described supervision in the laboratory as being very participatory.

It is interesting to note that the less successful Carmel laboratory had more of its decisions made at the top. Because of this, there was a definite feeling by the scientists that their particular expertise was not being effectively used in choosing projects.

Relation with others. The people at Akron perceived a great deal of similarity among themselves in background, prior work experiences, and approaches for tackling job-related problems. They also perceived the degree of coordination of effort among colleagues to be very high. Because Akron's task was so precisely defined and the behavior of its members so rigidly controlled around the automated lines, it is easy to see that this pattern also made sense.

By contrast, Stockton's scientists perceived not only a great many differences among themselves, especially in education and background, but also that the coordination of effort among colleagues was relatively low. This was appropriate for a laboratory in which a great variety of disciplines and skills were present and individual projects were important to solve technological problems.

Time orientation. As we would expect, Akron's individuals were highly oriented toward a relatively short time span and manufacturing goals. They responded to quick feedback concerning the quality and service that the plant was providing. This was essential, given the nature of their task.

Stockton's researchers were highly oriented toward a longer time span and scientific goals. These orientations meant that they were willing to wait for long-term feedback from a research project that might take years to complete. A scientist in Stockton said:

"We're not the kind of people here who need a pat on the back every day. We can wait for months if necessary before we get feedback from colleagues and the profession. I've been working on one project now for three months and I'm still not sure where it's going to take me. I can live with that, though."

This is precisely the kind of behavior and attitude that spells success on this kind of task.

Managerial style. Finally, the individuals in both Akron and Stockton perceived their chief executive to have a "managerial style" that expressed more of a concern for the task than for people or relationships, but this seemed to fit both tasks.

In Akron, the technology of the task was so dominant that top managerial behavior which was not focused primarily on the task might have reduced the effectiveness of performance. On the other hand, although Stockton's research task called for more individualistic problem-solving behavior, that sort of behavior could have become segmented and uncoordinated, unless the top executive in the lab focused the group's attention on the overall research task. Given the individualistic bent of the scientists, this was an important force in achieving unity of effort.

All these differences in climate characteristics in the two high performers are summarized in Exhibit III.

As with the formal attributes, the less effective Hartford and Carmel sites and organization climates that showed a perceptibly lower degree of fit with

Exhibit III. *Differences in "climate" characteristics in high-performing organizations*

Characteristics	Akron	Stockton
1. Structural orientation	Perceptions of tightly controlled behavior and a high degree of structure	Perceptions of a low degree of structure
2. Distribution of influence	Perceptions of low total influence, concentrated at upper levels in the organization	Perceptions of high total influence, more evenly spread out among all levels
3. Character of superior-subordinate relations	Low freedom vis-à-vis superiors to choose and handle jobs, directive type of supervision	High freedom vis-à-vis superiors to choose and handle projects, participatory type of supervision
4. Character of colleague relations	Perceptions of many similarities among colleagues, high degree of coordination of colleague effort	Perceptions of many differences among colleagues, relatively low degree of coordination of colleague effort
5. Time orientation	Short-term	Long-term
6. Goal orientation	Manufacturing	Scientific
7. Top executive's "managerial style"	More concerned with task than people	More concerned with task than people

their respective tasks. For example, the Hartford plant had an egalitarian distribution of influence, perceptions of a low degree of structure, and a more participatory type of supervision. The Carmel laboratory had a somewhat top-heavy distribution of influence, perceptions of high structure, and a more directive type of supervision.

COMPETENCE MOTIVATION
Because of the difference in organizational characteristics at Akron and Stockton, the two sites were strikingly different places in which to work. But these organizations had two very important things in common. First, each organization fit very well the requirements of its task. Second, although the behavior in the two organizations was different, the result in both cases was effective task performance.

Since, as we indicated earlier, our primary concern in this study was to link the fit between organization and task with individual motivation to perform effectively, we devised a two-part test to measure the sense of competence motivation of the individuals at both sites. Thus:

The *first* part asked a participant to write creative and imaginative stories in response to six ambiguous pictures.

The *second* asked him to write a creative and imaginative story about what he would be doing, thinking, and feeling "tomorrow" on his job. This is called a "projective" test because it is assumed that the respondent projects into his stories his own attitudes, thoughts, feelings, needs, and wants, all of which can be measured from the stories.[5]

The results indicated that the individuals in Akron and Stockton showed significantly more feelings of competence than did their counterparts in the lower-fit Hartford and Carmel organizations.[6] We found that the organization-task fit is simultaneously linked to and interdependent with both individual motivation and effective unit performance. (This interdependency is illustrated in Exhibit IV.)

Exhibit IV. *Basic contingent relationships*

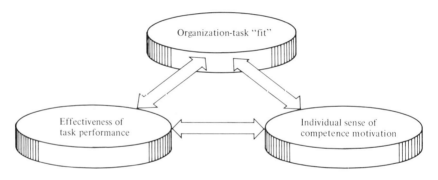

Putting the conclusions in this form raises the question of cause and effect. Does effective unit performance result from the task-organization fit or from higher motivation, or perhaps from both? Does higher sense of competence motivation result from effective unit performance or from fit?

Our answer to these questions is that we do not think there are any single cause-and-effect relationships, but that these factors are mutually interrelated. This has important implications for management theory and practice.

CONTINGENCY THEORY

Returning to McGregor's Theory X and Theory Y assumptions, we can now question the validity of some of his conclusions. While Theory Y might help to explain the findings in the two laboratories, we clearly need something other than Theory X or Y assumptions to explain the findings in the plants.

For example, the managers at Akron worked in a formalized organization setting with relatively little participation in decision making, and yet they were highly motivated. According to Theory X, people would work hard in such a setting only because they were coerced to do so. According to Theory Y, they should have been involved in decision making and been self-directed to feel so motivated. Nothing in our data indicates that either set of assumptions was valid at Akron.

Conversely, the managers at Hartford, the low-performing plant, were in a less formalized organization with more participation in decision making, and yet they were not as highly motivated like the Akron managers. The Theory Y assumptions would suggest that they should have been more motivated.

A way out of such paradoxes is to state a new set of assumptions, the Contingency Theory, that seems to explain the findings at all four sites:

1. Human beings bring varying patterns of needs and motives into the work organization, but one central need is to achieve a sense of competence.

2. The sense of competence motive, while it exists in all human beings, may be fulfilled in different ways by different people depending on how this need interacts with the strengths of the individuals' other needs—such as those for power, independence, structure, achievement, and affiliation.

2. Competence motivation is most likely to be fulfilled when there is a fit between task and organization.

4. Sense of competence continues to motivate even when a competence goal is achieved; once one goal is reached, a new, higher one is set.

While the central thrust of these points is clear from the preceding discussion of the study, some elaboration can be made. First, the idea that different people have different needs is well understood by psychologists. However, all too often, managers assume that all people have similar needs. Lest we be accused of the same error, we are saying only that all people have a need to feel competent; in this *one* way they are similar. But in many other dimensions of personality, individuals differ, and these differences will determine how a particular person achieves a sense of competence.

Thus, for example, the people in the Akron plant seemed to be very different from those in the Stockton laboratory in their underlying attitudes toward uncertainty, authority, and relationships with their peers. And because they had different need patterns along these dimensions, both groups were highly motivated by achieving competence from quite different activities and settings.

While there is a need to further investigate how people who work in different settings differ in their psychological makeup, one important implication of the Contingency Theory is that we must not only seek a fit between organization and task, but also between task and people and between people and organization.

A further point which requires elaboration is that one's sense of competence never really comes to rest. Rather, the real satisfaction of this need is in the successful performance itself, with no diminishing of the motivation as one goal is reached. Since feelings of competence are thus reinforced by successful performance, they can be a more consistent and reliable motivator than salary and benefits.

Implications for Managers

The major managerial implication of the Contingency Theory seems to rest in the task-organization-people fit. Although this interrelationship is complex, the best possibility for managerial action probably is in tailoring the organization to fit the task and the people. If such a fit is achieved, both effective unit performance and a higher sense of competence motivation seem to result.

Managers can start this process by considering how certain the task is, how frequently feedback about task performance is available, and what goals are implicit in the task. The answers to these questions will guide their decisions about the design of the management hierarchy, the specificity of job assignments, and the utilization of rewards and control procedures. Selective use of training programs and a general emphasis on appropriate management styles will move them toward a task-organization fit.

The problem of achieving a fit among task, organization, and people is something we know less about. As we have already suggested, we need further investigation of what personality characteristics fit various tasks and organizations. Even with our limited knowledge, however, there are indications that people will gradually gravitate into organizations that fit their particular personalities. Managers can help this process by becoming more aware of what psychological needs seem to best fit the tasks available and the organizational setting, and by trying to shape personnel selection criteria to take account of these needs.

In arguing for an approach which emphasizes the fit among task, organization, and people, we are putting to rest the question of which organizational approach—the classical or the participative—is best. In its place we are raising a new question: What organizational approach is most appropriate given the task and the people involved?

For many enterprises, given the new needs of younger employees for more autonomy, and the rapid rates of social and technological change, it may well be that the more participative approach is the most appropriate. But there will still be many situations in which the more controlled and formalized organization is desirable. Such an organization need not be coercive or punitive. If it makes sense to the individuals involved, given their needs and their jobs, they will find it rewarding and motivating.

CONCLUDING NOTE

The reader will recognize that the complexity we have described is not of our own making. The basic deficiency with earlier approaches is that they did not recognize the variability in tasks and people which produces this complexity. The strength of the contingency approach we have outlined is that it begins to provide a way of thinking about this complexity, rather than ignoring it. While our knowledge in this area is still growing, we are certain that any adequate theory of motivation and organization will have to take account of the contingent relationship between task, organization, and people.

Notes

1. Douglas McGregor, *The Human Side of Enterprise* (New York, McGraw-Hill Book Company, Inc., 1960), pp. 34–35 and pp. 47–48.

2. See for example Paul R. Lawrence and Jay W. Lorsch, *Organization and Environment* (Boston, Harvard Business School, Division of Research, 1967); Joan Woodward, *Industrial Organization: Theory & Practice* (New York, Oxford University Press, Inc., 1965); Tom Burns and G. M. Stalker, *The Management of Innovation* (London, Tavistock Publications, 1961); Harold J. Leavitt, "Unhuman Organizations," HBR July–August 1962, p. 90.

3. McGregor, op. cit., p. 245.

4. See Robert W. White, "Ego and Reality in Psychoanalytic Theory," *Psychological Issues,* Vol. III, No. 3 (New York, International Universities Press, 1963).

5. For a more detailed description of this survey, see John J. Morse, *Internal Organizational Patterning and Sense of Competence Motivation* (Boston, Harvard Business School, unpublished doctoral dissertation, 1969).

6. Differences between the two container plants are significant at .001 and between the research laboratories at .01 (one-tailed probability).

Project Organization:
Factors Affecting the Decision Environment
Bruce N. Baker, Dalmar Fisher,
and David C. Murphy

This paper presents some of the initial findings of a study designed to detail the relationships among situational, structural, and process variables as they relate to project effectiveness. The emphasis of this paper is upon investigating the project organization and decision making environmental variables as they relate to project success. The overall study was conducted by the School of Management, Boston College, and sponsored by the National Aeronautics and Space Administration.

The overall study is believed to be the largest and most comprehensive investigation to date on the subject of project management effectiveness. A sample of 646 responses to a 17 page questionnaire represented a variety of industries (34% manufacturing, 22% construction, 17% government, and 27% services, transportation and others). Most of the respondents themselves had been directly involved in the particular project they chose to describe in their questionnaire. Of the total sample, 50% had been the project manager, 31% had been in other positions on the project team, and another 10% had been the project manager's direct superior. About one-third of the projects were described as being public in nature, the remaining two-thirds being in the private sector. The types of contracts or agreements involved included cost plus fixed fee (32%) in-house work orders (28%), fixed price (21%), and fixed price with incentives (14%). The major activity or end product involved in the projects included construction (43%), hardware or equipment (22%), new processes or software (14%), and studies, services and tests (11%).

The data were analyzed in several ways. First, product-moment correlations were performed on the project characteristics with six success items. These correlations indicated linear relationships of the project characteristics with the success items. It was found that the overall subjective item—"All things considered, the project was a success"—presented a fair overall measure of success.

Next, in order to simplify the data and to enhance the understanding of the project characteristics, a factor analysis was performed on the variables

Paper presented to the Midwest Conference, American Institute for Decision Sciences, Minneapolis, Minnesota, May 1974. Reprinted by permission of AIDS.

Item	Factor loading
Satisfaction with outcome—client	.734
Satisfaction with outcome—parent	.701
Satisfaction with outcome—project team	.683
Project was a success	.678
Satisfaction with outcome—end users	.670
Technical adequacy of end result	.588

describing each project. While the correlations allow us to study the relationships of specific items or project characteristics, factor analysis allows us to move a step closer toward understanding the total pattern of relationships among all of the variables. Factor analysis is a statistical technique which can analyze the relationships between any number of variables and produce a set of "factors" or underlying dimensions each representing an interrelated "cluster" of the original variables. Thus when, say, five variables tend to "travel together" they are "boiled down" to a single factor for analysis purposes. This has the important advantage of reducing the number of variables to be studied.

One of the factors which emerged in the factor analysis provided us with a measure of project success. This factor, which we called "Perceived Success of the Project," was comprised of the following individual questionnaire items:

A total of thirty-three other identifiable and distinct factors were derived from the variables. Each of the factors was correlated with the factor, "Perceived Success of the Project."

In order to identify any non-linear relationships among the factors and perceived success or failure, an F-test analysis of variance was performed on the factors with success items categorized by degree.

In addition, a path analysis diagram was constructed based upon a series of multiple regressions.

Some of the results run counter to traditional practice. Some can be considered counter-intuitive in nature. A few of the findings which may be considered to fall into these types of categories are presented below. In each case, a statement is presented which the reader is asked to declare as true or false before proceeding.

A matrix form of project organizational structure is the least disruptive to traditional company functional organizational patterns and is also most likely to result in project success.

False. Although there are no clear definitions of the different forms of project organizational structures which have attained widespread acceptance, there are some terms which imply certain patterns. The matrix form of organization is well understood by experienced project management personnel but the authority which goes with such a matrix form of structure varies considerably. In order to provide a spectrum of choices which attempted to avoid preconception of terms, the following organizational patterns were presented for describing the organizational structure of the project team as it existed during the peak activity period of the project:

- Pure Functional-Project Manager, if any, was merely the focal point for communications, he had no authority to direct people other than by persuasion or reporting to his own superior.
- Weak Matrix-Project Manager was the focal point for controls; he did not actively direct the work of others.
- Strong Matrix or Partially Projectized-Project Manager was the focal point for directions and controls; he may have had some engineering and control personnel reporting to him on a line basis, while remainder of the Project Team was located administratively in other departments.
- Projectized-Project Manager had most of the essential elements of the Project Team under him.
- Fully Projectized-Project Manager had almost all of the employees who were on the Project Team under him.

An F-test of these different forms of organizational structure compared with project success revealed that the projectized form of organizational structure was most closely associated with success. Therefore, it is important for the project manager to have most of the essential elements of the project team under him.

The question remains, however, how should the decision making authority of the project manager relate to the decision making authority of the client organization (the organization which sponsored, approved, and funded the effort), and the parent organization (the organization structure above the level of the project manager but within the same overall organization)?

When a project is critical to the overall success of a company and/or it is critical to the client organization, the parent organization and/or the client organization should take a strong and active role in internal project decision making.

False. It is important for the client organization to establish definitive goals for a project. Similarly, and especially for in-house projects, the parent organization must also establish clear and definitive goals for the project. When there is a good consensus among the client organization, the parent organization, and the project team with respect to the goals of a project, then success is more readily achieved. A path analysis revealed that success criteria clarity and consensus were especially important for:

- projects with complex legal/political environments,
- projects which are relatively large, and

- projects undertaken within a parent organization undergoing considerable change.

Once success criteria have been clarified and agreed upon by the principal parties involved with a project, i.e., the client, the parent, and the project team, then it is essential to permit the project team to "carry the ball" from there on out with respect to internal decisions.

Because some decisions require the approval of the client organization, it was found that the authority of the client contact should be commensurate with the authority of the project manager. Projects characterized by strong project manager authority and influence and strong client contact authority and influence were strongly associated with success. Unfortunately, many client organizations and parent organizations tend to believe that the more closely they monitor a project and the more intimately they enter into the internal project decision process, the more likely the project will be successful. Close coordination and good relations patterns were found to be the most important factors contributing to project success. Nonetheless, there is a very important distinction between "close" and "meddling" and there is just as important a distinction between "supportive" and "interfering" relationships. Many factors and relationships pointed to the need for the client and the parent organization to develop close and supportive working relationships with the project team but to avoid meddling or interfering with the project team's decision making processes. The lesson is clear: the project manager should be delegated sufficient authority to make important project decisions and sufficient authority to direct the project team.

Once given this authority, how should the project manager arrive at decisions and solve problems?

Because participative decision making and problem solving can tend to slow up the decision making and problem solving processes, these behavioralistic approaches should not be employed on complex, crash projects.

False. First of all, participative decision making and problem solving within the project team was highly correlated with success for the total sample of projects. Second, a path analysis revealed that under conditions of adversity, such as a highly complex project, or one where initial over-optimism prevailed regarding the time and cost for completing the project, it was especially important to employ participative approaches to overcome these adversities.

If this pattern is successful, should the public also participate in project decisions affecting the public interest?

Public participation is an essential ingredient of success for projects affecting the public interest.

False. Although the trend of the past eight to ten years has certainly been in this direction, i.e., to encourage, or at least to facilitate, public participation in the decision making process for public projects, and although value judgment may lean heavily toward this approach, the facts are that public participation delays and hampers projects and reduces the probability of success.

Therefore, from a management standpoint (not from a value judgment standpoint), public participation should be avoided or circumvented as much as possible.

If public participation hampers success, can the cooperation and participation of several agencies help to safeguard the public interest and result in a more successful overall effort than a project undertaken by a single agency?

> Public projects involving the cooperation, funding, and participation of several governmental agencies are more likely to be successful than projects undertaken by a single agency.

False. Again, the trend is certainly in this direction. There has been a great deal of emphasis upon:

- inter-agency cooperative efforts, e.g., Departments of Labor, Commerce, and Transportation;
- inter-governmental cooperative efforts, e. g., Federal, state, and local jointly funded efforts.
- the creation of new, integrative agencies, e.g., regional commissions combining the efforts of several states, counties, or cities to attack common problems.

Although the creation of these jointly-funded, jointly-managed organizational mechanisms may be desirable from the standpoint of integration of efforts, they tend to result in less successful projects as compared to projects undertaken by a single source of funding and authority. Such cooperative efforts result in the creation of elaborate bureaucratic structures, decision delays, red tape, and relatively diminished success.

What types of project tools contribute to better project decisions and relatively greater project success?

> The use of PERT-CPM systems is the most important factor contributing to improved decision making and project success.

False. PERT-CPM systems *do* contribute to project success, especially when initial over-optimism and/or a "buy-in" strategy has prevailed in the securing of the contract, but the importance of PERT-CPM is far outweighed by another factor involving project tools entitled, "systems management concepts." This factor included the use of, and value of, work breakdown structures, life cycle planning, systems engineering, configuration management, and status reports. The over-use of PERT-CPM systems was found to hamper success. It was the *judicious* use of PERT-CPM which was associated with success.

As stated earlier, some of these findings run counter to traditional project management practice and some may be considered counter-intuitive.

When establishing organizational structures and decision making patterns for a project the following guidelines should be kept in mind:

- Design a projectized form of organizational structure.
- Delegate sufficient authority to the project manager for internal project decisions and to the principal client contact for decisions requiring client organization approval.
- A project manager should seek to maximize his influence and to employ participative approaches to problem solving and decision making.
- Avoid or minimize public participation.
- Seek to establish single agency funding and direction for public projects.
- Avoid pre-occupation with, or over reliance upon PERT-CPM.

These guidelines alone cannot assure project success, they can only contribute to it. Another aspect of the study has shown that there are:

- twenty-nine project management characteristics which strongly affect the preceived failure of a project,
- twenty-three project management characteristics which are strongly associated with perceived success of a project, and
- ten project management characteristics linearly related to both perceived success and perceived failure.

It is not generally possible to include all the characteristics which contribute to success nor to exclude all those which affect failure. Where a choice exists, however, it is important to know which choice will contribute to project success and/or which choice will contribute to project failure. This study contributes to a better understanding of how to make those choices.

INFORMATION FLOW

Cost Control, Production and People
Chris Argyris

Budgets and the budgeting process are central features of our highly industrial-ized society. To produce a product at a profit, management needs more than machines and technical processes. Management also needs a means of keeping score—calculating the score for the total organization at appropriate time intervals and also calculating the score for each unit making up that total, so that the contributions of the units can be evaluated.

Budgets are generally prepared annually, and they are often broken down into monthly and weekly totals. Each budget can be looked upon as a goal for the organization, as determined by top management. The goal is based in part upon past experience but also represents a projection of a future desired state of affairs. The budget may specify goals for production, labor costs, maintenance costs, materials costs, amount of waste or scrap, and so on.

In terms of our scheme of analysis, what are budgets? They are symbols designed to represent a planned state of organizational performance. The symbols have effects upon the sentiments of people and in turn affect their activities and interactions. In this way, the impact of budgets is felt throughout the social system even by those who give little direct attention to budgets. The purpose of this chapter is to explore some of the ways in which budgets affect sentiments, interactions, and activities in the social system.

Most of the material in the present chapter is drawn from *The Impact of Budgets on People.*[1]

WHAT DO BUDGET SYMBOLS MEAN TO PEOPLE?
In a study of four plants, Argyris and Miller asked each factory supervisor to name the department which affected him most and then the second most

A paper prepared for Controllership Foundation, Inc., under the direction of S. Hos-lett, with the assistance of F. Miller, Jr., Ithaca, New York: Cornell University School of Business and Public Administration, 1952, pp. 11. Reprinted by permission of Chris Argyris.

important department. A total of 56 percent considered production control as most important and 44 percent named the budget department; *all but one* supervisor who named production control first chose the budget department as the second most important department.

These sentiments should be interpreted in terms of the flow of interactions and activities within the plants. If we just looked at the efficient functioning of production departments, we might assume that their supervisors would consider the maintenance department as the most important one for them. One could argue that without efficient maintenance, production would break down. However, as a general rule the production departments initiate interactions and activity changes for the maintenance department, whereas production control and cost control constantly initiate interactions and activity changes for the production departments. The budget people also have control of one of the key sets of symbols in the organization and thereby indirectly bring rewards and penalties to the production supervisors.

How do the budget people see their own role? One man says, "If I see an inconsistency, I'll go to top management and report it. No, I never go to the supervisor in charge. It is our job to report any inconsistencies to the top management."

Another man gives this picture:

> As soon as we examine the budget results and see a fellow is slipping, we immediately call the factory manager and point out, "Look, Joe, you're behind on the budget. What do you expect to do about it?"
>
> True, he may be batting his brains out already on the problem, but our phone call adds a little more pressure—er—well, you know, we let them know we're interested.
>
> The important thing for us to do is follow up. The supervisor's interest lags unless someone is constantly checking up on him. A little pressure. If you don't, the tendency is to lag. You can't blame supervisors. They are interested in the machines.
>
> I think there is a need for more pressure. People need to be needled a bit.
>
> I think a man is inherently lazy and if we could only increase the pressure . . . I think budgets would be more effective.

The factory managers, superintendents, and higher level supervisors see budgets in much the same light. Consider these two comments:

> The job of budgets is to see to it that we *never forget* we've got a job to do. Sure, we apply pressure with budgets. I guess budgets aren't worth much unless they have a kick in them.
>
> I go to the office and check that budget everyday. I can then see how we're meeting the budget. If it's O.K., I don't say anything. But if it's no good, then I come back here (*smiles*) and give the boys a little . . .

you know what . . . the old needle.

The factory foremen take quite a different view of budgets. Budgets represent pressures on them—that they cannot pass down to the workers. These two comments are illustrative:

> You can't use budgets with the people. Just can't do anything like that. People have to be handled carefully and in our plant, carefully doesn't mean budgets. Besides, I don't think *my* people are lazy.

> No sir, I can't use budgets to increase production. I don't dare go up and say to a man, "My budget is *up* $5,000 this year, John." He'd look at me in scorn. No sir, anything like that is using a *whip*. And the men *don't like it.*

How do the workers see budgets? They often recognize that management people are worried about costs, but with the foremen afraid to put the cost situation to them, they remain uninvolved in the struggle.

PROBLEMS WITH BUDGETS

This discussion suggests several important problems involved in the application of this set of symbols.

1. *Pressure.* The budgets are seen as sources of severe psychological pressure on the part of management people. This problem may be perhaps most acute at the foreman level, because the foreman receives the pressure and has no one to whom he can pass it on without fear of damaging reactions.

2. *Budget results indicate the score but do not reveal the plays that went into making up the score.* As one factory supervisor said:

> Let's say the budget tells me I was off. I didn't make it. That's of interest. But it doesn't tell me the important thing of why I didn't make it, or how I am going to make it the next time. Oh sure, they might say all I need to do is increase production and cut out waste. Well, I know that. The question is how to do it.

3. *The goal is always rising.* As one man commented:

> If I meet this budget, those guys up there will only raise it. Oh, you can't let them know that you made the budget without too much trouble. If you do they'll up it as sure as hell.

4. *It is often charged that the goal is too high.* One factory supervisor made this comment:

> Budgets should be realistic. They should reflect the true picture. Take the error budget for example. There is something. The error figure is way too low. I know it. The people know it and so do the financial people know it.

So I suggested to the financial people that they should increase it. They refused. They feel that if they increase the budget to a realistic level and the people meet it, they'll have no reason to cut down errors.

We, on the other hand, feel differently. Our people see the figure and they know it is ridiculously low. So they say, "Oh, those financial guys do that so they can have the opportunity to wave the flag."

5. *In many situations, production management people do not participate in the goal-setting process.* At least this is true at the level of factory superintendent and below.

Most of the controllers interviewed spoke about encouraging the participation of the line people in the budget-making process, but they seemed to view the budget people as the active agents and the supervisory people as the passive accepters in this so-called participation process. Argyris paraphrases the comments of a number of controllers in this way:

We bring them in, we *tell* them that we want their frank opinion, but most of them just sit there and nod their heads. We know they're not coming out with exactly how they feel. I guess budgets scare them. . . . Some of them don't have too much education. . . .

Similarly, the controllers refer to another phase of the participation process as they outline what happens when they present the budget to the supervisor:

Then we request the line supervisor to sign the new budget. Then he can't tell us he didn't accept it. We found the signature helps an awful lot. If anything goes wrong, they can't come to us, as they often do, and complain. We just show them their signature and remind them they were shown exactly what the budget was made up of. . . .

Needless to say, the supervisor who is asked to sign on the dotted line —and knows he has no alternative—can hardly feel that he is participating in the budget-setting process.

THE IMPACT OF PEOPLE

What impact do these budget-making and enforcing procedures have on the sentiments, activities, and interactions of people?

1. *The budget man achieves his successes by pointing out the failures of departmental managements.* The procedures described put budget people and supervisors in a competitive transaction situation. Furthermore, the transactions tend to be "rigged" so that the supervisors cannot win. If they meet the budgets established for their departments, they escape penalties, but they do not win. Only by exceeding the budget standards can the supervisors win. Since the budgeteers control the symbols of success and failure, they are inclined to set the standards so high that surpassing them is highly unlikely.

There is no doubt that this system stimulates the supervisors to take budget and costs very seriously. At the same time, it leads to strongly negative sentiments toward budget people on the part of factory supervisors. Is this a necessary price that must be paid for developing an efficient and cost-conscious organization?

2. *Budget and cost control procedures, as often used, tend to put and keep supervisors in a failure situation.* In fact, some controllers and other executives seem to feel that the only way to get supervisors highly motivated regarding costs is to have the budgets so tight that supervisors are nearly always falling at least somewhat short of meeting the budgets. The assumption seems to be that men are naturally lazy and will relax as soon as they have reached a goal set before them. If this assumption were true, it would then follow that great care must be taken to set goals that are rarely reached.

On the other hand, if we assume that most people in industry are concerned with doing a conscientious job and would get especially strong satisfaction in meeting or exceeding the goal set before them, then it is obviously a mistake to set goals that can rarely be met.

Research suggests that constant failure to meet goals has a depressing effect upon both the morale and productivity of the individuals involved. This does not, however, suggest that the lower the goal, the better the morale and performance. People seem to perform best and to achieve the greatest satisfactions when they are called upon to put forth special efforts to meet the goal, but then do find it within their reach.

3. *As often administered, budgets promote interdepartmental friction and an orientation toward the past.* That is, budgets provide supervisors with an incentive to discover faults in other departments so that they and their departments may escape blame. Wherever the blame is finally placed, the effort to pin down responsibility involves a canvassing of past events and may divert considerable time from current activities and planning for the future.

An illustration of this effect is provided by a case presented by Argyris in these words as he describes a management meeting and the events that followed:

Present at the meeting were the supervisors of the two departments, two budget people, the supervisor of the department that supplies the material, and the top executive whom we shall call the leader.

Leader: I've called you fellows down to get some ideas about this waste. I can't see why we're having so much waste. I just can't see it. Now (*turns to one of the supervisors*), I've called in these two budget men to get some ideas about this waste. Maybe they can give us an idea of how much some of the arguments you're going to give are worth.

Cost Man 1 to Leader (*Slightly red—* seems to realize he is putting the supervisors "on the spot."): Well, er—we might be wrong, but I can't see how. There's an entire 1 percent difference and that's a lot.

Supervisor A to Supervisor B (*Trying to see if he could place the blame on Supervisor B.*): Well, maybe—maybe—some of your boys are throwing away the extra material I sent back to your department.

Supervisor B (*Becomes red, answers quickly and curtly.*): No, no, we're reworking the extra material and getting it ready to use over again.

Supervisor A (*Realizing that the argument wasn't going to hold much water.*): Well—you know—I've been thinking, maybe it's those new trainees we have in the plant. Maybe they're the cause for all the waste.

Leader: I can't understand that. Look here—look at their budget, their [trainees'] waste is low.

The meeting continued for another 20 minutes. It was primarily concerned with the efforts of Supervisors A and B to fix the blame on someone except themselves. The leader terminated the meeting as follows:

Leader: All right, look here, let's get busy on this—all of you—all of us, let's do something about it.

Supervisor B left the meeting, flushed, tense, and obviously unhappy. As he passed through the door, he muttered to himself, "Those g—— d—— budgets!" (Note that the budgets are immediately blamed for the unhappiness.)

Supervisor B hurried down to his area of the plant. He rushed in the office and called his subordinates abruptly. "Joe—get over here—I want to speak to you—something's up."

The subordinates came in, all wondering what had occurred. As soon as they had all assembled, the supervisor started:

Supervisor B: Look, we've just got to get at this waste. It makes me look like ——. Now let's put our heads together and get on the ball.

The supervisors set to work to locate the causes for the waste. Their methods were interesting. Each one of them first checked to see, as one of them put it, "that the other guys (departments) aren't cheating us." A confidential statement finally arrived in Supervisor B's hands from one of the subordinates to the effect that he had located the cause for waste in another department.

Supervisor B became elated, but at the same time was angry at the fact that he had been made to look "sick" at the meeting with the leader.

Supervisor B: . . . I'm going to find out why they are making the waste. I don't mind taking a little ——, as long as it's me that's doing the trouble.

Supervisor B roared out of his office and headed straight for the office of Supervisor A, where the confidential sources had reported the waste. Supervisor A saw him coming, and braced himself for the onslaught.

Supervisor B:——, I found out that it's your boys causing the waste.——, I want to know why——. . . .

Supervisor A (*Cuts off Supervisor B . . . spits out some tobacco and says*): Now, just hold on to your water. Don't get your blood up. I'll tell you. . . .

Briefly, we have tried to show, by a running account of one small problem, the effects budgets can have upon people. In this cost-conscious plant, five or six people on the supervisory level spent many man-hours trying to place the blame on someone else.

4. *As usually administered, the budget process does not involve workers.* As the foremen point out, it is probably fortunate for management that the process does not reach workers—as it is ordinarily carried out. If the foremen did indeed transmit to workers the cost pressures they themselves feel, the losses incurred by management would certainly outweigh any gains that could be made. On the other hand, the behavior of workers is certainly of great importance in creating the figures that the budget process reports. Therefore, it does seem ironic that workers are left out of the process altogether. We may ask whether there might not be some way of involving workers in the process without incurring the losses that would normally be expected.

THE BUDGET-MAKING PROCESS

The process by which the budget is made up has important consequences for the reactions of operating people to that budget. Let us consider two contrasting cases.

The first is taken from the company in the Argyris-Miller study, where production supervisors reported feeling under the most extreme budget pressures. Here we found a common belief that accountants were running the company. In fact we found that a very high proportion of the men in top management were accountants by educational background.

Let me digress to point out the general significance of this phenomenon. While most large companies recruit men of a variety of educational backgrounds and promote to higher management levels men from the several functional specialties, we often do find that one particular category of men has much more than its proportionate share in the higher positions. Thus we find members reporting that company A is run by engineers, company B by salesmen, company C by accountants, and so on.

The effects of such a promotional emphasis may go far beyond the careers of individual members. Men of a given category are likely to see the organization and its problems in similar ways, and when they hold the dominant positions, they are able to impose their own views upon the structure and procedures of the organization.

In the accountant-dominated company, the controller in the main office was naturally a powerful figure. Furthermore, his power extended into every plant. Reporting directly to the controller, and independent of the plant manager, the plant controller was responsible for the direction of the plant office and also for the budgets for office and plant. The controller would hand down to each plant controller the targets they should seek to establish so that the figures for each plant would fit into the overall company budget the controller was to recommend to the president and board of directors. The plant controller would then work out the figures for departments and the plant as a whole.

In this process, the plant controller was not required to seek out the collaboration of operating management. Collaboration did not generally take place, and sharp conflicts between plant manager and plant controller were commonly observed. In the one case where we found collaboration, it seemed something more than a coincidence that the plant manager himself was an accountant. While this may have helped to smooth relations between the two men, it did nothing to relieve budget pressures perceived at lower operating levels. In fact, we see the plant manager calling cost men into meetings with superintendents to help him apply the pressure to them.

In the second case, while we have much less systematic information, the process seemed to be quite different. In this company, the vice-president and controller was considered to be a staff man responsible for establishing the cost control and accounting procedures for the company as a whole. He was also looked upon as a technical consultant to the cost control people in the plant. However, each plant manager had a plant controller reporting directly to him. It was the plant manager who presented the preliminary budget for his plant to the general manager and the president of the company. At least in some cases, this preliminary budget grew out of considerable discussion that the plant manager held with his superintendents and with his controller.

The president then reviewed with his general manager the preliminary budgets submitted from the plants. He reported that he sometimes acted to tighten up a plant budget but at least as often decided that the goals set were unrealistically high and should be somewhat reduced. It was his aim to establish budgets that *could be met.* The involvement of the supervisors in the budget-making process and the establishment of goals that seemed reasonable to them combined to make them feel under less budget pressures than the supervisors in the first case reported.

SUMMARY AND CONCLUSIONS
Budgets provide the primary set of symbols by which the performance of managers and supervisors is judged. The budget-making and implementation process is therefore highly *salient* not only to the budget makers but especially to the people whose performance is so judged. Supervisors are not likely to be indifferent toward the budget and cost control people.

If budgets are established without any participation in the process by departmental supervisors, we can expect the supervisors to hold strongly negative sentiments toward the budgeteers. The budget makers are likely to have a negative view of human nature and feel that men will be too lazy to perform well unless they have exacting standards imposed upon them. Supervisors who work under such tight standards that they find themselves constantly experiencing failure tend to become demoralized.

As often administered, budgets tend to focus supervisory attention on the past rather than on present or future. If higher management relies heavily upon budgets to control subordinates, the supervisors find themselves so often called upon to justify past failures to meet the standards that they find it difficult to think of the present and plan for the future.

Pressure from budgets tends to promote interdepartmental friction. If the departmental supervisor is called to account by superiors for falling short of his budget, he may consider three possible strategies of response:

1. Undertake to do better in the future.
2. Claim that the budgetary standards are unfair.
3. Claim that sub-par performance was due to problems created for one's own department by some other department.

The first strategy provides no immediate solution. It will take some time to demonstrate this improved performance, whereas the superior is applying "the needle" to past performance. Furthermore, the supervisor assumes that if he really does better in the future, the standards will be raised further so that he will again be in a failure situation. The second strategy is no more promising. The manager who is trying to apply pressure with the budget is not likely to respond favorably to a strategy that would tend to disarm him. Thus the third strategy may appear to the supervisor as his only possible escape. He therefore tries to blame other supervisors for his apparent failure—and at the same time to be on guard against others who, in the same situation, would like to pin the blame on him.

Can these negative effects of budgets and cost control be avoided—without the loss of performance? Suppose we ask each supervisor to make up his own budget. To relieve him further from pressure from above, suppose we even leave it to him to report to superiors at the end of each period how he did in relation to his own standards.

We can imagine this strategy working well in a small organization and as part of a general program to involve supervisors in decision making. We cannot imagine the strategy working in a large organization, no matter what the leadership philosophy of top management. Budgets are not used simply to put pressure on supervisors. They are used by higher management in relation to current performance figures to assess the relationship between past plans and current performance, to plan future production and financial requirements.

We assume that higher management must continue to be involved in budget setting, but we do not have to assume that the process will be carried out without any participation of the supervisors whose performance is being judged. Supervisors will respond less negatively to budgets and budgeting specialists if they themselves play a more prominent role in the process than is generally the case

We also suspect that few managements are exploiting budgets in terms of their teaching and learning potential for budget specialists and supervisors alike. One supervisor gave us this clue in these words:

> So they tell me that I didn't make my budget. Well, that is of interest, but the real question is: Why didn't I make the budget? They don't give me any help in answering that question.

In many plants, the cost control specialists present their findings on departmental performance not to the supervisor but to his superior. The cost control man may interact with the supervisor only when he is called in by a manager to help prove to the supervisor how badly he performed. In this highly negative situation, the supervisor is not likely to admit that he does not fully understand the budget or ask the cost control man to help him to interpret it and to use it more effectively in his department.

This suggests an approach along different lines: In this approach, the supervisor and the budget specialist work together in preparing the departmental budget. Each month they again get together to review performance figures against the budget. The budget specialist uses the budget not as a club but, in relation to performance figures, as a diagnostic instrument. He tries to help the supervisor to understand the budget so that he can even arrive at his own diagnosis. In the process, the budget specialist gains from the supervisor a far more realistic picture of departmental operations and problems that he would otherwise have. Thus, even if he alone prepares the first draft of the departmental budget, it is more likely that the supervisor will find it realistic and reasonable. The process also should influence the budget specialist's sentiments toward the supervisor. With this approach, he is less likely to consider the supervisor a lazy man who needs to be "needled" and more likely to consider him a responsible individual who is eager to improve his performance.

Since we do not have research data to back up this proposed approach, the argument must remain speculative. Nevertheless, note how we have gone about changing the sentiments of supervisors toward budget specialists (and vice versa) and the sentiments supervisors have toward themselves and their jobs. We have proposed a reorganization of the interactions and activities of budget specialists and supervisors. We proceed on the assumption that if changes are introduced in I and A, changes in S will necessarily follow. If this fundamental assumption is correct, then our framework can at least guide us to changes that are worth trying out.

References

Argyris, Chris, under the direction of Schuyler Dean Hoslett, with the assistance of Frank B. Miller, Jr. *The Impact of Budgets on People.* Ithaca, N.Y.: Cornell University School of Business and Public Administration, 1952. The first organizational behavior study of the human impact of cost control and budgeting procedures and still the best thing of its kind.

Gardner, Burleigh B., and Moore, David G. *Human Relations in Industry,* rev. ed. Homewood, Ill.: Richard D. Irwin, Inc., 1964. See Chapter 7, "The Factory Organization and the Division of Labor," especially section on "Control Organizations," pp. 205–14. A good, brief introduction.

Discussion Questions

1. Select an organization with which you are familiar. How are the symbols of success/failure established? Who participates in the goal and standard-setting process? With what consequences?

2. Interview a person with some experience in a work organization where he has been involved either in setting up the symbols of success/failure or in having them applied to him. Answer the same questions as above.

The Impact of Computerized Programs on Managers and Organizations: A Case Study in an Integrated Manufacturing Company
Edgar F. Huse

This is a case study describing the impact that computerized programs have on managers and organizations, particularly when such programs cut across departmental lines within a company. Because this paper is concerned with the "people" problems involved in the implementation of information systems, only enough technical information concerning the programs will be provided to give an over-all understanding of the mechanized programs.

Neither the computer programs themselves nor the technical problems involved will be described in detail. Rather, the report will provide specific recommendations for management and others to follow in the design and implementation of automated programs such as those described in this report. The recommendations have to do with the "human" aspects of the change process. The recommendations will also deal primarily with the impact on middle management, since it was this group that was the most affected by the design and implementation of the information systems.

The integrated information system (IIS) consisted of a series of twelve major computer programs with numerous subsidiary programs. The programs would be integrated in the sense that one program would lead into the next without the necessity for human intervention. These would include the following: processing of orders for original equipment and spare parts into manufacturing; scheduling of assembly and spare parts requirements; assembly and manufacturing schedules; inventory control; prediction of man and machine requirements; and measuring performance vs. commitments for the marketing, manufacturing, and purchasing departments.

Anticipated benefits were expected to include: reductions in cycle time from receipt of the customer order to shipment of original equipment and spare parts; reductions in inventory; more efficient use of manpower and machinery; reduced costs through elimination of indirect manufacturing expense jobs, and

Reprinted from *The Impact of Computers on Management,* by Charles A. Myers, ed., by permission of The M.I.T. Press, Cambridge, Mass. Copyright © 1967, pp. 282–302.

more timely, accurate schedules and management measurement reports. The system would replace or integrate in some modified fashion a multitude of manually maintained or partially mechanized systems existing in the company.

Savings resulting from the installation of the integrated information system (IIS) were estimated to be in the neighborhood of one million dollars per year, stemming from such sources as reduced cycle times, reduced inventory, and the reduction of the labor force by 70 to 100 people, particularly indirect labor.

THE ORGANIZATION

The study was conducted in an integrated manufacturing company employing approximately seven thousand people. The company manufactures a line of highly complex pieces of equipment used for a variety of defense and civilian purposes. In addition to the original equipment, it manufactures and supplies a complete line of spare parts and related materials for the maintenance and repair of the original equipment.

The business has expanded consistently in recent years, with marked sales increases each year. In 1965, the equipment was marketed in more than ten different countries in addition to the United States. The company produces seventeen different models of its original equipment, although the units can be classified into three basic types. This diversity requires the organization to maintain over 25,000 different engineering drawings of specific parts. One-year's business can be visualized as consisting of approximately 2,500 pieces of original equipment, plus approximately 22,000 separate orders for spare parts (some of which are purchased in large lots). On an annual basis, almost 6,000,000 parts are manufactured or processed. Approximately three million day and piecework vouchers are processed each year through the computer, which also handles the records for 47,000 tools, fixtures and dies, as well as 1,500 individual machines. Internal lot shipments and receipts number approximately 250,000 per year.

Manufacturing cycles are on the order of twelve to fifteen months. There are approximately twelve major production-schedule changes per year. Each major schedule change requires, if done manually, approximately 15,000 man hours to perform the more than 200,000 hand calculations required in the change. On an annual basis, approximately nine man years are required to make the 2,400,000 hand calculations needed to develop the production planning schedule. Since it takes forty working days to develop a schedule change on a manual basis and since, as the business expands, major schedule changes have been occurring on a more frequent basis, new schedule changes frequently occur *before* the last schedule has been finalized. This has meant that the assembly and manufacturing shops have been in a constant state of flux with constantly shifting schedules. Before the last schedule is finalized, a new one has been started.

The proposed programs would reduce the time necessary for a schedule change to an estimated four to five days, including reviews for accuracy and to less than a hundred hand calculations, with a proportionate increase in accuracy.

THE NATURE AND PURPOSE OF THE INTEGRATED INFORMATION SYSTEM (IIS)

As the business done by the Company expanded, two things happened in the area of mechanization. First, more and more data were put on the computer and secondly, the need for even more mechanization became apparent. The first real attempt to mechanize production scheduling occurred in the period from 1959 to 1963 in one of the "make" shops in manufacturing. For example, in 1961, a computerized system known as PASS (Production Automated Scheduling System) was implemented into the organization. Although it eventually failed after several years of work, much was learned from this and other work done in the organization in the period between 1959 and 1964.

The specific history of IIS, in this report, extends through the period between January, 1964 to January, 1966, a two-year span. In early 1964, a twelve-man integrated information systems task force was established to design, develop, and implement the programs. The task force was composed of representatives from manufacturing management, systems analysts, and computer programmers. In addition to the actual task-force members, functional representatives were assigned to work with the task force. Their role was primarily as liaison between the task-force members and specific groups of operating personnel. There were originally six such representatives.

The task-force members were working full time on the integrated system. Their function consisted in studying and analyzing activities, defining the scope of the twelve original computer programs, establishing detailed time schedules, formulating the program logic, and programming the computer, as well as remaining in contact with operating management for implementation and training purposes.

The functional representatives remained full time on their respective jobs. Their role consisted of maintaining contact with both operating management and task-force personnel to ensure that full communications were established and maintained.

As mentioned earlier, the original plans called for the development and implementation of twelve computer programs which would be integrated in the sense that one program would lead into the next without necessity for human intervention. The basic programs were:

OEO—Original Equipment Orders*
SPO—Spare Parts Ordered
APO—Assembly Parts Lists
ABB—Assembly Build-Up Books
AS I& II—Assembly Schedules (General and Detailed)
GMS—General Make Schedule
DMS—Detailed Make Schedule by Manufacturing Area
PLS—Parts List Maintenance Schedule
PPS—Purchased Parts Schedule†
IIM—Internal Inventory Movement
MCLRF—Machine Capacity and Labor Requirements Forecasting
IF—Inventory Forecasting
PMML—Parts Man-Machine Load

The following diagram shows an overly simplified flow of the major programs:

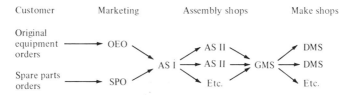

In other words, the orders for new equipment or for spare parts lead into the assembly schedules which, in turn, lead into the general and detailed make schedules. Each of these "executive routines" has, of course, a large number of subroutines. Internal inventory movement (IIM), as an "independent" program, provides up-to-date information and feedback as to what parts are where in the manufacturing and shipping cycle.

The programs were originally designed for the IBM 7044 computer, with plans to switch over to the GE 625 early in 1966. The year 1964 was devoted primarily to the design and development of the computer logic for the twelve major programs of IIS. It was during this period of time that the major systems analysis and charting took place.

The original timetable had called for the programs to be implemented in the period between February and June, 1965, with all programs to be completely implemented by July 1, 1965. In actual fact, *all* of 1965 was heavily

---

*Original equipment orders are primarily hand posted so that this is not actually a mechanized program.

†Not a part of the original schedules, but added late in 1964 at the request of Manufacturing Management.

involved in the implementation effort. By January 1, 1966, none of the major programs was completely "operational," and some were being revised and corrected, with considerable emphasis being placed on redesign and reimplementation.

It was too soon to tell, by January, 1966, whether the programs would eventually become successful, or whether, like PASS (the 1961 attempt), the programs would ultimately fail. However, the literature on mechanized programs, as well as this organization's experience with PASS and IIS, provides us with information that can be very helpful to any management group faced with a similar problem of development and installation of computerized and mechanized programs that cut across unit and department lines as did IIS.

RECOMMENDATIONS FOR FUTURE INSTALLATIONS

For two years, the author attended meetings and interviewed managers, task-force personnel, systems analysts, functional representatives, and others involved with the design and implementation of IIS. Based on that experience, this section of the report will provide specific recommendations for management and others to follow in the design and implementation of similar programs.

The problem of implementation of automated information systems is primarily a problem of the administration of change. For this reason, the recommendations have to do with the "human" aspects of the change process, rather than with the technical aspects of the programs themselves. The recommendations will also deal primarily with the impact on middle management, since it was this group that was the most affected by IIS. This, of course, was one of the major points made by Leavitt and Whisler in their article, "Management in the 1980's."[1]

Although the recommendations will be handled fairly independently, they are highly interrelated and the distinction between them is semantic, rather than real and actual. An organization is a total entity and one of the basic principles of organizational theory is that a stress, strain, or change in one part of the organization will have an impact on all parts of the organization, as Schein has pointed out.[2] Therefore, the principles should be considered as being somewhat different viewpoints of the *same* problem.

A. Hard Work and Sincere, Dedicated Effort are not Enough

The loyalty, hard work, and effort expended by the personnel at all levels in the company, including both task-force and operating personnel, were impressive. They put in many hours of overtime in the face of production pressures and pressures to design and implement the mechanized programs, yet the computer programs fell far behind schedule. Clearly, hard work and sincere, dedicated effort are not enough.

B. Top Management Needs to be Highly Involved

In a very real sense, the establishment of major mechanized schedules has far-reaching effects on the organizational structure. For this reason, it is essential that top management be highly involved in the design and implementation flow and organizational structure.

When the project originally started, it was solidly backed by the then vice-president of manufacturing and approved by the president. However, there was only limited involvement, at the beginning, by other department managers. When the vice-president of manufacturing changed jobs and a new vice-president was appointed, the amount of support for the programs dropped materially for a considerable period of time. As a result, the whole effort lagged. In addition, because top management remained detached, decisions were made which did not maximize the goals and aims of the organization. As one person put it, "One of the biggest problems about this whole program is the fact that it affects most of the organization but the actual decisions are made in little small groups with insufficient data as to how the decisions affect others."

Involvement by top management as an active group is the primary vehicle by which the other recommendations in this report will be implemented. Such involvement cannot be passive, nor can it be delegated. It must be personal. Naming a personal representative or sitting through "informational" meetings is not sufficient. Such techniques are essentially passive.

It is top management that can reduce the role conflict and ambiguity seen in the IIS study. By top management is not meant one manager only. Rather, if the organization is to become committed to supraordinate goals rather than subordinate goals, this means that the top management group must be involved *as a group* and that the interest and involvement of single managers is not enough.

As Thurston puts it, "Specialists have had too much responsibility for information systems and operating managers too little . . . the specialist should not dominate . . . companies would do well to give considerably more responsibility to *operating* managers."[3] The development and installation of integrated information systems is far too important to leave completely in the hands of the systems people.

C. Shift From Subordinate to Supraordinate Goals

With the advent of mechanized programs, work groups that in the past have been quite independent become much more interdependent. The walls between groups, units, and sections begin to crumble as the programs and information flow out across and through them.[4] Currently, the possibility of losing "control" of one's own operation and being dependent upon other areas is quite threatening, especially to the manager of what has been an autonomous area.

For example, the concept of IIS was that the programs would be "integrated"; that is, one program would feed directly into another. The possibility of losing control caused (1) a great deal of massive resistance on the part of managers, particularly at the unit and subunit level and (2) the demand that the programs, at the interface between different sections or subsections, come under manual control of the individual manager.

This was particularly true since the programs were "integrated." This means, in organizational terms, that data generated in marketing would, basically, control the activities in the assembly areas and the assembly areas would, in turn, control the activities in the make-shop areas. This fear and concern occurred early in the development of IIS, especially in the summer of 1964. It remained dormant until late spring of 1965 when the programs were about to be implemented and caused almost a complete halt to the further development of the programs until late fall of 1965. In December, 1965, the conflict, although still not resolved, had been reduced in intensity through the "expedient" method of providing what were, essentially, manual inputs as data moved from one section of the company to another. The manual inputs, rather than integrated programs, were necessary because the conflict had not been resolved and because the different groups displayed a high degree of mistrust of input data received from other groups, from marketing to assembly to the make shops.

Currently, most managers are rewarded (pay increases, promotions, etc.) for their "independent" accomplishments of the subordinate, specific goals in their own section, subsection or unit, rather than for assisting in the attainment of the supraordinate goals of the total organization. It cannot be too strongly stressed that this reward system will need to be extensively modified if "integrated" computerized and mechanized programs are to be successful.

As Katz[5] puts it, "There are inevitably differential returns to individuals. . . . They include rewards of status, prestige, power and psychological satisfactions. . . . If there is too rigid a hierarchy . . . this makes for vested interest in each group's position in the organizational hierarchy."

D. Careful Analysis of Information Flow and Information Usage

In most organizations, because of the commitment to subordinate goals, managers at all levels play the "numbers game." This has been a well-accepted and hallowed tradition in American industry and has been necessary if one is to "look good" to top management (meaning anyone higher). However, this is one of the consequences of the concentration on rewards for accomplishing subordinate, rather than supraordinate goals, as discussed in the immediately preceding section.

Under nonautomated systems, the "numbers game" is, essentially, relatively harmless because allowances can be made for it. It does considerably increase the cost of doing business in terms of such concepts as "water" in the schedule, increased inventory and the like, but these costs have not been insurmountable. Now, with integrated programs, the costs become much greater. Increasing reliance on accurate input becomes essential for computerized programs.

For example, one of the programs was designed to predict machine capacity and labor requirements by work station. Trial runs indicated the program feasibility but essentially erroneous data as output. This was because some of the input to the program was based upon the labor voucher—analysis showed a 35 per cent error rate in the labor voucher. As one foreman put it, "You tell me what you want my boss to look good on and boy, will he look good!"

This kind of "fudging" of data is not new, nor is it isolated. Every manager and every supervisor, in almost every company, knows how to play the "numbers game." However, although the informal system can live with this shifting of data, computer programs cannot. Their outputs are completely dependent upon the accuracy of their inputs. As the programmers put it, "GIGO—That means garbage in, garbage out."

Attempts to develop tighter and stricter controls, particularly at the managerial level, will have the same effect they have always had—better attempts to "beat the system." For this reason, much more careful attention to information flow is necessary under EDP. The issue is not in terms of whether data flow should be centralized or decentralized. Rather, the issue is more basic—who is the appropriate person in the organization to get specific data? How can we ensure that data are used by the appropriate person as a means of improving decision-making and are not used as a means of punishing or catching the individual? This will require careful planning on the part of top management if the accuracy of the programs is not to be destroyed by the "numbers game."

Zannetos[6] suggests giving managers some time to utilize information provided by the centralized EDP system to take corrective action before they are exposed to checks and queries from above. Another approach would be to make certain that information is appropriately sent to the individual or individuals responsible for taking action with higher management receiving only broader, more globally based reports.

E. Involvement of Operating Personnel

As we mentioned earlier, the installment of a new series of EDP programs is basically a problem in the management of change. Those installations that have clearly involved their operating personnel in the *design* as well as the implementation of the systems have tended to be considerably more successful in the implementation of the programs than those organizations that have not brought their operating personnel into the design stage. This, of course, means that the design stage takes longer than it would under "normal" conditions of having the systems people develop the design—but the implementation is considerably shorter and the implementation problems tend to vanish. Mann and Neff[7] have described the implementation of a successful conversion and make the following points about managing change:

1. The organization had been concentrating the effort of its managerial and supervisory personnel on increasing interunit coordination and effective functioning for three years before beginning to plan for an EDP conversion. . . .

2. All supervisory personnel—not just a selected few—were familiar with and had participated several times in the organization's procedure for initiating changes.

3. Membership on fact-finding committees was designed to bring people together from several departments to work on a given problem. A "total" organization view—as distinct from a "sub-system" view—had been established. . . .

Late in the present study, a member of the IIS Task Force was asked, "If you had it to do over again, what would you do differently?" His response was:

If we had to do it over again, we should have done a better job of bringing the operating people into the team. It was never *their* responsibility, always *ours*.

If management cannot bring itself to involve operating personnel thoroughly at all levels, then it may be forced to take the exactly opposite alternatives: that is, develop the programs in the normal fashion, by the systems people, and then have the systems people completely responsible for the implementation of the programs until they have been error-free for a minimum of three months of "parallel" operation before beginning the change-over.

The "mixed" approach leads to comments such as those made by an operating manager at the close of the study:

I'm unhappier about the system than the last time we talked. I tell them (the Task Force) what is wrong and needs to be fixed and they ignore me. Then they come back and tell me, "It's your responsibility. You've got to make it work."

F. Requirements for Additional Manpower in the Implementation Stage

No matter which alternative discussed immediately above is followed, considerable additional manpower will be necessary in the implementation stage. It will be necessary to provide this manpower from either the ranks of operating personnel or from the systems area, but the additional manpower is necessary to maintain "parallel" operations for the time that the new programs are being implemented and modified. As we have seen, this can well be a lengthy and tedious process. The attempt to do this on an "overtime" basis means that a great deal of role conflict occurs in the conflicting demands for time to meet production pressures and for time to check, recheck, and modify the programs to fit the operating situation. Installation of EDP is an expensive process and requires investment, not only in computer and similar time, but in manpower, particularly at the implementation stage.

If management does not plan for these requirements for additional manpower in the implementation stage, "expedient" rather than systematic and organized steps will be taken to solve the problem.

G. Role Conflict and Ambiguity

The concept of role has been reexamined in recent years, especially in work by Kahn *et al.*[8] Each person in an organization is expected to fulfill a role in his job. The role is the sum total of the expectations that the others with whom the individual has contact have of him. This includes supervisors, subordinates, peers, outside vendors and customers and others, depending on the particular job. To the extent that the individual does not know what those expectations are or is unclear about the expectations, he has *role ambiguity*. To the extent that the individual understands the expectations of others but the expectations differ so that all the expectations cannot be satisfied, the individual has *role conflict*. Both conditions reduce the effectiveness of the individual. For example, under conditions or role conflict, the individual tries to resolve the conflict through such methods as withdrawal and isolation. Both role conflict and role ambiguity were much in evidence as IIS progressed.

For example, role conflict was present at all levels in manufacturing. It was manifested in a number of different ways: the conflict between production pressures and the demands by task-force personnel to "help" with reviewing programs for errors and the like; the conflict with other units in manufacturing and with marketing; the conflict between moving toward the task force and being perceived as a "traitor" to one's own group—these were but a few.

The role ambiguity was also high. For example, for a long time there was no real definition on the part of manufacturing personnel as to the extent of their responsibility for implementing the program. One perception was held by the task force and a quite different perception was held by manufacturing personnel. As one supervisor said to a task-force man, "It's your program." Also, it was quite unclear to many in manufacturing as to the position their boss was taking toward the new system.

The functional representatives had even more marked role conflict and ambiguity than many others. Not only were they conflictual about their participation in the face of production pressures, but also they did not want to be traitors to their own units. Their role was never very clear. As one functional representative put it, "When I first became a functional representative, I wasn't certain what I was supposed to do. I wanted to make suggestions about the programs, but the logic was already developed, so I just attended the meetings and then finally stopped."

H. The Role of Personnel—the Change Agent

The role of the personnel department in a change process of this magnitude is highly important, particularly in the area of conflict resolution. Blake, Shepard, and Mouton[9] have pointed out that industry currently provides little adequate machinery for conflict resolution to develop solutions that are truly the best for the organization as a total entity.

The emerging role of a "change agent" is one that is becoming important in the literature. For example, Bennis[10] summarizes some of the current literature on the utility and purpose of the change agent. In brief, the appointment of a change agent is an essential step in conflict resolution. The role of the change agent is to work with both line and staff personnel, gather data, anticipate organizational and people problems, improve communications, reduce defensiveness between groups and individuals, promote problem-solving conflict resolution, and provide feedback of data to all levels. He should be appointed as soon as the mechanized programs are decided upon, rather than waiting for the inevitable conflicts to occur, and should report to the personnel manager or above, depending upon the circumstances and the organization. He should have a good knowledge of psychological and sociological principles and be able to work well, at all levels, with both individuals and groups.

This active intervention of the change agent can be helpful in reducing the role conflict and ambiguity discussed in the preceding section.

I. Establishment of Realistic Goals and Time Deadlines

The history of mechanized programs is a history of missed and extended due dates. As Mann and Neff[11] put it:

> It is essential to set realistic expectations about what a change will mean to those directly affected. New complex man-machine systems usually require an initial break-in or shakedown period of some duration. Overly optimistic announcements . . . can create expectations for both men and management which may in turn contribute to a good deal of subsequent frustration and misunderstanding.

IIS was no exception. IIS was to have been fully completed and implemented by July 1, 1965. By January 1, 1966, the major programs were still not actually operational.

Realistic goals and deadlines need to be established for major EDP programs. Probably even these should be regarded as only tentative. Managerial pressure to meet these deadlines may well result in over-emphasis on meeting due dates with corresponding reduction in the completeness and accuracy of the programs. For example, it was apparent in the "installation" of IIS that managerial pressure for meeting due dates resulted in the dates being "met" with poor programs.

As an operating manager put it:

> The programs are not reviewed for accuracy before they are sent out but, instead, are reviewed with a time deadline in mind.

A personnel department official put it this way:

Looking back, we should have taken one program at a time and really cleaned it up. We tried to do too much, too fast, too soon. This caused massive resistance, particularly on the part of the managers, and each person found himself being reinforced by the resistance of the other guy.

This, then, is the real cost of unrealistic goals and schedules. A more appropriate timetable would be to establish an implementation schedule that is at least two to three times the maximum time necessary to design the programs and, in effect, to leave time for a "second stage" of redesign and reimplementation, particularly if lower-level operating personnel are not highly involved in the original design stage.

J. Turnover of Systems and Operating Personnel

The design and installation of a major series of mechanized programs is a lengthy and time-consuming process taking, at best, several years and, in actual practice, four to five years. During this time, there will be extensive turnover. For example, not only are systems people in role conflict, but they are also in very short supply and will have many opportunities to move on to bigger and better jobs, not only within a company but outside. The same will be true of operating managers.

The turnover within the company of both operating managers and task-force personnel approached the 100 per cent mark during the two-year history with which this report is concerned. Although this may seem high, a comparable turnover will be found in other organizations—in the systems area, if not in the operating areas.

This means that planning for turnover is essential. It also means that documentation of the system's logic and, perhaps, duplication of effort will also be highly necessary. It may be less expensive, in the long run, for two or more systems people to be thoroughly familiar with a specific program than for only one person, who can well be expected to leave sometime during the program design and implementation stage.

K. The Role of the Functional Representative

Functional representatives, as described earlier in this report, were appointed to work with the task force from each operating area. They were usually the production planning managers from the appropriate assembly and make areas. Their role was to continue doing their regular job while acting as a liaison between operating personnel and task-force members. Such an approach provides a partial compromise between involvement of operating personnel as a team working with systems people in designing and implementing the programs and the other extreme, which more usually happens, of the systems people generally working by themselves in the actual design of the programs.

However, several things militated against the success of this concept. The first was the fact that the functional representatives had high production pressures and, therefore, role conflict, as we discussed earlier. The second was the fact that they were never really involved in the design of the systems and, therefore, never really felt that they were members of the task force, which factor led to role ambiguity. Two modifications need to be made in the concept of the functional representative if this route is to be followed. The first (mentioned earlier) is that the functional representative should be brought in much earlier and actively involved with the design of the systems, thus reducing the role ambiguity. The second modification is that *two* rather than *one* functional representatives be used. Two people, forming their own subgroup, have much less role conflict and much more possibility of influencing the behavior of the other referent groups than can an individual person by himself.

L. The Programs Themselves

As discussed earlier in this report, the twelve major programs were to include processing of requests for quotations and customer orders into manufacturing, scheduling of original equipment and spare parts requirements, assembly and component parts manufacturing schedules, inventory control, prediction of man and machine requirements, and measuring performance vs. commitments for the manufacturing, marketing, and purchasing departments.

The extent and complexity of these programs is tremendous. It represents an extremely ambitious attempt to develop integrated programs that would, literally, cut across departmental lines.

In view of the history of the programs, their complexity and the massive resistance of middle managers, the question can be raised: "In the future, would it be wiser to begin with less ambitious programs?" As long as managers are committed to subordinate goals; as long as the numbers game is played in industry; as long as managers are measured and rewarded on their attainment of the goals of their own area rather than on their contribution to the total organization—under these conditions, the attempt to develop programs that are truly integrated may be unsuccessful. Given this situation, it may be more appropriate to develop smaller, pay-as-you-go programs.

SUMMARY AND CONCLUSIONS

In summary, this report has provided a brief description of an attempt to develop and implement major mechanized computer schedules in a large company. The nature and scope of the programs and the two-year history of the integrated information system has been described. At the end of the observation period—January, 1966—it was still too early to tell whether or not the programs would eventually be successful, but enough had been learned to identify a number of roadblocks which inhibit and delay implementation of programs of this nature.

The development, design and implementation of computerized programs which cut across departmental lines is essential for major organizations if they are to remain competitive. However, the success of such programs is highly dependent upon the reactions of the "users" at a number of levels, from the production clerk up to and including the vice-presidential levels. The person most affected, and most resistant to the change, is the middle manager. His involvement, cooperation, and support are essential if the programs are to succeed.

Notes

1. Harold J. Leavitt and Thomas L. Whisler, "Management in the 1980's." *Harvard Business Review,* 1958, 36, No. 6, 441–48.

2. Edgar H. Schein, *Organizational Psychology,* Englewood Cliffs, N.J.: Prentice-Hall, Inc., 1965.

3. Philip H. Thurston. "Who Should Control Information Systems?" *Harvard Business Review,* 1962, 40, No. 6, 135–139.

4. Charles A. Myers, "The Impact of EDP on Management Organization and Managerial Work" Working Paper, Sloan School of Management, Massachusetts Institute of Technology, Cambridge, September, 1965.

5. Daniel Katz, "Approaches to Managing Conflict," in Elise Boulding (Ed.), *Conflict Management in Organization,* Ann Arbor: Foundation for Research on Human Behavior, 1961.

6. Zenon S. Zannetos, "On the Theory of Divisional Structures: Some Aspects of Centralization and Decentralization of Control and Decision-Making," *Management Science,* 1965, 12, No. 4, B49–68.

7. F. C. Mann and F. W. Neff, *Managing Major Change in Organizations,* Ann Arbor: The Foundation for Research on Human Behavior, 1961.

8. R. L. Kahn, D. M. Wolfe, R. P. Quinn, and J. D. Snock, *Organization Stress: Studies in Role Conflict and Ambiguity,* New York: John Wiley & Sons, Inc., 1964.

9. R. R. Blake, H. A. Shepard, and J. S. Mouton, *Managing Intergroup Conflict in Industry,* Houston: Gulf Publishing Company, 1964.

10. Warren C. Bennis, *Changing Organizations,* New York: McGraw-Hill Book Co., Inc., 1966.

11. F. C. Mann and F. W. Neff, *op. cit.,* p. 31.

ORGANIZATION DEVELOPMENT

The Effects of the Managerial Grid Lab on
Organizational and Leadership Dimensions
Michael Beer and Stephen W. Kleisath

In the past several years laboratory training has gained much attention and prominence as a means for developing managers and changing organizations. Behavioral scientists see in the laboratory method a powerful tool for changing attitudes and behavior. Those of us who have participated in a laboratory session cannot deny its power to involve and make an impact. The T group or sensitivity training is the best known and researched of these laboratory techniques.

The Managerial Grid is an outgrowth of T group training—conceived to overcome some of its shortcomings. I will not dwell on a detailed description of Grid since I assume that most of you here are familiar with it. However, it is important to understand the main difference between sensitivity training and Grid. First, the Managerial Grid provides the trainee with a well defined cognitive framework for thinking about managerial behavior. Participation, openness in communication, and integration of concern for production and concern for people are some of the key concepts. Although these represent years of research by others, Blake and Mouton have developed a model and a language which communicate these concepts to the layman in a simple and clear manner. Appendix A shows Blake's Grid. The vertical axis of the grid represents concern for people on a 1 to 9 scale. The horizontal axis of the grid represents concern for production on a 1 to 9 scale. All styles of management described by Blake are expressed as coordinates on this grid. The optimum

Paper presented at the Annual Meeting of the American Psychological Association as part of a symposium, Research on the Impact of Using Different Laboratory Methods for Interpersonal and Organizational Change, Washington, D.C., September 1971.

style, 9, 9, is in the upper right-hand corner of the grid and represents 9 units of concern for people and 9 units of concern for production. One clearly sees reflected in this grid past research on the relation of initiating structure and consideration to grievances and turnover. All this lends support to the cognitive framework. Secondly, while a sensitivity laboratory is completely unstructured, Grid is completely structured. Every minute of the one-week laboratory is fully planned and instrumented. Competitive exercises between small groups on various concepts to be learned is the main characteristic. Finally, Grid departs from T groups by its emphasis on organization development. The one-week laboratory is merely the first of six phases of development. The five subsequent phases are intended to exploit cognitive learning and attitude change through formal steps to be taken by boss and subordinates at work. There are reexaminations of primary work group functioning, confrontations between departments which work together, and always the setting of goals for individual and organizational improvement. Starting at the top of the organization, everyone in the organization attends Grid.

In all phases the Grid is an attempt to overcome some of the shortcomings attributed to sensitivity training. Anxiety and the possibility of psychological damage to individuals are minimized by a high degree of structure which forces participants to deal with surface behavior only. In its emphasis on two to three years of follow-up, Grid formalizes a procedure designed to change the many organizational forces which influence individual behavior. All this is theoretically sound, but does Grid change individuals and organizations?

RESEARCH OBJECTIVES AND SETTING
The study covered by this report was intended to evaluate the effects of the full six-phase organization development program on a division of the CORNING GLASS WORKS. This report covers only the effects of Phase I, the laboratory phase. Some 230 salaried employees, the total managerial and professional force of the division, participated in this phase during a one-year period. The Grid Laboratories were run by an organization change agent who reported directly to the division manager and whose duties also included counseling with managers on application of Grid concepts.

EXPERIMENTAL DESIGN
It would be worthwhile to look at Appendix B. This is a model of how we viewed Grid and its effects on the organization. It guided us in the design of the evaluation.

As you can see, we hypothesized that Grid would affect a number of organizational process variables specified by Blake and Mouton in their book, "The Managerial Grid." Each phase of Grid is primarily aimed at one of these process variables: Phase I, individual and managerial behavior; Phase II, group process; Phase III, intergroup relations; and Phases IV through VI, all process variables but particularly operations. A change in these variables was hypothesized by us to effect the organizational output variables of employee commitment and organizational morale (enthusiasm for work, organizational support, drive), productivity, and employe satisfaction and organizational integration. Our output variables reflect the organizational model proposed by Stogdill (1959), but essentially they reflect Blake's claim for Grid—9,9 management should increase commitment and productivity. Whereas Blake may view commitment as a process variable, we were not satisfied with this conception. Clearly, improvement in managerial behavior and group process could increase employe commitment and morale without increasing productivity and profitability. Productivity is a function of many factors other than commitment. Nevertheless, commitment is a worthwhile organizational goal in and of itself and therefore should be viewed as an output. Finally, although Blake and Mouton do not mention employe satisfaction explicitly, it is clear that 9,9 management should increase it, and with such an increase should come increased organizational integration as measured through turnover. (Research by Fleishman and Harris (1962) would support this hypothesis.)

Our evaluation of the Grid is based primarily on a measurement of the organizational variables in the model before and a little more than a year after all salaried personnel attended the one-week Managerial Grid Laboratory. This was done by means of an Organizational Behavior Questionnaire administered to all salaried employes of the division and a group of technicians and clerical personnel in the division who did not attend the one-week laboratory. The questionnaire is a compilation of several established scales developed at Ohio State and the University Of Michigan and some items developed by us specifically for this research. A list of all dimensions measured and their definitions is cited in Appendix C. All previously developed scales were reported to have acceptable reliabilities. Leadership behavior was measured by asking employes to describe their supervisor's behavior using eight dimensions of the revised Ohio State Leadership Scales. Estimates of participation, use of groups in managing, and employe influence on work were measured by means of items developed by Seashore and Bowers (1963) in an evaluation of an organization development program. Perceived responsibility, authority and delegation were measured by means of the Ohio State RAD scales. Four group process dimensions were measured—integration, peer supportiveness of achievement, peer supportiveness of affiliation, and group norms. Intergroup relations were measured by means of three scales named, "Intergroup Dependence," "Intergroup Cooperation," and "Definition Among Departments." These scales emerged from a post hoc factor analysis of items included in the questionnaire to measure these process variables. Four scales provided a measure of informal work communication, upward communication, downward communication, and intergroup communication. The organizational output of satisfaction was measured by eleven dimensions ranging from satisfaction with supervisor to satisfaction with management and advancement. Three of the dimensions are part of an overall satisfaction factor, also shown in our results. The output variables of commitment were measured by four dimensions including enthusiasm for work, support for company objectives, and effort. Productivity was the only weak link in our model from the standpoint of measurement. We looked at several financial measures of success but found most of them inadequate as valid and reliable criteria. Finally, to establish the relationship of the forty-one dimensions to organizational effectiveness, we obtained paired comparison ratings from the two top managers in the division on eleven departments for which we had complete data. A relationship between the process and output dimensions measured by questionnaire would at least be an indication of their relevance to organizational effectiveness as seen by the top management of the division. The aforementioned constitutes our approach to measuring organizational attitudes, behavior and productivity before and after the program of development—two snapshots of the organization over a year apart.

To substantiate our questionnaire findings, to add a qualitative feel for what happened, and to try to establish Grid as the cause of any changes observed, we interviewed seventy salaried employes in the division and asked them to describe changes in themselves, their peers, and their department as a whole. We also asked their opinions of Grid, degree of support at the top for the program, and chief blocks to change in the division.

Two other aspects of our design need to be mentioned before going on to our findings. At the end of the one-week Grid Laboratory, we asked participants to indicate in a questionnaire their evaluation of the program. In addition, we obtained through a Leadership Opinion Questionnaire administered immediately before and immediately after the laboratory, participants' feelings concerning ideal leadership behavior. These opinions were measured on the same eleven dimensions on which we planned to obtain a description of supervisory behavior. Thus, we were able to obtain an estimate of attitude change due to the laboratory on the same dimensions for which we obtained measures of leadership behavior change. Would there be an attitude change as a result of the laboratory and would this be translated into behavior change?

The essence of our research approach was organizational. Grid is an organizational development program designed to change an organization, and we wanted to measure organizational variables.

There are many difficulties in this kind of research created by transfers of individuals from one department to another or out of the division; but because an effective organization development program must change the modus operandi of an organization despite these difficulties, we took it upon ourselves to evaluate the program from a total organization point of view.

RESULTS AND DISCUSSION

Participant Evaluation

Let me briefly review data obtained by means of the participant evaluation. A content analysis of some of the questions is presented in Appendix D. Participants felt that their learning included a better understanding of their managerial style and a better appreciation and knowledge of team management. Participants said they planned to keep an open mind and listen better on the job, and 52% said they planned to practice team management and gain the involvement and commitment of their subordinates. As we shall see later, these observations by participants immediately after Grid are reflected in some of the questionnaire data and post-Grid interviews. In general, the participant evaluations and the observations of the trainers indicated a high degree of acceptance and enthusiasm for Grid. Although the positive feelings toward Grid is not evidence of attitude change or behavior change, it is a necessary if not sufficient condition for such change to occur. Unless trainees are involved and enthusiastic, no training program can succeed—particularly not a training program aimed at attitude and behavior change.

Leadership Opinion Questionnaire

Data from the Leadership Opinion Questionnaire indicates the laboratory changed participant opinion concerning ideal leadership. Appendix E presents pre- and post-Grid means and standard deviations for eleven leadership opinion dimensions Mean differences and their statistical significance using a two-tailed t test for correlated means are also shown. It is immediately clear that there was considerable change in opinions. All dimensions which are related to a concern for production or structure went down appreciably. These dimensions are Representation, Persuasiveness, Initiating Structure, Role Assumption, and Production Emphasis. The dimensions of Participation, Emphasis On Group, and Employe Influence On Work, which represent a concern for people and their involvement in work, went up quite significantly. Only Tolerance Of Freedom went down significantly. Consideration, which was high to begin with, stayed substantially the same. Integration, which does not fall into either category and is the leader's willingness to facilitate teamwork, also increased significantly.

The division of the leadership dimensions into production and people factors not only represents Blake's two-dimensional conception of leadership, but also reflects a post hoc factor analysis of the leadership behavior dimensions to be discussed later. In this factor analysis ten of the eleven dimensions clearly loaded on one of the factors. Only integration loaded equally on both factors.

The pattern of change in opinions is clear. Concern for people and their involvement in work went up Concern for production and structure went down. Integration, which is related to both, went up. The only change that is inconsistent is the drop in Tolerance Of Freedom. It would seem that the Grid Laboratory has created a greater balance between the two concerns. This change is in line with Blake's objectives of 9,9 management.

A correlational analysis of this data before and after Grid was not completed at the time this report was written, but we would bet that correlations between dimensions on the two factors increased. As we shall see, this is exactly what happened with the leadership behavior dimensions.

Organizational Behavior Questionnaire

Were the changes in attitude concerning leadership and supervision translated into behavioral change back in the organization? Our data from the Organizational Behavior Questionnaire, presented in Appendix F, shows us that it was. Taking the division as a whole, thirty-eight of the forty-one dimensions changed in the expected direction—thirty-seven positively and one negatively. Of these changes, one was statistically significant at the .10 level and fourteen at the .05 level.

Among the fourteen leadership dimensions, thirteen changed positively and one stayed the same. The significant changes were Emphasis On Group, Employe Influence On Work, Responsibility, Authority, and Delegation. Participation and Integration also increased appreciably, but the changes were short of statistical significance at the .05 level. Although the specific direction of change in the first eleven dimensions is not the same in all cases as in the opinion questionnaire data just presented, the pattern is similar. Dimensions representing concern for production showed only slight positive changes. The dimensions representing concern for people and their involvement in work showed larger, and in the case of Employe Influence On Work and Group Emphasis, significant changes. The leader's facilitation of cooperation and teamwork, as measured by integration, also increased appreciably. Once again, as in the opinion questionnaire, a greater balance between concern for production and people emerges as the major finding.

An examination of the correlation coefficients between the leadership dimensions before and after Grid confirms that the integration of supervisors' concern for production and their concern for people and their involvement in work has increased during the one-year period. Appendix G shows just a sample of these intercorrelations. It is clear that on the whole the correlations between production- and people-oriented leadership behavior increased while the correlations between dimensions within the same factor stayed substantially the same. For instance, the correlation between Initiating Structure and Tolerance Of Freedom increased from .07 to .55 and the correlation between Initiating Structure and Consideration from .30 to .50.

These findings are much more significant than the absolute changes observed. One of the objectives of Grid is to develop in individuals a managerial style which integrates concern for people and production. We think the data shows that this has happened.

Group process was measured by four scales measuring degree of group integration, support by peers of achievement, support by peers of affiliative behavior, and group pressure for conformity. All scales changed positively as expected, but none significantly. However, we did not expect change in this category until Phase II—the team development phase of the organizational development program.

We measured intergroup relations by means of three scales—group interdependence, cooperation, and definition among departments. Interdependence and cooperation among groups increased significantly as expected. The changes were statistically significant at the .05 level. Contrary to expectations, definition among departments decreased but not significantly. The positive changes observed in this category were not expected until Phase III which is designed to solve interdepartmental problems.

In the communications category we can see that upward and downward communication improved—downward communication significantly at the .05 level. Informal work communication, which ascertained the degree of non-work oriented conversations, decreased as expected. It is gratifying that a dimension we expected to go down did so. Unexpectedly, intergroup communication declined significantly at the .05 level. There is no clear apparent explanation for this, particularly in view of the improvement in intergroup cooperation and dependence.

The organizational output of overall satisfaction increased significantly at the .05 level. All eleven dimensions of satisfaction increased. Satisfaction with management, division, security, and freedom increased significantly at the .05 level. Other relatively large increases included satisfaction with supervisor and recognition. We can safely say that satisfaction in the division increased during the one-year period.

The organizational output of commitment also increased as measured by four dimensions. Increases in support for company objectives and effort were statistically significant at the .05 level.

In summary, when the division was taken as a whole, changes in all but two dimensions were in the expected direction. However, it seemed to us that differences between plants and departments would exist depending on support of the program by managers and the specific situational forces for and against change. Appendices H, I and J show data on the same dimensions described above for two separate plants in the division and a third group composed of the sales force and a new developing business. Even a quick glance shows that there are marked differences. Plant A, which was isolated geographically from headquarters (500 miles away), generally shows the same pattern of change as the total division, but the changes are much more pronounced. Eight of forty-one dimensions changed significantly at the .10 level and twenty-five at the .05 level. On the other hand, only eight of forty-one dimensions in Plant B were found to change at the .05 level and two at the .10 level. This plant was in the same location as headquarters, and the data include many divisional staff people. As our observations indicated at the time and the interviews later confirmed, the general manager did not support Grid as it progressed and found it difficult to adopt a 9,9 style as his personal style of management. This, we think, partially explains the differences between Plants A and B. Appendix J shows data for the sales force and the new business. We can see that in these groups changes were often negative and contrary to expectations. Why? There were numerous problems in the management of these groups that may have prevented change but are too lengthy to go into here. However, it is important to note that function was not the key variable. One of the sales managers and his group showed remarkable, positive change.

Additional data on individual groups and departments are available. These show marked differences in change between groups and between managers. They also show that the significance of positive and negative changes for given dimensions must be viewed in terms of their initial level and the level of other dimensions. The subtlety of these considerations is lost in the overall means.

Appendix K shows differences between pre- and post-organizational process and output variables as described by Plant A's clerical personnel and technicians. These personnel did not attend Grid. The results are unmistakable. The differences in pre- and post- means are large, indicating that changes obtained in this research are not a function of laboratory attendance. Two dimensions changed significantly at the .10 level and twenty at the .05 level. For instance, satisfaction with supervision increased from 3.54 to 4.14. Consideration increased from 3.49 to 3.91. These indicate that the effects of Grid carried down to at least this level of employee.

Interviews

The interview was our fourth approach toward measuring the effects of Grid. Seventy interviews with salaried personnel in the division were content analyzed. A summary of this analysis is contained in Appendix L. Approximately half of the interviewees saw no change or could not comment about change in their department's operations or its members. The rest saw more openness in communication, more use of groups in managing, better meetings, and better relations with other departments. In the self category much change was reported, with only 10% seeing no change in themselves. Key changes included greater openness in communication, greater insight into behavior of self and others, greater knowledge of management behavior, and greater group orientation in managing. You will remember that these were areas in which participants said, after the labs, they would try to change. The report of increased communication and greater use of groups was also confirmed by the organization behavior questionnaire. It is not surprising that over half of the interviewees saw no change in their department operations. Not until later phases were such changes expected.

One of the most interesting findings of the interviews relates to perceptions of supervisory support for the Grid program and values. While 78% of the interviewees saw their immediate supervisor as supporting Grid, only 29% felt certain that the next level up supported Grid. Finally, only 4% were certain that top management in the division supported Grid, while 4% indicated that top management did not support Grid. The rest could not comment, indicating a lack of knowledge which psychologically is equivalent to lack of support. In fact, there was little or no support for the program at the top of the division. As mentioned earlier, the General Manager's initial support turned into skepticism as the program progressed. In view of this, it was amazing to us to find as much change as we did.

The greatest barrier in applying concepts of Grid was felt to be the lack of follow-up. Production pressures were felt to prevent an investment of time in follow-up. Personal observations on our part support this notion. An organizational development program can only be successful if time is allotted to it regardless of other pressures. Of course, Phases II through VI are designed to provide such follow-up and they had not occurred at the time these interviews were conducted. Other mentions of difficulties in applying Grid concepts included lack of top support and resistance of others, confirming our earlier statements.

But, what of sales and production measures? It would be an oversimplification to assume that Grid could have direct and measurable effects on these gross financial criteria. Too many other variables completely beyond the control of individuals within the organization and unrelated to the intended effects of Grid are responsible for the ultimate criteria of sales, productivity and profitability.

To overcome this problem we relied very little on financial criteria as measures of the effectiveness of Grid. Our way of relating the changes observed in organizational processes to organizational performance was by means of rankings of performance. We obtained rankings of effectiveness on eleven managers and their departments from the two top managers in the division by means of the paired comparison method. The rank order correlation between the rankings of these two managers was .982. These rankings were then compared to our independent rankings of the same eleven managers based on the questionnaire data obtained. Our rankings were based on how high each manager was on all of the dimensions measured. The Rho for the relationship between the division manager's rankings and ours was .67. The Rho for the relationship between the rankings of the second highest manager in the division and our rankings was .61. More importantly, there was perfect agreement concerning the four poorest managers. In other words, the four lowest managers on the forty-one questionnaire dimensions were also ranked lowest in effectiveness by top management. In fact, several management changes ensued independent of our research which confirmed our findings. Although this does not directly demonstrate the effects of Grid on productivity, it does indicate that the organizational processes and outputs measured and observed to change during Grid had some relevance to top management's performance criteria.

One final word about turnover. As you recall, organizational integration as measured by turnover was one of the organizational outputs in our model. We expected and hoped that Grid would affect turnover—particularly the rate of quits in the division. Appendix M clearly shows that turnover in 1966, the year during which the final laboratories were run decreased for the total division. A more positive conclusion about the relationship between Grid and turnover comes from an analysis of turnover in Plants A and B. You will recall that Plant A started at a lower level than Plant B on the process variables and employee satisfaction. However, the dramatic changes in Plant A during the one-year period resulted in its surpassing Plant B in almost all dimensions by the time the program ended. The relative changes in organizational processes and employe satisfaction are clearly seen in the turnover data. Plant B had lower turnover than Plant A before the program started. During 1965 when the program was underway the two plants reversed positions even though turnover increased for both due to common reasons unrelated to Grid. In 1966 while Grid Labs were being completed, Plant A's turnover dropped much more than Plant B's. Thus, turnover exactly follows trends in organizational process changes observed in the two plants as a result of Grid. Although this still is not positive proof of the direct effects of Grid on turnover, it considerably strengthens the probability of a cause-and-effect relationship.

CONCLUSIONS AND PERSPECTIVE

There is little question in our minds that the Grid Laboratories had an impact on the organizational process and outputs of the experimental division. The important changes were in the managers' use of groups, participation, and employe influence on work, all of which increased. Perceived responsibility and authority increased from fairly low levels as did delegation reported by supervisors. Managers' integration of people-oriented managerial behavior and production- and planning-oriented behavior increased, accomplishing one of the key objectives of Grid Laboratories. In addition, intergroup relations improved and in one plant communications and group process improved significantly.

With respect to output variables, we can only say with certainty that employe satisfaction improved and turnover decreased more in the plant which changed most. Thus, the laboratories seem to have had a positive effect on organizational integration. Similarly, commitment, the second of three output variables, increased as measured by two of four scales. The effects on sales, production and profitability are much harder to assess and may not even be good criteria in evaluating Grid. We can only conclusively say that the more effective managers had higher scores on organizational process and output variables. Thus, the variables which changed as a result of Grid are related to what management views as effective management. It is important to note that all the changes just described are of a social psychological nature. The interviews indicate that little or no change in the operations and structure of the organization occurred. These must occur if individual change is to be permanent. Of course, such changes were not expected until later phases.

We feel particularly confident about our conclusions because all the research methods used—participant evaluations, Leadership Opinion Questionnaires, Organizational Behavior Questionnaires, and interviews—indicated change. In most instances, one method confirmed change observed in another. For instance, many of the intentions by participants to change, as expressed after the laboratories, were confirmed by the Leadership Opinion Questionnaire, were later observed as changes in the pre and post organizational behavior questionnaire data, and were confirmed by post-program interviews. The best example of this was the expressed intention to use groups and teamwork in managing.

Observations of outsiders also confirm that changes occurred in the division. Unsolicited comments by two such outsiders indicate that they noticed a marked change in their ability to deal with individuals in the division. Openness in communication, good meetings, better listening, and a problem orientation were the main changes observed.

Finally, I would like to mention only briefly that post-Phase I data from a plant outside this division indicate that means on the forty-one dimensions measured are higher than the experimental division's post data. Although we have no pre data, if we assume the same baseline as in our experimental division, we can say that even more change has occurred as a result of Phase I in this plant.

We can make no absolute statements about cause and effect simply because there was no control division. However, the differences in change between plants, departments and managers indicate that the division's performance which improved substantially in this period, was not the cause of the change in process and output variables. All departments and plants were working in approximately the same economic environment. Therefore, change or lack of it must be attributed to the interaction of Grid with individual managers' willingness to change, proper support by top management, and other situation characteristics. The change perceived by weekly employees, who did not attend Grid, eliminates the possibility that the changes reflect verbal learning on the part of Grid participants.

The differences between Plants A and B make good sense from an organizational change theory point of view. Plant B and the division's top management were in the same location. Lack of change in Plant B can be attributed to the poor climate for change. In addition, any changes in Plant B may have been dampened by other events which occurred just shortly before the post-Grid questionnaire was administered. First, the headquarters group located at Plant B had been told that they were moving to the company's headquarters location. This caused much upset and unhappiness which can be seen in the decline of the Family dimension of satisfaction. This dimension ascertains the employee's perceptions of his family's attitudes towards his employment with the company. Secondly, a nationally known company built a large plant in town. For the first time, Plant B was faced with a competitor in the labor market offering high salaries and good opportunities. The effects of this can be seen in the decline of two satisfaction dimensions—Friends and Advancement. These dimensions ascertain the employe's satisfaction with his job relative to his friends' jobs and their satisfactions with promotional progress. What other dimensions were affected by these events is hard to judge, but there is no question that the events described dampened any possible changes in satisfaction and other variables that might have changed as a result of Grid.

It was amazing to us to find as much change as we did after the laboratory phase of Grid. Frankly we expected no change in most of the organizational variables measured until the later phases of Grid forced changes in situational variables. Only in the leadership category did we expect change because the laboratory is specifically designed to change individual managerial behavior.

Why did the laboratory work? I think the answer lies in the cognitive framework provided participants and in the dynamic and involving qualities of a structured laboratory. The involvement of individuals in the laboratories can only be appreciated if observed directly. The competitive nature of the exercises caused individuals to identify closely with their group and become subject to their influence through feedback. Invariably the 9,9 style was the one to which individuals and groups tried to model themselves. One could almost see the values of individuals change as the week progressed. In our opinion, any laboratory which provides a catchy and easily understood cognitive framework and a format that involves individuals would be successful. Grid merely saves someone the considerable work of designing a laboratory with these general qualities. It is these qualities of Grid rather than its specific characteristics which make it a powerful tool for changing behavior. We think the data just presented support this conclusion.

OD Techniques and their Results in 23 Organizations: The Michigan ICL Study
David G. Bowers

Data collected by the Michigan Inter-Company Longitudinal Study from more than 14,000 respondents in 23 organizations are analyzed in terms of the organizational development treatments that intervened between pre- and postmeasures. Four "experimental" treatments (Survey Feedback, Interpersonal Process Consultation, Task Process Consultation, *and* Laboratory Training) *and two "control" treatments* (Data Handback *and* No Treatment) *are compared to determine their relative association with improved organizational functioning as measured by the Survey of Organizations questionnaire. The results indicate that* Survey Feedback *was associated with statistically significant improvement on a majority of measures, that* Interpersonal Process Consultation *was associated with improvement on a majority of measures, that* Task Process Consultation *was associated with little or no change, and that* Laboratory Training *and* No Treatment *were associated with declines. In addition, organizational climate emerges as a potentially extremely important conditioner of these results, with* Survey Feedback *appearing as the only treatment associated with substantial improvement in the variables of this domain.*

In 1966, staff members of the University of Michigan's Institute for Social Research launched a five-year program of organizational projects, the *Inter-Company Longitudinal Study* (ICLS). This ambitious undertaking addressed itself to a number of substantive questions of organizational behavior and change research within a framework containing the following features:

1. *Continuity of site* (over a period of one or more years);

2. *Use of a common survey instrument* (as a benchmark measure of the functioning of the human organization);

3. *Organizational development as a beneficial tool* (to increase payoff to participating firms and to ensure the presence of constructive movement for research purposes);

Reproduced by special permission from the *Journal of Applied Behavioral Science,* **9**, 1, pp. 21–43. Copyright © 1973, NTL Institute for Applied Behavioral Science, associated with the National Education Association. Reproduced by permission of David G. Bowers and the publisher.

4. *Research on organizational change techniques* (to permit the acquisition of systematic knowledge about the comparative effect of a number of possible interventions).

After an initial year of instrument development, staff acquisition, and pilot projects, the main phase of the study began. The hopes and aims sketched in the four precepts listed above were in varying degrees brought to fulfillment. Continuity of site proved to be greater than has been the case in the great majority of previous studies: Most organizations remained committed to and involved in an ICLS project for at least two years. They did not, however, endure for the full five years (although some may well ultimately do so).

A common instrument, the Survey of Organizations questionnaire, was developed and refined. It has been used, in one of its editions, in each site and data collection wave. Most participating organizations underwent at least two measurement waves using that instrument, with some form of change, development, or intervention occurring in the interval between the two; some had as many as five successive measurements. Relevant portions of this instrument generated the substance of the data examined in this article.

All organizations, with the exception of a very few in which no action plan was intended and in which none evolved, undertook some program of organizational development; as we shall see, the specific nature of the activity varied from one site to another.

Organizational change research is an uncharted territory in many aspects, and the research staff has had, of necessity, to feel its way along quite gradually. Many of the findings are only now slowly entering into the professional purview. As the reader can imagine, content analysis of five years of documents and multivariate analysis of a mountain of quantitative data is a lengthy, difficult task. I wish to forewarn the reader who anticipates a detailed chronicling of intervention strategies that I will present less of that than he (or I) might wish. Instead, my present purpose is an overview of results from this study's large number of cases and their possibilities for comparative analysis.

At the end of five years, work in some form has been underway in 31 organizations (plants or separate marketing regions) in 15 companies. Data from 23 of these organizations in 10 companies are included in the present analysis. Six organizations, in four companies, were excluded because no repeat measurements have as yet been obtained. One company was excluded because it was primarily involved in an ancillary activity unrelated to organizational research and change of the kind considered here.

The 23 organizations comprise 14,812 persons, in white-collar and blue-collar positions, and constitute a wide array of industries—paper, chemicals, petroleum refining, aluminum, automobiles, household products, and insurance, in the areas of continuous process manufacturing, assembly-line manufacturing, components fabrication, marketing, and research and development.

CHANGE TREATMENTS TO BE COMPARED

Six forms of intervention can be identified as having occurred in one or more of the 23 organizations. For the most part they are not "pure" treatments, since nearly all involved at least some form of return of tabulated survey data. Nevertheless, they are sufficiently different from one another to have been the source of conflicts between the change agents who used them and to have been regarded as different by the client systems who experienced them.

Survey Feedback

No authoritative volume has as yet been written about this development technique, although a number of article-length references exist.[1]

Many persons mistakenly believe that survey feedback consists of a rather superficial handing back of tabulated numbers and percentages, and little else.

On the contrary, when employed with skill and experience, it becomes a sophisticated tool for using the data as a springboard to development. In the sites classified as having received *survey feedback* as a change treatment, this treatment formed the principal substance of the intervention. Data were tabulated for each group engaged in the project, as well as for each combination of groups that represented an area of responsibility in the organizational pyramid. Data appeared in the format shown in Figure 1.

Each supervisor and manager received a tabulation of this sort containing data from the responses of his own immediate subordinates; the measures, descriptions of their basis, and meaning; and suggestions concerning their interpretation and use. A resource person, from ISR or the client system's own staff, usually counseled privately with the supervisor-recipient about the contents of the package and then arranged a time when the supervisor could meet with his subordinates to discuss the findings and their implications. The resource person ordinarily agreed to attend that meeting in order to help the

Fig. 1 *Typical format of survey feedback tabulation*

```
*  *  *  *  *  *  *  *  *  *  *
*    GROUP NUMBER 99999    *
*  *  *  *  *  *  *  *  *  *  *
```

Item	(1)	(2)	(3)	(4)	(5)	Mean	Std. dev.	N
7 CO USES NEW WK METHODS	8	0	17	42	25	3.82	1.11	11
8 CO INTEREST IN WELFARE	8	8	17	25	33	3.73	1.29	11
22 DISAGREEMTS WKED THRU	0	8	50	17	8	3.30	0.78	10
38 OBJECTIVS SET JOINTLY	17	8	25	17	17	3.10	1.37	10

(Columns (1)–(5): Percentage distribution)

participants with the technical aspects of the tabulations and the process aspects of the discussion.

Feedback procedures typically vary from site to site, and did so within the ICLS sites that received this treatment. In certain instances, a "waterfall" pattern, in which the feedback process is substantially completed at superordinate levels before moving to subordinate groups, was adopted. In other instances, feedback to all groups and echelons was more or less simultaneous.

Time and space do not permit a lengthy discussion of the various forms which feedback may take. It should be stated, however, that an effective survey feedback operation helps an organization's groups move from a discussion of the tabulated perceptions, through a cataloguing of their implications, to commitment to solutions to the problems identified and defined by the discussion.

This technique has long been associated with organizational development and change work conducted by the Institute for Social Research and was considered at the outset of this study as likely to constitute a more or less standard tool. That it was not as universally employed as this statement might suggest forms the basis for its identification as a distinct treatment.

Interpersonal Process Consultation

This treatment bears at least some resemblance to what Schein (1969) has termed "Process Consultation." The change agent most closely identified with this treatment attaches great importance to developing, within the client groups themselves, a capacity for forming and implementing their own change program. Considerable importance is attached to the change agent's establishing himself from the outset as a trustworthy, helpful adjunct to the group's own process. A great deal of effort and emphasis is placed on his catalyzing a process of surfacing data in areas customarily not plumbed in work organizations (attitudes, feelings, individual needs, reasons for conflict, informal processes, and so on). In behavioral specifics, the change agent employs the posing of questions to group members; process-analysis periods; feedback of observations or feelings; agenda-setting, review, and appropriateness-testing procedures; and occasional conceptual inputs on interpersonal topics. Work is sometimes undertaken with members singly, but more often in natural work-groupings. Human, rather than technical, processes are generally assumed to have primacy for organizational effectiveness.

Task Process Consultation

This treatment is oriented very closely to task objectives and the specific interpersonal processes associated with them. A change agent who adheres to this pattern typically begins by analyzing a client unit's work-task situation privately, after extensive interviews concerning its objectives, potential resources, and the organizational forces blocking its progress. He consults privately with the supervisor at frequent intervals to establish rapport and to gain commitment to objectives and desired future courses of action. He sets the stage for client group discussions by introducing select bits of data or by having another person do so. He encourages group discussion and serves as a process observer, but also uses role playing, some substantive inputs at timely points, as well as nondirective counseling techniques, to guide the discussion toward commitment to desired courses of action.

Laboratory Training

As practiced within ICLS projects, this intervention technique more nearly approximates the interpersonal relations laboratory than the intrapsychic or personal growth session. A "family group" design was followed almost exclusively, with the entire laboratory lasting from three days to two weeks, depending upon circumstances and organizational schedule requirements. Sessions were ordinarily conducted at a motel or resort away from the usual work place. Experimental exercises (e.g., the NASA Game or "Moon Problem," the Ten-Dollar Exercise, the Tower-Building Problem) were interspersed with unstructured discussion time. During the years of the study, a number of terms were used by those conducting the training to describe it. Initially it was referred to as "T-Group Training"; in later years it was termed "Team Development Training," or simply "Team Training." The content, however, remained relatively constant in kind, if not in exact substance. The change agents who conducted the training were not novices; on the contrary, they had had many years of experience in conducting it and were judged by those familiar with their work to be competent

Data Handback

Not truly a change treatment, this forms instead a control or comparison condition. In certain sites no real survey feedback work was conducted. Data were tabulated and returned in envelopes to the appropriate supervisors, but no effort was made to encourage group problem-solving discussions concerning those data. Nor did any other treatment occur in these sites.

No Treatment

In a few sites, data were tabulated and returned to the appropriate top or staff manager but were not shared by him with relevant managers and supervisors. They were instead filed away in a cabinet. Since no other development activities were undertaken in these sites, it seems justifiable to classify them as having had no treatment at all.

Survey Feedback was earlier described as the "principal substance of the intervention" in sites labeled as such in the study. It was also stated that some form of tabulated survey data was returned to someone in all sites. Both statements are true. A system is classified in this article as having received

Survey Feedback as its treatment when survey feedback, *and that alone* was used, both with capstone groups (those groups at the top management rungs of the organizational ladder) and with all groups below them which were involved in the project. Where Interpersonal Process Consultation, Task Process Consultation, or Laboratory Training are the reported treatments, the principal intervention *with the capstone groups* consisted of that particular treatment. These groups, along with all other participating groups in their organization, also received tabulated data, and ordinarily spent a varying amount of time discussing it.[2] Change agents who used these treatments characteristically placed survey feedback work in a distinctly secondary role. In some instances, after a few brief and sometimes superficial sessions, groups were encouraged to move on to the "real" change activity; in other instances, the nonfeedback activity began before survey data were made available, and the data were used only occasionally (perhaps by the change agent himself) to underscore a point or a development. Data feedback, to the extent that it went on at all, was often left in these sites to partially trained, and normally overloaded, internal resource persons, who were often more attracted to the more glamorous activities modeled by the external change agent.

Thus events, schedules, and the personal style preference of the change agents combined to produce a contrast between sites in which Survey Feedback was truly and thoroughly conducted at all levels and without other treatments, and sites in which a rather half-hearted effort at data discussion was overshadowed by other treatments with capstone groups.

Finally, a word must be said about the way in which organizations came to receive different treatments. In a true experiment, assignment to treatment category is random. No pretense can be made that a purely random assignment procedure was employed in this multicompany study. Still, if not random, it appears to have been less than systematic. Change treatment was determined on a basis having little, if anything, to do with the nature of the client system; it was instead determined by change agent preference, i.e., by the preferred and customary techniques of the change agent assigned to the site. In short, treatment was determined by change agent selection, which was in turn determined by sheer availability at the time of contract.

MEASUREMENT AND ANALYSIS PROCEDURES

The dependent variables in the analyses reported below are measures of organizational functioning obtained from repeated administrations (ordinarily one year apart) of the Survey of Organizations questionnaire (Taylor & Bowers, 1972), particularly the 16 critical indices that constitute the core of that instrument. The content of this instrument was originally developed from the many studies which ISR had conducted over the years prior to 1966. Subsequently the content of this questionnaire has been subjected to a number of analyses, employing both smallest-space analysis and hierarchical cluster analysis, which suggest that the total may really comprise the limited number of multi-item indices employed in this present study. Six are measures of the organizational conditions that surround any particular focal group to form the environment within which it must live. These conditions, outside and especially above a particular manager's group, are really nothing more than the perceived accumulated effects of the ways in which other groups function. Helpful or harmful policies, for example, are the output of higher-echelon groups with good or poor leadership, respectively. We call these accumulated effects *organizational climate,* and attach to that term essentially the same meaning given it by Evan (1968), i.e., a concrete phenomenon reflecting a social-psychological reality, shared by people related to the organization, and having its impact on organizational behavior. We do *not* imply by the term the alternative meaning sometimes given it, that of a general flow of behavior and feeling within a group (cf. Halpin, 1966).

Four other indices measure managerial leadership behavior of an interpersonal (support and interaction facilitation) and task (goal emphasis and work facilitation) nature. Four similar measures tap the peer leadership area, and together these eight measures reflect what has come to be called the "Four-Factor" theory of leadership (Bowers & Seashore, 1966; Taylor & Bowers, 1972). The remaining two measures tap Group Process and Satisfaction, respectively.

High scores on these 16 measures, for any organization or group, are considered to be reasonably reflective of a general state of organizational effectiveness; lower scores, of a less effective state. The content of the measures, like their place in a conceptual scheme, is based upon the Likert "meta-theory" of the human organization as a social system (Likert, 1961, 1967), which itself represents an integration of a large array of empirical findings. The questionnaire has been subjected to extensive analyses, and the healthy and inquisitive skeptic is directed to Taylor and Bowers (1972), where both reliability and validity data are presented in considerable detail. For present purposes, a brief summary of content and reliability is presented in Table 1. Evidence concerning validity is perhaps best summarized by the following statement, taken from the basic reference:

> Fairly clear evidence exists that the *Survey of Organizations* measures relate appropriately to both efficiency and attendance criteria. Relationships to efficiency extend across all four time periods and reach levels as high as .80. Relationships to attendance attain only slightly lower levels, and, where data are available, show every sign of extending across all time periods.[3]

> Relationships to other criteria present patterns which are far less definitive. In the case of Product Quality, no clear pattern emerges at all. In the Human Cost area, organizational climate seems to have appropriate and significant relationships to all three measures available for analysis: minor injuries, physical health, and grievance rate (Taylor & Bowers, 1972).

Table 1 *Summary of content and reliability of 16 indices of the survey of organizations questionnaire*

Area-measure	Description	No. of items	Internal consistency reliability coefficient
ORGANIZATIONAL CLIMATE			
Human resources primacy	Whether the climate indicates that people, their talents, skills, and motivation are considered to be one of the organization's most important assets.	3	.80
Communication flow	Whether information flows effectively upward, downward, and laterally in the organization.	3	.78
Motivational climate	Whether conditions and relationships in the environment are generally encouraging or discouraging to effective work.	3	.80
Decision-making practices	How decisions are made in the organization: whether they are made effectively, at the right levels, and based upon all the available information.	4	.79
Technological readiness	Whether the equipment and resources are up to date, efficient, and well maintained.	2	.58
Lower-level influence	Whether lowest-level supervisors and employees feel they have influence on what goes on in their department.	2	.70
MANAGERIAL LEADERSHIP			
Support	Behavior toward subordinates that lets them know they are worthwhile persons doing useful work.	3	.94
Interaction facilitation	Team building, behavior that encourages subordinates to develop close, cooperative working relationships with one another.	2	.89

Table 1 (Cont.)

Area-measure	Description	No. of items	Internal consistency reliability coefficient
MANAGERIAL LEADERSHIP (Cont.)			
Goal emphasis	Behavior that stimulates a contagious enthusiasm for doing a good job (*not* pressure).	2	.85
Work facilitation	Behavior that removes road-blocks to doing a good job.	3	.88
PEER LEADERSHIP			
Support	Behavior by subordinates toward one another that enhances their mutual feeling of being worth-while persons doing useful work.	3	.87
Interaction facilitation	Behavior by subordinates toward one another that encourages the development of close, cooperative working relationships.	3	.90
Goal emphasis	Behavior by subordinates toward one another that stimulates a mutually contagious enthusiasm for doing a good job.	2	.70
Work facilitation	Behavior that is mutually helpful; helping each other remove road-blocks to doing a good job.	3	.89
GROUP PROCESS	How the group functions; does it plan and coordinate its efforts, make decisions and solve prob-lems, know how to do its job, share information; is it motivated to meet its objectives, is it adaptable, is there confidence and trust among its members?	7	.94
SATISFACTION	Whether employees are satisfied with economic and related rewards, adequacy of their immediate supervisor, effectiveness of the organization, compatibility with fellow employees, present and future progress within the organi-zation, and their job as a whole.	7	.87

Two successive measures are considered simultaneously for the analyses to be reported here: those preceding and following (a year later) the occurrence of a particular change treatment. In certain instances, index measures for the premeasure or the postmeasure are considered separately, and are therefore reported as arithmetic means on a five-point Likert scale (high score = desirable condition, low score = undesirable condition). In other instances, change itself is the focal concern; for these purposes, the first (or pre-) measures have been subtracted from the second (or post-) measures. Thus a "positive" change score indicates enhanced effectiveness; a "negative" score, deterioration.

The balance of the article considers findings which, within the confines of the ICLS setting, help answer the following research questions:

1. *Were the treatments differentially effective in producing change in organizational functioning, as measured by the Survey of Organizations questionnaire?*

2. *What is the relationship between change in organizational climate and the effects of these various treatments?*

RESULTS

We begin with a consideration of change or gain scores for each of the 16 critical indices for each treatment, presented in Table 2. The reader may note that, for each treatment, two sets of scores are given for each variable category. One comparison is labeled "Whole Systems," and refers to grand response mean gain scores for all respondents combined within organizations receiving that treatment for the first and second waves of measurement (ordinarily one year apart). The other comparison is labeled "Capstone Groups" and refers, within the Interpersonal Process Consultation, Task Process Consultation, and Laboratory Training treatments, to persons in groups that actually received that particular treatment. For comparison purposes, persons in groups of a similar nature (ordinarily the top management groups) are presented for the Survey Feedback, Data Handback, and No Treatment clusters.

The findings presented in Table 2 may be summarized as follows:

1. *Laboratory Training* is associated with negative change in organizational climate for both capstone groups and systems as a whole. Although group process improves at both levels, peer support declines for capstone groups, and both peer and managerial support decline for the systems in which these groups are located, as does overall satisfaction.

2. *Interpersonal Process Consultation* contains so few cases within capstone groups, and the changes are of such a (low) magnitude, that firm conclusions cannot be drawn. For their systems *in toto*, however, 7 of the 16 measures reflect significant, positive changes, largely in the managerial and peer leadership areas. Organizational climate, group process, and satisfaction measures change scarcely at all.

Table 2 Changes in questionnaire indices, from first to second survey waves, by variable and change treatment

	Treatment											
	Laboratory training		Interpersonal process cons.		Task process cons.		Survey feedback		Data handback		No treatment	
Area-measure	Caps. gps N=116	Whole sys. N=3417	Caps. gps N=12	Whole sys. N=3788	Caps. gps N=38	Whole sys. N=1847	Caps. gps N=85	Whole sys. N=3893	Caps. gps N=55	Whole sys. N=932	Caps. gps N=51	Whole sys. N=935
Organizational climate												
Hum. resources prim.	-.42*	-.18*	+.10	-.02	-.04	-.17*	+.35*	+.15*	+.13	-.05	-.59*	-.61*
Communication flow	-.19*	-.12*	+.10	+.12*	+.16	-.06	+.22*	+.15*	+.23*	-.12*	-.02	-.06
Motiv'l conditions	-.13*	-.12*	-.22	+.02	+.03	-.04	+.24*	+.01	+.04	-.16*	-.09	-.09
Dec-making prac's	-.15*	-.13*	-.17	+.03	+.21*	-.14*	+.30*	+.17*	+.04	.00	-.32*	-.52*
Tech. readiness	-.01	+.13*	-.25	-.07	+.02	-.11*	+.39*	+.05	+.02	-.08	NA†	NA†
Lower-level infl.	+.03	-.10*	-.23	+.05	+.11	+.03	+.26*	+.01	-.33*	-.18*	-.47*	-.23*
Managerial leadership												
Support	-.10	-.11*	+.31	+.11*	-.11	-.19*	+.07	+.18*	+.18	+.01	-.16	-.32*
Inter. facilitation	-.04	+.02	-.05	+.20*	+.07	.00	+.11	+.36*	+.27*	+.15*	+.21*	.00
Goal emphasis	+.11	-.06	-.13	+.08	+.09	-.06	.00	+.17*	+.21*	+.06	-.11	-.11*
Work facilitation	+.12	-.08	+.29	+.21*	-.09	-.05	+.17	+.27*	+.33*	+.15*	-.09	-.16*
Peer leadership												
Support	-.20*	-.11*	-.24	+.02	+.17	-.13*	+.29*	+.06	-.01	+.03	-.19*	-.23*
Inter. facilitation	+.09	-.04	-.07	+.12*	+.08	-.06	+.30*	+.20*	+.06	+.20*	-.04	-.11*
Goal emphasis	-.05	.00	+.08	+.12*	+.22	-.02	+.21*	+.14*	+.15	+.12*	+.04	-.12*
Work facilitation	+.07	+.03	-.17	+.15*	+.04	-.03	+.36*	+.19*	+.09	+.20*	-.02	-.08
Group process	+.20*	+.27*	-.05	+.01	-.03	-.06	+.28*	+.21*	-.14	-.21*	NA†	NA†
Satisfaction	-.09	-.15*	-.04	+.04	+.32*	-.03	+.17*	+.09	+.07	-.02	-.07	-.23*

* Change large enough to be statistically significant at or beyond .05 level of confidence.
† Measures omitted in edition of questionnaire used in these sites.

3. *Task Process Consultation* is associated with little significant change among capstone groups; only two measures (Decision-Making Practices, Satisfaction) change, both in a positive direction. For whole systems, however, all significant changes are negative, and a majority of them occur in the area of organizational climate. Considering that the two measures of support (managerial and peer) also show a significant decline, the pattern shows at least some resemblance to that observed in conjunction with Laboratory Training.

4. *Survey Feedback* reflects positive and significant changes for capstone groups in every area except managerial leadership. For whole systems, 11 of the 16 measures show positive, statistically significant change. No measure, for either capstone groups or whole systems, reflects negative change.

5. *Data Handback* is associated in capstone groups with improved communication flow but a decline in the amount of influence attributed to lower organizational levels. Managerial leadership generally improves in these groups; all other measures show essentially no change. For their systems *in toto,* organizational climate is viewed as becoming worse, while peer leadership and some aspects of managerial leadership improve.

6. *No Treatment,* as a "treatment," is associated with general negative change for capstone groups and whole systems.

There are, therefore, clear differences in reported change among treatment categories. It would be premature, however, to discuss substantive implications of these results before considering the possible impact of several methodological or situational factors.

Regression Toward the Mean
One such factor is the familiar argument concerning "regression toward the mean." Although clients were assigned on a staff-availability basis, it is conceivable that client systems were assigned to change agents (and therefore to treatments) in a way which coincided with their initial positions on the characteristics measured. If so, and if regression toward the mean accounts for the observed results, we would expect those initially below the mean to exhibit positive change (toward the mean) and those initially above the mean to exhibit negative change (also toward the mean). We would also expect them to reflect significant differences at the outset; that is, to have been different from one another in the premeasure in ways congruent with a regression explanation. Table 3 presents an analysis of variance test of the differences among treatment categories at the time of the premeasure, and Table 4 shows a simple categorization of significant changes in terms of their consistency or inconsistency with a regression hypothesis.

There are clearly significant differences at the outset. Inspection of the treatment means shows that these differences do not, however, coincide with what would be expected if some form of regression toward the mean were to account for the contrasting results obtained with the various treatments. Task

Table 3 *Intertreatment differences in premeasures*

Area-measure	F	p		Treatments—Capstone Groups ($df = 5,350$)				
			Lab. training	Interpersonal process consult.	Task process consult.	Survey feedback	Data handback	No treatment
Organizational climate								
Hum. resources prim.	10.97	.001	4.00	3.46	3.92	3.80	3.46	4.46
Communication flow	4.94	.001	3.74	3.28	3.74	3.75	3.33	3.93
Motiv'l conditions	6.83	.001	3.92	3.64	3.98	3.86	3.47	4.20
Dec-making prac's	6.94	.001	3.28	3.11	3.49	3.53	2.90	3.60
Tech. readiness	2.09	N.S.	3.64	4.50	3.86	3.69	3.64	N.A.
Lower-level infl.	3.34	.01	2.96	2.54	2.97	2.96	2.86	3.43
Managerial leadership								
Support	5.02	.001	4.17	4.05	4.26	4.45	3.85	4.42
Inter. facilitation	8.93	.001	3.99	3.49	4.12	4.11	3.25	3.90
Goal emphasis	5.73	.001	4.14	4.08	4.41	4.49	3.85	4.40
Work facilitation	6.53	.001	3.38	3.21	3.68	3.70	3.10	3.79
Peer leadership								
Support	5.34	.001	4.09	4.06	3.76	3.91	3.87	4.38
Inter. facilitation	2.55	.05	3.45	3.17	3.31	3.53	3.16	3.71
Goal emphasis	1.70	N.S.	3.63	3.46	3.38	3.61	3.44	3.78
Work facilitation	1.69	N.S.	3.00	3.19	3.14	3.21	2.96	3.32
Group process	5.54	.001	3.52	4.00	3.74	4.00	3.63	N.A.
Satisfaction	4.68	.001	3.99	3.88	3.99	4.22	3.78	4.32

(Cont.)

Table 3

Area-measure	F	p	Lab. training	Interpersonal process consult.	Task process consult.	Survey feedback	Data handback	No treatment
				Treatments—Whole Systems ($df = 5$, inf.)				
Organizational climate								
Hum. resources prim.	236.78	.001	3.00	3.28	3.65	3.17	2.93	4.01
Communication flow	110.09	.001	2.94	2.98	3.27	2.94	2.96	3.57
Motiv'l conditions	99.25	.001	3.23	3.31	3.56	3.25	3.10	3.77
Dec-making prac's	164.16	.001	2.73	2.84	3.13	2.68	2.47	3.38
Tech. readiness	342.60	.001	2.80	3.47	3.70	3.37	3.53	N.A.
Lower-level infl.	61.81	.001	2.56	2.48	2.68	2.50	2.37	3.01
Managerial leadership								
Support	83.25	.001	3.78	3.84	4.04	3.82	3.77	4.44
Inter. facilitation	33.44	.001	3.20	3.20	3.37	3.11	2.98	3.48
Goal emphasis	50.52	.001	3.72	3.75	3.86	3.66	3.57	4.16
Work facilitation	75.13	.001	3.15	3.19	3.32	3.17	2.99	3.74
Peer leadership								
Support	51.97	.001	3.84	3.83	3.89	3.73	3.80	4.20
Inter. facilitation	44.98	.001	3.16	3.18	3.19	2.96	2.91	3.40
Goal emphasis	41.19	.001	3.30	3.36	3.36	3.21	3.15	3.60
Work facilitation	34.65	.001	3.10	3.20	3.12	2.98	2.85	3.22
Group process	95.33	.001	3.28	3.56	3.59	3.63	3.56	N.A.
Satisfaction	61.65	.001	3.60	3.73	3.74	3.68	3.51	4.07

Process Consultation sites, which began the effort around mid-range of the comparative distribution, show scarcely any change, and that which does occur is mixed as to its possible regression effects. Interpersonal Process Consultation and Data Handback treatment sites did, in fact, begin the change process from a somewhat lower scale point. Although capstone groups in Data Handback reflect a pattern in Table 4 that might suggest consistency with a regression hypothesis, the pattern for whole systems in this treatment is mixed, and that for whole systems in Interpersonal Process Consultation is clearly contrary to the hypothesis.

The contrary pattern presented by both Laboratory Training and Survey Feedback is even stronger. Laboratory Training, which began below the mean of the array and which would therefore be expected to show improvement, in fact declined. Survey Feedback, which started above the array mean and would be expected on a "regression toward the mean" hypothesis to decline, showed improvement.

Only in the case of whole systems experiencing No Treatment is there some substantial evidence for the regression hypothesis. In terms of the most striking differences in changes associated with various treatments it therefore seems reasonable to reject the hypothesis that they represent regression-toward-the-mean, methodological artifacts.

Table 4 *Consistency of significant changes with a regression hypothesis, by change treatment*

Treatment	No. consistent with regression hypothesis	No. inconsistent with regression hypothesis
Laboratory training		
Capstone	1	5
Whole systems	1	9
Interpersonal process consult.		
Capstone	0	0
Whole systems	0	7
Task process consult.		
Capstone	0	2
Whole systems	3	2
Survey feedback		
Capstone	0	12
Whole systems	0	11
Data handback		
Capstone	4	1
Whole systems	5	4
No treatment		
Capstone	1	4
Whole systems	10	0

Organizational Climate as a Mediating Factor

Still another possible explanation of the findings centers around the role played by organizational climate in conjunction with attempts at intervention. A quite plausible argument can be made (and indeed was made at the time, particularly by individuals connected with the Laboratory Training sites) that basically autocratic and punitive practices and policies contribute to an organizational climate that masks the true effects of the change treatment. Thus, the argument goes, if organizational climate could be controlled, the effects of the treatment on group member leadership behavior would show themselves to be positive.

What could not be controlled in the course of the projects can be controlled at least reasonably well by an analytic strategy employing Multiple Classification Analysis, which produces estimates of the effect of each of several predictors alone, after controlling for the effects of all others (Andrews, Morgan, & Sonquist, 1967). Table 5 shows change scores for the eight leadership indices, adjusted to remove the effects of organizational climate change.[4]

The results indicate considerable merit to the argument that the impact of a treatment is in part contingent upon the organizational climate in which it occurs, particularly in the case of Laboratory Training. The significant decline in managerial support present in the unadjusted scores disappears when adjustment is made for organizational climate, and the changes for managerial interaction facilitation and work facilitation, as well as for peer work facilitation, become positive. Only peer support remains significant and negative, although a decline in magnitude is apparent there as well.

Data Handback also benefits somewhat from controlling for level of organizational climate, with previously significant, positive changes increasing slightly in magnitude, and one additional measure attaining significance.

The remaining treatments (Interpersonal and Task Process Consultation, Survey Feedback, and No Treatment) show slight reduction in effects as a result of controlling for the effects of organizational climate.

SPURIOUS EFFECTS IN SURVEY FEEDBACK

An additional issue potentially affecting interpretation must be at least acknowledged before discussion of the overall implications of the findings. As an intervention technique, Survey Feedback usually employs the same instrument as a development tool that it uses to measure changes in the dependent variables. Therefore, the argument may be made, the results are likely to be confounded.

On reflection, this question breaks down into two separate issues: (a) the possibility that the feedback process subtly teaches organizational members how to respond to the questionnaire, and (b) the greater likelihood that issues tapped by the instrument will receive more attention during the work or change activities which intervene between pre- and postmeasures than will other issues.

Table 5 *Mean workgroup change scores, adjusted to remove effects of organizational climate change, by leadership measure, by treatment*

| | Treatment | | | | | | | | | | | |
| | N = 167 Lab. training | | N = 298 Interpersonal process consul. | | N = 109 Task process consult. | | N = 112 Survey feedback | | N = 98 Data handback | | N = 104 No treatment | |
Area-measure	Unadj.	Adj.	Unadj.	Adj.	Unadj.	Adj.	Unadj.	Adj.	Unadj.	Adj.	Unadj.	Adj.
Managerial leadership												
Support	-.15*	-.04	+.12*	+.04	-.25*	-.22	+.13	+.05	+.03	+.07	-.25*	-.18*
Inter. facilitation	+.07	+.20*	+.23*	+.13*	+.03	+.07	+.43*	+.33*	+.14	+.18*	+.05	+.14*
Goal emphasis	-.02	+.09	+.13*	+.05	-.09	-.06	+.14	+.06	+.06	+.09	-.08	-.01
Work facilitation	-.01	+.11*	+.22*	+.13=	-.09	-.05	+.24*	+.15	+.16*	+.21*	-.13*	-.05
Peer leadership												
Support	-.17*	-.11*	+.06	+.01	-.18*	-.17*	.00	-.06	+.07	+.08	-.22*	-.17*
Inter. facilitation	-.01	+.11	+.16*	+.06	-.09	-.06	+.17*	+.08*	+.20*	+.24*	-.12	-.03
Goal emphasis	-.04	+.05	+.15*	+.08=	-.06	-.04	+.10	+.04	+.16*	+.20*	-.10	-.03
Work facilitation	+.05	+.15*	+.24*	+.16=	-.10	-.08	+.25*	+.18*	+.22*	+.26*	-.05	+.02

* Statistically significant at .01 level of confidence.

The "subtle education" issue seems plausible on the surface, but with close examination proves less reasonable in the present setting. First, at least as employed within ICLS, questionnaires were administered by members of the ISR project staff, who literally took them to the sites and returned them to Ann Arbor. Large stocks of questionnaires left for scrutiny, memorization, or "boning up" were not available to member-participants. Second, the questionnaire contains over 100 items, and only a shorthand identification of the question stems appears on the computer print-out employed in feedback. Third, the tabulation sheets for any group or organization show considerable variation in response among members, as well as variation among the responses of any single respondent. Fourth, organizations of the type included in this study undergo a great deal of member rotation and turnover. Fifth, a substantial amount of evidence (not reported here) obtained from more detailed analyses within organizations reflects the construct validity of the measured changes. Changes in questionnaire indices relate differentially to one another in ways congruent with chronicled events in the project's history, with reports of change agents and top managers (obtained by content-analyzed interviews), and with performance measures from the operating records of the firm.

All in all, then, in order for the observed effects in the present study to represent a "subtle education" in how to respond, either an educative capability that would make organizational development itself obsolete or a conspiracy of organizational members so large and complex as to be mind-boggling would have had to occur. Consider: the invisible hand guiding such a process would have had to build into the memory banks of hundreds—often thousands—of persons (many of them relatively uneducated) exactly that correct combination of responses which would square with all or most of the appropriate comparisons internal to the data themselves, with data from operating records, and with events during the interim which had been flagged by project staff members. It would have had to accomplish this without inducing an undifferentiated, across-the-board rise in response positiveness, while taking into account a large percentage of members who were new to the setting. Finally, it would have had to arrange all of this some six to eight months after the overwhelming majority of persons within the organization had seen the instrument or any data tabulated from it!

The second problem, that greater attention is likely to be paid during the intervention to issues reflected in the survey rather than to issues not reflected in the survey, is not to be denied, but rather acknowledged. In its most basic form, this is not a "problem" (in the sense of something which distorts or obfuscates). Instead, it is the heart of the change process for any system attempting to adapt to changes in its environment by a process of information inputs concerning the effect of mid-course corrections. This so-called problem appears in any change treatment and any evaluation or self-monitoring system geared to corrective input short of ultimate survival or destruction.

Having said this, we must also acknowledge that a measuring instrument fails to the extent that it is parochial in content. It may well be, for example, that the questionnaire used in this study omits content areas of great significance for organizational effectiveness—areas which are targeted by non-Survey Feedback treatments. If that is the case, however, it becomes an error of omission, not of commission. Errors of commission only appear if the instrument or the meta-theory on which they are based are themselves invalid. To the extent that the questionnaire taps what it purports to tap, and to the extent that those characteristics *do* relate to valid outcomes, its use as an assessment device is appropriate.

THOUGHTS ABOUT THE IMPLICATIONS OF THESE FINDINGS

Although these findings emphasize the differences present among the several treatments, all the application methods used in the present study appear to be quite climate-impacted. If the organizational climate is not changing positively, none of the treatments show any likelihood of substantially enhancing supportive behavior, whether by managers or by peers, or of enhancing goal emphasis by managers. Similarly, the problem-solving behavioral combination of interaction facilitation and work facilitation, as well as mutual goal emphasis by peers, seems climate-prone, in the sense that it is enhanced by positive shifts in climate, and harmed by negative shifts.

In the sites and projects included in the present study, Laboratory Training clearly suffers from an organizational climate that is *becoming* harsher and more barren.[5] This may, in fact, explain the discrepancy between findings in the present study and findings reported elsewhere: it may be that laboratory-like, experiential learning is successful in organizations whose climate is, or is becoming, positive (e.g., a Harwood or a TRW; cf. Marrow, Bowers, & Seashore, 1967; or Davis, 1967), but unsuccessful in organizations whose superstructure is, or is becoming, more autocratic and punitive.

Survey Feedback, on the other hand, is the only treatment in the present study associated with large, across-the-board, positive changes in organizational climate. Controlling for these changes tends to *reduce* the raw, significant, and positive change observed in Survey Feedback sites for managerial and peer leadership variables. By way of contrast, Data Handback shows an increase, not a decrease, in positive change in managerial and peer variables when change in organizational climate is controlled statistically. In both treatments, the data format, content of the tabulation, and nature of the recipients are the same. Why, then, do we find a difference? The reason may be that the Survey Feedback process, in combination with the data, produces an attention to those issues related to organizational climate that must change if the system itself is to change. In fact, considering the intrinsic nature of the other treatments, it seems at least plausible that Survey Feedback is the only treatment of those considered which is likely to attend to these system-level issues in anything like a comprehensive form. Although the issue whether treatment itself effects climate change remains truly unanswered within these present data, a technical report (Bowers, 1971) investigates this particular problem and produces evidence to suggest that it does. In any event, more research on this question is needed; if treatments do not affect organizational climate positively or if other ways of accomplishing that end are not available, the present findings suggest that one would be best off following the rather barren practice of simply tabulating the data and handing them back!

Little more can be added to this point by way of interpreting the present findings. At the very least, they indicate that the different intervention strategies employed in ICLS had somewhat different outcomes. Beyond this, however, they add a degree of credence to the argument advanced by some that organizational change is a complex, sytems-level problem in organizational adaptation, not merely an additive end-product of participation in particular development activities.

Notes

1. See Bowers and Franklin (1972) for a discussion of the theoretical rationale for this treatment.

2. All items were in each instance returned to group participants. Thus, although selective attention may have occurred, treatments do not differ in the particular data returned.

3. A "time period" is a period of approximately four consecutive months; four such periods, covering an 18-month time span, are used in the validation analyses.

4. The technical report from which this analysis was drawn used workgroup means, not individual scores, as the analysis units. Thus the gain scores reported in Table 5 differ slightly from those reported in Table 2. The pattern, however, is substantially the same.

5. It is worth noting that it is the *change* in climate, not its original state, which seems impactful. Laboratory Training and Survey Feedback, for example, are almost identical in climate at the outset, but change differentially.

References

Andrews, F., Morgan, J., & Sonquist, J. *Multiple classification analysis.* Ann Arbor: Institute for Social Research, 1967.

Bowers, D. Development techniques and organizational climate: An evaluation of the comparative importance of two potential forces for organizational change. Technical Report, Office of Naval Research, 1971.

Bowers, D., & Franklin, J. Survey-guided development: Using human resources measurement in organizational change. *Journal Contemporary Business,* 1972, **1**, 43–55.

Bowers, D., & Seashore, S. Predicting organizational effectiveness with a four-factor theory of leadership. *Administrative Science Quarterly,* 1966, **11**, 238–263.

Davis, S. An organic problem-solving method of organizational change. *JABS,* 1967, **3**, 3–21.

Evan, W. A systems model of organizational climate. In R. Tagiuri and G. Litwin (Eds.), *Organizational climate.* Boston: Harvard University Press, 1968.

Halpin, A. W. *Theory and research in administration.* New York: Macmillan, 1966.

Likert, R. *New patterns of management.* New York: McGraw-Hill, 1961.

Likert, R. *The human organizations.* New York: McGraw-Hill, 1967.

Marrow, A., Bowers, D., & Seashore, S. *Management by participation.* New York: Harper & Row, 1967.

Schein, E. Process consultation: Its role in organization development. In E. Schein, W. Bennis, and R. Beckhard (Eds.), *Organization development.* Reading, Mass.: Addison-Wesley Publishing Co., 1969.

Taylor, J., & Bowers, D. *The survey of organizations: A machine-scored standardized questionnaire instrument.* Ann Arbor: Institute for Social Research, 1972.

Punching the Clock: When You Choose
David T. Cook

Boston

A growing number of U.S. workers can fearlessly ignore their alarm clocks.

These well-rested employees work for firms that have adopted "flexible hours"—a system allowing workers to select their hours—within company guidelines.

"Flex time" is now the fastest-growing humanizing trend on the American work scene, spreading "at a fantastic rate," says Janice Hedges, a U.S. Labor Department economist.

Growth of the four-day week is a more widespread trend—has "plateaued" says American Management Association consultant Kenneth Wheeler.

Flexible hours do not mean fewer hours of work. The system modifies rigid starting and quitting times—not total hours on the job. Thus workers who opt to snooze in the morning must continue to toil after early risers have quit for the day.

EMPLOYEES ENTHUSIASTIC

For example, at John Hancock Mutual Life Insurance Company—the latest major firm to try flex time—selected employees can report between 7:30 and 9 in the morning. Quitting times vary from 3:40 to 5:10 P.M. and are keyed to a worker's arrival.

At Scott Paper company, "great enthusiastic employee and management response" greeted the flex program, says James Gaylord, the firm's vice-president for industrial relations.

Employees at other companies appear equally enthused.

"Our office is near a beach, so in the warm weather you can go for a swim in the afternoon," says Lufthansa German Airlines employee Hoshab Jian.

Flexible hours are not offered to the line's airport employees. But staggered starting hours "do not create problems" in staffing the airline's Long Island headquarters office, says personnel manager David Buisch.

Some firm's plans are more flexible than others. At Hewlett-Packard, a California-based electronics manufacturer, the flexible-hour program can turn a lunch break into a siesta.

PRODUCTIVITY BY-PRODUCT

"You can take a two-hour lunch and make up for it by starting early or staying late," says HP executive John Kane.

Hewlett-Packard is one of the few firms that allows flexibility in an employee's midday break. The firm has 20,000 workers on flexible hours.

For workers, the appeal of flexible hours is convenience. For the keeper of the corporate purse, the plan appeals for other reasons.

Improved employee productivity appears to be a by-product of flex time, "although scanty data exists" to support this assumption, says Riva Poor, a Cambridge, Mass., management consultant.

As a result of its plan, Lufthansa cut it work force by 4 percent and nevertheless saw "a marked increase in the volume of work," company officials say.

Even without productivity increases, flexible hours are attractive since they combine employee appeal with low cost.

John Hancock's experiment with flexible hours will cause "not really any" cost increases, says Peter Janetos, a Hancock vice-president.

WORKERS SET OWN SALARY

With the exception of Hancock, no U.S. firm currently is offering employees both a four-day week and flexible working hours. At Hancock, workers eligible for the four-day week cannot participate in flexible time, and vice versa.

Efforts to bring even greater flexibility to working conditions often start at smaller firms.

For example, employees at a large Oakland, Calif., appliance store are allowed to set their own salary level and vacation length.

"I do not want anyone working for less than they think they are worth," says owner Arthur Friedman.

The majority of salary requests are reasonable, he says, and those he thought excessive produced a marked increase in worker productivity.

The program has had little impact on the store's profits. "They are about the same as they were," Mr. Friedman says, "but working is a lot more pleasant."

Job Enrichment: A Valuable Tool
for Company and Worker
Edgar F. Huse

A number of companies are finding that it is in their own interest to provide job enrichment for their workers.

This is true for the giant General Electric, Texas Instruments, American Telephone and Telegraph, and Corning Glass Workers as well as for small companies like Donnelly Mirrors in Holland, Mich., and Precision Castparts Corporation in Portland, Ore.

In essence, job enrichment refers to the deliberate redesigning of jobs and the way they are performed in order to provide more challenging content for the worker. By making the job more meaningful and interesting the worker is given the opportunity for growth, recognition, challenge, and achievement. Planning, evaluating, and doing are not separated; the worker does much of the planning, goal-setting and controlling of his own job.

Typically, job enrichment begins in a small company or in one section or plant of a larger organization, and the results are startling. As one worker at a Corning plant making precision electronic hospital testing equipment put it, "I just love it here. My husband is a supervisor in a different company, and I go home at night and tell him how he should be doing things in his company."

In another case, a group of female assembly workers were sitting in the cafeteria having a cup of coffee after punching out. They weren't griping: they were planning how to meet the manufacturing schedule! One of them turned to me and said, "Isn't this silly—we really should be home cooking dinner for our husbands, but we get so involved here."

After an assembly line was broken up and the workers were allowed to plan their own schedule and make their own instrument, productivity soared by 84 percent and morale, interest in the job, and quality of performance improved tremendously.

As one satisfied worker said, "I feel a lot better about my job, now that I am putting the whole instrument together. It is my instrument and I feel responsible for it."

Boston Globe, April 8, 1973. Courtesy of the Boston Globe.

In another organization, the maintenance supervisor began allowing the janitors more responsibility for establishing their own schedules and determining which waxes, cleaning powders, and scrubbing machines to buy.

Being given more responsibility and opportunity for achievement and recognition cured an alcoholic janitor; he has not been on the binge for two years, a previously unheard of record.

Another janitor said: "Before, my boss did all the thinking and made all the decisions for us. Now, we can make up our own schedules and make our own decisions. The job is a lot more interesting and fun than it used to be."

At Non-Linear Systems in Del Mar, Calif. (making electronic instruments) the reaction to job enrichment has been highly positive. Productivity and morale have gone up. As one person explained, "Where I worked before, other people did all your planning and thinking for you. Here, people respect you as a human being and listen to you and your ideas."

In a textile plant, rearrangement of the work according to job enrichment principles produced the same kind of results: Production and morale went up; absenteeism and scrap went down.

In another organization, a manufacturing plant was shut down on a Friday afternoon and groups were formed to identify problems. Every individual in the organization was present—janitors, guards, secretaries, technicians, and engineers. Each group had representatives from every department in the organization.

The groups were asked to identify problems that would either (1) make the organization a better place to work or (2) make the organization more effective. About 60 or 70 major problems were identified and for two months, the organization was shut down every Friday afternoon so that the groups could work on the problems. The organization not only reduced manufacturing costs by 45 percent in five months, but as one clerk put it, "When they shut the plant down and asked us for our ideas, and then when I saw some of my ideas being put into effect, it made me feel great.

"For the first time, I felt important and felt that I had something to contribute to the job."

A union member put it this way, "Now they are really listening to us. It's tremendous."

In one municipality the truck drivers rather than their boss were given the option of deciding who got the new truck to drive. Their reaction, of course, was highly positive; they felt more satisfied with their decision than they had in the past with the boss's decision.

The basic idea behind job enrichment is to give employees at all levels more opportunity to make decisions about their goals, schedules, methods of doing the job, and more responsibility for the completed product. This means, of course, that management must be willing to delegate authority and to accept the fact that workers can make intelligent decisions when given proper data and information.

This does not mean that the manager abdicates—rather, he allows decisions to be made by those who are most involved and qualified to make the decisions.

Sometimes, this is hard to take, because managers feel that their right to make decisions is being taken away by people who have little or nothing to contribute to the planning and evaluating of the job.

In one case, a group of female assembly workers had increased their productivity by more than 300 percent and were solving problems that outside consultants had been unable to solve. Yet when a new manager came into the organization, he thought that the group was not being supervised closely enough and sent in a new foreman to "straighten the place out." Soon, many of the workers quit or transferred to different jobs, and productivity dropped drastically.

Job enrichment is a tougher way to manage, since it means that the supervisor can no longer "go by the book" and treat employees as automatons. It is much easier to have the restrooms painted or put in a new insurance plan and hope that the workers will be mollified.

At a conference attended by some 40 personnel managers of plants in one corporation, each personnel manager had been instructed to interview a number of hourly workers before the conference and then report on his findings. Most of the personnel managers reported that the workers in their plants were unhappy about such things as rest periods, vacation plans, and fringe benefits. The personnel manager from the only plant having an organizational development and job enrichment program reported that the two biggest gripes that the hourly workers in his plant had were parts shortages and poor product design.

Currently, only a small minority of American organizations are using job-enrichment programs. Yet, if the job is to have any real meaning, if America's workers at all levels are to avoid further de-humanization, work must be made more meaningful, challenging, and intrinsically interesting.

As one worker summarized her own job-enrichment experience, "Those other girls are deprived and they don't even know it!"

The Internal OD Consultant: Issues and Questions
Carol Weiss Heine

The intent of this paper is to share some insights and questions on the role of the internal OD consultant. The starting place is an evaluation study of internal OD consultants within industrial systems. The role of internal consultant is a marginal, lonely one. The process of differentiating the organizational forces that contribute to this state of affairs is needed.

This study was based on an adaptation of the Lippett, Watson and Westley model of planned change. The LW&W model is a problem-solving model for the external consultant. The model of practices presented in this study was intended to describe the OD process of the internal OD consultant.

The LW&W problem-solving model is:

Phase 1: development of a need for change.

Phase 2: establishment of a change relationship.

Phase 3: clarification or diagnosis of the client's problem.

Phase 4: examination of alternative change goals and strategies, and establishment of specific change goals and strategies.

Phase 5: institutionalizing the change.

Phase 6: terminating the change relationship.[1]

The Heine model tested in the study is:

Phase 1: *Entry:* how the relationship between the client and consultant begins.

Phase 2: *Contracting:* boundary setting for client-consultant relationship, including initial problem definition.

Phase 3: *Strategy Planning and Implementation:* knowledge gained in first two phases is used to further focus problem definition and planning of the form and function of the intervention.

Phase 4: *Evaluation:* looking at the impact of each intervention and the total OD effort.

Phase 5: *Institutionalization:* building self-renewing skills and processes into the system to maintain an optimal state of operation.[2]

Reprinted by permission of Carol Weiss Heine. Unpublished manuscript.

The LW&W model describes the process of an external consultant setting up a temporary system to solve explicit problems. The external consultant works with the temporary system in such a way that it is neither in conflict or interfaces with the daily operation and existence of the established system. The goal of a temporary system is to either improve or change the operations of the established system. The improvements or changes are applied to the established system once they have been tested in the "laboratory" of the temporary system. The temporary system is a simulation of reality where alternatives and solutions can be tested before they are applied to the established system.

The Heine model describes a framework for a model of OD practices of internal OD consultants. The model was based on the assumption that an internal OD consultant, by nature of his job, collaborates with his client to increase their problem-solving capacity. This model falls short in the Strategy Planning and Implementation, Evaluation and Institutionalization phases. Perhaps the model falls short because it focuses only on problem-solving and collaboration as an approach to the OD process. A more viable model describing the OD process would incorporate the problem-solving process within an on-going organization. This would be combined with a systems analysis approach to organizational life. A systems analysis approach would introduce a conceptual framework for dealing with dynamics of the system's structure or the core processes of the organization. This would include managerial subsystems, organizational structure, organizational environment and climate, and organizational goals and values. A model which incorporates both problem-solving and systems analysis would describe both *how* to facilitate changing and *what* to focus on changing.

Use of the Heine model demonstrates that one cannot simply assume that the external consultant and internal consultant role and process is interchangeable. The differences between the two go beyond the meaning of the adjectives preceding "consultant."

One of the differences noted during the study was that the internal OD consultant role is less clear-cut than that of the external consultant. Internal OD consultants found difficulty in articulating their "role" to clients. Unclear role definitions affected the way internal OD consultants carried out their job. Organizational climate also affects consultant behavior. The effect that organizational climate has on the internal OD consultant's behavior is an interesting question. Certainly, the climate of an organization is more apt to affect the behavior of an internal OD consultant than an external OD consultant.

Internal consultants seem to be concerned with accommodating the needs of the on-going system. The internal OD consultants most typically work with team-building. They work toward improving quality of meetings and deal with specific personnel problems. Their work suggests the value of modifying and accommodating to "what is" as contrasted to an examination

of the subsystem norms and working towards changing. The external consultant appears to be freer to look at pervasive system and subsystem norms. This
is because he is not part of either system.

An internal consultant is inside the system. His knowledge of system
norms both inhibits and facilitates his usefulness to the system, since he is
subject to the same company norms as other employees. A consultant would
be doing his client an injustice to tamper with norms that he knew were set
by top management and which could not be changed without executive consent. Working with overall system norms precludes a concern for more focus
on overall system issues and long range goals. Sometimes an internal consultant does not have access to the groups that deal with these issues.

It may be that the limitations of an internal OD consultant are not
explicit to either the consultant or management. Internal OD consultants are
implicitly more accountable to the company than external consultants. Top
management may prefer to hire internal OD consultants because in the long
run the fees are less expensive than external consultants. Too much is expected
of internal OD consultants, both by themselves and by others.

Returning to the three phases where the Heine model falls short—
Strategy Planning and Implementation, Evaluation, and Institutionalization—
several other issues become explicit.

The LW&W model calls for joint problem-solving. The Heine model
focuses on collaboration (between client and consultant) as a process toward
which OD goals can be achieved. However, during the Strategy Planning and
Evaluation phases collaboration between consultant and client was not
achieved. Perhaps collaboration is not relevant to the on-the-job practice of
OD. Categorically this cannot be true. This is a point at which a model based
on systems theory could shed some light. The issue is how to proceed at this
point in the process. During the Strategy Planning and Implementation phase
the systems issues of how will the change affect other parts of the organization
comes to the foreground. It may even appear sooner.

In the study it was also discovered that very little energy was spent on
self-renewal by either consultants or clients. The question arises: Is self-
renewal a concept perhaps still too new to be explicitly incorporated in the OD
process for an internal OD consultant? It appears that establishing specific
skills and structures for self-renewal within a subsystem is not relevant for an
internal consultant. The fact that an internal consultant does not terminate his
relationship with the client the way an external consultant does may contribute
to self-renewal not being a part of the OD effort.

Whatever the reason, it is clear that self-renewal is a concept not practiced by internal OD consultants. To actualize the concept of self-renewal
within an organization, some structure or process is needed to help people
within the organization collect and feedback operational data. Self-renewal, to
exist at all, must be endorsed by top management. And it may well be that the

external consultant is in the best possible position to work on the specifics of the self-renewal process.

The internal OD consultant does not terminate his relationship in the same way the external OD consultant does. The internal OD consultant is more accessible than the external consultant. Geographic and organizational proximity makes termination unrealistic. Therefore perhaps the issue is to determine how an internal OD consultant can follow up on work done within a subsystem without inhibiting the client's growth and change. A modified model of OD practices for an internal consultant needs to speak to this issue rather than termination of the relationship.

OD PROCESS

It is assumed that climate affects the OD process. Therefore one can say that the organizational climate influences the OD process. Interesting questions arise. How does climate influence process? How does a competitive environment affect the collaborative process? The studies done by Deutsch[3] on the effect of competition and collaboration on individual behavior and group functioning provide an explanation as to the influence of organizational climate on the OD process.

In his study, Deutsch points out that in a competitive climate productivity, conflict and norms are affected. The norms of a competitive situation support separateness, individuality and the need to achieve and surpass others. This drive also causes a certain amount of tension. It creates lack of open communication. Conflicts are left unresolved and insecurity grows out of the expectation of hostility from others. This environment created by competition among groups and group members also affects the group cohesion. One of the indicators of a cohesive group is the degree of collaboration among the members. There is little in a competitive environment that encourages collaboration among members, except the cohesion that occurs as group joins forces against an external force or the enemy. Thus, one can assume that collaboration in a competitive environment is hard to achieve.

In the study it was discovered that collaboration during the Strategy Planning and Implementation phases was too difficult to attain. Likert[4] suggests a rationale for this state of affairs. He says that traditional organizations structured hierarchically tend to nurture competition rather than collaboration. The companies studied are described as hierarchical organizations. The OD process has been incorporated into these systems structurally. Collaboration between client and consultant was difficult to attain although there was no indication that they were competing with one another in the relationship.

In theory and practice it seems unrealistic to expect client and consultant to collaborate early in the OD process particularly during the data gathering, diagnosis and intervention phases. In organizations which are managed traditionally status becomes the currency of exchange for relationships. It seems clear that competitive relationships will be the norm rather than collaborative relationships. The internal OD consultant is working towards counternorms and is bound to have difficulty if he becomes myopic around the collaborative approach.

From these considerations it becomes clear that organizational structure, climate, and norms do affect the OD process. It becomes clear also that in order to facilitate effective planning changes one must look at OD models other than that of the external consultant.

In the past five years, a number of organizations have created internal OD consultant groups, which have replaced external OD consultants. On the other hand, the turnover rate for internal OD consultants is high. Perhaps some combination of internal and external OD consultants would fulfill OD objectives more satisfactorily. In order to do this there needs to be more clarity about the respective roles and responsibilities of the internal and external OD consultants. One trend that has developed over the last year is that internal OD consultants are becoming line managers with line responsibility. They use their OD technology and skill in their management position.

During the study some other interesting discoveries were made. These differ from the differences between internal and external OD consultants. These involve: organizational structure, organizational environment and the OD process. These discoveries are based on perceptions of events and processes while doing the study.

ORGANIZATION STRUCTURE

Data were gathered from consultants about their respective company's organizational structure as it related to the location of the OD department. In one company the OD group is most closely connected to top management. They talked about their autonomy and freedom. In another company the OD department is part of the Personnel Department. Consultants from this company indicated that every time they went out to a new client they perceived that their effectiveness was minimized because of the "personnel" stigma. They also talked about the accountability process. They perceived that the written reports required of them hampered their relationship with the clients. In a third company the OD groups also talked about accountability and authorization. Structurally they reported to two bosses. The consultants reported that his dual accountability and authorization led to much uncertainty when decisions outside their immediate concerns had to be made.

This leads me to wonder about the relationship between effectiveness of an OD group and the location of the OD department in the organizational hierarchy. Secondly I wonder about the impact of unclear accountability and authorization procedures on the effectiveness of the OD process.

ORGANIZATIONAL ENVIRONMENT

The climate for acceptance of OD within the companies seemed to emerge as an organizational force affecting the practice of OD. At specific points it appeared that organizational environment influenced the effectiveness of the OD process. One of the three companies studied was seen to be more accepting of OD than the others. The degree of acceptability facilitated or inhibited making decisions of moving from planning to action. Value of the consultant resources brought to the job, and access to clients throughout the company was affected. The degree of acceptability also influenced the amount of time employees were given to work on their own professional growth and development.

Notes

1. Ronald Lippett, Jeanne Watson, and Bruce Westley, *The Dynamics of Planned Change,* (New York: Harcourt, Brace & World Co., 1958).

2. Carol W. Heine, *An Evaluation of Organizational Development Practices of the Inter-Company Laboratory According to Criteria of a Theoretical Model,* (Unpublished Dissertation: Boston University, School of Education, 1972).

3. Morton Deutsch, "An Experimental Study of the Effects of Cooperation and Competition upon Group Processes," *Human Relations,* 1949.

4. Rensis Likert, *New Patterns of Management* (New York: McGraw-Hill Book Company, Inc.), 1961.

INTEGRATED APPROACHES

OD Interventions—An Overview
Wendell L. French and Cecil A. Bell, Jr.

The term *OD interventions* refers to the range of planned programmatic activities clients and consultants participate in during the course of an organization development program. These activities are designed to improve the organization's functioning through enabling organization members better to manage their team and organization culture. OD interventions constitute the continually evolving technology—the methods and techniques—of the practice of organization development. Knowing the OD intervention armamentarium and knowing the rationale underlying the use of different interventions contributes substantially to understanding the philosophy, assumptions, nature, and processes of organization development. In these five chapters on interventions, we examine the techniques involved in applying behavioral science theory and practice to change and improve ongoing systems. In this chapter we look at issues, definitions, rationale, and several classificatory schemata related to interventions. In Chapters 10 through 13 we extend the discussion through an examination of the current inventory of OD interventions.

A DEFINITION OF OD INTERVENTIONS
The term OD interventions is currently being used in several different ways. On the one hand, this seems to be due to confusion and lack of definition; on the other hand, it is due to the fact that it quite accurately (if not precisely) refers to several orders of meaning in terms of level of abstraction. Is an OD

intervention something that someone does to an organization, or is it something that is going on, that is, an activity? It is both. We prefer, however, that emphasis be placed on the activity nature of interventions; interventions are "things that happen," activities, in an organization's life.

One use of the term that is common with practitioners and laymen alike is that an intervention is something the outside consultant does to the client system. The major shortcomings of this definition are, first, that it does not provide for the client system doing something to itself without the assistance of an external, or even internal, consultant; and, second, it denies the joint collaboration that takes place between consultant and client. In OD programs, individuals and units within the organization often initiate activities designed to improve their functioning and do so on their own. These activities can clearly constitute OD interventions.

The term is often used to refer to any learning technique or method available to the practitioner. Thus, any one of the extant methods available, what Burke and Hornstein call "the social technology of OD,"[1] is an intervention according to this use. (These techniques are available both to the client system and to consultants.) This is probably the most common use, and it is an appropriate one. The technology of OD consists of educational activities, methods, and techniques; some "things to do" and "things to be sure not to do"; questionnaires, observation and interview schedules, and so forth. Any of these can appropriately be considered an intervention when it is used to bring about organization improvement.

Common usage also finds the term applied to the following different levels of activities:

A single task, say, a two-hour decision-making exercise

A sequence or series of related tasks designed around some theme or objective; for example, Beckhard's *confrontation meeting* is a series of tasks designed to surface an organization's major problems, determine the priorities for solving the problems, and assign responsibilities for actions[2]

A "family" of activities that are related but may be quite different; for example, the set of activities called team-building interventions are a wide variety of diverse activities all designed to improve a team's effectiveness as a unit, and the activities may relate to ways to perform the task better or to ways to improve the relations between the team members

The overall plan for relating and integrating the organization improvement activities that an organization might be engaged in over a period of years (this is generally referred to as the *intervention strategy,* the *strategy of intervention,* or the *OD strategy* of the organization development program)

All of these are correct uses of the term intervention, but they relate to different levels of abstraction and can thus be confusing at times.

Finally, to give our definition of the term: OD interventions are *sets of structured activities* in which selected organizational units (target groups or individuals) engage with a task or a sequence of tasks where the task goals are related directly or indirectly to organizational improvement. Interventions constitute the action thrust of organization development; they "make things happen" and are "what's happening."

The OD practitioner is a professional versed in the theory and practice of organization development. He brings four sets of attributes to the organizational setting: a set of values; a set of assumptions about man, organizations, and interpersonal relationships; a set of goals and objectives for himself and for the organization and its members; and a set of structured activities that are the *means* to implementing his values, assumptions, and goals. These activities are what we mean by the word *intervention*.

A BRIEF WORD ABOUT THE NATURE OF OD INTERVENTIONS

In the chapter on the nature of organization development, the characteristics, nature, and scope of OD interventions were discussed in relation to the OD process. Many of the characteristics ascribed to OD inhere also in OD interventions. The foundations and characteristics of the OD process are given there as follows: it is data based and experience based, with emphasis on action, diagnosis, and goal setting; it frequently utilizes work teams as target groups; it rests on a systems approach to organizations; it is a normative–re-educative strategy of changing; and it is an ongoing process. In this section we deal explicitly with OD interventions, covering some new materials and some old materials in a new way.

OD interventions are structured activities of selected target groups. Some "secrets" of OD are contained in this statement, because there are "better" ways and "worse" ways to structure activities in order for learning and change to take place. OD practitioners know how to structure activities in the "better" ways through attending to the following points:

> Structure the activity so that the relevant people are there. The relevant people are those affected by the problem or the opportunity. For example, if the goal is improved team effectiveness, have the whole team engage in the activities. If the goal is improved relations between two separate work groups, have both work groups present. If the goal is to build some linkages with some special group, say, the industrial relations people, have them there and have the linking people from the home group there.

> This preplanning of the group composition is a necessary feature of properly structuring the activity.

Structure the activity so that it is (1) problem oriented or opportunity oriented and (2) oriented to the problems and opportunities generated by the clients themselves. Solving problems and capitalizing on opportunities are involving, interesting, and enjoyable tasks for most people, whether it is due to a desire for competence or mastery (as suggested by White),[3] or a desire to achieve (as suggested by McClelland),[4] or whatever. This is especially true when the issues to be worked on have been defined by the client. There is built-in support and involvement, and there is a real payoff when clients are solving issues that they have stated have highest priority.

Structure the activity so that the goal is clear and the way to reach the goal is clear. Few things demotivate an individual as much as not knowing what he is working toward and not knowing how what he is doing contributes to goal attainment. Both of these points are part of structuring the activity properly. (Parenthetically, the goals will be important goals for the individuals if the second point above is followed.)

Structure the activity so that there is a high probability of successful goal attainment. Implicit in this point is the warning that expectations of practitioners and clients should be realistic. But more than that, manageable, attainable objectives once achieved produce feelings of success, competence, and potency for the people involved. This, in turn, raises aspiration levels and feelings of self- and group-worth. The task can still be hard, complicated, taxing—but it should be attainable. And if there is failure to accomplish the goal, the reasons for this should be clear so they can be avoided in the future.

Structure the activity so that it contains both experience-based learning and conceptual/cognitive/theoretical-based learning. New learnings gained through experience are made a permanent part of the individual's repertoire when they are augmented (and "cemented") through conceptual material that puts the experience into a broader framework of theory and behavior. Relating the experience to conceptual models, theories, and other experiences and beliefs helps the learning to become integrated for the individual.

Structure the climate of the activity so that individuals are "freed up" rather than anxious or defensive. Setting the climate of interventions so that people expect "to learn together" and "to look at practices in an experimenting way so that we can select better procedures" is what we mean by climate setting.

Structure the activity so that the participants learn both how to solve a particular problem and "learn how to learn" at the same time. This may mean scheduling in time for reflecting on the activity and teasing out learnings that occurred; it may mean devoting as much as half the activity to one focus and half to the other.

Structure the activity so that individuals can learn about both *task* and *process.* The task is what the group is working on, that is, the stated agenda items. The term process, as used here, refers to *how* the group is working and *what else is going on* as the task is being worked on. This includes the group's processes and dynamics, individual styles of interacting and behaving, etc. Learning to be skillful in working in both of these areas is a powerful tool. Activities structured to focus on both aspects result in learnings on both aspects.

Structure the activity so that individuals are engaged as whole persons, not segmented persons. This means that role demands, thoughts, beliefs, feelings, and strivings should all be called into play, not just one or two of these. Integrating disparate parts of individuals in an organizational world where differentiation in terms of role, feelings, thoughts is common probably enhances the individual's ability to cope and grow.

These features are integral characteristics of OD interventions and also of the practitioner's practice theory of organization development. Little attention is given to characteristics of structuring activities in the literature, but knowledge of them helps to take some of the mystery out of interventions and may also be helpful to people who are just beginning to practice OD.

A different approach to the nature of OD interventions is provided by Warren Bennis when he lists the major interventions in terms of their underlying themes.[5] He describes the following kinds of interventions: (1) *discrepancy intervention,* which calls attention to a contradiction in action or attitudes that then leads to exploration; (2) *theory intervention,* where behavioral science knowledge and theory are used to explain present behavior and assumptions underlying the behavior; (3) *procedural intervention,* which represents a critiquing of how something is being done to determine whether the best methods are being used; (4) *relationship intervention,* which focuses attention on interpersonal relationships (particularly those where there are strong negative feelings) and surfaces the issues for exploration and possible resolution; (5) *experimentation intervention,* in which two different action plans are tested for their consequences before a final decision on one is made; (6) *dilemma intervention,* in which an imposed or emergent dilemma is used to force close examination of the possible choices involved and the assumptions underlying them; (7) *perspective intervention,* which draws attention away from immediate actions and demands and allows a look at historical background, context, and future objectives in order to assess whether or not the actions are "still on target"; (8) *organization structure intervention,* which calls for examination and evaluation of structural causes for organizational ineffectiveness; and (9) *cultural intervention,* which examines traditions, precedents, and practices—the fabric of the organization's culture—in a direct, focused approach.

Bennis' typology helps to provide a more thorough understanding of the nature of OD interventions while at the same time affording a classification scheme against which specific activities may be compared.

The nature of OD intervention—the structured activities designed to bring about system improvement—is complex and multifaceted. But certain themes recur in many interventions, the dynamics of the intervention process itself are becoming better understood, and there is a growing body of concepts that relates to the process of planned change. Considerable understanding of the nature of OD interventions is available to practitioners and clients alike as a result of this process. Just as an example, and to close this section on a serendipitous note: the *decision* to participate in an OD intervention may itself be a cause of organizational improvement. Just making the decision will signal to the members involved that the culture is changing, that new ideas and new ways of doing things are becoming more of a possibility and reality. This signal may itself cause changes in the direction of improvement. Our evaluation techniques and our theories of the intervention process are not sophisticated enough to handle such interactional complexities. That is for future practitioners at future times.

THE MAJOR FAMILIES OF OD INTERVENTIONS

Not all OD programs contain all the possible intervention activities, but a wide range of activities is available to the practitioner. As we see it, the following are the major "families" or types of OD interventions.

Diagnostic Activities: fact-finding activities designed to ascertain the state of the system, the status of a problem, the "way things are." Available methods range from projective devices like "build a collage that represents for you your place in this organization" to the more traditional data collection methods of interviews, questionnaires, surveys, and meetings.

Team-building Activities: activities designed to enhance the effective operation of system teams. They may relate to task issues, such as the way things are done, the needed skills to accomplish tasks, the resource allocations necessary for task accomplishment; or they may relate to the nature and quality of the relationships between the team members or between members and the leader. Again, a wide range of activities is possible. In addition, consideration is given to the different kinds of teams that may exist in the organization, such as formal work teams, temporary task force teams, and newly constituted teams.

Intergroup Activities: activities designed to improve effectiveness of interdependent groups. They focus on joint activities and the output of the groups considered as a single system rather than as two subsystems. When two groups are involved, the activities are generally designated intergroup or interface activities; when more than two groups are involved, the activities are often called *organizational mirroring*.

Survey-Feedback Activities: related to and similar to the diagnostic activities mentioned above in that they are a large component of those activities. However, they are important enough in their own right to be considered separately. These activities center around actively working the data produced by a survey and designing action plans based on the survey data.

Education and Training Activities: activities designed to improve skills, abilities, and knowledge of individuals. There are several activities available and several approaches possible. For example, the individual can be educated in isolation from his work group (say, in a T-group comprised of strangers), or he can be educated in relation to his work group (say, when a work team learns how better to manage interpersonal conflict). The activities may be directed toward technical skills required for effective task performance or may be directed toward improving interpersonal competence. The activities may be directed toward leadership issues, responsibilities and functions of group members, decision making, problem solving, goal setting and planning, etc.

Technostructural Activities: activities designed to improve the effectiveness of the technical or structural inputs and constraints affecting individuals or groups. The activities may take the form of (1) experimenting with new organization structures and evaluating their effectiveness in terms of specific goals, (2) devising new ways to bring technical resources to bear on problems.

Process Consultation Activities: activities on the part of the consultant "which help the client to perceive, understand, and act upon process events which occur in the client's environment."[6] These activities perhaps more accurately describe an approach, a consulting mode in which the client is given insight into the human processes in organizations and taught skills in diagnosing and managing them. Primary emphasis is on processes such as communications, leader and member roles in groups, problem solving and decision making, group norms and group growth, leadership and authority, and intergroup cooperation and competition. Emphasis is also placed upon learning how to diagnose and develop the necessary skills to be effective in dealing with these processes.

Grid Organization Development Activities: activities invented and franchised by Robert Blake and Jane Mouton, which comprise a six-phase change model involving the total organization.[7] Internal resources are developed to conduct most of the programs which may take from three to five years to complete. The model starts with upgrading individual managers' skills and leadership abilities, moves to team-improvement activities, then to intergroup relations activities. Later phases include corporate planning for improvement, developing implementation tactics, and concluding with an evaluation phase assessing change in the organization culture and looking toward future directions.

Third-Party Peacemaking Activities: activities conducted by a skilled consultant (the *third party*), which are designed to "help two members of an organization manage their interpersonal conflict."[8] They are based on confrontation tactics and an understanding of the processes involved in conflict and conflict resolution.

Coaching and Counseling Activities: activities that entail the consultant or other organization members working with individuals to help them (1) define learning goals; (2) learn how others see their behavior; (3) learn new modes of behavior to see if these help them to achieve their goals better. A central feature of this activity is the nonevaluative feedback given by others to an individual. A second feature is the joint exploration of alternative behaviors.

Life- and Career-Planning Activities: activities that enable individuals to focus on their life and career objectives and how they might go about achieving them. Structured activities lead to production of life and career inventories, discussions of goals and objectives, and assessment of capabilities, needed additional training, and areas of strength and deficiency.

Planning and Goal-Setting Activities: activities that include theory and experience in planning and goal setting, utilizing problem-solving models, planning paradigms, ideal organization vs. real organization "discrepancy" models, and the like. The goal of all of them is to improve these skills at the levels of the individual, group, and total organization.

Each of these families of interventions has many activities and exercises included in it. They all rely on inputs of both conceptual material and actual experience with the phenomenon being studied. Some of the families are directed toward specific targets, problems, or processes. For example, the team-building activities are specific to intact work teams, while the life-planning activities are directed to individuals, although this latter activity takes place in group settings. Some interventions are problem-specific: examples of this are the third-party peacemaking activities and the goal-setting activities. Some activities are process-specific—that is, specific to selected processes: an example of this is the intergroup activities in which the processes involved in managing interfaces are explored.

Additional interventions used in OD exist and are discussed in the following chapters. Examples of important interventions that in themselves do not constitute a family are the confrontation meeting, sensitivity training, force field analysis, the role analysis technique (RAT), and so forth.

SOME CLASSIFICATION SCHEMATA FOR OD INTERVENTIONS

There are many possible ways to classify OD interventions. Several have already been given: the families of interventions represent one approach, and

Bennis's types of interventions represent another approach. Our desire is to construct several classificatory schemata showing interventions from several perspectives. In this way, we can better accomplish our objective of examining OD from a kaleidoscopic rather than from a microscopic point of view.

One way to gain a perspective of OD interventions is to form a typology of interventions based on the following questions: (1) Is the intervention directed primarily toward individual learning, insight, and skill building or toward group learning? (2) Does the intervention focus on *task* or *process* issues? (Task is what is being done; process is how it is accomplished, including how people are relating to each other and what processes and dynamics are occurring.) A four-quadrant typology constructed by using these two questions is shown in Figure 1.

This classification scheme presents one approximation of the categories of various interventions; it is difficult to pinpoint the interventions precisely because a single intervention may have the attributes of more than one of the quadrants. Interventions simply are not mutually exclusive; there is great overlap of emphasis and the activity will frequently focus on, say, task at one time and process at a later time. Generally, however, the interventions may be viewed as belonging predominantly in the quadrant in which they are placed. It is thus possible to see that the interventions do differ from each other in terms of major emphasis.

Another way to view interventions is to see them as *designed to improve the effectiveness of a given organizational unit.* Given different organizational targets, what interventions are most commonly used to improve their effectiveness? This is shown in Figure 2. The elasticity of different interventions really becomes apparent in this figure, with many interventions being placed in several categories.

Examination of Figures 1 and 2 reveals redundancy and overlap in that specific interventions and activities appear in several classification categories. This may be confusing to the reader who is new to the area of organization development, but it nevertheless reflects the use to which various interventions are put. Perhaps a positive feature of the redundancy is that it suggests patterns among the interventions that the practitioner knows but that may not be readily apparent to the layman. Some of these patterns become more apparent in Figure 3.

Another conceptual scheme for categorizing the OD interventions rests on an attempt to determine the central, probable underlying causal mechanisms of the intervention, that is, the underlying dynamics of the intervention that probably are the cause of its efficacy. This scheme is more controversial: different authors might hypothesize different causal dynamics. This is due partly to the relative paucity of theory and research on interventions. But the practitioner chooses and categorizes interventions on the basis of assumed underlying dynamics of change and learning, and it might therefore be helpful to present a tentative classification scheme based on these mechanisms.

Fig. 1 *OD interventions classified by two independent dimensions: individual-group and task-process*

Task vs. Process Dimension	Individual vs. Group Dimensions: Focus on the individual	Individual vs. Group Dimensions: Focus on the group
Focus on task issues	Role analysis technique Education: technical skills; also decision making, problem solving, goal setting, and planning Career planning Grid OD phase 1 (see also below) Possibly job enrichment and Management by Objectives (MBO)	Technostructural changes Survey feedback (see also below) Confrontation meeting Team-building sessions Intergroup activities Grid OD phases 2, 3 (see also below)
Focus on process issues	Life planning Process consultation with coaching and counseling of individuals Education: group dynamics, planned change Stranger T-groups Third party peacemaking Grid OD phase 1	Survey feedback Team-building sessions Intergroup activities Process consultation Family T-group Grid OD phases 2, 3

Several hypothesized causal mechanisms inherent in OD interventions may lead to change and learning. These causal mechanisms are found to greater and lesser degrees in different interventions, and it is probable that the efficacy of the different interventions therefore rests on different causes. Some features of different interventions that may be causally related to learning and change are presented below. These are used to construct Figure 3.

Feedback: This refers to learning new data about oneself, others, group processes, or organizational dynamics—data that one did not previously take active account of. Feedback refers to activities and processes that "reflect" or "mirror" an objective picture of the real world. Awareness of this "new information" may lead to change if the feedback is not too threatening.

Awareness of Changing Sociocultural Norms: Often people modify their behavior, attitudes, values, etc., when they become aware of changes in the norms that are helping to determine their behavior. Thus, awareness of new norms has change potential because the individual will adjust his behavior to bring

Fig. 2 *Typology of OD interventions based on target groups*

Target group	Types of interventions
Interventions designed to improve the effectiveness of INDIVIDUALS	Life- and career-planning activities Role analysis technique Coaching and counseling T-group (sensitivity training) Education and training to increase skills, knowledge in the areas of technical task needs, relationship skills, process skills, decision making, problem solving, planning, goal setting skills Grid OD phase 1
Interventions designed to improve the effectiveness of DYADS/TRIADS	Process consultation Third-party peacemaking Grid OD phases 1, 2
Interventions designed to improve the effectiveness of TEAMS & GROUPS	Team building—Task directed —Process directed Family T-group Survey feedback Process consultation Role analysis technique "Start-up" team-building activities Education in decision making, problem solving, planning, goal setting in group settings
Interventions designed to improve the effectiveness of INTERGROUP RELATIONS	Intergroup activities—Process directed —Task directed Organizational mirroring (three or more groups) Technostructural interventions Process consultation Third-party peacemaking at group level Grid OD phase 3 Survey feedback
Interventions designed to improve the effectiveness of the TOTAL ORGANIZATION	Technostructural activities Confrontation meetings Strategic planning activities Grid OD phases 4, 5, 6 Survey feedback

it in line with the new norms. The awareness that "this is a new ball game" or that "we're now playing with a new set of rules" is here hypothesized to be a cause of changes in individual behavior.

Fig. 3 *Intervention typology based on principal emphasis of intervention in relation to different hypothesized change mechanisms*

Hypothesized change mechanism	Interventions based primarily on the change mechanism
Feedback	Survey feedback T-group Process consultation Organization mirroring Grid OD instruments
Awareness of changing sociocultural norms	Team building T-group Intergroup interface sessions First three phases of Grid OD
Increased interaction and communication	Survey feedback Intergroup interface sessions Third-party peacemaking Organizational mirroring Management by objectives Team building Technostructural changes
Confrontation and working for resolution of differences	Third-party peacemaking Intergroup interface sessions Coaching and counseling individuals Confrontation meetings Organizational mirroring
Education through: 1. New knowledge 2. Skill practice	Career and life planning Team building Goal setting, decision making, problem solving, planning activities T-group Process consultation

Increased Interaction and Communication: Increasing interaction and communication between individuals and groups may in and of itself effect changes in attitudes and behavior. Homans, for example, suggests that increased interaction leads to increased positive sentiments.[9] Individuals and groups in isolation tend to develop "tunnel vision" or "autism," according to Murphy.[10] Increasing communication probably counteracts this tendency. Increased communications allows one to check his perceptions to see if they are socially validated and shared.

Confrontation: This term refers to surfacing and addressing differences in beliefs, feelings, attitudes, values, or norms to remove obstacles to effective interaction. Confrontation is a process that actively seeks to discern real differences that are "getting in the way," surface those issues, and work on the issues in a constructive way. Many obstacles to growth and learning exist; they continue to exist when they are not actively looked at and examined.

Education: This refers to activities designed to upgrade (1) knowledge and concepts, (2) outmoded beliefs and attitudes, (3) skills. In organization development the education may be directed toward increasing these three components in several content areas: task achievement, human and social relationships and behavior, organizational dynamics and processes, and processes of managing and directing change. Education has long been an accepted change technique.

Some interventions emphasize one mechanism of change over others. A tentative typology based on these principal underlying change mechanisms is presented in Figure 3.

This classification scheme, while differentiating between interventions, also shows the many multiple emphases that are found in many of the activities. We are only beginning to understand the underlying mechanisms of change in interventions. As that knowledge increases, greater precision in the selection of intervention activities will be possible. The issue seems to be statable as follows: OD does in fact work; why it works is less well known and understood.

We find that another convenient classificatory scheme can be formed by categorizing OD interventions into those directed toward team improvement (Chapter 10), toward improving intergroup relations (Chapter 11), and toward the level of the total organization (Chapter 12) and those interventions that focus directly on personal, interpersonal, and group processes (Chapter 13). This scheme is similar to the typology based on target groups presented in Figure 2, but separates out the "process" interventions for special attention.

As a final note, in addition to knowledge about various interventions and knowledge about the appropriateness and timeliness of interventions, the OD practitioner is cognizant of the many dimensions inherent in each particular activity. Since an intervention contains the possibility for going in many directions, the practitioner attends to the range of alternatives in his own inputs.

For example, in a team-building meeting, the practitioner will have various dimensions in his head that guide his inputs and contributions. These dimensions can be explained through looking at the questions the practitioner may be asking himself:

> We are dealing with individual behavior right now; how can this learning be translated to learning for the group?

> We are dealing with group phenomena right now: how can this learning be translated to learning for the individuals?

We are focusing on task competencies and requirements; how do these relate to process issues and understanding of the group's dynamics?

We have just learned about a phenomenon by experiencing it; what theoretical or conceptual material would augment this learning?

We are dealing with issues and forces impinging on this group from outside the group; what activities must be designed to facilitate more appropriate handling of these interface issues?

We are dealing with an old problem in a new way; does that signal a change in the sociocultural norms of this group, and are the members aware of it?

We are diagnosing areas of interpersonal and intergroup conflict; what interventions are appropriate to deal with these issues?

SUMMARY

In this chapter we have taken an overview of OD interventions—the sets of structured activities in which selected organizational units (target groups or individuals) engage with a task or a sequence of tasks where task goals are related directly or indirectly to organizational improvement. Different definitions of OD interventions were discussed. The nature of interventions and several classifications of them were presented to gain a picture of interventions from several different perspectives. In the next several chapters OD interventions are described in greater detail in an inventory of most of the extant techniques and methods used in organization development.

Notes

1. W. W. Burke and H. A. Hornstein, "Introduction" to "The Social Technology of Organization Development," prepublication copy, 1971, p. 1.

2. Richard Beckhard, "The Confrontation Meeting," *Harvard Business Review,* (March–April 1967), 149–53.

3. R. W. White, "Motivation Reconsidered: The Concept of Competence." *Psychological Review,* 66 (1959), 297–334.

4. D. C. McClelland, J. W. Atkinson, R. A. Clark, and E. L. Lowell, *The Achievement Motive* (New York: Appleton-Century-Crofts, 1953).

5. Warren Bennis, *Organization Development: Its Nature, Origins, and Prospects* (Reading, Mass.: Addison-Wesley Publishing Company, 1969), pp. 37–39. We have paraphrased and interpreted his list extensively.

6. E. H. Schein, *Process Consultation* (Reading, Mass.: Addison-Wesley Publishing Company, 1969), p. 9.

7. R. R. Blake and J. S. Mouton, *Building a Dynamic Corporation through Organization Development* (Reading, Mass.: Addison-Wesley Publishing Company, 1969). This book is a treatise showing how grid organization development programs operate.

8. R. W. Walton, *Interpersonal Peacemaking: Confrontation and Third-Party Consultation* (Reading, Mass.: Addison-Wesley Publishing Company, 1969), p. 1. This entire book is devoted to an explication of this specialized intervention technique.

9. George C. Homans, *The Human Group* (New York: Harcourt, Brace & Co., 1950).

10. G. Murphy, "The Freeing of Intelligence," *Psychological Bulletin,* 42 (1945) 1–19.

Choosing the Depth of Organizational Intervention
Roger Harrison

There is a need for conceptual models which differentiate intervention strategies from one another in a way which permits rational matching of strategies to differing organizational change problems. A central concept in such a model could be the depth of individual emotional involvement in the change process. By depth we mean how deep, value-laden, emotionally charged, and central to the individual's sense of self are the issues and processes about which a consultant attempts directly to obtain information and which he seeks to influence. In order of increasing depth are the change strategies: operations analysis, management by objectives, the Managerial Grid, the T Group, and task group therapy.

As depth of intervention increases, so also do a number of concomitants of depth: dependence on the special competence of the change agent, centrality of the individual as the target of the change attempt, costs of intervention, and the risk of unintended consequences for individuals. These concomitants suggest a criterion for the depth of intervention: to intervene at a level no deeper than that required to produce enduring solutions to the problems at hand. *However, a countervailing trend tends to push the level of intervention deeper as organizational systems shift from greater external control to more autonomy and internal control for members. As the individual becomes more important, the level at which the processes which effectively determine his behavior operate becomes deeper, and the individual has increasing influence over the success or failure of the intervention. A case is presented for a radical shift of consultant orientation in the direction of accepting a client's felt needs and presented problems as being real and of working on them at a level where the client can serve as a competent and willing collaborator. This leads to the second criterion:* to intervene at a level no deeper than that at which the energy and resources of the client can be committed to problem solving and to change.

Since World War II there has been a great proliferation of behavioral science-based methods by which consultants seek to facilitate growth and change in individuals, groups, and organizations. The methods range from operations analysis and manipulation of the organization chart, through the use of Grid Laboratories, T Groups, and nonverbal techniques. As was true in the development of clinical psychology and psychotherapy, the early stages of this developmental process tend to be accompanied by considerable competition, criticism, and argument about the relative merits of various approaches. It is my conviction that controversy over the relative goodness or badness, effectiveness or ineffectiveness, of various change strategies really accomplishes very little in the way of increased knowledge or unification of behavioral science. As long as we are arguing about what method is better than another, we tend to learn very little about how various approaches fit together or complement one another, and we certainly make more difficult and ambiguous the task of bringing these competing points of view within one overarching system of knowledge about human processes.

As our knowledge increases, it begins to be apparent that these competing change strategies are not really different ways of doing the same thing—some more effective and some less effective—but rather that they are different ways of doing *different* things. They touch the individual, the group, or the organization in different aspects of their functioning. They require differing kinds and amounts of commitment on the part of the client for them to be successful, and they demand different varieties and levels of skills and abilities on the part of the practitioner.

I believe that there is a real need for conceptual models which differentiate intervention strategies from one another in a way which permits rational matching of strategies to organizational change problems. The purpose of this paper is to present a modest beginning which I have made toward a conceptualization of strategies, and to derive from this conceptualization some criteria for choosing appropriate methods of intervention in particular applications.

The point of view of this paper is that the depth of individual emotional involvement in the change process can be a central concept for differentiating change strategies. In focusing on this dimension, we are concerned with the extent to which core areas of the personality or self are the focus of the change attempt. Strategies which touch the more deep, personal, private, and central aspects of the individual or his relationships with others fall toward the deeper end of this continuum. Strategies which deal with more external aspects of the individual and which focus upon the more formal and public aspects of role behavior tend to fall toward the surface end of the depth dimension. This dimension has the advantage that it is relatively easy to rank change strategies upon it and to get fairly close consensus as to the ranking. It is a widely discussed dimension of difference which has meaning and relevance to practitioners and their clients. I hope in this paper to promote greater flexibility and rationality in choosing appropriate depths of intervention. I shall approach this task by examining the effects of interventions at various depths. I shall also explore the ways in which two important organizational processes tend to make demands and to set limits upon the depth of intervention which can produce effective change in organizational functioning. These two processes are the autonomy of organization members and their own perception of their needs for help.

Before illustrating the concept of ranking five common intervention strategies along the dimension of depth, I should like to define the dimension somewhat more precisely. We are concerned essentially with how private, individual, and hidden are the issues and processes about which the consultant attempts directly to obtain information and which he seeks to influence. If the consultant seeks information about relatively public and observable aspects of behavior and relationship and if he tries to influence directly only these relatively surface characteristics and processes, we would then categorize his intervention strategy as being closer to the surface. If, on the other hand, the consultant seeks information about very deep and private perceptions, attitudes, or feelings and if he intervenes in a way which directly affects these processes, then we would classify his intervention strategy as one of considerable depth. To illustrate the surface end of the dimension let us look first at operations research or operations analysis. This strategy is concerned with the roles and functions to be performed within the organization, generally with little regard to the individual characteristics of persons occupying the roles. The change strategy is to manipulate role relationships; in other words, to redistribute the tasks, the resources, and the relative power attached to various roles in the organization. This is essentially a process of rational analysis in which the tasks which need to be performed are determined and specified and then sliced up into role definitions for persons and groups in the organization. The operations analyst does not ordinarily need to know much about particular people. Indeed, his function is to design the organization in such a way that its successful operation does not depend too heavily upon any uniquely individual skills, abilities, values, or attitudes of persons in various roles. He may perform his function adequately without knowing in advance who the people are who will fill these slots. Persons are assumed to be moderately interchangeable, and in order to make this approach work it is necessary to design the organization so that the capacities, needs, and values of the individual which are relevant to role performance are relatively public and observable, and are possessed by a fairly large proportion of the population from which organization members are drawn. The approach is certainly one of very modest depth.

Somewhat deeper are those strategies which are based upon evaluating individual performance and attempting to manipulate it directly. Included in this approach is much of the industrial psychologist's work in selection, placement, appraisal, and counseling of employees. The intervener is concerned with what the individual is able and likely to do and achieve rather than with processes internal to the individual. Direct attempts to influence performance may be made through the application of rewards and punishments such as promotions, salary increases, or transfers within the organization. An excellent illustration of this focus on end results is the practice of management by objectives. The intervention process is focused on establishing mutually agreed-upon goals for performance between the individual and his supervisor. The practice is considered to be particularly advantageous because it permits the supervisor to avoid a focus on personal characteristics of the subordinate, particularly those deeper, more central characteristics which managers generally have difficulty in discussing with those who work under their supervision. The process is designed to limit information exchange to that which is public and observable, such as the setting of performance goals and the success or failure of the individual in attaining them.

Because of its focus on end results, rather than on the process by which those results are achieved, management by objectives must be considered less deep than the broad area of concern with work style which I shall term instrumental process analysis. We are concerned here not only with performance but with the processes by which that performance is achieved. However, we are primarily concerned with styles and processes of work rather than with the processes of interpersonal relationships which I would classify as being deeper on the basic dimension.

In instrumental process analysis we are concerned with how a person likes to organize and conduct his work and with the impact which this style of work has on others in the organization. Principally, we are concerned with how a person perceives his role, what he values and disvalues in it, and with what he works hard on and what he chooses to ignore. We are also interested in the instrumental acts which the individual directs toward others: delegating authority or reserving decisions to himself, communicating or withholding information, collaborating or competing with others on work-related issues. The focus on instrumentality means that we are interested in the person primarily as a doer of work or a performer of functions related to the goals of the organization. We are interested in what facilitates or inhibits his effective task performance.

We are not interested per se in whether his relationships with others are happy or unhappy, whether they perceive him as too warm or too cold, too authoritarian or too laissez faire, or any other of the many interpersonal relationships which arise as people associate in organizations. However, I do not mean to imply that the line between instrumental relationships and interpersonal ones is an easy one to draw in action and practice, or even that it is desirable that this be done.

DEPTH GAUGES: LEVEL OF TASKS AND FEELINGS

What I am saying is that an intervention strategy can focus on instrumentality or it can focus on interpersonal relationships, and that there are important consequences of this difference in depth of intervention.

When we intervene at the level of instrumentality, it is to change work behavior and working relationships. Frequently this involves the process of bargaining or negotiation between groups and individuals. Diagnoses are made of the satisfactions or dissatisfactions of organization members with one another's work behavior. Reciprocal adjustments, bargains, and trade-offs can then be arranged in which each party gets some modification in the behavior of the other at the cost to him of some reciprocal accommodation. Much of the intervention strategy which has been developed around Blake's concept of the Managerial Grid is at this level and involves bargaining and negotiation of role behavior as an important change process.

At the deeper level of interpersonal relationships the focus is on feelings, attitudes, and perceptions which organization members have about others. At this level we are concerned with the quality of human relationships within the organization, with warmth and coldness of members to one another, and with the experiences of acceptance and rejection, love and hate, trust and suspicion among groups and individuals. At this level the consultant probes for normally hidden feelings, attitudes, and perceptions. He works to create relationships of openness about feelings and to help members to develop mutual understanding of one another as persons. Interventions are directed toward helping organization members to be more comfortable in being authentically themselves with one another, and the degree of mutual caring and concern is expected to increase. Sensitivity training using T Groups is a basic intervention strategy at this level. T-Group educators emphasize increased personalization of relationships, the development of trust and openness, and the exchange of feelings. Interventions at this level deal directly and intensively with interpersonal emotionality. This is the first intervention strategy we have examined which is at a depth where the feelings of organization members about one another as persons are a direct focus of the intervention strategy. At the other levels, such feelings certainly exist and may be expressed, but they are not a direct concern of the intervention. The transition from the task orientation of instrumental process analysis to the feeling orientation of interpersonal process analysis seems, as I shall suggest later, to be a critical one for many organization members.

The deepest level of intervention which will be considered in this paper is that of intrapersonal analysis. Here the consultant uses a variety of methods to reveal the individual's deeper attitudes, values, and conflicts regarding his own functioning, identity, and existence. The focus is generally on increasing the range of experiences which the individual can bring into awareness and cope with. The material may be dealt with at the fantasy or symbolic level, and the intervention strategies include many which are noninterpersonal and nonverbal. Some examples of this approach are the use of marathon T-Group sessions, the creative risk-taking laboratory approach of Byrd (1967), and some aspects of the task group therapy approach of Clark (1966). These approaches all tend to bring into focus very deep and intense feelings about one's own identity and one's relationships with significant others.

Although I have characterized deeper interventions as dealing increasingly with the individual's affective life, I do not imply that issues at less deep levels may not be emotionally charged. Issues of role differentiation, reward distribution, ability and performance evaluation, for example, are frequently invested with strong feelings. The concept of depth is concerned more with the *accessibility* and *individuality* of attitudes, values, and perceptions than it is with their strength. This narrowing of the common usage of the term, *depth,* is necessary to avoid the contradictions which occur when strength and inaccessibility are confused. For instance, passionate value confrontation and bitter conflict have frequently occurred between labor and management over economic issues which are surely toward the surface end of my concept of depth.

In order to understand the importance of the concept of depth for choosing interventions in organizations, let us consider the effects upon organization members of working at different levels.

The first of the important concomitants of depth is the degree of dependence of the client on the special competence of the change agent. At the surface end of the depth dimension, the methods of intervention are easily communicated and made public. The client may reasonably expect to learn something of the change agent's skills to improve his own practice. At the deeper levels, such as interpersonal and intrapersonal process analyses, it is more difficult for the client to understand the methods of intervention. The change agent is more likely to be seen as a person of special and unusual powers not found in ordinary men. Skills of intervention and change are less frequently learned by organization members, and the change process may tend to become personalized around the change agent as leader. Programs of change which are so dependent upon personal relationships and individual expertise are difficult to institutionalize. When the change agent leaves the system, he may not only take his expertise with him but the entire change process as well.

A second aspect of the change process which varies with depth is the extent to which the benefits of an intervention are transferable to members of the organization not originally participating in the change process. At surface levels of operations analysis and performance evaluation, the effects are institutionalized in the form of procedures, policies, and practices of the organization which may have considerable permanence beyond the tenure of individuals. At the level of instrumental behavior, the continuing effects of intervention are more likely to reside in the informal norms of groups within the organization regarding such matters as delegation, communication, decision making, competition and collaboration, and conflict resolution.

At the deepest levels of intervention, the target of change is the individual's inner life; and if the intervention is successful, the permanence of individual change should be greatest. There are indeed dramatic reports of cases in which persons have changed their careers and life goals as a result of such interventions, and the persistence of such change appears to be relatively high.

One consequence, then, of the level of intervention is that with greater depth of focus the individual increasingly becomes both the target and the carrier of change. In the light of this analysis, it is not surprising to observe that deeper levels of intervention are increasingly being used at higher organizational levels and in scientific and service organizations where the contribution of the individual has greatest impact.

An important concomitant of depth is that as the level of intervention becomes deeper, the information needed to intervene effectively becomes less available. At the less personal level of operations analysis, the information is often a matter of record. At the level of performance evaluation, it is a matter of observation. On the other hand, reactions of others to a person's work style are less likely to be discussed freely, and the more personal responses to his interpersonal style are even less likely to be readily given. At the deepest levels, important information may not be available to the individual himself. Thus, as we go deeper the consultant must use more of his time and skill uncovering information which is ordinarily private and hidden. This is one reason for the greater costs of interventions at deeper levels of focus.

Another aspect of the change process which varies with the depth of intervention is the personal risk and unpredictability of outcome for the individual. At deeper levels we deal with aspects of the individual's view of himself and his relationships with others which are relatively untested by exposure to the evaluations and emotional reactions of others. If in the change process the individual's self-perceptions are strongly disconfirmed, the resulting imbalance in internal forces may produce sudden changes in behavior, attitudes, and personality integration.

Because of the private and hidden nature of the processes into which we intervene at deeper levels, it is difficult to predict the individual impact of the change process in advance. The need for clinical sensitivity and skill on the part of the practitioner thus increases, since he must be prepared to diagnose and deal with developing situations involving considerable stress upon individuals.

The foregoing analysis suggests a criterion by which to match intervention strategies to particular organizational problems. It is *to intervene at a level no deeper than that required to produce enduring solutions to the problems at hand.* This criterion derives directly from the observations above. The cost, skill demands, client dependency, and variability of outcome all increase with depth of intervention. Further, as the depth of intervention increases, the effects tend to locate more in the individual and less in the organization. The danger of losing the organization's investment in the change with the departure of the individual becomes a significant consideration.

AUTONOMY INCREASES DEPTH OF INTERVENTION

While this general criterion is simple and straightforward, its application is not. In particular, although the criterion should operate in the direction of less depth of intervention, there is a general trend in modern organizational life which tends to push the intervention level ever deeper. This trend is toward increased self-direction of organization members and increased independence of external pressures and incentives. I believe that there is a direct relationship between the autonomy of individuals and the depth of intervention needed to effect organizational change.

Before going on to discuss this relationship, I shall acknowledge freely that I cannot prove the existence of a trend toward a general increase in freedom of individuals within organizations. I intend only to assert the great importance of the degree of individual autonomy in determining the level of intervention which will be effective.

In order to understand the relationship between autonomy and depth of intervention, it is necessary to conceptualize a dimension which parallels and is implied by the depth dimension we have been discussing. This is the dimension of predictability and variability among persons in their responses to the different kinds of incentives which may be used to influence behavior in the organization. The key assumption in this analysis is that the more unpredictable and unique is the individual's response to the particular kinds of controls and incentives one can bring to bear upon him, the more one must know about that person in order to influence his behavior.

Most predictable and least individual is the response of the person to economic and bureaucratic controls when his needs for economic income and security are high. It is not necessary to delve very deeply into a person's inner processes in order to influence his behavior if we know that he badly needs his income and his position and if we are in a position to control his access to these rewards. Responses to economic and bureaucratic controls tend to be relatively simple and on the surface.

Independence of Economic Incentive

If for any reason organization members become relatively uninfluenceable through the manipulation of their income and economic security, the management of performance becomes strikingly more complex; and the need for more personal information about the individual increases. Except very generally, we do not know automatically or in advance what styles of instrumental or interpersonal interaction will be responded to as negative or positive incentives by the individual. One person may appreciate close supervision and direction; another may value independence of direction. One may prefer to work alone; another may function best when he is in close communication with others. One may thrive in close, intimate, personal interaction; while others are made uncomfortable by any but cool and distant relationships with colleagues.

What I am saying is that when bureaucratic and economic incentives lose their force for whatever reason, the improvement of performance *must* involve linking organizational goals to the individual's attempts to meet his own needs for satisfying instrumental activities and interpersonal relationships. It is for this reason that I make the assertion that increases in personal autonomy dictate change interventions at deeper and more personal levels. In order to obtain the information necessary to link organizational needs to individual goals, one must probe fairly deeply into the attitudes, values, and emotions of the organization members.

If the need for deeper personal information becomes great when we intervene at the instrumental and interpersonal levels, it becomes even greater when one is dealing with organization members who are motivated less through their transactions with the environment and more in response to internal values and standards. An example is the researcher, engineer, or technical specialist whose work behavior may be influenced more by his own values and standards of creativity or professional excellence than by his relationships with others. The deepest organizational interventions at the intrapersonal level may be required in order to effect change when working with persons who are highly self-directed.

Let me summarize my position about the relationship among autonomy, influence, and level of intervention. As the individual becomes less subject to economic and bureaucratic pressures, he tends to seek more intangible rewards in the organization which come from both the instrumental and interpersonal aspects of the system. I view this as a shift from greater external to more internal control and as an increase in autonomy. Further shifts in this direction may involve increased independence of rewards and punishments mediated by others, in favor of operation in accordance with internal values and standards.

I view organizations as systems of reciprocal influence. Achievement of organization goals is facilitated when individuals can seek their own satisfactions through activity which promotes the goals of the organization. As the satisfactions which are of most value to the individual change, so must the reciprocal influence systems, if the organization goals are to continue to be met.

If the individual changes are in the direction of increased independence of external incentives, then the influence systems must change to provide opportunities for individuals to achieve more intangible, self-determined satisfactions in their work. However, people are more differentiated, complex, and unique in their intangible goals and values than in their economic needs. In order to create systems which offer a wide variety of intangible satisfactions, much more private information about individuals is needed than is required to create and maintain systems based chiefly on economic and bureaucratic controls. For this reason, deeper interventions are called for when the system which they would attempt to change contains a high proportion of relatively autonomous individuals.

There are a number of factors promoting autonomy, all tending to free the individual from dependence upon economic and bureaucratic controls, which I have observed in my work with organizations. Wherever a number of these factors obtain, it is probably an indication that deeper levels of intervention are required to effect lasting improvements in organizational functioning. I shall simply list these indicators briefly in categories to show what kinds of things might signify to the practitioner that deeper levels of intervention may be appropriate.

The first category includes anything which makes the evaluation of individual performance difficult:

A long time span between the individual's actions and the results by which effectiveness of performance is to be judged.

Nonrepetitive, unique tasks which cannot be evaluated by reference to the performance of others on similar tasks.

Specialized skills and abilities possessed by an individual which cannot be evaluated by a supervisor who does not possess the skills or knowledge himself.

The second category concerns economic conditions:

Arrangements which secure the job tenure and/or income of the individual.

A market permitting easy transfer from one organization to another (e.g., engineers in the United States aerospace industry).

Unique skills and knowledge of the individual which make him difficult to replace.

The third category includes characteristics of the system or its environment which lead to independence of the parts of the organization and decentralization of authority such as:

An organization which works on a project basis instead of producing a standard line of products.

An organization in which subparts must be given latitude to deal rapidly and flexibly with frequent environmental change.

I should like to conclude the discussion of this criterion for depth of intervention with a brief reference to the ethics of intervention, a problem which merits considerably more thorough treatment than I can give it here.

The Ethics of Delving Deeper

There is considerable concern in the United States about invasion of privacy by behavioral scientists. I would agree that such invasion of privacy is an actual as well as fantasied concomitant of the use of organizational change strategies of greater depth. The recourse by organizations to such strategies has been widely viewed as an indication of greater organizational control over the most personal and private aspects of the lives of the members. The present analysis suggests, however, that recourse to these deeper interventions actually reflects the greater *freedom* of organization members from traditionally crude and impersonal means of organizational control. There is no reason to be concerned about man's attitudes or values or interpersonal relationships when his job performance can be controlled by brute force, by economic coercion, or by bureaucratic rules and regulations. The "invasion of privacy" becomes worth the cost, bother, and uncertainty of outcome only when the individual has achieved relative independence from control by other means. Put another way, it makes organizational sense to try to get a man to *want* to do something only if you cannot *make* him do it. And regardless of what intervention strategy is used, the individual still retains considerably greater control over his own behavior than he had when he could be manipulated more crudely. As long as we can maintain a high degree of voluntarism regarding the nature and extent of an individual's participation in the deeper organizational change strategies, these strategies can work toward adapting the organization to the individual quite as much as they work the other way around. Only when an individual's participation in one of the deeper change strategies is coerced by economic or bureaucratic pressures, do I feel that the ethics of the intervention clearly run counter to the values of a democratic society.

ROLE OF CLIENT NORMS AND VALUES IN DETERMINING DEPTH

So far our attention to the choice of level of intervention has focused upon locating the depth at which the information exists which must be exchanged to facilitate system improvement. Unfortunately, the choice of an intervention strategy cannot practically be made with reference to this criterion alone. Even if a correct diagnosis is made of the level at which the relevant information lies, we may not be able to work effectively at the desired depth because of client norms, values, resistances, and fears.

In an attempt to develop a second criterion for depth of intervention which takes such dispositions on the part of the client into account, I have considered two approaches which represent polarized orientations to the problem. One approach is based upon analyzing and overcoming client resistance; the other is based upon discovering and joining forces with the self-articulated wants or "felt needs" of the client.

There are several ways of characterizing these approaches. To me, the simplest is to point out that when the change agent is resistance-oriented he tends to lead or influence the client to work at a depth greater than that at which the latter feels comfortable. When resistance-oriented, the change agent tends to mistrust the client's statement of his problems and of the areas where he wants help. He suspects the client's presentation of being a smoke screen or defense against admission of his "real" problems and needs. The consultant works to expose the underlying processes and concerns and to influence the client to work at a deeper level. The resistance-oriented approach grows out of the work of clinicians and psychotherapists, and it characterizes much of the work of organizational consultants who specialize in sensitivity training and deeper intervention strategies.

On the other hand, change agents may be oriented to the self-articulated needs of clients. When so oriented, the consultant tends more to follow and facilitate the client in working at whatever level the latter sets for himself. He may assist the client in defining problems and needs and in working on solutions, but he is inclined to try to anchor his work in the norms, values, and accepted standards of behavior of the organization.

I believe that there is a tendency for change agents working at the interpersonal and deeper levels to adopt a rather consistent resistance-oriented approach. Consultants so oriented seem to take a certain quixotic pride in dramatically and self-consciously violating organizational norms. Various techniques have been developed for pressuring or seducing organization members into departing from organizational norms in the service of change. The "marathon" T Group is a case in point, where the increased irritability and fatigue of prolonged contact and lack of sleep move participants to deal with one another more emotionally, personally, and spontaneously than they would normally be willing to do.

I suspect that unless such norm-violating intervention efforts actually succeed in changing organizational norms, their effects are relatively short-lived, because the social structures and interpersonal linkages have not been created which can utilize for day-to-day problem solving the deeper information produced by the intervention. It is true that the consultant may succeed in producing information, but he is less likely to succeed in creating social structures which can continue to work in his absence. The problem is directly analogous to that of the community developer who succeeds by virtue of his personal influence in getting villagers to build a school or a community center which falls into disuse as soon as he leaves because of the lack of any integration of these achievements into the social structure and day-to-day needs and desires of the community. Community developers have had to learn through bitter failure and frustration that ignoring or subverting the standards and norms of a social system often results in temporary success followed by a reactionary increase in resistance to the influence of the change agent. On the other hand, felt needs embody those problems, issues, and difficulties which have a high conscious priority on the part of community or organization members. We can expect individuals and groups to be ready to invest time, energy, and resources in dealing with their felt needs, while they will be relatively passive or even resistant toward those who attempt to help them with externally defined needs. Community developers have found that attempts to help with felt needs are met with greater receptivity, support, and integration within the structure and life of the community than are intervention attempts which rely primarily upon the developer's value system for setting need priorities.

The emphasis of many organizational change agents on confronting and working through resistances was developed originally in the practice of individual psychoanalysis and psychotherapy, and it is also a central concept in the conduct of therapy groups and sensitivity training laboratories. In all of these situations, the change agent has a high degree of environmental control and is at least temporarily in a high status position with respect to the client. To a degree that is frequently underestimated by practitioners, we manage to create a situation in which it is more unpleasant for the client to leave than it is to stay and submit to the pressure to confront and work through resistances. I believe that the tendency is for behavioral scientists to overplay their hands when they move from the clinical and training situations where they have environmental control to the organizational consulting situation, where their control is sharply attenuated.

This attenuation derives only partially from the relative ease with which the client can terminate the relationship. Even if this most drastic step is not taken, the consultant can be tolerated, misled, and deceived in ways which are relatively difficult in the therapeutic or human relations training situations. He can also be openly defied and blocked if he runs afoul of strongly shared group norms; whereas when the consultant is dealing with a group of strangers, he can often utilize differences among the members to overcome this kind of resistance. I suspect that, in general, behavioral scientists underestimate their power in working with individuals and groups of strangers, and overestimate it when working with individuals and groups in organizations. I emphasize this point because I believe that a good many potentially fruitful and mutually satisfying consulting relationships are terminated early because of the consultant's taking the role of overcomer of resistance to change rather than that of collaborator in the client's attempts at solving his problems. It is these considerations which lead me to suggest my second criterion for the choice of organization intervention strategy: *to intervene at a level no deeper than that at which the energy and resources of the client can be committed to problem solving and to change.* These energies and resources can be mobilized through obtaining legitimation for the intervention in the norms of the organization and through devising intervention strategies which have clear relevance to consciously felt needs on the part of the organization members.

THE CONSULTANT'S DILEMMA:
FELT NEEDS VS. DEEPER LEVELS

Unfortunately, it is doubtless true that the forces which influence the conditions we desire to change often exist at deeper levels than can be dealt with by adhering to the criterion of working within organization norms and meeting felt needs. The level at which an individual or group is willing and ready to invest energy and resources is probably always determined partly by a realistic assessment of the problems and partly by a defensive need to avoid confrontation and significant change. It is thus not likely that our two criteria for selection of intervention depth will result in the same decisions when practically applied. It is not the same to intervene at the level where behavior-determining forces are most potent as it is to work on felt needs as they are articulated by the client. This, it seems to me, is the consultant's dilemma. It always has been. We are continually faced with the choice between leading the client into areas which are threatening, unfamiliar, and dependency-provoking for him (and where our own expertise shows up to best advantage) or, on the other hand, being guided by the client's own understanding of his problems and his willingness to invest resources in particular kinds of relatively familiar and nonthreatening strategies.

When time permits, this dilemma is ideally dealt with by intervening first at a level where there is good support from the norms, power structure, and felt needs of organizational members. The consultant can then, over a period of time, develop trust, sophistication, and support within the organization to explore deeper levels at which particularly important forces may be operating. This would probably be agreed to, at least in principle, by most organizational consultants. The point at which I feel I differ from a significant number of workers in this field is that I would advocate that interventions should *always* be limited to the depth of the client's felt needs and readiness to legitimize intervention. I believe we should always avoid moving deeper at a pace which outstrips a client system's willingness to subject itself to exposure, dependency, and threat. What I am saying is that if the dominant response of organization members indicates that an intervention violates system norms regarding exposure, privacy, and confrontation, then one has intervened too deeply and should pull back to a level at which organization members are more ready to invest their own energy in the change process. This point of view is thus in opposition to that which sees negative reactions primarily as indications of resistances which are to be brought out into the open, confronted, and worked through as a central part of the intervention process. I believe that behavioral scientists acting as organizational consultants have tended to place overmuch emphasis on the overcoming of resistance to change and have underemphasized the importance of enlisting in the service of change the energies and resources which the client can consciously direct and willingly devote to problem solving.

What is advocated here is that we in general accept the client's felt needs or the problems he presents as real and that we work on them at a level at which he can serve as a competent and willing collaborator. This position is in opposition to one which sees the presenting problem as more or less a smoke screen or barrier. I am not advocating this point of view because I value the right to privacy of organization members more highly than I value their growth and development or the solution of organizational problems. (This is an issue which concerns me, but it is enormously more complex than the ones with which I am dealing in this paper.) Rather, I place first priority on collaboration with the client, because I do not think we are frequently successful consultants without it.

In my own practice I have observed that the change in client response is frequently quite striking when I move from a resistance-oriented approach to an acceptance of the client's norms and definitions of his own needs. With quite a few organizational clients in the United States, the line of legitimacy seems to lie somewhere between interventions at the instrumental level and those focused on interpersonal relationships. Members who exhibit hostility, passivity, and dependence when I initiate intervention at the interpersonal level may become dramatically more active, collaborative, and involved when I shift the focus to the instrumental level.

If I intervene directly at the level of interpersonal relationships, I can be sure that at least some members, and often the whole group, will react with anxiety, passive resistance, and low or negative commitment to the change process. Furthermore, they express their resistance in terms of norms and values regarding the appropriateness or legitimacy of dealing at this level. They say things like, "It isn't right to force people's feelings about one another out into the open;" "I don't see what this has to do with improving organizational effectiveness;" "People are being encouraged to say things which are better left unsaid."

If I then switch to a strategy which focuses on decision making, delegation of authority, information exchange, and other instrumental questions, these complaints about illegitimacy and the inappropriateness of the intervention are usually sharply reduced. This does not mean that the clients are necessarily comfortable or free from anxiety in the discussions, nor does it mean that strong feelings may not be expressed about one another's behavior. What is different is that the clients are more likely to *work with* instead of *against* me, to feel and express some sense of ownership in the change process, and to see many more possibilities for carrying it on among themselves in the absence of the consultant.

What I have found is that when I am resistance-oriented in my approach to the client, I am apt to feel rather uncomfortable in "letting sleeping dogs lie." When, on the other hand, I orient myself to the client's own assessment of his needs, I am uncomfortable when I feel I am leading or pushing the client to operate very far outside the shared norms of the organization. I have tried to indicate why I believe the latter orientation is more appropriate. I realize of course that many highly sophisticated and talented practitioners will not agree with me.

In summary, I have tried to show in this paper that the dimension of depth should be central to the conceptualization of intervention strategies. I have presented what I believe are the major consequences of intervening at greater or lesser depths, and from these consequences I have suggested two criteria for choosing the appropriate depth of intervention: first, *to intervene at a level no deeper than that required to produce enduring solutions to the problems at hand;* and second, *to intervene at a level no deeper than that at which the energy and resources of the client can be committed to problem solving and to change.*

I have analyzed the tendency for increases in individual autonomy in organizations to push the appropriate level of intervention deeper when the first criterion is followed. Opposed to this is the countervailing influence of the second criterion to work closer to the surface in order to enlist the energy and support of organization members in the change process. Arguments have been presented for resolving this dilemma in favor of the second, more conservative, criterion. The dilemma remains, of course; the continuing tension under which the change agent works is between the desire to lead and push, or to collaborate and follow. The middle ground is never very stable, and I suspect we show our values and preferences by which criterion we choose to maximize when we are under the stress of difficult and ambiguous client-consultant relationships.

REFERENCES

Byrd, R. E. Training in a non-group. *J. humanistic Psychol.*, 1967, 7 (1), 18–27.

Clark, J. V. Task group therapy. Unpublished manuscript, Univer. of California, Los Angeles, 1966.

A Systems Approach to
Organization Development
Michael Beer and Edgar F. Huse

Organization development (OD) efforts are often exclusively oriented to one method, one set of theoretical concepts, or one organizational variable. An input-process-output model of an organization was used as a framework for planned change.[1] *The program dealt with many organizational dimensions and used several intervention strategies and OD technologies. The effort resulted in substantial changes in organizational inputs, processes, and outputs. A number of findings about organization development have emerged from this OD experience and include the following: (1) OD efforts must not always start at the top; (2) the organization itself is the best laboratory for learning; (3) structural and interpersonal changes must complement and reinforce each other; (4) adult learning starts with behavioral change rather than cognitive change; and (5) the selection of change leaders as initial targets for the change program is a useful OD strategy.*

Excerpted and reproduced by special permission from the *Journal of Applied Behavioral Science,* **8,** 1, pp. 79–101. Copyright © 1972, NTL Institute for Applied Behavioral Science, associated with the National Education Association.

This article is written to provide the reader with an understanding of the systems organizational model that guided our efforts as change agents; to describe the varied approaches used for organizational change; and to describe the results and what we have learned about the process of change and its prospects in large, complex organizations. Rather than consigning the conclusions to the end, we shall underscore our major findings as we proceed through the sections of the case study.

The organizational development program took place in a plant designing and manufacturing complex instruments for medical and laboratory use.

Through the efforts of the personnel supervisor, enough interest existed initially for our holding a series of seminars which contrasted traditional approaches with newer approaches based on behavioral research findings and theory. Although these seminars never succeeded in getting an explicit decision on the pattern of management that would prevail in the plant (indeed, as will be discussed later, there was considerable resistance to "theory"), they did start to unfreeze the managerial group (which was steeped in the tradition of the parent organization) sufficiently to commit themselves to "trying" some new approaches on a very limited basis. This constituted much less than commitment to a new pattern of management, but it did open the door to experimentation and examination.

Overworked Theories

A number of practitioners of OD stress the importance of top management commitment to OD if such a program is to be successful. As one author puts it, "Without such support, we have found no program of this kind can ever succeed. . . . First, we worked with top managers to help them fully understand. . . . This proved vital, not only in helping their understanding of the concepts but also in earning their commitment to the program" (Roche & MacKinnon, 1970). In the same vein, Beckhard (1969) and Blake and Mouton (1969) stress that OD must be planned and managed from the top down.

Certainly no one would dispute the proposition that top management commitment to OD is highly valuable and helpful. However, our experience in this study [*Finding 1*] indicates that *a clear-cut commitment at the top of the organizational unit to a particular OD approach is not necessary for a development program to succeed.* Indeed, an attempt to obtain too strong a commitment from top management in the early stages may be threatening enough to cause the withdrawal of any commitment to planned change, especially since the concept of OD and its technologies (e.g., Theory *Y,* job enrichment, sensitivity training, and the like) are foreign and threatening to the established beliefs of many managers.

Moreover, we found [*Finding 2*] that *total top management understanding of where the OD process will lead and the state of the organization at the end is not necessary for successful programs to take place.* Indeed, given the current state of the art, the OD practitioner himself may not have a clear view of the road ahead, except in very general terms.

What *is* necessary is that someone in a strategic position feel the need for change and improvement. In our plant, that person was the personnel supervisor. Although the plant manager was mildly interested in the initial stages, he was mainly submitting to pressures from the personnel man. Throughout his tenure in the plant, the plant manager's commitment and interest mildly increased, but he was never a strong proponent nor the most skilled manager in some of the new approaches. Furthermore, the plant manager's "boss" never fully knew what was going on in the plant nor did he ever commit himself in any way to the OD program. We now believe that it is possible to change a relatively autonomous unit of a larger organization without the total commitment or understanding of top management in that unit and, in larger and more complex organizations, even without their knowledge.

Initial Commitment to New Approaches
In addition to felt need, the second essential condition is that there be, somewhere in the organization, some initial commitment to experimentation, application, and evaluation of new approaches to present problems. A case study report by the second author (Huse, 1965) describes a successful OD program that took place because a middle manager in a large organization felt the need for change and requested help. He could not have cared less about specific OD principles. He simply wanted help in improving his organization. Davis (1967) points out, in his now classic case study, that top management was not really involved at the beginning and that a majority of the effort was expended in "on-the-job situations, working out real problems with the people who are involved with them."

Of course, it is obvious that top management support of both theory and practice makes it easier for the change agent; conversely, the lack of such support increases the risk involved for consultants and managers, and causes other systems problems, as we shall discuss later in this article. Furthermore, the conditions of a felt need, a strong and self-sufficient commitment to change, and relative unit autonomy are needed. What we *are* saying is that the commonly heard dicta that one must start at the top and that top management must be committed to a set of normative principles are overworked. *Change can and does begin at lower levels in an organization* [*Finding 3*].

A CONCEPTUAL MODEL
If the client system and its management in this case did not (need to) have specific OD concepts in mind, who did? The change agents did.

It is important that the change agent have in mind an organizational model and a flexible set of normative concepts about management with a systems orientation. The organizational model should be general and reflect

Fig. 1. *Systems model of an organization*

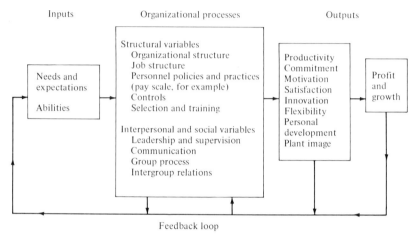

the complex *interactive* nature of systems variables. The concepts must be updated and changed as new research findings become available and as more is learned about the functioning of the client system, the environment in which the client system operates, and the effects of changes made in the client system. This is, of course, an iterative procedure.

Figure 1 represents the model of organizational change which guided our efforts. This model has some basic characteristics which must be understood if we are to see how it can shape the planning of a change effort. It represents an organization as an open system engaged in a conversion process. Employee needs, expectations, and abilities are among the raw materials (inputs) with which a manager must work to achieve his objectives.

Organizations have many processes. Figure 1 includes only the more important ones in general terms, and these exist at both the structural and interpersonal levels. Leadership and communication, for example, are two of the interpersonal dimensions which serve to pull together, integrate, and shape the behavior of organizational members. They convert into effort and attitudes the potential brought to the organization in the form of needs and abilities of individuals. The structure or formalized dimensions of the organization obviously cannot exist independently of the interpersonal variables, but they are different from the interpersonal variables in terms of their susceptibility to managerial control, the means by which they might be changed, and the timing of their change. Previous literature on organizational change has emphasized interpersonal variables; more recent literature (Lawrence & Lorsch, 1969) has emphasized structural variables. It is our opinion, based upon experience, that both interpersonal and structural variables are crucial to effective organizational change. The effects of organizational design or managerial control systems on employees have been researched and documented but are still insufficiently understood. For example, we are convinced that an operant conditioning model can be used to understand the behavior of managers with respect to controls. "Beating" goals and looking good on standard measures are like food pellets to the manager.

In the output column, we have listed multiple outcomes. These are not completely independent, but they are conceptually distinctive enough in their relationship to the organizational process variables that it is useful to think of them individually. It is the optimization of the organizational outputs that leads to long-term profitability and growth for employees and the organization. Other final outcomes could be listed if we were discussing organizations with different objectives.

Inherent in this model are several basic notions: An organization is an open system which, from the human point of view, converts individual needs and expectations into outputs. Organizational outputs can be increased by improving the quality of the input. An example of this would be the selection of people with higher levels of ability and needs. However, because there are costs associated with selecting personnel of higher quality, we might say that efficiency has not increased. The organization may improve its performance, but this gain has been obtained only because the input, i.e., the quality of personnel has improved, not because there has been a change in the manner in which the organization *utilizes* its human resources.

Since organizations are open systems, organizational performance can also improve by unleashing more of the potential inherent in the human resources. If you will, outputs will increase because we have made the conversion process more efficient. This can be done, for example, by designing organizational processes which better fit the organization's environment or by changing organizational processes so that human resources can be fully unleashed and brought to bear on the task and objectives of the organization. The adjustment of organizational processes to reflect more accurately the needs of the environment and of the persons in it is one of the key objectives of our organizational development program.

Figure 1[1] does not cover some of the more traditional but vitally important concepts of an organization as a total system. For example, capital budgets, the R & D thrust of an organization, overhead or indirect budgets, and the marketing direction of an organization are extremely important aspects which need to be considered. Blake and Mouton (1969) have developed the Corporate Excellence Rubric as a means of assessing the health of the organization through a traditional functional framework. Furthermore, current research (Lawrence & Lorsch, 1969) points up the fact that the differentiation of functional units has a tremendous influence upon the effectiveness of an organization. However, for purposes of brevity, these aspects are not covered in this article.

Mechanisms of Change

We chose an eclectic approach to create change in the organizational processes listed in Figure 1, with the basic belief that a variety of approaches to change should be used with the plant in question. The primary mechanism was consulting, counseling, and feedback by a team of four. The primary change agents were the personnel man within the organization (there have been four different ones since the OD effort began); Beer as an external-to-the-plant agent but internal to the organization, and Huse as the outside change agent. The fourth member of the team was a research assistant whose responsibility it was to interview and gather data in the client system for diagnostic and feedback uses by the change agents.[2]

We began a basic strategy of establishing working relationships with individuals at all levels of the organization. We operated as resource persons who could be used to solve specific problems or initiate small experiments in management; we tried to encourage someone or some organizational component to start implementing the concepts inherent in our model of an organization. Managers gained familiarity with these ideas through consultation and, to a much lesser extent and without full understanding, from the initial few seminars that we held. The main ingredients were a problem or a desire to change and improve, combined with action recommendations from the change agents. Soon there were a few individuals throughout the organization who began, with our help, to apply some new approaches. Because most of these approaches were successful, the result was increased motivation to change. To a degree, nothing succeeds like success!

Models for Learning

There are at least two basic models for learning. The traditional method, that of the classroom and seminar, stresses theory and cognitive concepts before action. As Argyris (1967) points out, "The traditional educational models emphasize substance, rationality. . . ." However, a number of authors (Bartlett, 1967; Bradford, 1964; Schein & Bennis, 1965) make the point that behavior is another place to start. For example, Huse (1966) has shown that one's own facts are "much more powerful instruments of change than facts or principles generated and presented by an outside 'expert.' " The process of change in this OD effort started with behavioral recommendations, was followed by appropriate reinforcement and feedback, and then proceeded to attitudinal and cognitive changes.

Figure 2 summarizes the basic concept from our experience. *Effective and permanent adult learning [Finding 4] comes after the individual has experimented with new approaches and received appropriate feedback in the on-the-job situation.* This approach is analogous to, but somewhat different from, the here-and-now learning in the T Group.

Fig. 2. *The learning process*

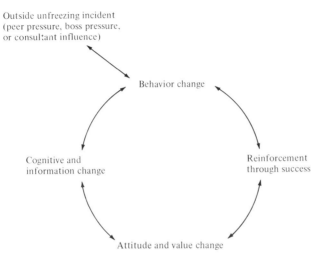

In other words, a manager might have a problem. Without discussing theory, the change agent might make some recommendations relating to the specific situation at hand. If, in the here-and-now, the manager was successful in the attempt to solve the problem, this would lead to another try, as well as to a change in his attitude toward OD. This approach capitalizes upon the powerful here-and-now influence which the job and the organizational climate can have upon the individual. Indeed, such changes can occur without *any* knowledge of theory.

Either model of learning can probably work to produce change in the individual. However, if one starts with cognitive facts and theory (as in seminars), this may be less effective and less authentic than starting with the individual's own here-and-now behavior in the ongoing job situation. In any case, the process is a cyclic one, involving behavior, attitudes, and cognition, each reinforcing the other. In our case, there was an early resistance to seminars and the presentation of "Theory." However, after behavior and attitude changes occurred, there began to be more and more requests for cognitive inputs through reading, seminars, and the like. It is at this later stage that seminars and "theory inputs" would seem to be of most value.

That learning starts with behavior and personal experience has been one of the most important things we have learned as we have worked to effect organizational change. The process is quite similar to what is intended to happen in laboratory training. What we have found [*Finding 5*] is that *the operating, ongoing organization may, indeed, be the best "laboratory" for learning.* This knowledge may save us from an overreliance upon sensitivity training described by Bennis (1968) when he states that "when you read the pages of this Journal, you cannot but think that we're a one-product outfit with a 100 per cent fool-proof patent medicine." This finding may also be the answer in dealing with Campbell and Dunnette's (1968) conclusions that "while T-Group training seems to produce observable changes in behavior, the utility of these changes for the performance of individuals in their organizational roles remains to be demonstrated."

The unfreezing process. What triggers an individual to unfreeze and to allow the process to begin, if it is not "theory"? First, there are some individuals who are ready to change behavior as soon as the opportunity presents itself in the form of an outside change agent. These are people who seem to be aware of problems and have a desire to work on them. Sometimes all that they need are some suggestions or recommendations as to different approaches or methods they may try. If their experiences are successful, they become change leaders in their own right. *They then [Finding 6] are natural targets for the change agent, since they become opinion leaders that help shape a culture that influences others in the organization to begin to experiment and try out new behaviors.* As Davis (1967) points out, it is necessary to "provide a situation which could initiate the process of freeing up these potential multipliers from the organizational and personal constraints which . . . kept them from responding effectively to their awareness of the problems." Davis used "strangers" and "cousins" laboratories. In our case, the unfreezing process was done almost exclusively in the immediate job context.

An early example of the development of change leaders in our work with this company was the successful joint effort of an engineer and a supervisor to redesign a hotplate assembly operation which would eliminate an assembly line and give each worker total responsibility for the assembly of a particular product. It resulted in a productivity increase of close to 50 per cent, a drop in rejects from 23 per cent, controllable rejects to close to 1 per cent, and a reduction in absenteeism from about 8 per cent to less than 1 per cent in a few months. Not all the early experiments were successful, but mistakes were treated as part of the experiential learning process.

As some in the organization changed and moved ahead by trying out new behaviors, others watched and waited but were eventually influenced by the culture. An example of late changers so influenced was the supervisor of Materials Control, who watched for two years what was going on in the plant but basically disagreed with the concepts of OD. Then he began to feel pressure to change because his peers were trying new things and he was not. He began by experimenting with enriching his secretary's job and found, in his own words, that "she was doing three times as much, enjoying it more, and giving me more time to manage." When he found that this experiment in managerial behavior had "paid off," he began to take a more active interest in OD. His next step was to completely reorganize his department to push decision making down the ladder, to utilize a team approach, and to enrich jobs. He supervised four sections: purchasing, inventory control, plant scheduling, and expediting. Reorganization of Materials Control was around product line teams. Each group had total project responsibility for their own product lines, including the four functions described above. We moved slowly and discussed with him alternative ways of going about the structural change. When he made the change, his subordinates were prepared and ready. The results were clear: In a three-month period of time (with the volume of business remaining steady), the parts shortage list was reduced from 14 I.B.M. pages to less than a page. In other words, although he was a late-changer in terms of the developing culture, his later actions were highly successful.

The influence of the developing culture was also documented through interviews with new employees coming into the plant. The perception by production employees that this was a "different" place to work occurred almost immediately, and changes in behavior of management personnel were clear by the second month.

In other words, while seminars and survey feedback techniques were used in our work with this plant, the initial and most crucial changes were achieved through a work-centered, consulting-counseling approach, e.g., through discussion with managers and others about work-related problems, following the model of adult learning described earlier.

So much for the manner in which the unfreezing process occurred and some of our learning about this process. What were some of the normative concepts applied and why? A brief overview of our approaches and findings follows.

A NORMATIVE MODEL

Communications
In this phase we attempted to open up communications at all levels. We started monthly meetings at every level of the organization, as well as a weekly meeting between the plant manager and a sample of production and clerical employees. The aim was to institutionalize the meetings to serve as a means for exchanging information and ideas about what had happened and what needed to happen. The meetings, especially between first-line supervisors and production workers, began primarily as one-way communications downward. Little by little, qualitative changes occurred and the meetings shifted to two-way communications about quality, schedules, and production problems. This effort to communicate (which was also extended through many other approaches) was an entire year in attaining success. It was an agonizingly slow process of change. In retrospect, this was a critical period during which trust was building and a culture conducive to further change was developing. Out of this, we concluded [*Finding 7*] that *organizational change occurs in stages: a stage of unfreezing and trust building, a take-off stage when observable change*

occurs, and a stabilization stage. Then the cycle iterates. In addition to the communication type of meeting described above, confrontation meetings between departments were also held (Blake, Shepard, & Mouton, 1964). These, too, improved relationships between departments, over time.

Job Enrichment

A second area of change was in job structure, primarily through the use of job enrichment, or, as it has been called in the plant, "the total job concept." We have already discussed the importance of the job for psychological growth and development—our findings in this area parallel those of Ford (1969). Our first experience of tearing down a hotplate assembly line has already been discussed. This was followed by similar job enrichment efforts in other areas. In one department, girls individually assemble instruments containing thousands of parts and costing several thousand dollars. The change here allowed production workers to have greater responsibility for quality checks and calibration (instead of trained technicians). In another case, the changeover involved an instrument which had been produced for several years. Here, production was increased by 17 per cent with a corresponding increase in quality; absenteeism was reduced by more than 50 per cent.

The plant is presently engaged in completely removing quality control inspection from some departments, leaving final inspection to the workers themselves. In other departments, workers have been organized into autonomous workgroups with total responsibility for scheduling, assembly, training, and some quality control inspection (the source for the supervisor's laudatory quote at the beginning of this case study). Changes in these areas have evolved out of an attempt to utilize the positive forces of cohesive workgroups. However, like Ford (1969), we have found that not everyone in the assembly workforce responds positively to such changes, although a high majority do so over time.

Mutual goal setting has also been widely adopted. Instead of standards established by engineering (a direction in which the plant was heading when we started), goals for each department are derived from the plant goal, and individual goals for the week or month are developed in individual departments through discussions between the boss and subordinates. Our interview data clearly show that in this way workers understand how their individual goals fit into the plant goal structure and can work on their own without close supervision for long periods of time.

Changes toward a pay process more clearly based on merit (including appraisals for hourly and weekly salaried clerical and technical employees as well as for managerial and professional personnel) were made to reinforce and legitimate an escalating climate of work involvement. More and more employees are now involved in questions of production, quality, department layout, and methods. Assembly workers give department tours to visitors, including vice presidents. Organization-wide technical and product information sessions are held. Concerned more with strategy than with daily problems, the top team has for some time molded itself into a business team, meeting periodically to discuss future plans.

More recently, changes in organizational structure are taking place to move a functionally oriented organization to a matrix organization, using concepts derived directly from Lawrence and Lorsch (1969). This involves, among other approaches, the use of "integrators" at varying levels within the organization.

Systems Interaction

A systems approach requires that mutually consistent changes in *all* subsystems be made in affecting the organizational processes listed in our model. In other words, [*Finding 8*] *multiple changes in the subsystems are needed for the individual employee to change behavior and perceptions of his role.* For example, participative supervision should be accompanied by redesign of jobs to allow more responsibility, by a pay system that recognizes performance, by a communication system that is truly open, and by corresponding changes in other subsystems throughout the organization. Past attempts to change organizations through a nonsystem approach, e.g., through such single media as supervisory training or sensitivity training, have had limited success because other key leverage points have not been changed in the total system. Further, an attempt to change one subsystem too quickly or too drastically can have severely harmful results, as pointed out in the "Hovey and Beard Company" case (Lawrence, Bailey, Katz, Seiler, Orth, Clark, Barnes, & Turner, 1961). Whether structural *or* interpersonal changes should take precedence in a given period of time depends upon the readiness of the system to change and the key leverage points. The key concept [*Finding 9*] is that *structural and interpersonal systems changes must reinforce and legitimate each other.* Figure 3 presents this concept. The change can be in either direction in the model.

We also learned [*Finding 10*] that *systems changes set off additional interactive processes in which changes in organizational functioning increase not only outputs but also develop the latent abilities of people.* We have concluded that the real potential in organizational development lies in setting in motion such a positive snowball of change, growth, and development. For example, as assembly workers took on additional responsibility they became more and more concerned about the total organization and product. "Mini-gripes" turned into "mega-gripes," indicating a change in the maturity of the assembly workers (Huse & Price, 1970). At the same time, this freed up management personnel to be less concerned about daily assignments and more concerned about long-range planning.

To illustrate this, at the beginning of the OD effort, the organization had a plant manager, a production superintendent, and three first-line supervisors,

Fig. 3. *The sequence of organizational change*

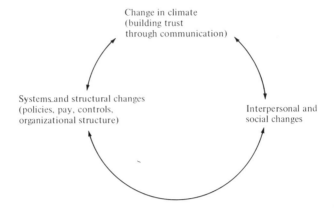

Change in climate
(building trust
through communication)

Systems and structural changes
(policies, pay, controls,
organizational structure)

Interpersonal and
social changes

or a total of five supervisory personnel in the direct manufacturing line. As the assembly line workers took on more responsibility, the five have been reduced to three (the plant manager and two first-line supervisors). The number of inspection and quality control personnel has also been reduced.

A Subsystem Within the Larger Organization
Up to this point in the case study we have been considering the plant as a system in its own right. However, changes set in motion here have also provided the first step in a larger plan for change and development to occur in the parent corporation (consisting of some 50 plants). As a subsystem within the larger system, this plant was to serve as a model for the rest of the corporation—as an example of how change should be planned and implemented. It was our hope that the systems approach to change would create such a clearly different culture in this plant that it would become visible to the rest of the corporation; that people from other segments of the larger organization would visit and become interested in trying similar models and mechanisms of change. Our hopes have been realized. Indeed, both authors are now applying OD concepts to other areas of the organization.

Influence is also exerted upward, with greater acceptance of these concepts by individuals at higher levels in the organization [Finding 11]. It is our perception that changes in organizational subsystems can have strong influences on the larger culture if the change is planned and publicized; if seed personnel are transferred to other parts of the system; if a network of change agents is clearly identified; and if careful planning goes into where and how change resources are to be used. Once again, top management commitment is not a necessary commitment for evolutionary change in a complex, multidivision, multilocation organization. (*Sometimes,* the tail begins to wag the dog.)

Fig. 4. *Equity model*

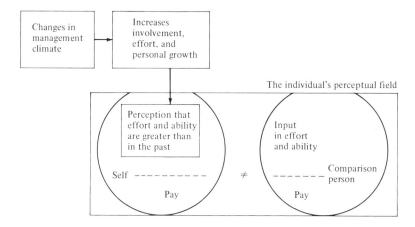

Subsystem Difficulties

However, this change process may cause some difficulties in the area of inter-face between the smaller subsystem and the larger system. For example, the increased responsibilities, commitment, and involvement represented by job enrichment for assembly workers are not adequately represented in the normal job evaluation program for factory workers and are difficult to handle adequately within the larger system. So pay and pay system changes must be modified to fit modern OD concepts. Figure 4 is a model which shows the effects of change in climate on individual model perceptions of equity in pay.

In addition to the larger system difficulties over wage plans, there still exists a great deal of controversy as to the importance of pay as a motivator (or dissatisfier). For example, Walton (1967) takes a basically pessimistic approach about participation through the informal approach, as opposed to the more formal approaches embodied in the Scanlon Plan (Lesieur, 1958), which "stress the economic rewards which can come from [formal] participation." On the other hand, Paul, Robertson, and Herzberg (1969) review a number of job enrichment projects and report: "In no instance did management face a demand of this kind [higher pay or better conditions] as a result of changes made in the studies." In a recent review of the Scanlon Plan (Lesieur & Puckett, 1969), the authors point out that Scanlon's first application did not involve the use of financial incentives but, rather, a common sharing between management and employees of problems, goals, and ideas. Indeed, Ford (1969) reports on the results of a series of job enrichment studies without ever mentioning the words "pay" or "salary." In the plant described in this case, no significant pressures for higher pay have been felt to date.

However, there has been sufficient opportunity for promotion of hourly employees to higher level jobs as the plant has grown.

It is certainly not within the scope of this article to handle the controversy regarding the place of pay as a motivator. We do want to make the point that standard corporate job evaluation plans are only one instance of the difficulties of interface between the client plant as a subsystem and the larger system. In our experience, these and other areas have been minor rather than major problems, but they have been problems.

Changes in Consumption of Research Findings

An important by-product of our experience has been [*Finding 12*] that *the client system eventually becomes a sophisticated consumer of new research findings in the behavioral sciences.* As mentioned earlier, there was early resistance to "theory"; but as the program progressed, there was increasing desire for "theory." We also found that a flexible and adaptable organization is more likely to translate theory into new policies and actions. Perhaps this is where behavioral scientists may have gone wrong in the past. We may have saturated our client systems with sophisticated research studies before the culture was ready to absorb them. This would suggest that a more effective approach may be carefully planned stages of evolution from an action orientation to an action-research orientation to a research orientation. This implies a long-range plan for change that we often talk about but rarely execute with respect to the changes in organizations that we seek as behavioral scientists.

RESULTS OF THE ORGANIZATIONAL DEVELOPMENT PROGRAM

To a great extent we have tried to share with you our results and findings throughout the article. In addition, we are retesting these concepts in several other plants. In retrospect, how much change really occurred at the client plant, and how effective have been the new approaches introduced? We have only partial answers since a control plant did not exist and since the plant was relatively new; no historical data existed against which to compare performance. However, considerable data do exist to support the thesis that change has occurred and that new managerial approaches have created an effective organization. (In addition, the second author is conducting ongoing research in another plant in the organization which has historical data. Before- and aftermeasures have already shown dramatic change: e.g., reduction in manu-turing costs for the plant of 40 to 45 per cent.)

Extensive interviews by the researcher and detailed notes and observa-he change agents indicate considerable improvement after our work t. Communication is open, workers feel informed, jobs are inter-lenging, and goals are mutually set and accomplished.

In each of the output dimensions, positive changes have occurred which we think, but cannot always prove, would not have occurred without the OD effort. Turnover has been considerably reduced; specific changes in job structure, organizational change, or group process have resulted in measurable productivity changes of up to 50 per cent. Recent changes in the Instrument Department have resulted in productivity and quality improvements. We have witnessed the significant changes in maturity and motivation which have taken place among the assembly workers. A change to a project team structure in the Materials Control Department led to a reduction of the weekly parts shortages. Following the findings of Lawrence and Lorsch (1969), the use of "integrators" and project teams has significantly reduced the time necessary for new product development, introduction, and manufacture. A fuller evaluation of the integrator role and the project organization as it affects intergroup relations and new product development is reported elsewhere (Beer, Pieters, Marcus, & Hundert, 1971).

Several recent incidents in the plant are evidence of the effect of the changes and bear repeating. An order called for in seven days and requiring extraordinary cooperation on the part of a temporary team of production workers was completed in fewer than seven days. A threatened layoff was handled with candor and openness and resulted in volunteers among some of the secondary wage earners.

New employees and managers now transferred into the plant are immediately struck by the differences between the "climate" of this plant and other locations. They report more openness, greater involvement by employees, more communication, and more interesting jobs. Even visitors are struck immediately by the differences. For example, one of the authors has on several occasions taken graduate students on field trips to the plant. After the tour, the consensus is, "You've told us about it, but I had to see it for myself before I would believe it." Managers transferred or promoted out of the plant to other locations report "cultural shock."

SUMMARY AND CONCLUSIONS

The Medfield Project (as it can now be labeled) has been an experiment in a systems approach to organizational development at two systems levels. On the one hand, we have regarded the plant as a system in and of itself. On the other hand, we have regarded the plant as a subsystem within a larger organization. As such a subsystem, we wanted it to serve as a model for the rest of the organization. Indeed, as a result of this study, OD work is going forward elsewhere in the parent company and will be reported in forthcoming articles.

Although we have shared our findings with you throughout the article, it seems wise now to summarize them for your convenience, so that they may be generalized to other organizations and climates.

Findings

1. A clear-cut commitment to a particular OD approach is not necessary (although desirable) for a successful OD program to succeed.

2. Total top management understanding of where the OD process will lead and the state of the organization at the end is not necessary for organizational change to occur.

3. Change can and does begin at lower levels in the organization.

4. Effective and permanent adult learning comes after the individual has experimented with new approaches and received appropriate feedback in the on-the-job situation.

5. Rather than the T Group, the operating, ongoing organization may be the best "laboratory" for learning, with fewer problems in transfer of training.

6. Internal change leaders are natural targets for the change agent, since they become influence leaders and help to shape the culture.

7. Organizational change occurs in stages: a stage of unfreezing and trust building, a take-off stage when observable change occurs, and a stabilization stage. Then the cycle iterates.

8. Multiple changes in the subsystems are needed for the individual employee to change behavior and perceptions of his role.

9. Structural and interpersonal systems changes must reinforce and legitimate each other.

10. Systems changes set off additional interactive processes in which changes in organizational functioning not only increase outputs but also develop the latent abilities of people.

11. Influence is also exerted upward, with great acceptance of these concepts by individuals at higher levels in the organization.

12. The client system eventually becomes a sophisticated consumer of new research findings in the behavioral sciences.

Perhaps the most important and far-reaching conclusion is that as organizational psychologists we have viewed our role too narrowly and with an insufficient historical and change perspective. Our research studies tend to be static rather than dynamic. We need to do a better job of developing a theory and technology of changing and to develop a flexible set of concepts which will change as we experiment with and socially engineer organizations. We are suggesting a stronger action orientation for our field and less of a natural science orientation. We must be less timid about helping organizations to change themselves. We must create a positive snowball of organizational change followed by changes in needs and expectations of organizational members, followed again by further organizational change. The objective of change agents should be to develop an evolving system that maintains reasonable internal consistency while staying relevant to and anticipating changes and adaptation to the outside environment. As behavioral scientists and change agents, we must help organizations begin to "become."

Notes

1. Cf. The traditional aspects included in the conceptual model developed by Huse (1969).

2. We should like to acknowledge the help and participation of Mrs. Gloria Gery and Miss Joan Doolittle in the data-gathering phase.

References

Argyris, C. On the future of laboratory training. *J. appl. Behav. Sci.,* 1967, 3 (2), 153–183.

Bartlett, A. C. Changing behavior as a means to increased efficiency. *J. appl. Behav. Sci.,* 1967, 3 (3), 381–403.

Beckhard, R. *Organization development: Strategies and models.* Reading, Mass.: Addison-Wesley, 1969.

Beer, M., Pieters, G. R., Marcus, S. H., & Hundert, A. T. Improving integration between functional groups: A case in organization change and implications for theory and practice. Symposium presented at Americam Psychological Association Convention, Washington, D.C., September 1971.

Bennis, W. G. The case study—I. Introduction. *J. appl. Behav. Sci.,* 1968, 4 (2), 227–231.

Blake, R. R., & Mouton, J. S. *Building a dynamic corporation through grid organization development.* Reading, Mass.: Addison-Wesley, 1969.

Blake, R. R., Shepard, H. A., & Mouton, J. S. *Managing intergroup conflict in industry.* Houston, Tex.: Gulf, 1964.

Bradford, L. P. Membership and the learning process. In L. P. Bradford, J. R. Gibb, and K. D. Benne (Eds.), *T-Group theory and laboratory method: Innovation in re-education. New York: Wiley, 1964.*

Campbell, J. P., & Dunnette, M. D. Effectiveness of t-group experiences in managerial training and development. *Psycholog. Bull.,* August 1968, 70, (2), 73–104.

Davis, S. A. An organic problem-solving method of organizational change. *J. appl. Behav. Sci.,* 1967, 3 (1), 3–21.

Ford, R. N. *Motivation through the work itself.* New York: American Management Association, 1969.

Huse, E. F. The behavioral scientist in the shop. *Personnel,* May/June 1965, 42 (3), 50–57.

Huse, E. F. Putting in a management development program that works. *California Mgmt Rev.,* Winter 1966, 73–80.

Huse, E. F., & Price, P. S. The relationship between maturity and motivation in varied work groups. *Proceedings of the Seventieth Annual Convention of the American Psychological Association,* September 1970.

Lawrence, P. R., & Lorsch, J. W. *Organization and environment.* Homewood, Ill.: Richard D. Irwin, 1969.

Lawrence, P. R., Bailey, J. C., Katz, R. L., Seiler, J. A., Orth, C. D. III, Clark, J. V., Barnes, L. B., & Turner, A. N. *Organizational behavior and administration.* Homewood, Ill.: Irwin-Dorsey, 1961.

Lesieur, F. G. (Ed.) *The Scanlon plan: A frontier in labor-management cooperation.* Cambridge, Mass.: M.I.T. Press, 1958.

Lesieur, F. G., & Puckett, E. S. The Scanlon plan has proved itself. *Harvard Bus. Rev.,* Sept./Oct. 1969, 47, 109–118.

Paul, W. J., Robertson, K. B., & Herzberg, F. Job enrichment pays off. *Harvard Bus. Rev.,* Mar./Apr. 1969, 47 (2) 61–78.

Roche, W. J., & MacKinnon, N. L. Motivating people with meaningful work. *Harvard Bus. Rev.,* May/June 1970, 48 (3), 97–110.

Schein, E. H., & Bennis, W. G. *Personal and organizational change through group methods: The laboratory approach.* New York: Wiley, 1965.

Walton, R. E. Contrasting designs for participative systems. *Personnel Admin.,* Nov./Dec. 1967, 30 (6), 35–41